Contents

Preface

Acknowledgements

Michael Witherick
Visiting Fellow, University of Southampton

Michael Carr
Senior Research Associate, Homerton College,
Cambridge University

of

pective

Hodder & Stoughton

A MEMBER OF THE HODDER HEADLINE GROUP

British Library Cataloguing in Publication Data

Witherick, M. E.
  Changing Face of Japan: Geographical
    Perspective
  I. Title II. Carr, Michael
  915.2

ISBN 0 340 55576 9

First published 1993

Typeset by Serif Tree, Kidlington, Oxon.

Printed in Great Britain for Hodder & Stoughton Educational,
a division of Hodder Headline Plc, Mill Road, Dunton Green,
Sevenoaks, Kent TN13 2YA by Thomson Litho Ltd, Scotland.

Preface

The fast approach of the 21st century is seen increasingly to mark what commentators refer to as 'the dawn of the Pacific era.' The phrase is significant for it implicitly acknowledges a fundamental shift taking place in the worldwide distribution of economic and political power. The scale of development recently achieved by territories fronting the Pacific Ocean, notably Japan and the west coast regions of USA and Canada, has already established this quarter of the globe as the leading sunrise region. At present, the economic centre of gravity, and therefore the power base, is clearly located in the Northern Hemisphere. Whilst this is unlikely to change in the foreseeable future, an important shift has already begun to take place within that hemisphere. The balance of power is gradually moving away from the American towards the Asian shore. The postwar economic success of Japan has been largely responsible for initiating this shift, but more recently it has been given added impetus by the emergence of the 'Asian tigers', the newly-industrialising economies like South Korea and Taiwan. The future supremacy of the Asian Pacific region seems further assured by the gradual awakening of the sleeping giant, China. It may be, too, that reorganisation of the former Soviet Union will allow its successor, the Commonwealth of Independent States (CIS), and the Russian Federation in particular, some scope to orientate more towards the Pacific, thereby lending further weight to the Asian sector.

Given this changing global scenario, it is highly desirable that people in the Atlantic region should be well-informed about events and developments taking place in the Asian Pacific region. What happens there inevitably and increasingly has an impact on the West, often in a challenging and sometimes an adverse manner. In particular, there is need for a much fuller knowledge and understanding of what to date has been the Pacific region's star performer, Japan. Despite its rise to the status of an economic superpower, despite its supposed 'westernisation' during the second half of the twentieth century, and despite the increasing overseas travel of its citizens, Japan remains curiously detached and remote from the caucus of the global community. To a considerable degree, this situation reflects what the Japanese want for themselves. But they are torn between this wish to be different, a people apart, and a general desire to conform and be accepted by others. These deep-felt and apparently contradictory aspirations are understood by few outside Japan; they are thoroughly misconstrued by many. They are an essential part of the Japanese enigma; they undoubtedly underlie the suspicion with which much of the world continues to view the country's progress.

For us in the West to become better informed about Japan is, in many respects, easier said than done. There undoubtedly exists a communications barrier. From a Western perspective, this is mainly the outcome of a difficult language, made less accessible by the use of unfamiliar systems of writing, and the prevalence of a unique culture that manifests itself in values and attitudes which are often fundamentally different from our own. The barrier is being lowered by degrees as the Japanese show great willingness to improve their communication with the rest of the global community. Most obviously, they are making strenuous efforts through their education system to ensure that all young people achieve a competence in the English language. The preparation of English versions of a whole range of publications, from planning strategies to official statistics, from company reports to ministerial documents, is also symptomatic of this desire to facilitate communication. The reasoning is that improved communication, in its turn, will help achieve those twin goals of being accepted and respected and yet recognised as being different.

It is in a context of improved information – exchange that this book has been prepared. Its theme is change, its emphasis is economic and social, and its perspective is geographical. Modern Japan is examined at two different spatial scales. In the first instance, attention focuses on the changing internal patterns of development and significant moulding factors – physical, historical and cultural. This is followed by an analysis of the spreading web of linkages which increasingly bind Japan with the international community and through which it exercises so much power and influence worldwide. Finally, attention turns to those issues which confront Japan, both at home and abroad, at the approach of the Pacific era. For all its postwar success and global strength, it is now clear that Japan faces a future which in some respects threatens to be less certain and secure.

Whilst our hope is that the book will appeal to a wide readership, we confess that it has been written with the student and teacher very much in mind. The need for a work of this type is acute, especially now that English-speaking nations as far afield as the UK, the USA, Australia and New Zealand are recognising that some study of Japan should be incorporated in the school and college curriculum. The book should also be of interest and use to those enrolled on a variety of university courses, from economics to geography, from politics to Asian and Pacific studies. To these 'educational' sectors of our readership, attention needs to be drawn to the resource materials and the potential which they offer, when pulled together from different chapters, to pursue some themes in more detail than has been possible within the overall scope and constraints of the book. For example, by pooling Figures 4.5 to 4.8, 5.2, 7.2, 9.1 and Tables 5.1 and 7.1, one can put together maps, graphs and statistics which provide the basis for a detailed investigation of population change in Japan over more than two centuries. Similarly, a combination of Figures 2.5 and 8.6 with Photos 1.10, 2.10, 7.4, 7.6, and 13.3 provides material for a closer analysis of the topical environmental issue of land reclamation.

Michael Witherick
Southampton

Michael Carr
Cambridge

Acknowledgements

We would like to acknowledge all those who, in diverse ways, have contributed to the completion of this book, be they seminal influences, data donors, illustrators, editorial experts or providers of vital domestic support! It would be invidious to single out particular people. Let it simply be said that our gratitude to them all is immense. Through their help, guidance and encouragement, we are now able to dedicate this analysis of the changing face of Japan to our Japanese friends and colleagues. Our wish is to contribute to a better international understanding of a country and its people destined in the Pacific era to play an even more important role in global affairs.

Every effort has been made to contact the holders of copyright material but if any have been inadvertently overlooked the publisher will be pleased to make the necessary alterations at the first opportunity.

Cover, The J Allan Cash Photolibrary.
P. 2 left to right; Robert Harding Picture Library; Jim Holmes; The J Allan Cash Photolibrary.
P. 4; p. 5; p. 6 Japanese Embassy/Japan Information & Cultural Centre.
P. 11 top, Professor Ian Simmonds, Dept. of Geography, University of Durham.
P. 11 lower, The J Allan cash Photolibrary.
P. 15 left to right, Nissan Motors (GB) Ltd; Michael Witherick.
P. 16 top left Jim Holmes
P. 16 top middle, right, lower; p. 17 Japan Information and Cultural Centre.
P. 18 Japanese Embassy/Japan Information & Cultural Centre.
P. 21 left to right, Jim Holmes; Culley/Greenpeace Communications Ltd; Jim Holmes; Japan Information and Cultural Centre.
P. 22 left to right, Robert Harding Picture Library; Japan National Tourist Organisation.
P.24; p. 25; Japan Information & Cultural Centre.
P. 27, Michael Witherick.
P. 29, Les Gibbon.
P. 30, Simone Ling.
P. 33, Japan Information & Cultural Centre.
P. 35, Jim Holmes.
P. 38, Michael Witherick.
P. 41 both; p. 42 top, Japan Information & Cultural Centre.

P. 42 lower, Michael Witherick.
P. 47, Japan Information & Cultural Centre.
P. 48 left Japanese Embassy/Japan Information & Cultural Centre
P 48 right The Hulton-Deutsch Collection.
P. 51, Japan Information & Cultural Centre.
P. 58, The Hulton-Deutsch Collection.
P. 71, John Greenlees.
P. 73, p. 80 both, Japan Information & Cultural Centre.
P. 95, John Greenlees.
P. 97, Japan Information Centre.
P. 110, Japan National Tourist Organisation.
P. 111, Michael Witherick.
P. 112, Jim Holmes.
P. 113, R.J. Harrison-Church.
P. 118 left to right, Jim Holmes; Michael Witherick; Japan Information & Cultural Centre.
P. 124 Japan Information & Cultural Centre.
P. 133; p. 135 top Simone Ling.
P. 135 lower; p. 146, Japan Information & Cultural Centre.
P. 151 Japan National Tourist Organisation.
P. 155 Jim Holmes.
P. 167 Michael Witherick.
P. 176 left to right, Japan Information and Cultural Centre; University of Reading.
P. 180, Nissan Photographic Department; Ron Giling/Panos Pictures.
P. 187, Richard Willson © Times Newspapers Ltd. 1991
P. 189 Sony Manufacturing Company Uk.
P. 201 left to right, Mark Edwards/Still Pictures; The J Allan Cash Photolibrary; John Greenlees.
P. 220, Japan Information and Cultural Centre.
P. 223, Jim Holmes.
P. 224, Planet Earth Pictures.
P. 225, International Society for Educational Information Inc.
P. 227; p. 233 The Hutchison Library.
P. 238 John Greenlees.
P. 249, Nissan Motors (GB) Ltd.
P.250 Planet Earth Pictures.
P.252 Ron Giling/Panos Pictures.

An introductory portrait

1 Images and Realities

Bullet trains, motor cars, electronic gadgetry and horrendous TV games are among the things commonly associated with modern Japan. Popular traditional images of the country include Mount Fuji, cherry blossom and wooden temples, *sumo* wrestlers and the tea ceremony. The Japanese themselves are widely perceived to be efficient and hardworking, competitive and heartless. On the basis of associations and perceptions such as these, promoted mainly through the mass-media, many around the world would claim that they 'know' about Japan and its people (Photo 1.1). But such 'knowledge' is, at best, partial and biased; at worst, it is downright untrue. The fact of the matter is that relatively few foreigners have anything more than a passing knowledge or shallow understanding of Japan and the Japanese. Given its status as an economic superpower, and the increasing influence it wields in the global community, it is very much in our interests to become more enlightened about the realities of modern Japan. We need to be better informed about the land, its people and their international relationships.

In seeking to describe and explain the changing face of Japan, this book puts the emphasis on developments which have occurred since the end of the Second World War. Of particular interest are the processes and patterns of change experienced since the **Oil Shocks** (as the Japanese refer to them) of the 1970s. The mammoth hikes in oil prices during 1973 and 1979/80 were to prove to be a major turning-point in Japan's development. Japan was required to rethink almost from scratch its energy and industrial strategies. It was also forced to reappraise its international relationships and security.

The geographical perspective adopted in this book has two distinct, but related dimensions. First, there is the internal face of the country which is basically the product of the physical environment and the human exploitation of that environment. Particularly important in a geographical perspective are the changing patterns of settlement and development produced by cultural, economic and technological progress. Crudely put, the internal geography requires asking, what goes

(b)

(a)

Photo 1.1 *Popular images of Japan (a) Sumo wresting, (b) Kofukiji Temple in Nara, and (c) Mount Fuji*

on where and why? Additionally, and often neglected in geographical studies of countries, there is the external face of Japan. Few, if any, nations live in complete isolation. They need to interact with others for a variety of purposes, such as buying and selling goods, investment and defence, giving or receiving aid. In one sense, the external geography provides what the internal geography cannot. Each of these external linkages produces a spatial pattern of relationships. Again, crudely put, the external geography requires asking what are those patterns and why?

In the remainder of this introductory chapter, two things need to be attempted. First, it is desirable to identify what are in effect some of the distinctive geographical attributes of modern Japan. Their significance is signalled by the frequent references made to them in subsequent chapters. As such, these characteristics might be regarded as providing the book with strands of continuity or underlying themes. Secondly, it is necessary to promote some preliminary knowledge of place and location in Japan. For example, we need to know about the major divisions of the country, their relative location and character. In short, it is necessary to have a spatial framework on which to hang the geographical detail of later chapters.

1.1 SELECTED ATTRIBUTES OF MODERN JAPAN

The intention here is to do no more than briefly signal what are deemed to be some of the outstanding characteristics of modern Japan. These need to be identified and recognised as being intrinsically or distinctively Japanese. In some instances, their significance is increased by the fact that they have operated as causal factors exercising considerable influence on various aspects of the changing face of modern Japan.

Economic superpower – Asia's first and only

Of all the attributes associated with modern Japan, none is more widely recognised by foreigners than the strength and global influence of its economy. Its competitiveness and strength have raised Japan to the status of an economic superpower. That achievement is all the more remarkable bearing in mind three things.

First, Japan was a relatively late starter in terms of economic development. The processes of large-scale industrialisation and urbanisation were not initiated until the second half of the 19th century, some 100 years behind the leading nations of the West. Thus, compared with countries such as Germany, the UK and USA, with which it has now caught up (and some would say, passed), the completion of the industrial revolution in Japan was achieved in about half the time (Table 1.1). Indeed, it might be argued that the rise to superpower status has largely been attained in less than 50 years. The modern Japanese economy has emerged phoenix-like from the ashes of comprehensive defeat and wholesale destruction suffered during the Second World War (Photo 1.2).

Secondly, and adding to this distinguished record, is the fact that Japan has become Asia's first highly industrialised and urbanised nation. Indeed, it has the distinction of being the first of its kind outside Europe and North America. Recently, however, its pioneering pathway in the eastern hemisphere has begun to be followed by the so-called **newly-industrialising countries** (NICs) of Hong Kong, Singapore, South Korea and Taiwan,

Table 1.1 Per capita GNP and GNP growth rates for selected advanced countries (1990)

	Per capita GNP (US$)	Mean annual growth 1986–1990 (%)
JAPAN	24 786	5.6
Switzerland	28 756	2.8
Sweden	22 031	2.1
USA	21 116	2.8
Canada	20 392	3.2
West Germany	20 132	3.1
Australia	17 912	3.4
France	17 505	3.1
Belgium	16 194	3.1
Netherlands	15 491	2.5
Italy	15 280	3.0
UK	14 844	3.1

Photo 1.2 Wartime destruction

been one of Japan's supreme achievements. Conquering the handicap speaks volumes for the quality and resourcefulness of Japan's population.

Economic success has brought with it calls for Japan to exercise a more broadly-based type of leadership, particularly in the Asian Pacific region. The argument increasingly put forward is that as one of the world's leading economies, the onus is on Japan to do more for others, such as increasing its aid, heading regional alliances and generally acting as minder to less-developed nations. But it would seem that Japan is reluctant to become too embroiled in the political affairs of other countries, in global diplomacy and in matters of defence and security. It appears to be far happier leaving all that to other advanced nations and concentrating instead on the maintenance and improvement its own economy.

also referred to as the '**Asian tigers**' (Figure. 1.1). However, despite superior growth rates, these countries still lag behind Japan in terms of per capita GDP.

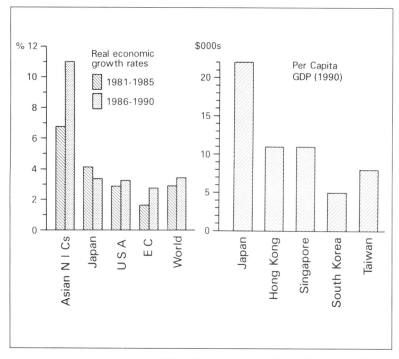

Fig. 1.1 *Japan and the Asian tigers: some economic indicators*

Thirdly, the speed and geographical uniqueness of Japan's economic development become even more impressive when it is realised that Japan simply has never commanded those material resources normally regarded as the prerequisites of industrialisation. Its sources of energy are meagre; its mineral resources are even more so. Three-quarters of Japan's primary energy supply has to be imported; apart from coal, it has no economically-viable mineral deposits. Overcoming these serious resource deficiencies has

An inhospitable environment

The meagreness of Japan's resource base is not just confined to the industrial realm. Limitations on agriculture include acute shortages of flat land and cultivable soils, whilst the climate of the northern half of the country offers a restricted growing-season. Then there is the unwelcoming nature of the environment to human settlement. The prevalence of a mountainous terrain restricts settlement in all parts of Japan to a patchwork of fragmented lowlands, most of which are located along the coast (Photo 1.3). The intervening mountains have made the provision of transport links both difficult and expensive; accessibility is never easy. Along the Japan Sea coast and in northern Honshu and Hokkaido, the harshness of the winters and shortness of the summers add to the general inhospitability of the environment.

But the tale of woe continues in that Japan's physical environment is also rich in natural hazards. Volcanic eruptions, earthquakes and their associated **tsunamis** are all a consequence of Japan's unfortunate location at the junction of three of the world's major **tectonic plates**. Typhoons and flooding are two climatic events which each year cause much damage to property and loss of life, whilst the combination of torrential rain and steep slopes results in frequent landslides which constantly plague transport lines in the mountainous interior.

It is indeed difficult to say much that is positive about Japan's environment. Attention might be drawn to the climate of the southern half of the country which is altogether more conducive to agriculture and settlement. The deep snows of the hard northern winters are beginning to be exploited in the context of winter sports. Abundant forests have been a traditional source of fuel and building materials. But these pluses pale into insignificance when compared with the many entries on the debit side of the environmental ledger.

The Japanese

An immense amount has been written about the Japanese, and it would take more than a series of volumes to give proper consideration to all those things that go to make up national character, such as the beliefs, values, attitudes, perceptions and behaviour of the people. At the real risk of indulging in dangerous over-generalisation, attention will be drawn here only to a small selection of Japanese traits, namely those regarded as having a direct bearing on the ensuing analysis of Japan's changing geography.

A long history of global isolation has instilled in the Japanese the belief that they are a people apart – a distinct race. The reality is otherwise, in that three different racial stocks may be identified: (i) the aboriginal Ainus in the north – a very hairy people apparently of Caucasian origin, but now largely greatly reduced in number by intermarriage; (ii) a relatively tall, white-skinned, fine-featured stock which probably came in prehistoric times from what is now northern China, Manchuria and Korea, and (iii) a Polynesian-type of stock, comprising rather squat, heavily muscled and brown-skinned people who came from South East Asia and the Pacific islands.

There are two particular outcomes of this belief in their own homogeneity.

Photo 1.3 *Mountains and small fragmented lowlands along the coast*

First, there is a general wish to maintain it so that, for example, intermarriage with *gaijin* (foreigners) is generally not condoned. Secondly, there is in all Japanese people a deep and in-built urge to conform, not so much as regards physical characteristics, but in terms of society as a whole. The latter is effected largely through what is termed **groupism**. The Japanese are inherently group-oriented. There is nothing that they crave more than to be accepted as a conforming member of a group. There are few greater insults than to suggest that a Japanese person is a *kojinteki* (an individual). An old Japanese proverb states that 'the nail which sticks up is quickly hammered down'. The individual is willing to suppress their own identity and point of view in return for *amae*, the dependence, protection and psychological security that come from being an accepted group member. The prevalence of this groupism and the desire to conform clearly make for a well-ordered society.

Next, it is possible to identify a number of attributes which relate to the work place and that are particularly significant when it comes to explaining Japan's economic success (Photo 1.4). Above all else, the Japanese are motivated by a strong work ethic. Society demands that work is an activity requiring the giving of one's best, whether one is a middle manager in a Tokyo head office or a junior worker on the assembly line. Compared with the West, working hours are longer and holidays shorter; indeed, it might be claimed that the Japanese are workaholics.

Photo 1.4 *An industrious, committed and conforming labour force*

The employer-employee relationship is also rather different. There is intense worker loyalty which flows in part from the widespread custom that once a person is put on a company's payroll, there is the prospect of a job for life. The company is very paternalistic towards its employees. In addition to a guaranteed job, it may provide housing and schooling, arrange marriages and holidays, and in many other ways look after employee well-being. In return, of course, the company reaps the benefits of a grateful and committed labour force. The need for Japan as a nation to regain face in the eyes of the international community after its humiliating defeat in 1945 has also been an important driving force behind this worker commitment. There has been a widespread wish to demonstrate the superiority of Japan, this time by means of economic achievement rather than military conquest.

As a consequence of this worker loyalty and commitment, company management is rather different, perhaps easier. The 'them and us' syndrome does not prevail in the Japanese firm. Although trade unions were introduced as one of the postwar reforms, they are not regarded as being particularly relevant to today's labour relations. Labour disputes are uncommon. Management decisions will rarely be challenged by subordinates, but the latter will nearly always expect to have been consulted. Sceptics suggest that the widely adopted consultative practice is something of a cosmetic – a ploy to win worker support for decisions really made by employers.

It is claimed that the Japanese are not a very inventive people. If that is true, then possibly some of the blame must fall on the highly regimented and unimaginative education system. But what the Japanese have shown themselves to be good at is innovation. In particular, they show great flair when it comes to seeing the practical applications and commercial potential of new technology; much is invested in research and development. They are also shrewd operators in business and meticulously thorough in their market research.

Finally, a summary of these and other aspects of Japanese character is provided by the following quite remarkable piece of self-analysis:

> "We have the same basic beliefs, traits and language, no matter what part of the country we live in. Our strongest national characteristic is being group-oriented; nothing is more important than conforming . . .
>
> We are consistent in the way in which we react to most situations and will use standard expressions. We are emotional and governed more by emotion than by intellect. We are intelligent rather than intellectual. We are affected very much by intangible and nebulous moods that drift across our society more than we are by straight facts and clear issues.
>
> We are not governed by religious ethics. Far more, we have very strong social ethics which dictate how we should live and what is expected of us, and we are more likely to be concerned about what is proper and improper, acceptable and unacceptable to our society and individuals than with religious ethics telling us what is right and what is wrong.

We are very enquiring people and anxious about what others think of us, and what we fear most is loss of face."

(Nakata, 1979).

The significance of the last observation cannot be overstated. The deep-rooted desire to maintain face (*tatemae*) and thereby command the respect of others is fundamental to the psyche of the Japanese. It is closely bound up with their wish to conform and to be an accepted group member. However, the quotation should not be taken as providing a complete list of Japanese traits. Certainly, one should add that the Japanese are inherently a polite, honest and law-abiding people. There is great personal safety in all parts of Japan (mugging is virtually unheard of). Their concern about personal cleanliness and health verges on hypochondria. They follow strict codes of conduct.

Crowded islands and uneven development

Today, the Japanese population amounts to over 120 million; they are crowded together in an area which is 50 percent larger than the United Kingdom. The mean population density is nearly ten times the global average, and Japan ranks as one of the most densely-populated countries in the world. Whilst homogeneity is something to which the Japanese aspire at an individual level, their aggregate distribution throughout Japan is far from uniform. Something approaching three-quarters of Japan is either unsettled or very sparsely populated. The corollary to this is that the settled areas are characterised by exceptionally high population densities, generally in excess of 1 000 persons per km².

Although the population distribution pattern largely reflects the occurrence of fragmented lowlands, the lowlands show considerable differences in population density. These differences, in turn, are the outcome of dissimilarities in the type and degree of development. At the macro-scale, the most densely-populated lowlands are those along the Pacific coastlands of the main island,

Honshu, running west of Tokyo and spilling over into northern Kyushu (Figure 7.4). Here is to be found the main generator of the Japanese economic powerhouse, a remarkable concentration of urban and industrial development. This is the **core** of the Japanese space economy. Whilst the lowlands elsewhere, in what might be termed the **periphery** of Japan, have their cities and concentrations of secondary and tertiary employment, their general ambience is much less pressured and intense. Significantly, the urban demand for space here is less voracious and allows many of the lowlands to continue to perform a vital agricultural role.

The disparity in the levels of development, as between the lowlands of the core and those of the periphery, is to be explained, as in other parts of the world, in terms of the latter's distance and inaccessibility from the main national markets. That inaccessibility has until recently been exacerbated by insularity; it is only since the late 1980s that Hokkaido and Shikoku have had direct transport links with Honshu. For northern Honshu and Hokkaido, explanation of the disparity also has an historical dimension, in that the relatively harsh environment of northern Japan has until this century deterred settlement and development.

Japan Inc. moves offshore

During the postwar period, the Japanese economy has undergone two distinct, but related changes. It has grown immensely in size. In terms of real GNP, it expanded nearly forty-fold during the period 1950 to 1990. At the same time, because of the increasing needs of this highly dynamic economy, it has been transformed from an economy largely contained within its own national boundaries to one that is truly global in dimension. The Japanese economy now has roots in, and draws growth from, almost all corners of the world. Initially, Japan reached offshore for supplies of food, and shortly after that for industrial raw materials and energy (Figure 1.2). Later, the overseas search turned to seeking even larger markets for its ever-increasing output

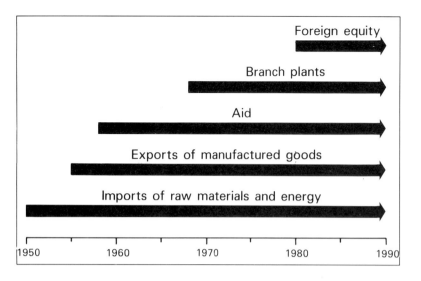

Foreign equity

Branch plants

Aid

Exports of manufactured goods

Imports of raw materials and energy

1950   1960   1970   1980   1990

Fig. 1.2 *Growing dimensions of Japan's economic involvement overseas*

of manufactured goods. Most recently, the offshore moves have tended to take two forms. Branch plants are being established in many countries in an attempt to take advantage of lower labour costs and to substitute local production for direct exports. Japan is also investing the profits of its successful economy to make even more money. This is being achieved by acquiring equity in foreign companies.

Because of these offshore moves, the Japanese economy has become thoroughly integrated into the global economic system. Because of its status in that system, the situation today is such that any change in the Japanese economy now reverberates around the world. Tokyo-watching is an everyday part of today's global business practice.

A special relationship

Of all its overseas contacts, none are more important than those with the USA. It may be rightly claimed that Japan has a special relationship. That relationship was born in 1945 as the American's led the Allied defeat and occupation of Japan. For the first five years of the postwar period, Japan was to all intents and purposes governed by the Americans. They were largely instrumental in drawing up the present Japanese Constitution; they also insisted on a whole range of reforms. Initially, the Americans showed themselves to be compassionate conquerors, supplying food to a population close to starvation and providing materials for the reconstruction of the country. The

Korean War (1950–1953) proved critical to the blossoming of the relationship. In return for its willing cooperation, mainly as an offshore military and supply base, Japan won three things – a peace treaty, the protection of American defence and favourable trading terms. The relationship has since gone from strength to strength, particularly on the economic side, to the point that the USA is Japan's number one trading partner and leading reciprocal investor. However, the balance in the flows of both goods and investment between the two countries now tips very much in Japan's favour. The implied reversal of fortunes, with the Japanese emerging as top dog, is clearly placing a strain on the American side of that special relationship.

Prefectures and central government

A final attribute requiring particular attention at this early stage is the Japanese system of government. Understanding this system provides the key to understanding much in the changing geography of Japan. This follows from the fact that the way in which a country governs itself incalcates and influences many different aspects of modern society. In a geographical perspective, it is seen to impact on a range of things, from the location of industry to the directions of overseas trade and investment, from the pattern of agriculture to the nature of the urban system.

Figure 1.3 shows the main islands of Japan and the division of the national territory into 47 prefectures. The prefectures are very unequal in terms of size. For example, Hokkaido, by far the largest prefecture, occupies an area 45 times that of the smallest, Osaka; Tokyo prefecture, with a population of about 12 million, contains 20 times more people than Tottori.

The prefecture is essentially the Japanese equivalent of the English county, but with one important difference. Although Japan has a centralised form of government, operating from Tokyo, within that unitary system the prefecture enjoys a much greater degree of freedom than its English

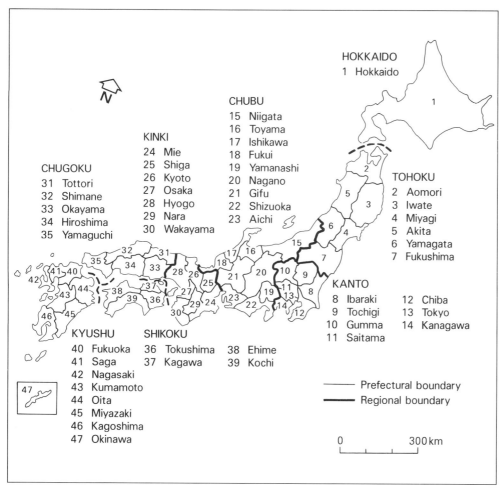

HOKKAIDO
1 Hokkaido

CHUBU
15 Niigata
16 Toyama
17 Ishikawa
18 Fukui
19 Yamanashi
20 Nagano
21 Gifu
22 Shizuoka
23 Aichi

KINKI
24 Mie
25 Shiga
26 Kyoto
27 Osaka
28 Hyogo
29 Nara
30 Wakayama

CHUGOKU
31 Tottori
32 Shimane
33 Okayama
34 Hiroshima
35 Yamaguchi

TOHOKU
2 Aomori
3 Iwate
4 Miyagi
5 Akita
6 Yamagata
7 Fukushima

KANTO
8 Ibaraki
9 Tochigi
10 Gumma
11 Saitama
12 Chiba
13 Tokyo
14 Kanagawa

KYUSHU
40 Fukuoka
41 Saga
42 Nagasaki
43 Kumamoto
44 Oita
45 Miyazaki
46 Kagoshima
47 Okinawa

SHIKOKU
36 Tokushima
37 Kagawa
38 Ehime
39 Kochi

—————— Prefectural boundary
━━━━━━ Regional boundary

0   300 km

Fig. 1.3 *The prefectures and regions of Japan*

equivalent. Central government control is less tight. In practice, this means that each prefecture has the power to enact and enforce its own legislation in such matters as taxation and financial budgets, economic development and social services. There is great scope for prefectural governments to be enterprising and innovative. They can make their own quite effective interventions in key aspects of everyday life, from building houses to constructing airports, from providing schools to reclaiming land, from setting up business parks to offering industrial incentives. Awareness of this greater autonomy of the Japanese prefecture is absolutely crucial in understanding the changing internal face of modern Japan. The policies and actions of individual prefectural governments can and do make considerable impact.

The prefectures are subdivided into local government areas with the distinction drawn between *shi* (urban) and *gun* (rural) districts. In the other direction, the prefectures are organised into eight *chiho* or regions (Figure 1.3). But there is no regional tier in the hierarchy of government; there is nothing between the central and prefectural levels of government. The regions are merely recognised in the compilation of official statistics and in the formulation of meso-scale planning strategies.

One of the popular misconceptions of modern Japan is that it represents the supreme example of the free market economy. That has not been the case during the postwar period; nor was it so before. Not only is there strong government at a prefectural level, but particularly in the economic sphere there has been, and still is, much intervention and direction by central government. To date, this has ranged from supplying private companies with information about overseas market opportunities to the protection of Japanese farming from foreign competition, from encouraging overseas investment to the promotion of high-tech industries, from the formulation of energy policies to subsidising major transport improvements. In short, Japan Incorporated has been carefully nurtured by government.

1.2   ROUND THE REGIONS

Table 1.2 presents some comparative statistics for the eight regions of Japan, whilst Figure 1.4 provides additional information. The ensuing commentary is intended merely to highlight the salient characteristics of each region. This introductory regional round-up should yield three vital things: (i) a basic spatial framework for future reference, (ii) an indication of the spatially variable character of Japan, and (iii) an impression of the broad geographic pattern produced by the processes of development up to 1990.

Hokkaido

Hokkaido is unique in the sense that it exists at two levels (Figure 1.3). This northernmost island is both a single prefecture and a *chiho*. The most strik-ing geographical feature is the mismatch between its shares of Japanese territory and population; less than 5 percent of the population is to be found on just over 20 percent of the land area (Table 1.2). By Japanese standards, it is distinctly sparsely popu-lated (Figure 1.4). The key to this lies in the island's rather inhospitable envi-ronment (Photo 1.5). Because of this and the general inaccessibility both within the island and from outside, much of Hokkaido is still at a pioneer stage. However, that is changing with the implementation of government-

backed development programmes, the recent opening of a direct rail link through the Seikan Tunnel under the Tsugaru Straits and the upgrading of airports and air services.

The resource-base of Hokkaido is quite varied. Fishing, coal-mining and forestry are three longstanding primary activities, but they are now outshone by agriculture. Quite remark-able achievements in plant breeding have meant that rice is now cultivated throughout almost the whole of Hokkaido. Today, however, the agricultural reputation of the island rests rather more on dairying and live-stock-rearing, and the cultivation of temperate cereals and root crops. These lines of farming have come into their own as the eating habits of the Japanese have become westernised.

Manufacturing is a relative newcomer to Hokkaido. Much of it is concerned with the processing of timber and agri-cultural and marine products; there is also some shipbuilding, steel-making and oil-refining. One final element in the island's economy that needs to be acknowledged is tourism which has expanded significantly, thanks to the fine scenery and wilderness, the vol-canoes and hot springs, and the heavy and enduring winter snows. The hold-ing of the 1972 Winter Olympic Games at Sapporo did much to boost the winter sports industry. Sapporo, the capital of Hokkaido, is, without doubt, one of the most attractive of all Japan's leading cities; its gridiron street pattern is a constant reminder that it was planned by an American architect.

Table 1.2   *A statistical comparison of the eight regions of Japan (1990)*

Region	Area (km2)	Percentage share of total area	Percentage mountains	Population lowland	Population (millions)	Percentage share of total population	Population density (p/km2)	Percentage share of GDP	Percentage share of primary sector output	Percentage share of secondary sector output	Percentage share of tertiary sector output
Hokkaido	83 500	22.1	49.0	11.7	5.6	4.6	72	3.8	10.9	2.6	4.1
Tohoku	67 000	17.7	62.0	14.3	9.7	7.8	145	6.3	16.2	5.3	6.3
Kanto	32 000	8.6	40.4	20.7	38.6	31.2	1 203	36.6	16.5	35.7	38.3
Chubu	67 000	17.7	70.9	14.9	21.0	17.0	313	17.4	15.9	21.4	15.1
Kinki	33 000	8.7	64.1	16.9	22.2	18.0	672	18.2	8.2	19.5	17.9
Chugoku	32 000	8.4	74.1	9.6	7.8	6.3	243	5.9	6.4	6.2	5.7
Shikoku	19 000	5.0	79.9	10.1	4.2	3.4	221	2.6	6.4	2.3	2.7
Kyushu	44 000	11.8	62.7	12.3	14.5	11.7	330	9.2	19.5	7.0	9.9
JAPAN	377 500	100.0	61.0	13.8	123.6	100.0	327	100.0	100.0	100.0	100.0

Photo 1.5 *Hokkaido – an abundant wilderness.*

Tohoku

This is one of five regional subdivisions of the main island, Honshu; its six constituent prefectures account for the northern part of the island (Figure 1.3). Its percentage shares of land and population suggest that this is another relatively sparsely populated part of Japan (Table 1.2). Whilst that is true, it also should be pointed out that the mean population density is twice that of Hokkaido (Figure 1.4). Historically, Tohoku has been regarded as a relatively remote and undeveloped region. Interestingly, it used to be called *michinoku*, which literally means 'the end of the road.' But the remoteness has been greatly reduced by recent transport developments, notably the completion of the *shinkansen* from Tokyo as far as Morioka, en route for the Seikan Tunnel and Hokkaido, and the construction of the Tohoku expressway to the ferry port Aomori (Photo 1.6). Due to its mountainous spines, movement between the Pacific and Japan Sea coasts of Tohoku remains rather difficult.

Economically, Tohoku is today the leading rice-producing region of Japan, growing about a quarter of the national output. It accounts for the largest share of Japanese primary sector output (Table 1.2). In the post-war period, there has been much reclamation, both of coastal shores and inland waters, to increase the amount of land available for rice production. Tree crops are grown in the more hilly country. Also contributing to the importance of the primary sector are fishing and aquaculture along the Pacific coast and forestry in the interior. Manufacturing has a relatively short history here, but since the early 1960s the Japanese Government has sought to encourage industry at selected locations in Tohoku. Sendai, a

Photo 1.6 *Transport improvements – Tohoku no longer the end of the road.*

go-ahead city of 900 000, is the regional capital and has become a major centre of office employment.

Kanto

Kanto is the centre of Japan – geographically, demographically and economically (Table 1.2). The seven component prefectures together account for a little less than 10 percent of the land area, 31 percent of the population and 37 percent of the national GDP (Figure 1.3). It is without

Regional Variations – a Comparative Summary

Chubu

Chubu is the most balanced of the regions, but occupying the whole width of central Honshu is very much a region of three parts:

(a) The Tokai subregion of fragmented lowland along the Pacific coast was once a prosperous farming area but this has largely been displaced by large-scale industrial development, with Nagoya the main centre of a string of cities linked by the Tokaido *shinkansen* and expressways – originally noted for textiles, its manufacturing base is now very varied, including motor vehicles (Toyota), oil refining and petro-chemicals, metals and engineering.
(b) Intervening mountains offer fine scenery and recreation. Most noted is Fuji-Hakone-Isu National Park stretching from Mt. Fuji to the beautiful Izu Peninsula - most frequented of all recreational areas in Japan.

(c) The Hokuriku sub-region, is one of the main rice producing areas and fronts the Japan Sea. It is important for engineering and electrical industries. Development recently aided by *shinkansen* and expressway links through central Alps to the Pacific Belt from Niigata. The Alps are the leading hydro–electricity region.

Kinki

Kinki centred on the three great cities of Kyoto, Osaka and Kobe is the next most important economic region to Kanto.

Kyoto is at the cultural heart of Japan displacing Nara in 794 AD as the capital until this was moved to Tokyo in 1868. Next to Tokyo, Kyoto is the main tourist centre and retains fine traditional craft industries – silk, pottery, handmade paper and traditional furniture.
Osaka and Kobe are the heart of the Hanshin industrial area – initially a textile area which turned to heavy industries in the 1920s and remains important for iron and steel, chemicals, shipbuilding and fine engineering. Kobe provides the main port gateway and Osaka has a new international airport.

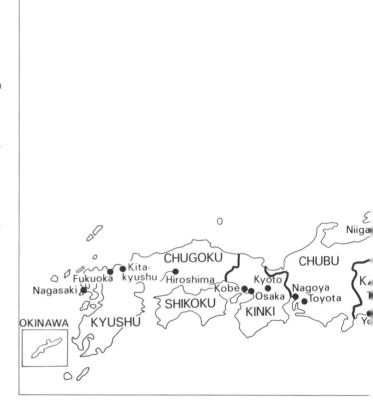

Chugoku

Makes up the 'toe' of Honshu. It is a small region and, in microcosm, is like Chubu, with the two coastal belts separated by a mountainous spine.

The Japan Sea belt known as *San-in* has very limited flat land, few natural harbours and poor accessibility. Thus development has been retarded. In contrast, the Inland Sea Belt (*San-yo*) has been one of Japan's most dynamic areas integrated with the Pacific Belt core by the *shinkansen*, expressways and the Inland Sea, (from early historical times a major artery). It has traditional industries but the emphasis is on heavy industries using imported raw materials and fuel. Hiroshima is developing a more diversifed industrial base due to increased accessibility and there are plans to develop an international airport. Shallow inshore water encourages aquaculture but also much land reclamation for industrial development.

Kyushu

Unlike Shikoku, Kyushu has for some time had the benefit of road and rail links to Honshu. The north developed as an important industrial region centred on Kitakyushu and Fukuoka. Based on coal, heavy industry developed but this, like shipbuilding at Nagasaki, has declined. But Kyushu has been successful in attracting high-tech industry, being second in this to the Kanto region. The south, with its mild winters and warm humid summers, is dominated by agriculture - rice, maize, vegetables and sub-tropical fruits. Tourism is of growing importance due to fine volcanic scenery and hot springs, displacing fishing on the coast as is tropical Okinawa island further south.**Okinawa** in part of the Nansei or Ryukyu islands stretching in a 1 000 km arc south west of Kyushu. Its sub-tropical climate is important for tourism though fishing remains significant.

Fig. 1.4

Hokkaido

The most sparsely populated region with 20% of Japan's area and only 5% of its population – because of its inhospitable environment and relative inaccessibility its development was late. It is now gathering pace due to the recent direct rail link via the Seikan tunnel under the Tsugaru Straits and the upgrading of airport links.

It has a varied primary resource base – coal-mining (declining), fishing and forestry – but these are overshadowed by the expansion of agriculture – temperate cereals, root crops, dairying and livestock distinguish it from the rest of Japan. But rice growing is now widespread as improvements in rice strains have enabled northward extension.

Manufacturing has expanded partly based on processing primary products – timber, agricultural, marine. In the 1960s shipbuilding, steelmaking and oil refining developed but are now declining. Some recent expansion of high-tech and light-industry, especially around Sapporo.

Tourism is now very important – fine scenery, wilderness, volcanoes, hot-springs and winter snows. Scene of 1972 Winter Olympics.

Tohoku

Though still relatively sparsely populated, the region has twice the mean density of Hokkaido. Accessibility greatly increased by completion of *shinkansen* line to Morioka and the motor expressway route to Aomori ferry port. Movement between the Pacific and Japan Sea coasts across Tohoku is difficult because of interior mountains.

This is the leading rice-producing area of Japan with 25% of the country's output, with much reclamation of coastal shores and inland waters increasing land available for rice. Tree crops are grown in more hilly areas plus some timber production. Fishing and aquaculture are important.

Since early 1960s the Government has encouraged industrial development. Better access has encouraged expansion of the Pacific Belt towards Sendai, the regional capital. Consumer and high-tech industry are likely to expand in the south of the region.

Kanto

Kanto is the heart of Japan geographically, demographically and economically. With only 10% of Japan's area it has 31% of its population with 37% national GDP. The core is South Kanto centred on Tokyo Bay with Tokyo, Kawasaki and Yokohama fused into a gigantic urban complex. Tokyo is the centre of the country's service, administrative and financial sectors and has a very varied manufacturing base. Yokohama is Japan's busiest port with the emphasis on port-related industries, whilst Kawasaki is a centre for heavy industry. Continued expansion of economic activity has led to severe land shortages, hence much coastal reclamation.

Despite large-scale urban development, the Kanto Plain remains an important agricultural region of very intensive land-use – rice production is significant, but the huge urban market encourages fruit, vegetables, flowers, dairying, poultry and pig rearing mainly under 'factory' conditions.

Severe conflict of land use between urban-based activities and housing on the one hand and farming on the other.

The Kanto Plain is fringed by scenic mountains with volcanoes, hot springs and lakes. Some of the best scenery is protected by inclusion in the Nikko and Chichibu–Tama National Parks, particularly attractive to day and weekend visitors from Tokyo metropolitan area. Hill and spa resorts offer a welcome and cool break from hot and humid conditions in the summer in the main cities and in winter snow cover on higher ground offers winter sports.

Shikoku

Smallest of the four main islands. It is 80% mountainous with settlement restricted to the discontinous coastal fringe, Southern Shikoku is one of the wettest and mildest parts of Japan and largely cut off by mountains – it is an agricultural area. In contrast, northern Shikoku is relatively dry and its accessibility increased by recent bridge links to mainland Honshu. It was mainly agricultural, productivity raised by large-scale irrigation schemes, but it is now developing industrially. The Government is concerned to improve this peripheral region and diversify its economic base.

doubt Japan's leading region; it is the true core of the Japanese space economy (Figure 1.4).

The greatest concentration of population in Japan occurs in the south of the region. Here the cities of Tokyo, Kawasaki and Yokohama are located so close together that they have become fused into a huge urban complex, crescentic in shape and wrapping around the shores of Tokyo Bay. As for the economic base, Tokyo flourishes on a mix of high-order tertiary and quaternary activities and a diverse portfolio of manufacturing (Photo 1.7). Yokohama's prosperity is rather more port-related (it is Japan's busiest port), whilst Kawasaki is an important centre of heavy industry. Around the eastern shore, there is much waterfront industry, such as oil-refining, iron and steel, chemicals and electricity generation. The whole of this industrial belt is known as the Keihin district. Its development has created a huge demand for industrial space, much of this being met by reclaiming large areas of land from Tokyo Bay.

Whether it is mere coincidence or not, it is worth noting that this vital region happens to occupy the largest lowland in the whole of Japan, the Kanto Plain. Despite the large-scale urban development, the Plain remains an important agricultural region (Table 1.2). From this arises one of the key issues in this region, namely the conflict between urban growth and farming and the former's erosion of a scarce resource. Rice is the dominant crop of the remaining farmland, but fruit and vegetables, poultry and pigs are other lines of agricultural production that flourish, thanks to the presence of the huge urban market.

To the north and west, the Kanto Plain is fringed by mountains. Due to their volcanic origin, hot springs abound and have given rise to many spas. The appeal of these areas to daytrippers and weekenders from the Tokyo conurbation is enhanced by the fine scenery. The national parks of Nikko and Chichibu-Tama now protect some of the best scenery. The altitude, in places in excess of 2 000m, offers a double recreational bonus. In summer, hill resorts like Karuizawa offer the opportunity for Tokyo-ites to cool off – to escape the hot, humid and enervating weather down on the plain proper. In winter, sub-zero temperatures and the persistence of a snow cover on the higher ground have encouraged the development of winter sports facilities.

Chubu

Of all the Japanese regions, Chubu is probably the best balanced in terms of its national percentage shares. Seventeen percent is the recurring value – it applies to Chubu's shares of land area, population and GDP (Table 1.2). The nine prefectures of Chubu provide a section across the width of central Honshu (Figure 1.3). For this reason, it is very much a region of three parts (Photo 1.8).

The corridor of fragmented lowlands along the Pacific coast of Shizuoka and Aichi is known as the Tokai region (Figure 1.4). Here, once prosperous farming has now been substantially displaced by large-scale industrial and urban development. The growth has been concentrated in a line of cities threaded together by the Tokaido *shinkansen* and expressway. Of these, the most important is Nagoya, Japan's fourth largest city and the centre of the Chukyo industrial district. Originally renowned for its textiles, Chukyo has since the Second World War become prominent in the manufacture of motor vehicles (Toyota), oil-refining and petrochemicals, metals and engineering. In stark contrast to the lowland pockets of dense development, the intervening mountains offer some

Photo 1.7 *Tokyo – a dynamic economic giant*

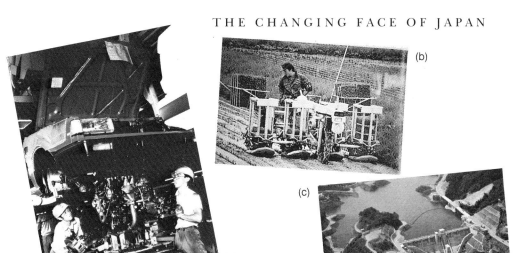

Photo 1.8 *The three parts of Chubu (a) motor vehicle manufacture at Toyota, (b) rice cultivation on the Niigata plain, and (c) HEP generation in the Central Highlands*

fine scenery and recreational opportunities. Most noteworthy is the Fuji-Hakone-Isu National Park, stretching from Mount Fuji (3 776m), the highest peak in Japan, down to the beautiful Izu peninsula. Given its location between the urban concentrations of the Tokai and Kanto regions, it is by far the most frequented of Japan's some 30 national parks.

Along the Japan Sea coast, and comprising the prefectures of Niigata, Toyama, Ishikawa and Fukui, is the Hokuriku region, the second major component of Chubu. This is one of the main rice-producing areas of Japan as well as an industrial region of some standing. Currently, it is enjoying renewed growth as the persistent handicap of isolation from the major national markets, caused by the great swathe of mountains referred to as the Japanese Alps, is gradually being overcome. Noteworthy has been the inauguration of the Joetsu *shinkansen*, which has reduced the travel time between Niigata and Tokyo to a mere two hours. Expressway links have also been completed to Tokyo, Osaka and Nagoya, and new ports created at Niigata and Toyama. However, for all their inaccessibility, the mountains are not without resources. Abundant hot springs have given rise to many spa resorts, whilst the remoteness and wilderness are being increasingly appreciated by people eager to escape the pressures of urban living for a few days. But even more important is the great HEP potential of the mountains. Exploitation of this resource in the postwar period has made the Alps the

leading HEP-generating region in Japan (Photo 1.8c).

Kinki

In terms of percentage share of population and GDP, the Kinki region just displaces Chubu as Japan's second most important region (Table 1.2). However, this status is achieved on a land area half the size, thanks mainly to a higher incidence of lowland. Just as Chubu is a region of three parts, so Kinki is a region of three cities – Kyoto, Osaka and Kobe (Figure 1.4). Kyoto, with a population of about 1.5 million, is Japan's fifth largest city. In 794 it superseded Nara as the capital city, a function which it retained until 1868 when Tokyo assumed the role. Because of that thousand years of involvement as the focus of Japanese society, Kyoto remains very much the cultural centre of the country and a tourist honeypot (Photo 1.9). It also remains an important centre of craft industries making such things as silk, pottery, hand-made paper and traditional furniture.

Osaka and Kobe, with populations of 2.5 and 1.5 million, are respectively the third and seventh largest cities in Japan. Both are important nodes in the Hanshin industrial district which has developed around the shores of Osaka Bay. This is Japan's second most significant industrial area. The early prosperity of Hanshin was based on the textile industry. During the 1920s it turned to heavy industries such as iron and steel, chemicals and shipbuilding. Since the Second World War, oil-refining, petrochemicals and motor vehicle manufac-

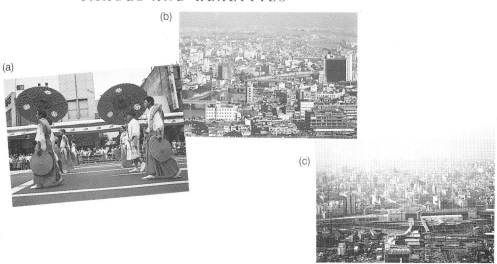

(a)

(b)

(c)

Photo 1.9. *Kinki's three cities (a) Kyoto, (b) Osaka and (c) Kobe*

ture have been added to the industrial portfolio. Although the Hanshin district currently has its problems, Osaka continues to enjoy a reputation as the industrial capital of Japan, whilst Kobe, its main gateway, remains the country's second busiest port.

Chugoku

The five prefectures of the Chugoku region make up the 'toe' of southern Honshu, a narrow peninsula lying between the Japan Sea and the Inland Sea (Figure 1.3). It is a small region,

accounting for 8 percent of the land area and 6 percent of Japan's total population and GDP (Table 1.2). It shows in microcosm the same three physical subdivisions as Chubu, namely two coastal belts of small, fragmented lowlands separated by a mountainous spine (Figure 1.4). The difference between the two coastal belts is considerable. The Japan Sea belt, known as *San-in* ('the shade of the mountains'), because of its much harder climate, less flat land, few natural harbours and poor accessibility, is one of the most retarded parts of Honshu in terms of development.

Photo 1.10 *Large-scale industrialisation around the Inland Sea*

In stark contrast, the Inland Sea belt, known as *San-yo*, has been one of the Japan's most dynamic areas (Photo 1.10). Since the Second World War, accessibility has been greatly improved. Along its length run the *shinkansen* and expressway linking Tokyo and northern Kyushu. The nature of Japan's postwar industrial development has also been a powerful incentive, in that the Inland Sea has provided an immense sheltered harbour for the huge ships bringing in oil, coal, iron and other industrial raw materials. The shallow in-shore waters have also allowed the reclamation of large amounts of land for the construction of industrial plants and modern port facilities. Today, perhaps because of its distance from the major domestic markets, the emphasis remains on heavy rather than consumer industry.

Shikoku

Shikoku is the smallest of the four main islands (Figure 1.3). Comprising four prefectures, it accounts for only 5 percent of the total land area of Japan (Table 1.2). It is overwhelmingly a mountainous island, with 80 percent of its terrain so classified. A discontinuous fringe of coastal lowlands accommodates the main settled areas (Fig. 1.4). Southern Shikoku is one of the warmest and wettest parts of mainland Japan; winters are especially mild. In contrast, northern Shikoku is relatively dry throughout the year. There are also some basic north-south contrasts in terms of development. Southern Shikoku is one of the most isolated parts of mainland Japan, being largely cut off by the east-west mountain spine. Its limited contribution to the national economy remains largely agricultural. The agricultural productivity of the northern part of the island has been significantly raised by some large-scale irrigation schemes. More importantly, it has enjoyed, but to a lesser degree, the same sort of postwar industrial development as has occurred in San-yo, on the opposite shores of the Inland Sea (Photo 1.10). However, as an industrial region, it has been seriously disadvantaged by the water separating it from the main urban markets on Honshu. At present, huge investments are being made in the construction of no less than three different island-hopping bridge links between Shikoku and Honshu (Photo 1.11). Already complete is the link between Sakaide and Kojima.

Kyushu

Unlike Shikoku, the island of Kyushu has for some time had the benefit of direct transport links with Honshu. There are road and rail tunnels running beneath the narrow straits at Shimonoseki as well as the Kaimon Bridge. But like Shikoku, Kyushu shows a strong north-south developmental contrast (Figure 1.3).

Two-thirds of the island's population is concentrated in the north, particularly in the prefecture of Fukuoka, where the two cities of Fukuoka and Kitakyushu each have populations in excess of 1 million. The latter is at the centre of one of Japan's four leading industrial regions. Although its fortunes have slipped somewhat in recent years, it remains an important for metals and chemicals, whilst to the west shipbuilding is a major activity at Nagasaki and Sasebo. Despite the industrial and urban development, agriculture is still significant and fishing remains a fairly prosperous activity along the north and north-western coasts (Table 1.2).

The southern two-thirds of Kyushu are still mainly preoccupied with farming.

Photo 1.11 *One of the new Honshu-Shikoku bridge links*

Photo 1.12 *Okinawa: a new conference centre*

Rice production dominates the coastal lowlands. But between harvests other crops are grown, such as vegetables and rushes for the weaving of *tatami*. Thanks to the winter mildness and improved transport, farmers are increasingly cashing in on the high prices paid in the large urban markets for early-season produce. On the hill slopes, the mandarin orange and other fruits become the main crops, while on the volcanic plateaus the cultivation of upland rice, maize, tobacco and vegetables is undertaken along with a certain amount of livestock-rearing. Attempts have been made to stimulate some industrial development. In the early postwar period, the aim was to take advantage of local supplies of timber and HEP and to exploit waterfront locations. More recently, Kyushu as a whole has met with some success in attracting modern high-tech industries. Fine volcanic scenery and abundant hot springs are the resources of a third component of the economy, a growing tourism.

A third part of the Kyushu region not to be overlooked is the Nansei (or Ryukyu) islands stretching for some 1000 km in a great arc southwestwards towards Taiwan. Administratively, most fall within the prefecture of Okinawa, the largest of the 60 or more inhabited islands. For 27 years after the Second World War, Okinawa was occupied by US troops. Although now returned to Japan, many American military installations remain. Servicing those bases and providing for the military personel have encouraged the urbanisation process, particularly around the capital city, Nara. Fishing remains a significant activity; the limited amount of manufacturing is mainly concerned with processing the output of a fairly productive agriculture, notably sugar and pineapples. The up-and-coming industry is tourism. The islands are popular with honeymooners and people taking short breaks to escape the hard winters of northern Japan. As an offshoot to tourism, determined efforts are being made to promote the international conference business (Photo 1.12).

That completes the regional round-up. Hopefully, together with the preceding section of this chapter, it has provided a flavour of Japan's geography and a starting point for the ensuing analysis of the changing face of the country. What should have emerged is that the regions exhibit both similiarities and differences. The similarities are largely to do with the unequal mix of lowland and upland, and the impact of the former and the coast on the location of settlement and development. The dissimilarities, such as are clearly indicated in Table 1.2 and Figure 1.4, stem in large measure from locational differences, primarily with respect to latitude, but also longitude. Locational differences lead to climatic contrasts which, in turn, impact on agriculture in particular and living conditions in general. Ultimately they are reflected in the pattern of uneven development.

2

The physical environment

2.1 OPPORTUNITIES AND CONSTRAINTS

The physical environment of any country is significant in a number of ways. Above all, it provides the very stage on which human settlement and development take place. But beyond that basic role of providing living space, it may be seen as operating in two essentially opposing ways. In a positive way, it offers opportunities. Most obviously, the physical environment can yield a whole range of resources, that is natural materials ranging from water and timber to minerals and energy, which are crucial to human progress. However, there are other and less direct ways in which that progress may be influenced in a positive way. For example, the occurrence of lowlands may well encourage the location of settlements and the concentration of agriculture. Indentations of the coast, particularly sheltered estuaries and bays, offer opportunities for the growth of ports. Snow-covered mountains may be exploited in the context of a winter-sports tourism. But very often the same features of the physical landscape can also be constraining in an essentially negative way. Those mountain areas may well prove to be inaccessible and a barrier to movement between different parts of the country. Those coastal embayments may be characterised by shallow water and therefore unusable by larger shipping. Those low-lying areas may be prone to regular flooding and therefore too hazardous for settlement and agriculture. Not everywhere is necessarily endowed with economically-exploitable mineral deposits and sources of energy.

This chapter describes and analyses the physical environment in these two ways. It seeks to identify the opportunities and the constraints and to make some sort of assessment of their relative impact on the course of Japanese development. The approach adopted is therefore essentially selective.

2.2 ISLANDS AND COASTS

A nation of islands

Japan is both an island nation and a nation of islands. It is a chain of some 3 900 islands stretching over 25 degrees of latitude, or approximately 3 000 km. The archipelago is dominated by the four main islands, which in order of size are Honshu, Hokkaido, Kyushu and Shikoku; together they account for 98 percent of the total land area (Table 2.1). The configuration of many of the small islands is controlled by a number of clearly defined tectonic arcs (Figure 2.1). To the north, the former Japanese islands of Sakhalin and the Kuriles coincide with two arcs which converge on Hokkaido. The Ryukyu arc runs through Kyushu and southwestwards out into the Pacific beneath the Nansei islands, thereby extending Japanese territory to within 100 km of Taiwan. The Bonin arc sets the alignment for the Izu and Ogasawara islands

Table 2.1 *The islands of Japan*

	Number of islands	Area (km²)	Area of main island (km²)	Length of coastline (km²)	Area per km of coastline (km²)
Hokkaido	263	83 520	78 073	2 447	31.9
Honshu	1 546	231 090	227 414	8 298	27.4
Shikoku	472	18 808	18 256	1 797	10.2
Kyushu	1 420	42 163	36 554	3 206	11.4
Okinawa	221	2 255	1 185	470	2.5
JAPAN	3 922	377 835	361 483	16 218	22.3

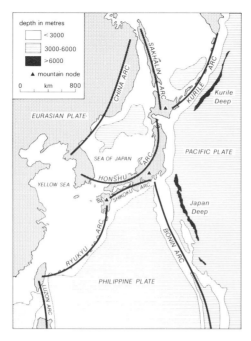

Fig. 2.1 *Tectonic arcs and ocean deeps*

Fig. 2.2 *Ocean currents*

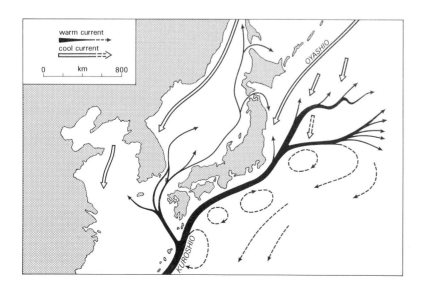

extending due south of Tokyo. These arcs coincide with the margins of tectonic plates. The last one, for example, coincides with the boundary between the Pacific and Philippine plates. Many of the islands, both here and along the other arcs, have been produced by volcanic activity.

This preponderance of islands has a number of significant consequences. It means that Japan has a very long coastline relative to its area; for every 22 km² of land, there is 1 km of coast (the ratio in the British Isles is 31 to 1) (Table 2.1). Nowhere is very far from the sea. The sea has been a strong and persistent influence throughout Japanese history. Because it is the

medium which separates the islands, the sea is to be seen as a divisive influence working against national unity. On the other hand, it has been a vital medium of transport and communication, a role emphasised by the mountainous nature of Japan and by the littoral location of many of the larger settlements. But the Japanese have looked to the sea, particularly the inshore waters, for another important reason – as a source of food. As elsewhere in the world, where there is a convergence of warm and cold ocean currents and a rich supply of plankton, so there have been rich and diverse stocks of fish (Figure 2.2). Fish, along with rice and *miso* (soya), form the traditional Japanese diet; fish is still eaten in immense amounts and in many different forms (raw, salted, smoked, cooked and as a soup stock). But the exploitation of the sea as a source of food involves much more than just fish; shellfish of all sorts and many varieties of seaweed are still consumed in large quantities (Photo 2.1).

Although Japan may justifiably be referred to as a maritime nation, it has not entirely matched the stereotype. Maritime nations have traditionally been outward looking and historically colonially oriented. The case history of Britain is a prime example, particularly between the 16th and 19th centuries, when it sought to explore overseas and gradually to acquire a vast overseas empire. But not so with Japan. For centuries, it literally closed its doors to the outside world; Japanese people scarcely ventured abroad. Only in the late 19th century did it begin to become ambitious in terms of overseas territory. From then onwards, however it quickly amassed an extensive empire in the western Pacific region, only to be totally divested of it when Japan surrendered at the end of the Second World War (1945) (Figure 10.1).

Coastal characteristics

The detail of the coast is subject to three major controls; the structural grain of the country, the impact of intense faulting and changes in sealevel. The outcome of these controls is that Japan may be divided into three distinct coastal regions (Figure 2.3).

Photo 2.1 *Exploiting the sea, (a) fishing boat unloading at port, (b) the Japanese whaling fleet factory ship Nisshin Maru, (c) drying seaweed and (d) fish farming*

The north-east region includes the Pacific coast of Honshu north of Tokyo, the Japan Sea coast north of Sakata and all of Hokkaido (Figure 2.3). For the most part this is an elevated coastline. As a result of uplifting, marine terraces are widespread, ranging in height from a little above the present high-tide line to over 300m above sea-level. Along the coastline, marine processes are tending to reduce irregularities, by infilling bays and cutting back headlands, and thereby gradually creating great sweeps of smooth coastline. Notable exceptions, however, include the coastline of eastern Hokkaido and of the Kitakami Mountains in northern Honshu. Along these stretches of coastline, drowning caused by land subsidence has accentuated the crenulations of the coast (Photo 2.2).

The coastline of the south-west region, which includes most of Kyushu and the Inland Sea between southern Honshu and Shikoku, is dominated by subsidence and therefore characterised by a highly-indented coastline (Figure 2.3). The Inland Sea is basically a huge, drowned, down-faulted basin. As the basin sank, so rocky inlets and small, rectangular fault-bound bays developed and former hilltops now poke above sea-level as small islands. Deposition is active in many of the bays

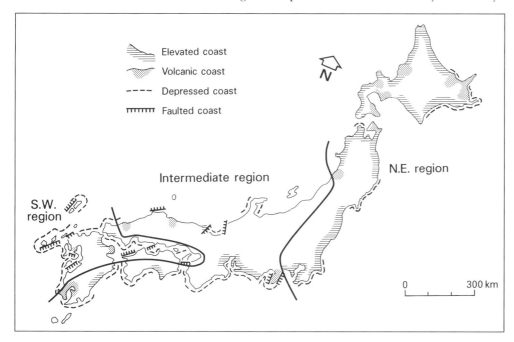

- ⎓⎓⎓ Elevated coast
- ⌒⌒⌒ Volcanic coast
- - - - Depressed coast
- ⊤⊤⊤⊤⊤ Faulted coast

S.W. region

Intermediate region

N.E. region

0   300 km

Fig. 2.3 *The three coastal regions*

Photo 2.2 *Contrasting coasts*

and inlets, leading to the formation of extensive bayhead marshes. The Inland Sea has offered much potential both in terms of sheltered shipping lanes and port development. Elsewhere, where the structural grain of the land runs at right angles to the coastline, long inlets and promontories, such as Nagasaki harbour and the Sadamisaki peninsula, have been formed.

The intermediate region comprises most of the Japan Sea coast of Honshu, the Pacific coast from Tokyo to the Inland Sea, and the southern coasts of Shikoku and Kyushu (Figure 2.3). Broadly speaking, subsidence has prevailed along the Pacific coast. Intense faulting has cut across the trend of the coastline breaking it into a series of impressive, fault-bound bays (Tokyo, Sagami, Suruga and Ize) and promontories (Boso, Miura and Izu) (Photo 2.2). In contrast, long stretches of the Japan Sea coast are characterised by extensive beaches and dunes backed by quite wide coastal plains. Here, the forces of sea, wind and river continue to work together to smoothen the coastline, infilling bays or sealing them off by the growth of lagoon-forming bars. Elsewhere, the general smoothness of the coastline derives from that fact that it runs parallel to a fault system along which downwarping has occurred. Only occasionally, as at Wakasa Bay, does the fault system cut across the coastline. Another notable

irregularity is the Noto peninsula with its indented coast. A little further to the north-east, it is possible that the island of Sato was once the distal end of a similar promontory which has since been breached by the sea.

2.3 THREE TYPES OF TERRAIN

Mountains and uplands

Over three-quarters of Japan is classified as mountainous, with land rising above 250m and sloping at more than 15° (Figure 2.4). There are some 15 peaks that exceed 3000m in altitude; nearly all are of volcanic origin and occur in the so-called **Japanese Alps** (Hida mountains) of central Honshu. The highest peak, Mount Fuji rises to 3776m . It is only in this central part of Japan that the mountains compare in size and grandeur with the European Alps. It is only here and in the high mountainous areas of Hokkaido that there has been glaciation. Elsewhere in Japan, the mountain landscape is made up of great slabs of elevated terrain. Although rarely rising above 1500m, they have been subjected to much folding, faulting and, most recently, deep dissection by V-shaped valleys. Separating the valleys are narrow ridges. The regularity of summit heights along many of these broken interfluves suggests that they may be

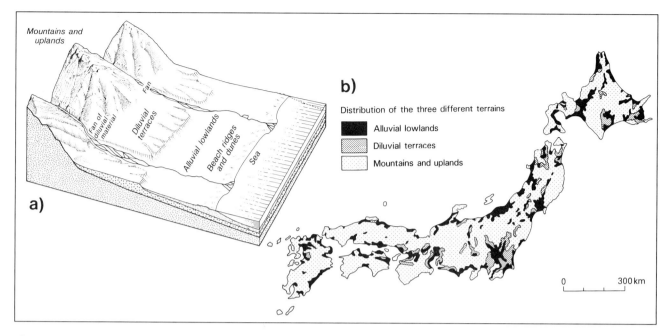

the remnants of former erosion surfaces.

In terms of settlement and development, the predominantly mountainous and deeply-cut terrain has been a persistent impediment to transport and national unity. Certainly, in the case of Honshu, historically the mountainous spine has tended to isolate settlements along the Japan Sea coast from those on the Pacific side. But the upland masses should not be written off as wholly negative areas. Indeed, probably they are beginning to be appreciated as they have never been before. A combination of the frenetic pressure of urban life today, and the rising leisure-consciousness of the Japanese, sees the upland interior being increasingly exploited for what they are, wilderness areas. They give Japan's urbanites the chance literally to get away from it all; a chance, in the Shinto tradition, to commune with nature and recharge the batteries.

Alluvial lowlands

In stark contrast to the all-prevailing uplands are the alluvial lowlands, accounting for no more than one-eighth of the land area of Japan (Figure 2.4). The typical alluvial plain is a stretch of water-borne sediments currently accumulating in either a coastal embayment or an upland basin. The former type prevails, but because the mountains frequently extend right

down to the sea in the form of promontories or steep, rocky cliffs, the coastal lowlands are discontinuous. So the overall topographic pattern of Japan is one of small, fragmented lowlands isolated by impenetrable uplands. Much the largest single lowland in Japan is the Kanto Plain of central Honshu. Extending to an area of 7000 km², it is significant that this plain now accommodates the burgeoning metropolitan area of Tokyo. Other lowlands of notable extent by Japanese standards are the Niigata, Nobi and Sendai plains of Honshu, the Ishikari and Tokachi plains of Hokkaido, and the Tsukushi plain of Kyushu. The significant point to be stressed here is that land suitable for human settlement is a very scarce resource in Japan. Throughout the 20th century, as Japan has been transformed into an urban society, so most of these lowlands have become battlefields between conflicting urban and rural interests. The outcome has been the progressive erosion of Japan's extremely small stock of farmland (particularly paddy-fields) by the relentless advance of the built-up area.

Diluvial terraces

Accounting for the remaining one-eighth of Japan is the third type of physical landscape, the **diluvial** terrain (Figure 2.4). It marks the transition between the steep upland slopes and the alluvial lowlands and is made up of

Fig. 2.4 *(a) Representative arrangement and (b) distribution of the different terrains*

sands and gravels deposited by turbulent streams as they debouch from the mountains. Each stream builds up its own fan or cone. The constituent material is graded, being coarsest at the upland margin and finest as it merges into the new alluvium of the lowlands. Often the streams are so close together that their fans coalesce to form a continuous piedmont belt. So great is the carrying power of many of these streams during times of flood that trains of diluvial material reach well out onto the plains. In all parts of Japan, it is common to find these diluvial areas cut into a series of terraces by geologically recent uplifting of the land. Each uplift has raised the diluvial deposits above the level of the newest alluvium and caused the streams to cut even more deeply into their fans. The diluvial terrain offers few opportunities in terms of economic development. Over the centuries, due to the ever-increasing demand for food, rice cultivation has been extended on to it from the alluvial lowlands. It has required intricate terracing of fans and their natural terraces (Photo 2.3). Traditionally, rice, tea and the mulberry (its leaves providing the staple diet of the silk worm) were widely grown. The paddy fields and tea bushes remain, but the mulberry groves have given way to orchards and in some places vineyards.

Photo 2.3 Diluvial terraces used for rice growing

Hazardous hydrology

Since nowhere in Japan is very far from the sea, rivers are typically short. The longest river, the Shinano flowing to the Japan Sea coast at Niigata, is a mere 367 km in length. The river Tone, which drains much of the Kanto plain, flows for only 322 km. Contrary to expectation, the Tone does not flow into Tokyo Bay. Instead, its lower course has deliberately been diverted eastwards to enter the Pacific at Choshi. In the mountains, the rivers are typically fast-flowing, tumbling down rocky channels. In the transitional zone of the diluvial terrain, the courses are gravel-choked and braided into numerous channels, whilst on the alluvial plains, except during periods of flooding, the rivers are shallow and flow in channels occupying only a small part of wide, boulder-strewn beds.

Not only are the rivers short, but because of the steepness of their mountain courses, they respond quickly to events such as the spring thaw, the intense rainfall of typhoons and the heavy downpours that occur during the two rainy seasons. In full spate, they have great erosive power. The material which is picked up and transported is then deposited to further extend the diluvial fans. They are also extremely prone to flooding and require much embanking, especially along their lower courses.

The pressure of human settlement on the scarce lowlands is such that deliberate risks are often taken with respect to the flood hazard (Photo 2.4). It is estimated that of all the damage caused by natural disasters in Japan, well over half is directly attributable to flooding. Table 2.2 itemises the damage caused by natural disasters in a typical year. Significant here is the secondary hazard of landslides, caused when flood water undercuts basal slopes and lubricates regolith.

On the positive side, it has been said that the resource potential of the rivers is very limited. They are not suited to shipping, but do provide water for both human consumption and irrigation of the paddyfields. Perhaps the most valuable aspect of Japan's hydrology are the many mountain lakes.

Persons – killed	187	Roads - places destroyed	4416
injured	653	Bridges – swept away	593
		Railways - places damaged	257
Buildings – ruined	742	Landslides	4556
swept away	239		
flooded	185 782	Boats – sunk	33
		swept away	15
Fields – swept away	7 283		
flooded	89 724	Communications broken	19 321

TOTAL COST OF DAMAGE – 797 billion yen

Table 2.2 *The typical extent of damage caused by natural disasters in one year (1975)*

Some have been exploited as reservoirs both for water supply and HEP generation. Others, particularly those occupying former volcanic craters, have great scenic appeal (Photo 2.5). Lakes such as Mashu and Toya in Hokkaido, Tazawa and Towada in northern Honshu, have become honeypots in the context of tourism; they also offer abundant opportunities for water-based recreation. By far the largest lake is Biwa (671 km²), occupying a fault basin to the east of Kyoto. For centuries, Biwa was a great source of inspiration in Japanese literature and poetry. It was well endowed with fish and much used for transportation. Today, however, due largely to its close proximity to the two major cities of Kyoto and Osaka, it is grossly overused as a source of domestic and industrial water, as a sewage outfall and as a recreational area. So great has been the pollution that many forms of biotic life have become extinct; there is also much concern about the great reduction in the lake's water-level.

Wetland reclamation

Reclamation of fluvial and coastal wetlands to create farmland and space for settlement has a long history in Japan, possibly dating back to the 9th century. There are few lowlands which have not been subject to some degree of reclamation. In many cases, it has simply involved embanking rivers and draining adjacent marshes. In other instances, lakes and ponds have been drained; for example, some 16 000ha of land have been recovered recently from Hachirogata, Japan's second largest lake. Coastal lagoons, tidal marshes, bay-heads and creeks have also experienced extensive reclamation.

Up until the 20th century, wetland reclamation was undertaken mainly to supplement the meagre amount of land suitable for agriculture, especially the growing of rice. Today, the prime motivators are urbanisation and industrial development. Nowhere in Japan have those pressures been greater than around Tokyo Bay, causing much modification of the original shoreline (Figure 2.5). An estimated 110 00ha of new land has been created here in order to provide additional space, not just for Tokyo, but also the other sizable cities that together make up the huge metropolitan area which now accommodates over 25 million people. The land has been put to a variety of uses: new port installations, heavy industrial developments such as oil refineries and steel works, housing, commercial growth, airport expansion

Photo 2.4 *The hazard of a swollen river during the spring thaw*

Photo 2.5 One of the 'honeypot' lakes

Fig. 2.5 Wetland reclamation around Tokyo Bay.

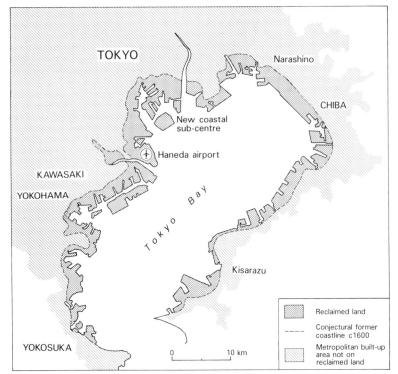

(as at Haneda airport) and the construction of basic urban services such as sewage treatment works and electricity generating stations.

2.4 VOLCANOES AND EARTHQUAKES

An abundance of active volcanoes

It has already been noted that Japan is located on a particularly unstable part of the earth's crust, where the Pacific and Philippine tectonic plates collide with and are subducted beneath the Eurasian plate (Figure 2.1). The immense forces associated with the collision have thrown up Japan's fold mountains, caused recurrent faulting and given rise to much volcanic activity. Today, Japan claims some 60 active volcanoes; they represent about one-tenth of the global stock. In the circumstances, it is fitting that one of the national symbols of Japan should be a volcanic cone, Mount Fuji (3 776m). Most of the active volcanoes lie along the Honshu arc, especially in Tohoku, where Mount Asama is the most renowned and feared (Figure 2.6(a)). In Hokkaido, notable volcanoes include Daisetsu and Tokachi; Showashinzan erupted first in 1944, and its cone now reaches to some 400m. Shikoku has no active volcanoes, but neighbouring Kyushu contains some of the best known, such as Mount Aso (one of the finest calderas in the world), Sakurajima and Unzen (Photo 2.6). Given its long geological history of vulcanicity, it is not surprising that a quarter of the land surface of Japan is made up of volcanic deposits.

Despite this abundance of active volcanoes, it has to be said that activity is not of the spectacular, cataclysmic type. Most regularly spew out either small amounts of lava or great clouds of fine ash and steam. Sakurajima, for

26

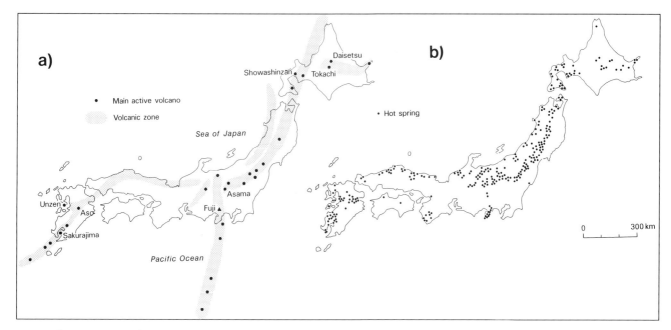

a)

- Main active volcano
~ Volcanic zone

Sea of Japan

Daisetsu
Showashinzan • • Tokachi

Asama

Unzen •
• Aso
Fuji ▲
Sakurajima

Pacific Ocean

b)

• Hot spring

0   300 km

example, constantly showers the nearby city of Kagoshima with ash and dust; Mount Aso bubbles away fairly benignly for the benefit of tourist hoards (Photo 2.6). Perhaps the worst aspect of the Japanese volcanoes is their habit of lying dormant for many years and then suddenly, without warning, springing into life. Mount Asama erupted in 1783 causing some 12 000 deaths; its next full eruption was not until 1912, followed by its most recent outburst in 1982. Miyaki, a volcanic island in the Bonin arc, was thought to be extinct, but suddenly exploded into life in October 1983. Most recently, Mount Unzen erupted in June, 1991, causing some fatalities. Mount Fuji, the highest mountain in Japan and the most perfect of volcanic cones, is declared to be dormant, and that is what it has been since 1708, but who knows for how much longer?

Because the perceived risk is thought to be small, farming and settlement have not been deterred from encroaching on the lower slopes of active volcanoes. But the encroachment has occurred because of the general pressure of population on the lowlands, not because of what is often the case, the lure of fertile soils. It is a sad fact that the lava of most Japanese volcanoes is acidic and that much of the total volcanic output is in the form of ash. As a consequence, the soils which develop on volcanic deposits are generally too porous and lack essential mineral nutrients to be of much agricultural value.

Minerals and energy

No less disappointing for Japan is the fact, that, despite prolonged tectonic and volcanic activity, the country has a pitifully meagre resource base of minerals. This alone makes all the remarkable Japan's rise as one of the world's leading industrial nations.

Fig. 2.6 *The distribution of (a) active volcanoes and (b) hot springs*

Photo 2.6 *Mount Aso caldera*

The most abundant mineral is coal. Annual production is in the order of 18 million tons. Domestic coal production accounts for about one-tenth of Japan's total primary energy budget. Coal is found at opposite ends of country, with Hokkaido and Kyushu each contributing about 40 percent of total output (Figure 2.7). This present equality of the two islands represents a considerable change in relative importance. Before the Second World War, Kyushu raised about 65 percent of Japan's domestic coal, and Hokkaido only 20 percent. The principal coalfields of Kyushu are all located in the north of the island at Chikugo, Sasebo, Amakusa and Miike. In Hokkaido, the main coalfields are at Ishikari, Kushiro and the offshore island of Rumoi. Of the coal produced, only 20 percent is coking coal and 5 percent bituminous coal. The remaining 75 percent is made up of steam coal, now mainly used for electricity generation. Because of its geological history of recurrent folding and faulting, coal seams are much disturbed and mining made difficult and expensive. Generally speaking, coal seams are thicker and of better quality in Hokkaido.

As regards other energy-giving minerals, Japan is almost destitute in terms of oil and natural gas. Less than one percent of its total needs of both fuels comes from domestic sources. The two main oil-bearing areas are at Akita and Hokuriku along the Japan Sea coast of northern Honshu (Figure 2.7). Natural gas is also extracted at Hokuriku and in Chiba prefecture near Tokyo.

Deposits of metallic ores are both small and rich in impurities. Japan produces about one-tenth of its iron ore requirements, this coming from small mines mainly in Hokkaido and Tohoku (Figure 2.7). The same areas are also the producers of small quantities of copper, lead and zinc. Finally, attention should be drawn to the fact that Japan does have its own sources of uranium.

Hot springs

Although Japanese volcanoes are a disappointment in terms of farming and minerals, they have yielded one valuable resource in the form of innumerable hot springs which occur throughout much of the country (Figure 2.6(b)). There are no less than a thousand hot spring areas designated within the volcanic zones of Japan, and most of these areas have developed their hot spring resorts. Taking a hot-spring bath is one of the traditional pastimes of the Japanese. As a custom, it is no less popular today than it was centuries ago. It is regarded not only as a hygienic and therapeutic practice, but also as a social occasion, a time to relax and chat. No weekend break or annual holiday taken in Japan would be

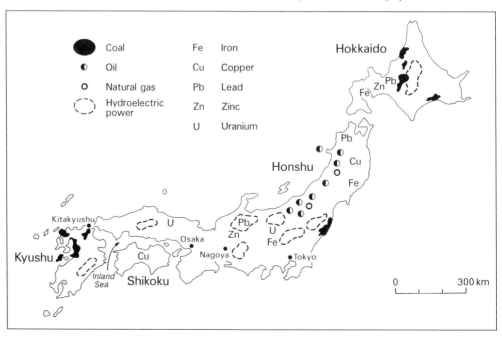

Fig. 2.7 *The distribution of industrial resources and energy*

regarded as complete without a few hours spent in a hot mineral bath. But for some, taking a hot-spring bath also has a more serious, medical side. Since the mineral qualities of the spring water vary from area to area, so too do the claimed medicinal properties. Thus particular areas have become famous for the treatment of particular medical disorders. Major spa resorts today include Beppu in Kyushu, Atami on the south coast of Honshu near Mount Fuji and Noboribetsu in Hokkaido. These coastal spas contain literally hundreds of hotels, each with its own supply and pools of hot-spring water where bathers soak and socialise. There are also many spa resorts up in the mountains; generally speaking, these are smaller but no less busy.

Thus vulcanity has produced a resource, the exploitation of which gives rise to a year-round tourism. That tourism is also boosted by the scenic appeal of the volcanic landscapes which more and more people are coming to appreciate given greater leisure time and the increased personal mobility provided by the motor car.

The geothermal energy of hot springs, although accounting for a very small part of Japan's total energy supply, has been harnessed for a diversity of purposes. It is used to provide heating for community housing projects, for glasshouses, for the evaporation of salt from sea-water, for drying fish and for fermenting soya bean curd.

Earthquakes

Earthquakes are very much a feature of everyday life. They represent the release of stress energy built up as the tectonic plates converge or slide past each other. In any one year, there may be as many as 5 000 earthquakes tremors. Most of these would be so weak as to be imperceptible to people. Gifu in central Honshu currently holds the record, with 516 noticeable earthquakes recorded in one year; Tokyo averages around 150 such tremors each year.

Japanese earthquakes are of two types. First, there are those that occur in the zone where the Pacific and Philippine

Photo 2.7 Hot spring resort

plates are subducted beneath the Eurasian plate (Figure 2.1). They are typically large-scale earthquakes with deep epicentres. Their strength is often so great that they cause major crustal disturbances and immense damage. But possibly their worst aspect is that, since their epicentres are located out at sea, they generate huge tidal waves, known as **tsumanis**. These waves can travel at speeds up to 110 kph and greatly increase in height, often to 30m, as they enter shallow inshore waters. Damage to property is overshadowed by the fact that many lives are lost due to drowning. The destructive potential of the tsunami is increased by the fact that so much of the Japanese population lives on low-lying coastal plains. Land subsidence is adding to their vulnerability. Osaka is sinking at a rate of about 5cm each year, and since 1935 its port area has subsided by 3m. The subsidence is caused here as elsewhere by the pumping of water from artesian wells and by the sheer weight of the built-up area compacting the ground. Another particular aspect of the earthquake hazard affects areas of reclaimed land. More vigorous tremors cause a 'liquefying' of the sands, gravels and other materials used in the reclamation process. As a consequence, heavy structures, such as apartment blocks, literally sink into the ground. What was a ground-floor flat can become a basement flat in a matter of minutes !

The second type of earthquake are those generated along major fault-lines at the rigid margin of the Eurasian plate. These are experienced almost everywhere in Japan and are the more frequent type. Their epicentres lie close to the surface. They affect both geological structures and the development of medium-scale landforms. They can cause considerable havoc, not just to buildings. Their shaking can trigger huge landslides, particularly during the wet seasons when hillslopes are highly lubricated; landslides, in their turn, cause much damage to roads and railway lines (Photo 2.8).

Undoubtedly, the worst Japanese earthquake on record occurred on 1 September 1923. In a matter of minutes, the Great Kanto Earthquake had killed over 100 000 people and destroyed some 300 000 buildings. The earthquake centred on Sagami Bay, 90 km south of Tokyo. So great was the force of the earthquake that the floor of the bay was split; the south coast was uplifted by nearly 2 m and the north coast depressed by a similar amount. There was also lateral displacement of up to 4 m. Even in distant Tokyo, there was an uplift of 10 cm and a horizontal displacement of 20 cm. Many of the deaths were not caused by falling building, but by the fires that resulted from stoves being overturned. Large areas of Tokyo and Yokohama, with their densely-packed wooden houses, were completely devastated by fires which raged for several days. Also adding to the fatalities, and even further afield, were the tsunamis which swept along the Pacific coast; ships were washed inland, people and buildings swept out to sea.

Although earthquake warning systems have improved immensely with modern technology, it remains easier to predict where an earthquake will take place rather than when. A whole range of precautionary measures are taken. Much housing is still built of light materials; larger buildings are constructed in such a way that they can withstand earthquake tremors up to a certain magnitude. Coastal defences are strengthened, and the general public are instructed in emergency procedures. But the risk remains, as does the fear that another Great Kanto Earthquake (more than 8 on the Richter scale) will strike one of Japan's largest cities. Will all those high-rise buildings survive? What of the hundreds of thousands travelling on the underground system during the rush hour? Will the spread of fire be contained? What about all those people living in apartment blocks built on reclaimed land? Will the coastal defences hold? The questions have yet to be answered, but posing them serves to underline the point that, for

Photo 2.8 *Minor, but frequent earthquake damage*

all the modern technology and precautionary measures, earthquakes remain a major hazard in Japan.

2.5 CLIMATIC CHARACTERISTICS

Climatically, the most significant aspect of Japan is its location at the mid-latitudinal margins of the Eurasian continent. As a result of that location, the climate reflects the impact of contrasting air mass influences – polar and tropical, continental and maritime – and their conflict along frontal zones. During the course of a year, the air-mass battleground makes a double passage across Japan and in so doing creates of climatic calendar of six seasons.

A year of six seasons

The mechanism responsible for this seasonal pattern is the **monsoon**, the twice-yearly reversal of pressure and wind systems. In winter, Siberia is dominated by high pressure; bitterly cold, north-westerly blasts of polar continental air prevail. Gradually, the high pressure gives way to the summer situation of low pressure and south-easterly winds of tropical maritime air. The transformation is a slow one, with the result that spring is a relatively long season of unsettled weather extending from late February to mid-June (Figure 2.8). But before spring turns to summer, there is a short rainy season, known as the *baiu*, which lasts from mid-June to mid-July. At this time, the polar front between polar continental and tropical maritime air masses passes north-westwards over Japan and causes great amounts of rainfall. High summer, with its hot, humid and enervating weather, lasts until early September, when the polar front retreats south-eastwards back across Japan and gives rise to another short rainy season, the *shurin*. The transition back to winter monsoon conditions is achieved quite quickly, so autumn is a relatively short season lasting from mid-October to mid-November.

Although all parts of Japan experience these six seasons, their relative duration and their temperature and precip-itation levels vary from place to place. Broadly speaking, it will be seen in Figure 2.8 that as one moves northwards, spring and autumn become longer as high summer shortens. That different parts of Japan should experience different temperatures is hardly surprising given that Japan spans some 25° of latitude. In January, when much of Hokkaido has a mean temperature of 8°C below freezing, southern Kyushu enjoys an average of 8°C above. Temperature contrasts are less marked in summer. In August, for example, the north-south difference is only 6°C. As a result of these seasonal temperature gradients, Hokkaido experiences a cool-summer continental climate, northern Honshu a warm-summer continental climate, and the rest of Japan a humid sub-tropical climate.

Patterns of precipitation

It is rather more difficult to generalise about the distribution of precipitation, because of the effects of local variations in altitude and aspect. Broadly speaking, there are three areas of above-average precipitation (greater than 200 cm per annum): (i) the Pacific side, south of 35°N, with its high mountains facing the on-shore winds of summer; (ii) the Japan Sea side, north of about 35°N, where high ground obstructs the polar air masses coming from the heart of Asia in winter, and (iii) the Japanese Alps of central Honshu (Figure 2.9). Notable areas of relative low precipitation (less than 150 cm) include the eastern half of Hokkaido, the eastern side of northern Honshu and the coastlands of the Inland Sea. A significant factor in the first two areas is the presence of the cold Oyashio ocean current along the Pacific coasts north of latitude 38°N (Figure 2.2). Onshore winds passing over this current are cooled and therefore made much more stable. Elsewhere around the shores of Japan, the warm Kuroshio ocean current prevails and is a factor encouraging rather than diminishing precipitation.

Because of the *baiu* and *shurin* seasons, precipitation is heavier during the summer half of the year, and amounts are generally higher on the Pacific side of Japan. In winter, the distribution pattern is reversed. Northwesterly

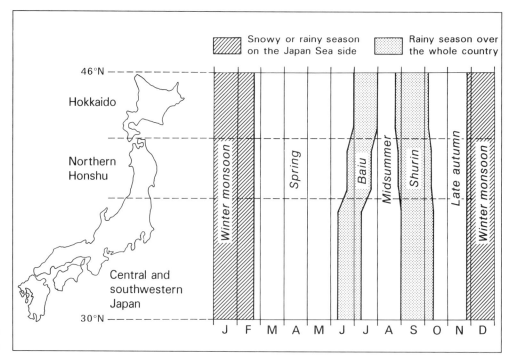

Fig. 2.8 *The seasons of Japan*

winds from the continent pick up moisture as they move across the Japan Sea and its branch of the warm Kuroshio current. The air is then uplifted by the mountains and most of the moisture squeezed out as snow. On the Pacific side of the mountains, the winter weather is altogether different. The northwesterly winds, having lost their moisture and strength, now permit clear, sunny days and very frosty nights. The winter differences between the two coasts may be illustrated by comparing Niigata on the Japan Sea coast with Tokyo on the Pacific side of the mountains. Niigata receives an average 56 hours of sunshine in January, whilst Tokyo, no more than 250 km away, enjoys 189 hours. In the same month, Niigata receives up to four times more precipitation.

Climate as a resource

Agriculture is probably the realm of human activity in which the Japanese climate is most exploited as a resource. Conditions are such that rice, the staple crop, can be grown virtually throughout the length of Japan. The timing of the two rainy seasons is fairly crucial, but even so irrigation is needed to supplement rainfall. Except in Hokkaido and on the eastern side of northern Honshu, winter temperatures are such that it is possible to grow a

second crop on the paddyfields. The range of climates experienced in Japan contributes significantly to the diversity of Japanese agricultural output. The cool climate of Hokkaido is well suited to the cultivation of temperate cereals and root crops; it also permits the growth of a good pasture for grazing livestock. In the southern half of Japan, the climate favours the production of a diversity of sub-tropical fruit, from mandarin to *nashi*, from peach to persimmon.

That same climatic diversity is also being increasingly exploited in the context of tourism. The mountain areas of Hokkaido and central and northern Honshu, with their heavy snowfalls, are being increasingly developed as winter sports resorts (Photo 2.9). Holding the 1972 Winter Olympics at Sapporo proved to be a powerful stimulus to the development of Hokkaido's great potential for skiing and ice-skating. At the other extreme, the sub-tropical climate of Kyushu and Okinawa appeals both to those taking their annual summer holiday, and those wishing to escape the harsh northern winter for a weekend break in the sun.

Climatic hindrances and hazards

Japan's climate is not all pluses; there

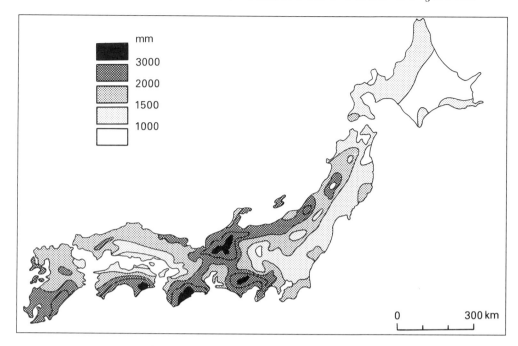

Fig. 2.9 The distribution of annual precipitation

are some constraining aspects. Transport and movement over much of northern Japan are often impeded in winter by heavy snowfalls (Photo 2.9). Flooding is all too common an occurrence, the outcome of the spring melt, the duration of the two rainy seasons and the passage of typhoons.

Typhoons, tropical revolving storms characterised by winds of very high velocity and torrential rainfall, constitute one of Japan's worst environmental hazards (Table 2.2). They occur principally between July and November and are disruptions to the normal seasonal weather patterns. The number in any one year can vary between 3 and 30. Originating out in the Pacific, typhoons take arcuate courses, first moving westwards and then turning towards the northeast. The main damage caused by the high winds, which blow at speeds up to 200 kph, includes destroying houses, felling power lines, flattening ripening rice and downing tree crops. Heavy rain, with 30 cm often falling in 24 hours,

Photo 2.9 Heavy winter snow – a resource and a hindrance

causes much flooding and many land-slides. Flooding in coastal areas is also exacerbated by the huge tidal waves whipped up by the wind, particularly where those waves are funnelled into inlets and bays. The western and southern coasts of Kyushu often suffer most at the hands of typhoons; also vulnerable are the Pacific coasts of Shikoku and Honshu.

2.6 ECOSYSTEMS AND BIOTIC RESOURCES

Attention has already be drawn in 2.2 to the aquatic resources of Japan (Photo 2.1). So it only remains under this section heading to consider the terrestrial resources of soils and vegetation.

Thin **lithosols** totally unsuited to cultivation characterise the mountains and uplands that account for nearly three-quarters of Japan's land surface. On the diluvial terraces, soils also tend to be immature and easily leached. In both types of terrain, soil erosion is a major problem, due to the combination of steep slopes, often made unstable by earthquakes and heavy precipitation. It is only on the alluvial lowlands, representing no more than 15 percent of the land area, that soils of any agricultural value are to be found. Despite careful husbandry, even these soils have become degraded by either the constant monoculture of rice or the demanding annual crop regime of rice followed by a winter cereal or vegetable. Heavy applications of human and animal waste have been the traditional way of maintaining the productivity of the alluvial soils.

Forests are the prevailing ecosystem type and constitute an outstanding feature of the Japanese landscape. Even today, such ecosystems cover something in the order of 65 percent of the land surface. This figure is unmatched by any other industrial nation. That so much forest should survive is mainly a reflection of the fact that the agricultural potential of the uplands and mountains has been so low as never to justify large-scale clearance. Inaccessibility has been another deterrent. Where clearance has taken place, sufficient time has generally been allowed to elapse for regeneration of the ecosystem. Wood has always been a vital article in Japanese civilisation, being the traditional building material and fuel. More recently, timber resources have been exploited for their woodpulp and as a source of rayon. The forests also add significantly to the beauty of the Japanese mountain scenery, and in a sense are being exploited today in the context of tourism.

The forest ecosystems of Japan are broadly of three types (Figure 2.10). In the north and east of Hokkaido, there are the coniferous forests made up largely of fir and spruce. These are exploited mainly for pulp, rayon and construction timber. The cool-temperate deciduous forest extends from southern Hokkaido down to central Honshu. Beech, maple, chestnut and oak are the most sought after hardwood species, being used for building purposes and in the manufacture of furniture. Unfortunately, it has been the custom to replant felled areas of

Fig. 2.10 *Vegetation regions and altitude zones*

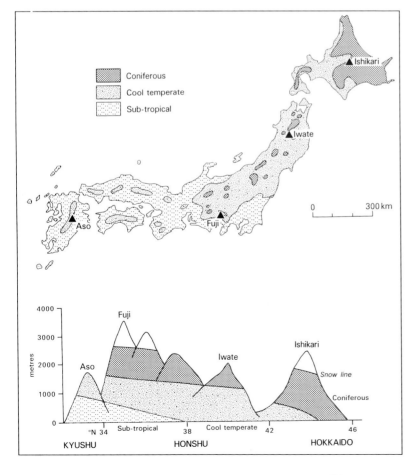

34

this forest with exotic conifers; so these broad-leaved forests are a dwindling ecosystem. In southern Honshu, Shikoku and Kyushu the forests are of a subtropical type, being made up of evergreen hardwoods such as the evergreen oak, camphor, myrtle, hemlock and cedar. The timber resources of these forests have not been so highly prized as the previous type, and here again there is a tendency to replant with more useful species of cedar and pine.

Outside the forests, on the lower ground, ecosystems have either been eliminated or drastically modified by human activity. In terms of the wellbeing of wildlife, possibly the most serious damage has been inflicted on wetland ecosystems. Large-scale reclamation and widespread canalisation of streams and rivers have greatly reduced their extent and seriously disturbed their food chains (Photo 2.10). One obvious consequence for bird populations has been the removal of breeding habitat and the loss of critical feeding areas used by migrants as they make their twice-yearly journey along the West Pacific flyway.

2.7 A MEAGRE AND HAZARDOUS ENVIRONMENT

Many geographical and historical studies of Japan frequently stress the inhospitable character of the physical environment. The preceding account has clearly demonstrated that there are aspects of that environment which have not been conducive to human settlement or to development in general. Five constraints would seem to merit highlighting, namely (i) the prevalence of a mountainous terrain, (ii) the diversity and severity of natural hazards (earthquakes, typhoons, floods, landslides and the occasional volcanic eruption), (iii) the meagre resource base of minerals and energy, (iv) the very limited amount of land suitable for agriculture, and (v) the duration and harshness of the winter along the Japan Sea coast of northern Honshu and in Hokkaido.

Looking at the physical environment in a positive way, that is in terms of its potential and opportunities, there is much less that can be said. There are fewer significant entries to be made on the credit side of the environmental ledger. Mention should be made of (i) the rich timber resources, (ii) the once rich fishery resources of its territorial waters, and (iii) the leisure opportunities of hot springs, water-based recreation, fine scenery and wilderness. Fourthly, Japan's climate has to be acknowledged in a number of different positive roles. In the same context of leisure and recreation, it provides the vital basis for the rising winter sports industry of northern Japan, as well as for the increasingly popular winter-sunshine breaks offered in parts of southern Japan. In an agricultural context, there is the suitability of the climate for rice cultivation and the production of a wide diversity of other crops.

On balance, it would seem that the constraints outweigh the opportunities. Such an evaluation makes all the more remarkable Japan's rise as one of the leading nations of the world – a case of resourcefulness triumphing over a dearth of resources!

Photo 2.10   River canalisation

The early development of Japan

3.1 THE GROWTH AND DISTRIBUTION OF POPULATION

Whilst Japan's postwar rise to the status of an economic superpower is remarkable, there is nothing startling in the way it has been achieved. Throughout a long history, its people have striven to make full use of the country's limited physical resources. At different times, exploitation of those resources has been supplemented by the utilisation of materials imported from abroad. Initially, these came from neighbouring countries, notably China and Korea, but today things such as industrial raw materials and energy are drawn from many different parts of the world.

Clearly a vital ingredient in Japan's economic success has been its population. In many respects, the attributes of that population have compensated for the meagre physical resource base. The size of population has been significant in terms of determining the dimensions of its potential labour force, whilst personal qualities such as the strong work ethic, unity of effort, good management, persistent application and foresightedness, have immeasurably increased its value to the economy. But those human resources too have in a sense been supplemented and enriched by importations from abroad. In particular, since the 16th century Japan has drawn heavily on the scientific and technological advances of the West and on its economic and education systems.

The exploitation of its own physical and human resources, and the supplementation of that resource base by judicious imports, have enabled an economic structure to be built up of sufficient strength to support Japan's large population of some 123 million at the high standard of living they currently enjoy. The foundations of this success have a history far longer than the postwar period. Similarly, many of the distinctive features of Japan's human geography today have roots reaching back over centuries rather than decades.

The rate of population growth at any given time is dependent on the rate of **natural increase** (the difference between crude birth and death rates) and the size of the population to which this relates, plus the balance of migration flows into and out of a country. One of the striking features about Japan's demographic history is that, apart from the return of 7 million Japanese ex-patriots and military personnel at the end of the Second World War, migration has had relatively little influence on the country's population growth since feudal times. The Japanese belief in their homogeneity as a people is clearly related to this record of very limited immigration. Thus, in analysing population growth in Japan, it is the difference between birth and death rates that is crucial. Changes in this difference have been strongly influenced by the interaction of factors arising from the people-environment relationships shown in Figure 3.1.

The historical anaylsis contained in this and the following chapter will seek to relate Japan's development to the stages defined in two models, namely that known as the **demographic transition** (Figure 4.5) and that produced by Rostow, the economist, the **stages of economic growth** (Figure 3.5).

The high stationary phase of the demographic transition

From the Middle Ages through to the

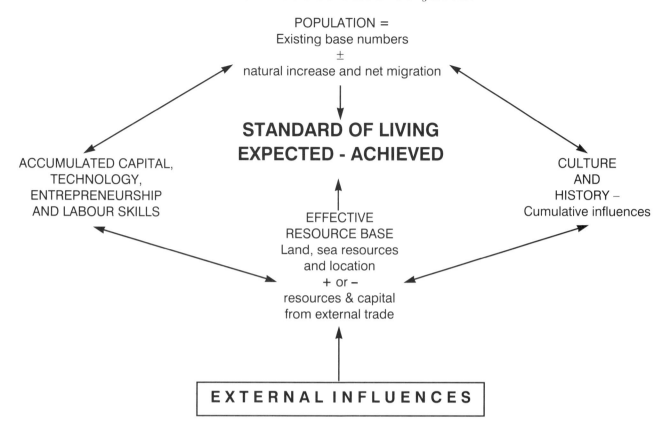

POPULATION =
Existing base numbers
±
natural increase and net migration

STANDARD OF LIVING
EXPECTED - ACHIEVED

ACCUMULATED CAPITAL,
TECHNOLOGY,
ENTREPRENEURSHIP
AND LABOUR SKILLS

EFFECTIVE
RESOURCE BASE
Land, sea resources
and location
+ or –
resources & capital
from external trade

CULTURE
AND
HISTORY –
Cumulative influences

EXTERNAL INFLUENCES

Fig. 3.1 *People-environment: basic components and linkages*

middle of the 19th century birth rates were moderately high. The intensive agricultural system underlying Japan's economy required a high labour input, and parents saw a reasonably large family as security in their old age. But there is evidence that right into the 19th century, because of poor medical care during child birth and famines causing the loss of unborn babies, the birth rate was kept in check. Although no means of artificial birth control were available, abortion and infanticide were practised at every level of society. During the Tokugawa period (1615 – 1867) as many as two out of every five babies were killed, usually females as they were seen as a financial burden. Whilst this deliberate reduction of population was to some extent prompted by limited food supplies, much of it was bound up with the many restrictions placed on the peasantry and with traditions that limited the size of families amongst the upper classes.

The death rate remained persistently high because of the harsh living conditions. Less than 15 percent of the land was cultivated and famines caused by floods, drought, frosts and typhoons, together with the poor transport system, severely reduced population numbers. For example, Japan suffered no less than 22 major famines between 1690 and 1840. From the 12th to the 17th century, Japan was also torn by internal wars (Photo 3.1). The death tolls of these wars, by seriously depleting the number of males of reproductive age, had a significant limiting effect on future rates of population growth. The widespread destruction of crops during these skirmishes also increased the level of mortality resulting from malnutrition and starvation.

In terms of the demographic transition model, Japan remained in the high stationary phase until the middle of the 19th century (Figure 4.5). Although birth rates were moderately high, population pressure on a limited resource base meant high death rates and therefore little population growth. During this time, the general situation of Japan in fact exhibited a number of characteristics emphasised by Malthus (1798). He had stated that growth in numbers would always keep the mass of the population's living standards at subsistence level. Because the 'passion between the sexes' would remain constant, leading to population increas-

Photo 3.1 *Old print depicting civil war*

ing in geometric ratio (1, 2, 4, 8, 16 ...), the limit to increasing food supplies for them would be set by the limited amount of new land available for cultivation. On this basis, food supply would only increase at an arithmetic rate (1, 2, 3, 4 ...). As a consequence, population would so press on resources that the natural and positive checks of famine, pestilence, war and high mortality rates amongst the weak would operate. The pressure would be mitigated only to a small extent by a conscious reduction in early marriages amongst the more educated in society and voluntary restraint from sexual intercourse.

Although the early demographic situation in Japan might be seen as exemplifying the Malthusian scenario, there were some distinctive differences. For example, attention has already been drawn to the deliberate attempt to control population growth by abortion and infanticide, measures which would have been abhorrent to Malthus. More importantly, however, from the 1860s onwards, Japan was able to break out of the Malthusian straightjacket of limited food supplies constantly checking population numbers. So the country moved from the high stationary to the early expanding phase, and population growth began to take off.

The momentum of a persistent distribution pattern

The general pattern of population distribution in feudal times was similar in its essentials to that which prevails today. The major concentration then, as today, was in what is usually referred to as the Pacific Belt, stretching westwards from Tokyo along the south coast of Honshu to as far as northern Kyushu. The long-established concentration is partly explained by the more favourable climatic conditions and by the occurrence of some large stretches of rich alluvial lowland. By comparison, much of the rest of the country, because of its mountainous character and harsher climate, was perceived to be less inviting.

In addition to the influences of terrain and climate, the attraction of settlement to coastal locations has been a significant factor (Figure 3.2). This may be partly explained by the coastal occurrence of most lowlands. Swift-flowing and heavily-laden rivers coming down from the mountainous interior have built up flood plains and deltas into bays and inlets. It is also explained by the rich fishing grounds that once existed in Japan's inshore waters. Even today, fish remains a vital part of the staple diet. Traditionally, a coastal location has also been important because the sea has provided an

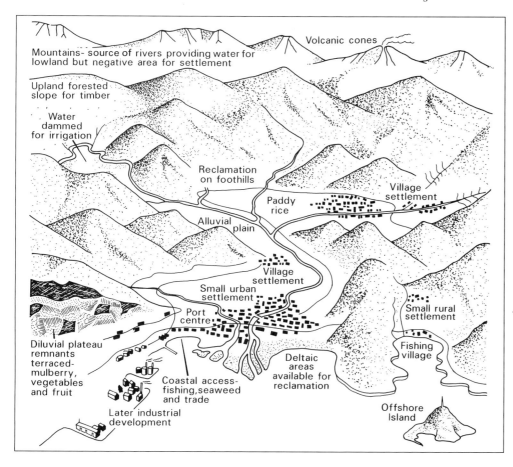

Fig. 3.2 *A sketch section to show typical landscape components and the human response to their resource potential*

important means of communication between different parts of Japan, thereby helping to avoid the difficulties of overland transport. More recently, that significance has increased as the Japanese economy has become more and more dependent on foreign trade. In this respect, the coastal lowlands around the Inland or Seto Sea were triply blessed with rich fisheries, sheltered anchorages and a good interconnecting transport artery. It was through the exploitation of these advantages that this particular stretch of the Pacific Belt became the initial focus of settlement and population.

However, the distribution of population cannot be explained wholly in terms of how well different parts of Japan were or were not naturally blessed with resources and opportunities. Population densities have a lot to do with historical and other human influences. Though Japan in very early times had a small indigenous population, the Ainus, the bulk of the population was descended from settlers migrating from what is now China and Korea and from the Pacific islands.

Both migration streams entered Japan through Kyushu and gradually pushed northwards. Consequently, the south of Japan, especially the Inland Sea basin, was the first part of the country to be settled, and by virtue of this became the country's historic core. In contrast, Hokkaido right up to modern times remained in the perception of most Japanese a remote, inhospitable frontier region.

Once established as the historic heart of the country, the Inland Sea basin graduated to become the **core**, that is the prime focus of most activity, cumulatively gaining more advantages as time went on and as Japan's economic and social structures were further built up. In contrast, the remainder of the country, the **periphery**, lagged behind the core region, a situation particularly well outlined and explained by the economist Myrdal's **cumulative causation process** (Figure 3.3). In this concept, Myrdal (1957) points out that one or more regions of a country may enjoy **initial advantages** over other parts and attract settlement. Once established, these centres of settlement

39

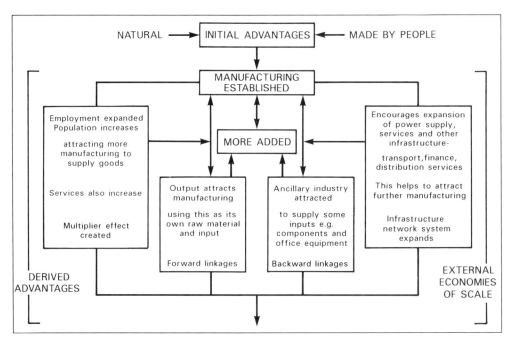

NATURAL → INITIAL ADVANTAGES ← MADE BY PEOPLE

↓

MANUFACTURING ESTABLISHED

Employment expanded
Population increases

attracting more
manufacturing to
supply goods

Services also increase

Multiplier effect
created

MORE ADDED

Output attracts
manufacturing

using this as its
own raw material
and input

Forward linkages

Ancillary industry
attracted

to supply some
inputs e.g.
components and
office equipment

Backward linkages

Encourages expansion
of power supply,
services and other
infrastructure-

transport, finance,
distribution services

This helps to attract
further manufacturing

Infrastructure
network system
expands

DERIVED
ADVANTAGES

EXTERNAL
ECONOMIES
OF SCALE

Fig. 3.3 Myrdal's
cumulative causation
process

attract resources, such as raw materials, people and investment, from other parts of the country and this leads to yet more growth. Thus to the initial advantages, **derived advantages** are added, giving the core impetus for further growth. So there is set in motion a cumulative causation process in which, whilst the core region grows and provides beneficial **spread effects** to the areas immediately around it, peripheral regions further away lose out and lag further behind. Not only are they starved of outside investment for growth, they are also drained of

some of their resources and labour by the pull of the prospering core, so the periphery suffered **backwash effects**.

The initial core region of the Inland Sea has since been enlarged north-eastwards, taking in central Honshu, to become the Pacific Belt or corridor. At the same time, the rest of the country has not only remained peripheral, but has been dominated by it. Regional imbalances have been created which continue to pose serious problems for modern Japan (see Chapter 9). The remainder of this chapter now traces the

Photo 3.2
Reconstructed buildings
and paddy fields of the
Yayoi period (300 – 100
BC) at Toro, Shizuoka

emergence of this elongated growth pole up to 1868; two stages are recognised (Figure 3.4).

3.2 THE EMERGENCE OF THE CORE REGION TO 1615

Whilst migration streams played a part in determining the initial location of Japan's core region, it was the better natural endowments of this part of

Photo 3.3 *Some of the products of old craft industries*

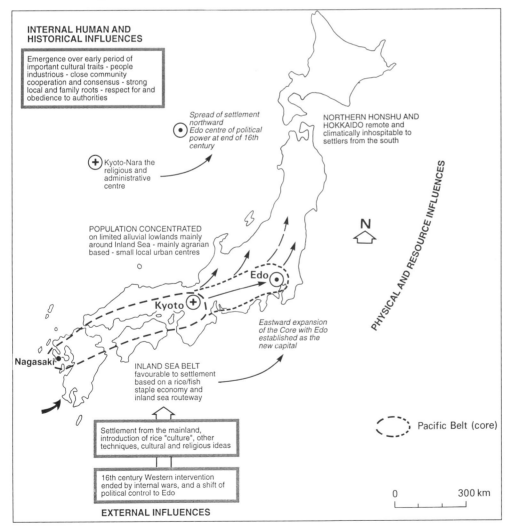

INTERNAL HUMAN AND HISTORICAL INFLUENCES

Emergence over early period of important cultural traits - people industrious - close community cooperation and consensus - strong local and family roots - respect for and obedience to authorities

Spread of settlement northward
⊙ *Edo centre of political power at end of 16th century*

NORTHERN HONSHU AND HOKKAIDO remote and climatically inhospitable to settlers from the south

⊕ Kyoto-Nara the religious and administrative centre

POPULATION CONCENTRATED on limited alluvial lowlands mainly around Inland Sea - mainly agrarian based - small local urban centres

PHYSICAL AND RESOURCE INFLUENCES

N

Edo ⊙

Kyoto ⊕

Eastward expansion of the Core with Edo established as the new capital

Nagasaki●

INLAND SEA BELT favourable to settlement based on a rice/fish staple economy and inland sea routeway

- - - Pacific Belt (core)

Settlement from the mainland, introduction of rice "culture", other techniques, cultural and religious ideas

16th century Western intervention ended by internal wars, and a shift of political control to Edo

EXTERNAL INFLUENCES

0   300 km

Fig. 3.4 *A summary of people-environment relationships in the early period of Japan's development*

needed to be carefully channelled and shared out if all the rice plots were to be flooded for planting and later drained for harvesting. Cultivation and harvesting also required a sustained cooperative effort. Thus from an early date, rural life was carefully regulated under the local feudal lord. The work ethic and the need for cooperation and consensus rather than confrontation, so evident in the economic life of the nation today, were instilled into the people even in these early times.

Whilst the economic base was an essentially agrarian one, founded on a staple diet of rice and fish, some localised industry did develop. Techniques of weaving, lacquering and metallurgy had been brought over from the Asian mainland and a flourishing cottage industry developed in some of the more enterprising areas in the Inland Sea core region (Photo 3.3). Processing of agricultural products also took place, rice wine (sake) for example being brewed. As mulberry growing on the diluvial terraces was extended, silk weaving became increasingly important. Though only at a craft stage, a growing amount of this work became concentrated in the emerging urban centres from which the local area was administered by the clan lord (daimyo). Since local economies were mainly self-sufficient, little of the food and manufactures entered into inter-regional trade. Nonetheless, some of the bases for the later industrialisation and urbanisation of the country were already being laid in the core region, thereby serving to reinforce its lead over other areas.

During this period a feudal system developed. Each lowland tended to be occupied by a semi-autonomous clan and its daimyo. Each clan was loosely subjected to an imperial authority. From the end of the 8th century, that authority was centred on Kyoto, the official residence of the Emperor. Although located away from the Inland Sea, Kyoto had good land and sea communications with the fringing lowlands. It was also well placed to serve the core region as it gradually extended towards Edo (Figure 3.4). Kyoto also became the main cultural and religious focus (Photo 3.4). Buddhism had been introduced from

Photo 3.4 *Garden of the Ryoanji zen temple, Kyoto*

Japan compared with the rest of the country which were the decisive influences. Once drained, the stretches of alluvial lowland bordering the Inland Sea, with their warm, humid climate, were suitable for paddy-rice cultivation which formed the basis of the early settlers' economy (Photo 3.2). The Inland Sea itself, with its rich fishing grounds, provided the protein necessary for human survival.

Although intensive rice-growing supplemented by fishing could support a high population, it required not only a very large labour input but close cooperation and organisation within the rural community. For example, water brought down by upland rivers

Photo 3.5 *Old print depicting expulsion of foreigners*

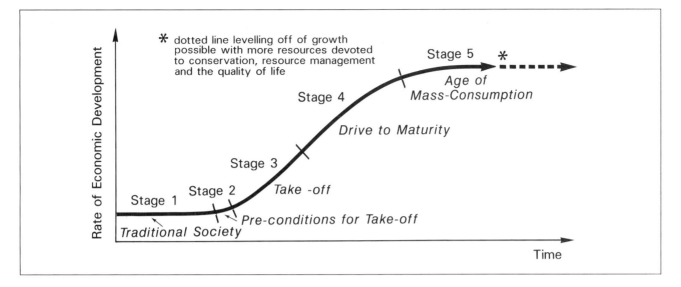

Fig. 3.5 Rostow's stages of economic growth

China in the third century AD and it came to flourish alongside Shintoism, the traditional set of beliefs rooted in the primeval worship of nature. Then, as now, people happily embraced both sets of belief. Ancestor worship and deification of the Emperor were important features of religious life, linking reverence for the family with respect and obedience to higher authority. These traits were important in establishing an orderly economic and social structure.

Power was gradually extended from Kyoto, not only over all of Kyushu, but northwards to central Honshu and beyond (Figure 3.4). With it there began to bud a sense of unity and national identity. This underpinned the economic links being forged between all but the most peripheral regions, notably stretches of the Japan Sea coast, Hokkaido and southern Shikoku. As a consequence, the political strength of the core region was increased.

Up to the middle of the 16th century, the only outside stimulus had come from nearby China and Korea. From that time onwards, however, Japan came under some Western influence, at first through Portuguese and Dutch traders from the East Indies. The introduction of firearms and Western techniques of castle-building, together with the playing off of one clan lord against another, placed pressure on the authority of the Emperor at Kyoto. The outcome was a period of instability and civil war. In the scramble for

power amongst the local war lords, Tokugawa Ieyasu, who held the fiefdom of Yedo (Edo), emerged as leader. Kyoto remained the religious and cultural heart, but the power of the Emperor was usurped and effective economic and political control transferred to Edo, later to become Tokyo (Figure 3.4).

Another consequence of the upheaval was the expulsion of foreigners from the country and the closing of Japan's doors to the outside world (Photo 3.5). This deliberate policy of isolation was to prove to be a vital factor in the further development of Japan. It meant that, unlike many parts of South East Asia, the country was not to become a colonial appendage of some Western power, but able to develop in its own distinctive way. This was important in enabling an integrated economy to develop, primarily based on domestic needs and not those of an external power. Also a strong national identity was nurtured, together with an 'us and them' attitude to foreigners that still persists today.

By the early 17th century, the initial core region of the Inland Sea had become enlarged eastwards to as far as Edo (Tokyo) (Figure 3.4). To its initial advantages had been added further derived advantages, setting in motion the cumulative causation process. The core's lead and dominance over the peripheral regions of the country was thus substantially reinforced. Within the extended core, Kyoto, Osaka and Edo became increasingly evident as

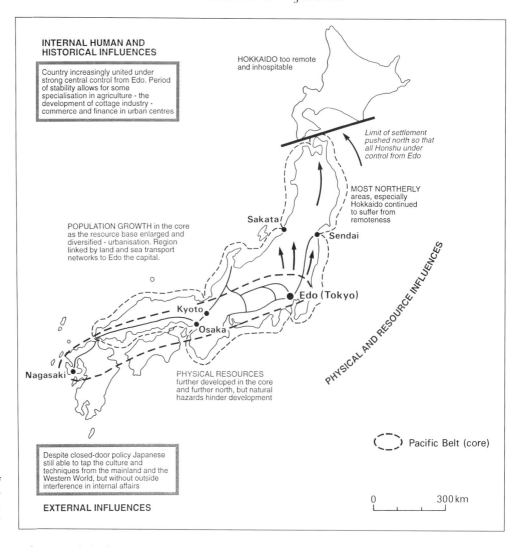

INTERNAL HUMAN AND HISTORICAL INFLUENCES

Country increasingly united under strong central control from Edo. Period of stability allows for some specialisation in agriculture - the development of cottage industry - commerce and finance in urban centres

HOKKAIDO too remote and inhospitable

Limit of settlement pushed north so that all Honshu under control from Edo

MOST NORTHERLY areas, especially Hokkaido continued to suffer from remoteness

POPULATION GROWTH in the core as the resource base enlarged and diversified - urbanisation. Region linked by land and sea transport networks to Edo the capital.

Sakata

Sendai

PHYSICAL AND RESOURCE INFLUENCES

Kyoto

Osaka

Edo (Tokyo)

Nagasaki

PHYSICAL RESOURCES further developed in the core and further north, but natural hazards hinder development

Despite closed-door policy Japanese still able to tap the culture and techniques from the mainland and the Western World, but without outside interference in internal affairs

EXTERNAL INFLUENCES

Pacific Belt (core)

0   300 km

Fig. 3.6 *A summary of people–environment relationships during the Tokugawa period*

urban and industrial nodes. Thus a number of the basic features which characterise the present human geography of Japan, both in its spatial aspects and its economic and social structures, have their origins in this early period of the country's development. Despite this and the signs of progress, Japan remained essentially at the traditional society stage in Rostow's model of economic growth (Figure 3.5).

3.3 PRE-CONDITIONS FOR TAKE-OFF AND MODERNISATION: THE TOKUGAWA PERIOD (1615 – 1867)

Under the Tokugawa *shoguns* (military rulers), political control was extended from the new capital at Edo over the whole country except Hokkaido. The country enjoyed 200 years of stability. This allowed for further economic progress and a modest increase in population to about 30 million (Figure 3.6). To support this growth in population, food production was raised by clearing and terracing more land on the lower slopes of the uplands and by extensive reclamation of riverine and coastal wetlands. Some regional specialisation of agriculture occurred, including mulberry-growing in Honshu along the borders of the Inland Sea and the cultivation of mandarin oranges in Kyushu. Some of the more prosperous and enterprising peasants began to process agricultural products and develop cottage industries such as cotton-weaving and sake-making. Some went in for trading and money-lending. Thus in the rural areas, there was some movement towards a moneyed economy with commerce becoming increasingly important.

As all this went on, urban areas also grew. The *daimyos* built new settlements

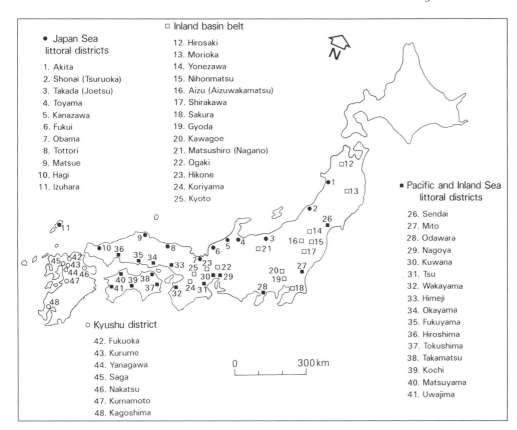

Fig 3.7 *Distribution of jokamachi*

(*jokamachi*) in association with castles (Figure 3.7). Many of these became centres of local commerce and increasingly important as administrative foci. Many survive today as prefectural capital cities (Photo 3.6). Since the feudal lords were now required to spend alternate years at Edo under the watchful eye of the Tokugawas, the city not only increased as the effective capital of Japan (Photo 3.7). It became an important social and commercial centre requiring many goods and services. By the close of the 18th century, it is claimed that Edo had a population of nearly 3 million, making it one of the largest cities in the world.

With the diversification of the economic base and the gathering pace of urbanisation, Japan began to move through the second stage of the Rostow model (Figure 3.5). But it still retained a strong feudal system, with the Tokugawa rulers exercising strict control over almost every aspect of economic life (Figure 3.8). Initially, this was beneficial to the development process, but eventually the old feudal order became a rigid straight-jacket unable to absorb the economic changes now under way. As so often happens,

economic change was running ahead of institutional change. The rural peasants were oppressed by increasingly heavy tax burdens to support the lavish living of the local lord, the vast bureaucracy at Edo, as well as the imperial court at Kyoto. In the towns, the *daimyos* and *samurai* (the old warrior guard) were in control and blocked the way to power for the increasing class of wealthy merchants and financiers.

To these growing tensions were added two more. First, there was the

Photo 3.6 *A prefectural capital with its castle intact*

45

Photo 3.7   *The procession of the daimyos to Edo*

Fig. 3.8   *The social hierarchy and class structure in Japan during the Tokugawa period*

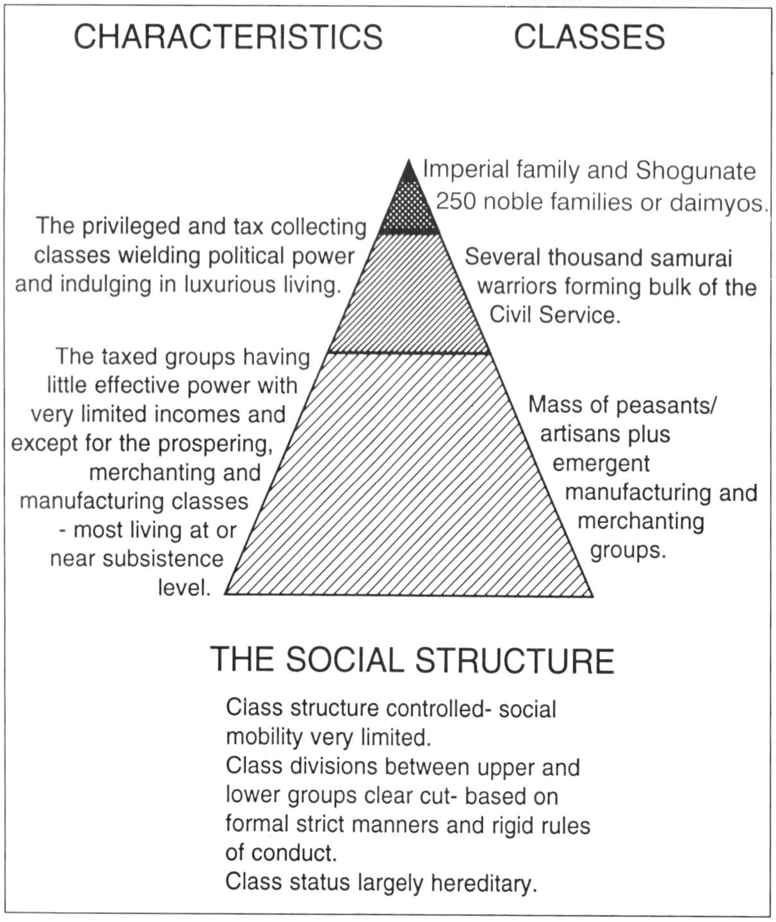

CHARACTERISTICS   CLASSES

Imperial family and Shogunate 250 noble families or daimyos.

The privileged and tax collecting classes wielding political power and indulging in luxurious living.

Several thousand samurai warriors forming bulk of the Civil Service.

The taxed groups having little effective power with very limited incomes and except for the prospering, merchanting and manufacturing classes - most living at or near subsistence level.

Mass of peasants/artisans plus emergent manufacturing and merchanting groups.

THE SOCIAL STRUCTURE

Class structure controlled- social mobility very limited.
Class divisions between upper and lower groups clear cut- based on formal strict manners and rigid rules of conduct.
Class status largely hereditary.

fundamental problem of population pressure. Although agricultural production had increased, much of the raised output was consumed by the towns, leaving little to feed the rapidly growing rural population. Recurrent natural disasters in the form of floods, typhoons and earthquakes added to the food shortage and widespread starvation. Secondly, there were mounting pressures from outside as foreign powers once again sought to break down the closed-door policy adopted by Japan's ruling faction. This time the pressures came not only from European nations, which by the mid-19th century had a colonial hold on much of South East Asia and footholds in neighbouring China, but also from the USA and Russia. Eventually, Japan was forced to concede and expose itself once more to outside influences, particularly in the context of trade.

This capitulation to foreigners and the ensuing disruption caused to the domestic economy by the opening of the country to Western trade resulted in an organised uprising led by *daimyos* from Kyushu. In 1867 they seized control from the Shogun at Edo and reinstated the Emperor as the effective leader of Japan. For once, the influence of a peripheral region was decisive in gaining control of the core. In the following year, Emperor Meiji and his court were transferred from Kyoto to Edo which, on becoming the imperial capital of the new Japan, was renamed Tokyo (Photo 3.7).

By the **Meiji Restoration**, as it is called, Japan set off along a conscious path towards modernisation. Modernisation was seen as the only effective way of countering Western colonial aspirations and protecting the integrity of Japan. The stage was set for a period of rapid industrialisation and urbanisation. However, it was not simply an upgrading of the economy that was set in train, but also a revamping of the political order. Japan adopted a constitution, a new judicial system and an administration, all fashioned along Western lines. But some aspects of the old order were deliberately carried through. The established fiefdoms were reconstituted as the modern prefectural divisions of the country and the *daimyos* appointed as governors, whilst *samurai* families continued to provide much of the civil service (Figure 3.8). In addition to this adherence to traditional regional and social divisions, many of the old social values continued to be encouraged, especially the norms and attitudes governing family and group relationships. As a result, Japan still managed to retain its own distinctive identity. Those long-established traits, nurtured during 250 years of isolation, continue to this day to set Japan apart from other industrial nations.

CHAPTER

4

The drive to modernisation
and industrialisation

4.1 THE ROLE OF GOVERNMENT

Under an administration remodelled on Western lines but retaining the Emperor as ruler, Japan was modernised at a rapid rate after 1868. By the turn of the century, it was well into the drive to maturity (Figure 3.5). The part played by government in this modernisation process needs to be emphasised from the outset. During the Tokugawa period, government had already begun to cooperate with leading business families. Its role after 1868 was even more forceful and has remained of great importance to the present. Much of the capital investment needed to develop the country's infrastructure and expand industry was raised by direct taxation. The Meiji Government established a modern banking and credit system. But it did much more besides. For example, it was responsible for setting up much of the new industry, especially basic industries. It also coordinated the development of transport and communications, including the nationalisation and extension of the rail network and the construction of a telegraphic network. The fundamental role of education was recognised if economic progress was to be achieved. A skilled and educated workforce was critical, as was able management at all levels. In short, the modernisation of Japan was very much centre-led.

4.2 INDUSTRIALISATION

The strategy

In its drive for modernisation, the Meiji Government identified industrialisation as the principal thrust. Japan's situation at the time may, to some extent, be compared with that of developing countries in recent times. On the one hand, the need to develop heavy,

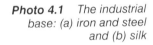

Photo 4.1 *The industrial base: (a) iron and steel and (b) silk*

(a)

(b)

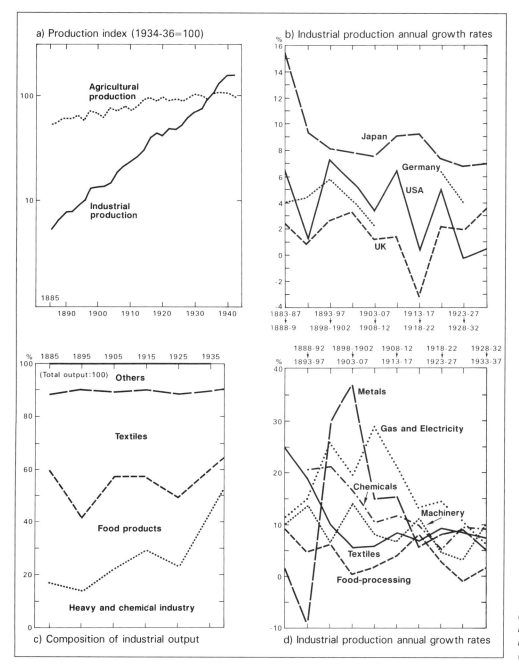

a) Production index (1934-36=100)

b) Industrial production annual growth rates

c) Composition of industrial output

d) Industrial production annual growth rates

Fig. 4.1 *Selected measures of industrialisation (1885 – 1940)*

capital-intensive industries, such as iron and steel, shipbuilding and heavy engineering, as a foundation for further industrialisation was fully recognised both by government and business interests (Photo 4.1). Additionally, this type of industrial development might be expected to give Japan more prestige in foreign eyes. On the other hand, since Japan had a cheap and plentiful workforce, these same parties saw the desirability of nurturing labour-intensive industries. Such industries could supply many of the needs of an expanding domestic

demand. They could also be particularly important in the export sector by earning foreign currency to pay for the raw materials and machine tools needed to develop heavy industries and to modernise the already-established lighter industries. Of all the industries, both new and old, textiles stood out as the single most important and formed the backbone of Japan's export trade. However, in order to benefit further from the advantages of its cheap, adaptable and committed labour supply, Japan began to extend its range of consumer manufactures to

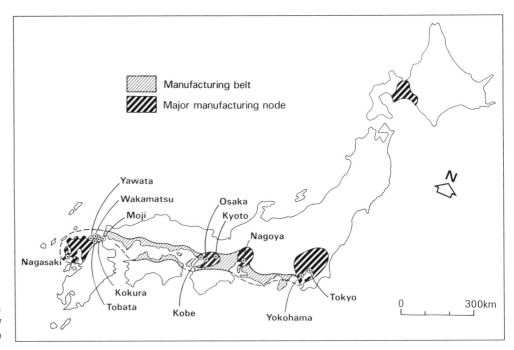

Fig. 4.2 *The manufacturing belt of Japan, circa 1930*

include such products as toys, bicycles and cigarettes.

Figure 4.1(a) gives some feel of the degree of industrial take-off, whilst (b) clearly indicates that Japan experienced higher rates of industrial growth than its three main international rivals throughout the 50-year period. During this time, the heavy industrial sector doubled its share of total industrial output and seemingly mainly at the expense of the food-processing industries (Figure 4.1(c)). Textiles appear to have enjoyed fluctuating fortunes. In terms of specific industries, Figure 4.1(d) indicates that metals, chemicals and machinery were the star performers. The apparent downward trend of the graphs for all industries after about 1900 should not be misconstrued. Although the annual growth rates declined, the compounding effect of these rates from one year to the next was such as to produce in nearly all industries an ever-increasing volume and value of output.

The spatial pattern

As for the distribution of this new industrial development, the core region of the Pacific Belt attracted most of the expansion, simply because of its momentum as the major concentration of population, and therefore of labour, and as the major domestic market (Figure 4.2). The region also held other cumulative advantages. For example, it was already the focus of most of the manufacturing that had taken place in Japan prior to the Meiji Restoration, and this provided a ready basis for further expansion. Here also lived the entrepreneurs, the merchants and financiers without whom industry could not flourish. It also had the best infrastructure, including good transport and communication networks and commercial services (Photo 4.2). But with overseas trade growing and the need to import much of the raw material needed for industry, the Pacific Belt held the additional advantage that a number of its leading cities, notably Tokyo and Osaka, occupied coastal locations with good sea access.

As the cumulative causation process continued and the Pacific Belt held an increasing capacity for self-sustained growth, so the peripheral regions largely lost out. There were, however, two exceptions to this generalisation. They were located at opposite ends of Japan, the larger in northern Kyushu and the other in Hokkaido (Figure 4.2). They owed their existence and status to the presence of coal and iron ore. Given the government backing of heavy industry, it was inevitable that these two industrial areas should flour-

ish. By virtue of their mininisation of raw material and energy costs, they were, in Weberian terms, classic **least-cost locations** (Table 4.1). Their only drawback was distance from the major markets in the Pacific Belt. Partly because of this factor, but rather more because the increasing demands of heavy industry could not be totally satisfied by domestic sources, the Pacific Belt also became a significant iron and steel-producing region. Yokohama was its major centre of pig-iron production, whilst steel-making was more dispersed, with Tokyo, Osaka and Kobe as leading centres using mainly imported rather than domestic pig iron.

A dual structure

The success of Japan's industrialisation can largely be put down to four factors, three having their roots in pre-Meiji times. These were the very close links between government and business interests as represented by a few powerful families, the loyalty and hard-work of the country's growing labour force and the very strong supportive infrastructure built up under government direction. But a fourth contributory factor to emerge during this period was a dual industrial structure, in which large-scale factory production was underpinned by thousands of small

family businesses and workshops (Photo 4.3). By sub-contracting work to the latter, the larger factories were able to reap the benefits of cheap, sweated labour. This, in turn, meant a competitive pricing of Japanese goods in overseas markets. This dual structure is still very evident today and remains an important factor in Japan's economic success.

Salient elements within each component of this dual structure were also influential. The Government, as has already been pointed out, built up strategic and basic industries, frequently importing modern plant machinery and machine tools from abroad. Many of the more prominent members of government, as today, came from those families who increasingly dominated both industry and business. These family concerns became known in business as the

Photo 4.2 *Old print of Tokyo-Yokohama railway*

Table 4.1 *Pig-iron production in Japan (1931)*

Location	Production (tonnes)
Northern Kyushu (Yawata & Tobata)	639 470
North-eastern Honshu (Kamaishi)	119 913
Hokkaido (Muroran)	62 287
Central Honshu (Yokohama)	61 490
Imports	407 376

(a) The home and workshop of a manufacturer of clothing

(b) A 'modern' factory making tabi or socks

Photo 4.3 *The dual structure of the industrial economy*

zaibatsu (Figure 4.3). Each *zaibatsu* began to adopt the corporate structure so evident in the conglomerates today. The group of industries and associated business making up the individual *zaibatsu* was controlled by a family council. The bank holdings financed the rest of the *zaibatsu's* industrial and commercial undertakings. This finance partly came from savings flowing back into the bank from the working- and middle-classes and partly from profits accrued from business undertakings. A number of the *zaibatsu* also developed great trading houses and shipping lines through which raw materials such as

cotton, wool and iron ore were imported and manufactured goods exported.

Within each *zaibatsu*, such as the Mitsubishi Corporation, a paternalistic policy was adopted by management towards its key workforce. In return for loyalty to the company and hard work, key employees were given job security and other benefits such as housing. In more recent times, these benefits have been extended to the workforce as a whole. Thus the sort of relationship that had existed in pre-Meiji times between a *daimyo* and his supporters,

The largest *zaibatsu* were Mitsui, Mitsubishi, Sumitomo, Yasuda. Their organisation varied a little, but the diagram shows a 'typical' organisation.

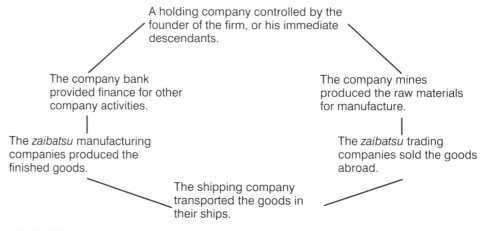

A holding company controlled by the founder of the firm, or his immediate descendants.

The company bank provided finance for other company activities.

The company mines produced the raw materials for manufacture.

The *zaibatsu* manufacturing companies produced the finished goods.

The *zaibatsu* trading companies sold the goods abroad.

The shipping company transported the goods in their ships.

Fig. 4.3 *The zaibatsu*

Each of these sub-sections controlled several affiliated companies. The whole process of production and sales was controlled by one, family-run, concern. This made the *zaibatsu* different from any other firms that existed in the world at that time.

together with the attitudes instilled by successive governments on the basis of Confucianism, Buddhism and Shintoism, were carried over into the 20th century. They have been important contributory factors to Japan's success as an industrial nation. Management and workers avoid confrontation and rely instead on consultation and consensus to resolve differences. Both parties recognise that the good of the company is to their mutual benefit.

Whilst key workers enjoyed security of employment within the emerging large corporations, nearly half the nation's workforce was employed in the myriads of small concerns that constituted the other component of the industrial structure. For them, no such benefit was available. Also hours were long, working conditions frequently harsh and wages low. Although many of these workshops were sub-contracted to make parts and ancillary products for the *zaibatsu*, they also produced goods sold directly to retailers and consumer markets.

A growing military dimension

Japan's industrial drive was thwarted by the global depression of the 1920s. Countries such as the USA, faced with a flood of cheap Japanese-made imports, adopted increasingly protectionist measures. These problems over-

seas were compounded by a series of financial crises at home which forced the Government to sell off many of the young state industries to private enterprise at very favourable prices. With the derived revenue, the Government managed to maintain some direct control over strategic industries, such as armaments and iron and steel. However, the effect of these developments was to weaken the Government and strengthen the power and influence of some of the old military families behind the *zaibatsu*. These families, together with hardliners who gradually infiltrated government, pursued an increasingly aggressive, expansionist policy to add to territory and resources already acquired as a result of the Russo-Japanese War (1903–04) and the annexation of Korea (1910). Amidst social and economic unrest at home, Japan had by 1937 taken much of East Asia from China, including Manchuria with its rich coal and iron deposits. This increased access to raw materials, combined with military expansion, helped to further stimulate heavy and strategic industries.

4.3 AGRICULTURAL DEVELOPMENT

Although industrialisation spearheaded the modernisation process, the agricultural sector was also to play its part.

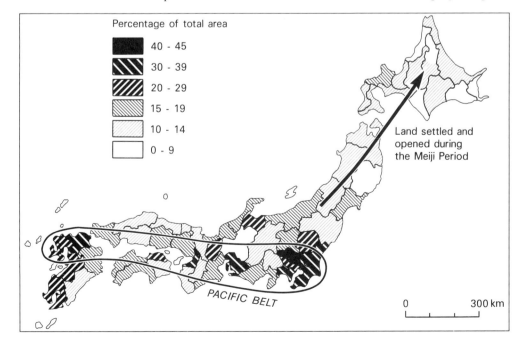

Fig. 4.4 *The distribution of arable land (1925)*

Size of holding (ha)	Farm households (number)	(percent)
Under 0.5	1 941 488	35
0.5 – 1.0	1 933 172	34
1.1 – 2.0	1 236 380	22
Over 2.0	522 760	9

Table 4.2   *The size of farm holdings (1930)*

Much of the finance for economic change came from this sector. Agricultural output had to be increased to feed the swelling urban population and provide important raw materials for consumer industries like textiles and brewing. Significantly, however, the increase in agricultural output was proportionately less than that of industrial production (Figure 4.1(a)).

Reform and recalcitrant problems

As part of the modernisation programme, and in order to encourage a

Farm occupancy	Farm households (number)	(percent)
Cultivating their own land exclusively	1 756 399	31
Cultivating their own land and leasing	2 382 091	42
Tenanting from landlords	1 495 310	27

Table 4.3   *Type of farm occupancy (1930)*

Crop	Area (000 ha)	Percent of total cultivated area
Irrigated rice	3 079	39.5
Dry crops	4 723	60.5
Wheat	497	6.4
Barley	377	4.8
Soyabeans	347	4.4
Sweet potatoes	259	3.3
Upland rice	133	1.7
Oats	118	1.5
Azuki beans	111	1.4
Potatoes	103	1.3
Mulberry	710	9.1
Vegetables	543	7.0
Green manure crops	424	5.4
Industrial crops	234	3.0
Fruit	77	1.0
Tea	38	0.5

Table 4.4   *Crop production (1930)*

rise in agricultural output, the peasantry, who had previously held land under a *daimyo*, were now granted legal ownership of their holdings. Subsidies and other price-support measures were introduced to stimulate more intensive cultivation and greater productivity. Under prevailing methods, since little more land was available for clearing, terracing and reclamation, so agriculture remained concentrated on the alluvial lowlands and in particular on those of the favoured core region (Figure 4.4). Even so, rice production rose by 50 percent between 1880 and 1915 and by a further 20 percent to 1926. But then the world recession brought a fall in agricultural prices and the Government could no longer afford to guarantee the high prices required to maintain the rise in output.

Although basic living standards had risen since 1868, few farmers could afford to introduce new methods as part of the drive to raise agricultural output. They continued to be reliant on traditional techniques which demanded a very high ratio of labour inputs to yield (Photo 4.4). The point was soon reached where, under existing methods, any further labour input failed to bring a commensurate increase in output. Indeed, by the interwar period, much of Japanese agriculture had reached the point of **diminishing returns**.

A further problem was the small size and fragmented nature of farm holdings. One-third were under one hectare in size and another third between only one and two hectares (Table 4.2). In order to increase the viability of their holdings, 42 percent of land-owning farmers were obliged to lease additional plots (Table 4.3). The size of holdings was also frequently reduced further because many farmers sold land as a way of clearing debts to local money-lenders. As a consequence, the money-lenders gradually rose to prominence as landlords in the villages.

Diversification and specialisation

Despite these inherent limitations in the structure and productivity of agriculture, progress was made towards greater diversification of output.

(b) Carrying rice

(c) Planting out the young rice shoots

(a) Irrigating rice field

Photo 4.4 *Labour-intensive farming in the 1920s*

Noteworthy was the introduction of more cash-cropping to meet the specific demands of growing urban markets (Table 4.4). Some regional specialisation in particular types of crop also occurred, particularly in Tohoku and Hokkaido as they were opened up for agriculture. Partially successful attempts were made to extend rice-growing further north using hardier rice strains. But much of the northern farmland was also given over to cool temperate cereals, like wheat and barley, root crops such as potatoes, and tree fruits, particularly apples. In Hokkaido, with government financial help and advice from overseas experts, cattle-rearing and dairying were promoted. In the southern half of Japan, much of the initiative for cash-cropping and some specialisation of output came from landlords in the villages and the more enterprising peasants who had taken over additional land. Here there was an increasing emphasis on the production of fruit, vegetables and poultry.

Diversification of total production at this time was not only a response to changing food requirements. Japan was heavily reliant on revenue from its exports of silk and cotton goods to help pay for the modernisation programme and for imports of raw materials and machinery. However, silk exports were dependent on increasing the area under mulberry to feed the yarn-producing silk worms. As a consequence, mulberry-growing on land above the alluvial lowlands expanded considerably in the south. But attempts to expand cotton-growing were not to prove successful. In the event, it became far cheaper to import raw cotton from traditional cotton-growing areas such as India and the USA.

In summary, then, the modernisation process saw Japanese agriculture responding to the changing demands of a rising urban market and an expanding textile industry. Output was raised, not so much by the application of new methods and greater mechanisation, as by the reorganisation of existing methods and an extension of the cultivated area by wetland reclamation and slope terracing. Increased production was also encouraged by breaking down the old feudal system and all its shocking restrictions. The sale of farmland was no longer tightly controlled, and much came into the hands of the

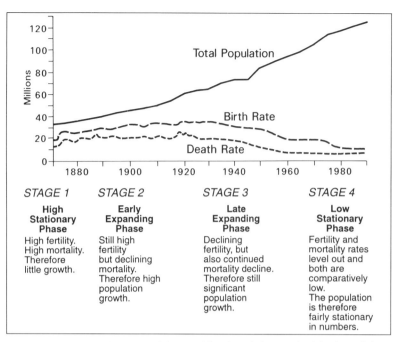

Fig. 4.5 *Japan's demographic transition in relation to the ideal model stages (births and deaths per 1000)*

4.4 EXPANDING PHASES OF THE DEMOGRAPHIC TRANSITION

The modernisation of industry launched by the Meiji Restoration, together with the improvement of agriculture, provided the means for the support of a much larger population. So Japan entered the expanding phase of the demographic transition (Figure 4.5). Stages 2 and 3 of the model are usually associated with a continued high birth rate and a rapid fall in the death rate due to better food supplies, improved sanitation and more medical knowledge. This was certainly a common explanation for the rapid population growth in those tropical countries which came under European colonial influence. But in Japan the great increase in population was not attendant on any significant lowering of the death rate due to the introduction of Western sanitation and medical science (Figure 4.6). These introductions did slightly lower mortality rates in the large cities, but rural areas remained unaffected. Famine did gradually disappear, but poor sanitation and harsh working conditions continued to keep the death rate at between 19 to 22 per 1000. Levels of mortality were particularly high amongst children up to the age of five.

In Japan's case, the main cause of the rapid population growth was a marked rise in the birth rate (Figure 4.5). In 1872 it stood at 17 per 1000; by 1928 it had doubled to 34 per 1000. This, on top of a growing base population, led to a doubling of the population from 33 to 66 million in a little over 50 years (Figure 4.6). The stimulation of the birth rate, which for centuries had only barely balanced annual deaths, was the result of a number of influences. There was a change in the attitude of the nation towards the size of the family. With the opening up of the country to the West, the Japanese leaders decided that a large population was necessary to provide the work force essential for the country's defence and the labour needed in the fields and factories. A large family was seen as a patriotic duty and a sign of national strength. But the propaganda for a large family could not have obtained such a firm hold on the population had there not been available at the same time more abundant means

better cultivators. Improvement of the transportation system put rural areas in contact with the growing urban and industrial markets, and this served as a stimulus to greater production. But for all the change, Japanese farming still retained some of its inherent structural weaknesses and its traditional preoccupation with rice. Intensification of production on existing paddyfields and an enlargement of the area devoted to rice meant that output of this staple food just about kept pace with the minimum subsistence needs of a growing population.

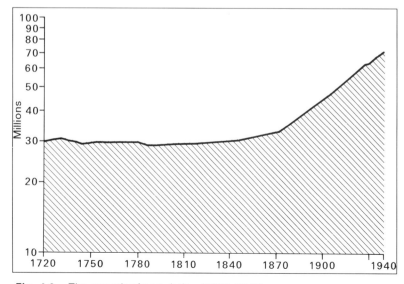

Fig. 4.6 *The growth of population (1720–1940)*

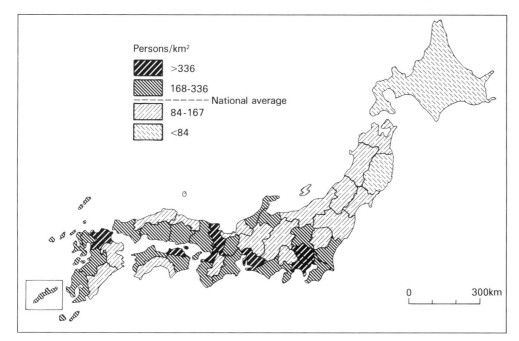

Fig. 4.7 *The distribution of population (1930)*

of feeding greater numbers.

This leads us to consider briefly the issue of the relationship between population growth and food supply. Boserup (1965), and others opposed to the Malthusian view, prefer to see population growth as stimulating technological developments and agricultural changes which, in turn, lead to an increased output of food. Population growth is also regarded as an essential trigger in the wider development process. Industrialisation and the export of manufactured goods are encouraged as a means of tapping overseas sources of food and other materials necessary to support growing numbers of people. Whilst in Japan's case demographic growth was an important element in the development process, providing for example the labour needed for industrialisation, unlike in Western countries it did not become particularly dependent on food imports. Nor did Japan experience a particularly profound revolution of agriculture. Instead, what were crucial were shifts of attitude and changes in the social and political climates. These encouraged and synchronised a rise in the birth rate and the modest reorganisation of agriculture. Up to the 1930s at least, the latter was able to provide sufficient food to support the former.

The increase in population was to have an impact on population density and

Year	Number of towns	Urban population (millions)	Urban population (percent of total population)
1878	99	3.4	9.8
1898	166	7.0	15.8
1920	232	14.2	26.1

Table 4.5 *The progress of urbanisation*

the pattern of distribution (Figure 4.7). At a cursory glance, the pattern in 1930 looked much the same as it had done at the end of the Tokugawa period, apart from some expansion of settlement north towards Hokkaido. Most people were where they had always been, that is on the coastal and alluvial lowlands of the Pacific Belt. In fact, however, the pattern became greatly intensified, as Japan's population grew and as an increasing proportion of them took up residence in urban centres. Whilst the number of farm households remained static at around 5.5 million and the agricultural labour force at 14 million, the urban population expanded from just over 3 million to 24 million (Table 4.5). In short, the density difference between urban and rural areas was amplified.

4.5 URBANISATION

Industrialisation and agricultural reorganisation in conjunction with the

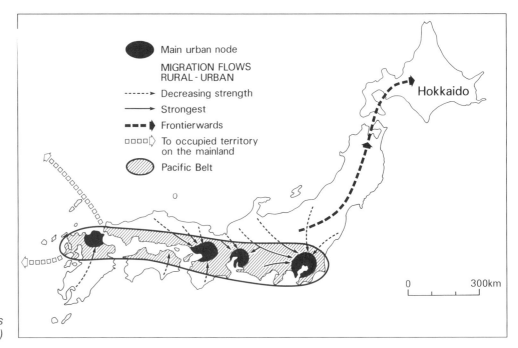

Fig. 4.8 *Migration flows (1868 – 1940)*

Photo 4.5 *An urban landscape of densely-packed wooden housing*

expanding population provided a powerful stimulus to the urbanisation process. Reflecting the population pattern, cities larger than 100 000 people were mainly concentrated in the Pacific Belt and its westward continuation into the northern part of Kyushu. By 1930, four major nodes or conurbations had become apparent in the corridor, namely Tokyo-Yokohama, Nagoya, Osaka-Kyoto-Kobe and northern Kyushu (Figure 4.8). These were the scenes of the most profound urbanisation (Photo 4.5). Much of the increase in urban popula-

tion, both here and elsewhere in Japan, was the outcome of rural-urban migration. Migration to the towns and cities was a consequence of the classic push-pull mechanism outlined in most migration studies, namely the lack of opportunities and lower living standards in rural areas set alongside and outweighed by the increased employment, educational and social openings of urban centres. Migration was also encouraged by the comparatively short distances between the most heavily-populated rural areas and the cities, both of which mainly occurred within

the Pacific Belt.

Whereas in Western Europe much of the labour migrating to the towns and cities resulted from increasing mechanisation of agriculture, in Japan it was almost entirely due to a rise in population which could not be absorbed within the agricultural sector. Only the eldest son, whether by birth or adoption, could inherit the family holding. Any male members of the family not needed on the holding drifted first into neighbouring towns looking for employment and later most moved on to the larger cities. Female migration also occurred but much of it was associated with marriage, since apart from agriculture and certain industries, notably textiles, there were few employment opportunities for women.

Whilst the largest number of rural migrants came from areas around the main industrial centres, the proportionate loss from the poorer and remoter peripheral regions was greater (Figure 4.8). These regions had fewer natural advantages to retain at least some part of the younger element in their populations. They therefore suffered the draining or **backwash effects** outlined by Myrdal in his cumulative causation model. In contrast, those rural areas nearer the towns and cities benefited from some **spread effects** as the urban demand for food and agricultural raw materials led to a more intensive and profitable farming which, in turn, encouraged retention of some of the younger, reproductive element in the population.

Initially, as in most cases of rural-urban migration, the majority of migrants were young men in their teens and early twenties, but over time the migration flows became more mixed, including an older age-range and more women. Some of the women took menial jobs in the textile industry and retailing, some entered a range of entertainment trades, but the vast majority came to town as a result of marriage arrangements. Since by tradition marriages were arranged by the elders of a family, the likelihood was that most male migrants would secure brides from their home area. Additionally, the flow of money and news back to the rural home, as well as frequent return visits, encouraged further migration and thereby gave added momentum to the urbanisation process.

4.6 JAPAN ON THE BRINK OF WAR

The outstanding feature of this period between the Meiji Restoration (1868) and Japan's involvement in the Second World War (1941) was, in Rostow's terms, the drive towards modernisation (Figure 3.5). Japan emerged as an important industrial nation, yet retained a strong agricultural base. The whole sectoral balance of the economy experienced a fundamental shift (Figure 4.9). The Pacific Belt became even more dominant, and within it there developed major concentrations of industry, services and urban population (Figure 4.10). Tokyo-Yokohama and Osaka-Kyoto-Kobe were already well established, but others appeared, notably Nagoya with its range of lighter industries, and northern Kyushu based on coal-mining and heavy industry.

Large-scale rural-urban migration served to exacerbate regional differ-

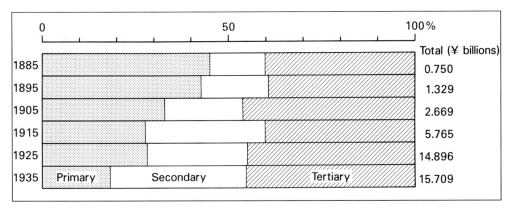

Fig. 4.9 *Sectoral shifts in the economy (1885 – 1935)*

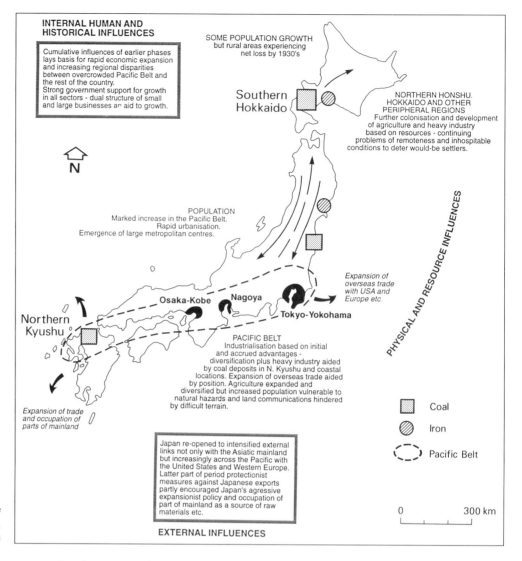

INTERNAL HUMAN AND HISTORICAL INFLUENCES

Cumulative influences of earlier phases lays basis for rapid economic expansion and increasing regional disparities between overcrowded Pacific Belt and the rest of the country.
Strong government support for growth in all sectors - dual structure of small and large businesses an aid to growth.

SOME POPULATION GROWTH but rural areas experiencing net loss by 1930's

Southern Hokkaido

NORTHERN HONSHU, HOKKAIDO AND OTHER PERIPHERAL REGIONS
Further colonisation and development of agriculture and heavy industry based on resources - continuing problems of remoteness and inhospitable conditions to deter would-be settlers.

N

POPULATION
Marked increase in the Pacific Belt. Rapid urbanisation. Emergence of large metropolitan centres.

Expansion of overseas trade with USA and Europe etc.

Osaka-Kobe   Nagoya

Northern Kyushu

Tokyo-Yokohama

PACIFIC BELT
Industrialisation based on initial and accrued advantages - diversification plus heavy industry aided by coal deposits in N. Kyushu and coastal locations. Expansion of overseas trade aided by position. Agriculture expanded and diversified but increased population vulnerable to natural hazards and land communications hindered by difficult terrain.

PHYSICAL AND RESOURCE INFLUENCES

Expansion of trade and occupation of parts of mainland

Japan re-opened to intensified external links not only with the Asiatic mainland but increasingly across the Pacific with the United States and Western Europe. Latter part of period protectionist measures against Japanese exports partly encouraged Japan's agressive expansionist policy and occupation of part of mainland as a source of raw materials etc.

Coal
Iron
Pacific Belt

0   300 km

EXTERNAL INFLUENCES

Fig. 4.10 *Summary of developments during the period 1868 to 1940*

ences. In the mountainous areas and the harsher climatic areas of the north, the structure of population was an ageing one. Eventually in some of those areas, there were too few people left in the reproductive age-range to provide enough children to replace the population lost by migration. So, it was that the more difficult areas actually suffered an absolute loss of population. This, in turn, made it difficult to attract other economic activities which might have helped to stem the tide of migration and so maintain the rural community at a viable level to support essential social services such as schooling and health. Hence the **downward spiral** was intensified to such an extent that only conscious intervention by government and local institutions could help reverse the trend. But the Government at this time was unwilling to intervene on behalf of rural areas.

Conversely, the urban centres particularly of the core had continued to expand. Because an increasing proportion of the urban population was of a reproductive age, so the rate of natural increase in the towns and cities rose considerably. Indeed, by the 1930s natural increase had become a more important factor affecting the rate of urbanisation than inward migration. With this rapid increase in urban population, and as a consequence of too little government investment in public goods and services, such as housing and medical care, the mass of that population was forced to live in appalling and overcrowded conditions. Added to this, there was the constant threat posed by natural hazards such as earthquakes, floods and typhoons. This was graphically illustrated by the Great Kanto earthquake of 1923 which triggered rapacious fires that swept through

THE CHANGING FACE OF JAPAN

great swathes of densely-packed, wooden housing in Tokyo and Yokohama. The result was a death toll measured in tens of thousands.

Whilst problems built up at home, Japan's aggressive overseas policy and its bid to control an Asian Pacific Empire culminated in the attack on the US base at Pearl Harbour in December, 1941. In so doing, Japan entered the Second World War, a venture which ended in the ruins of Hiroshima and Nagaski in August, 1945. Japan also suffered the destruction of much of its industry by the widespread and systematic Allied bombing. In surrendering, the Japanese people suffered what for them was the worst possible fate, a loss of face. The episode of the Second World War not only brought to a close the drive for modernisation and maturity, but that disaster and the rethink which followed were to usher in a new era for Japan. As will be shown in the following two sections, the nature of Japan's development since the war has been in many ways different from that before. At the same time, however, it can also be demonstrated that much of Japan's distinctive face today, as well as some of its current successes and failures, have foundations that can be traced back to the earlier periods just considered.

Expressions of postwar change inside Japan

5

Growth and transformation

Japan is now a highly-urbanised country with an advanced economy firmly based on manufacturing and increasingly dominated by services. The shift towards manufacturing was already well established by the 1930s and further consolidated by the war efforts of the early 1940s. The importance of the service sector has only become really conspicuous since the 1970s. The scale and pace of Japan's postwar economic growth has exceeded that of any other industrial country. The performance has often been referred to as an 'economic miracle'. From the early 1950s, by when Japan had largely made good its war damage and losses, its economy grew at an average annual rate of ten percent until the first Oil Shock of 1973 (Figure 5.1). Since then, very significant economic restructuring and adjustment have been taking place. Although the economic growth rate has slowed to an average of around 5 percent, Japan still outpaces most advanced countries (Table 1.1). Today, Japan is the world's second most important industrial nation, next to the USA. Given this status and the complex web of international relationships, clearly the continued well-being of Japan is crucial to the whole of the global economy.

5.1 THE DEMOGRAPHIC CONTEXT

Before examining the reasons for Japan's postwar economic success, it would be helpful to have some feel for the changing demographic situation of the country, particularly in the context of the demographic transition model (Figure 4.5).

Whereas Western European countries moved into the low stationary phase of the demographic transition during the inter-war period, and the transition was a gradual one, in Japan's case, the phase was delayed until after the

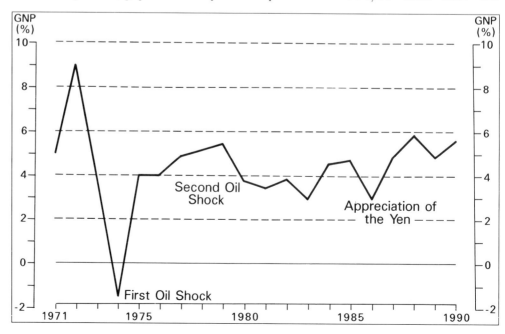

Fig. 5.1 *Changing rates of GNP growth (1971–1990)*

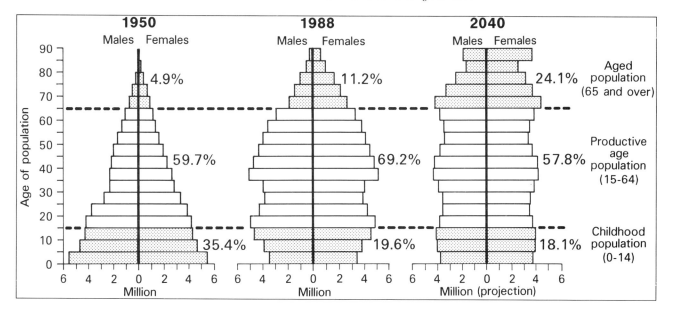

Second World War and, when it came, it was dramatic in its pace (Figure 4.5). Even as late as 1950, Japan's population structure was that of a country in the late expanding phase, as is well illustrated by the age-sex pyramid (Figure 5.2). Within 20 years, however, its structure became that of an ageing population. Due to a rapid fall in the birth rate, the base of the 1988 pyramid shows a marked narrowing. This, in turn, offers the prospect of a further lowering of the numbers coming into the reproductive age range. As standards of living have risen and good medical care has become generally available, so this reduction in fertility has been accompanied by a fall in the death rate and a rise in life expectancy. Life expectancy in Japan today is as high as anywhere in the world, being 76 years for men and 82 years for women.

The spectacular fall in the birth rate has been due to a number of circumstances, some of them particular to Japan but others common to all those industrialised countries which have entered the low-stationary phase. The dropping of the atomic bombs on Hiroshima and Nagasaki in the summer of 1945, and the psychological shock of military defeat, created a climate of great uncertainty about the future, altering attitudes to family size. Devastation of the economy and a loss of access to overseas resources made the Government anxious about over-population. Thus for the first time in

its history, family planning and birth control were encouraged, whilst abortion was made legal. By 1955 over a million abortions were being carried out annually, bringing a sharp drop in the birth rate.

As Japan moved into a period of high economic growth during the 1960s and standards of living rose, some of the influences already at work in bringing down the birth rate in the West became more effective. There was a trend to later marriages and a desire for a smaller family. These changes have arisen partly because of the wish to maintain material standards of living. They have also occurred because of the costs of housing and bringing up children, and the desire to ensure that any child has the best possible opportunities, including a good education. However, the wish of women to postpone or forego having children in order to pursue a career has not been a significant factor until recently .

Today, with a crude birth rate of just under 11/1 000 and a crude death rate of 6.5/1 000, Japan is now located as being well into the low stationary phase (Figure 4.5). Nonetheless, between 1945 and 1990 Japan's population increased by almost 75 percent (Table 5.1). But with a natural increase rate now at around 4.5/1 000, linked to a population of 123 million, the forecast is for population to continue growing slowly up to the year 2015. However, undoubtedly the greatest concern today is not about population

Fig. 5.2 *Changes in the population pyramid (1950 – 2040)*

Table. 5.1 *Population growth (1945–2040)*

Population (millions)			
Year	Actual	Year	Forecast
1945	72.1	1995	125.3
1950	83.2	2000	127.0
1955	89.3	2005	128.7
1960	93.4	2010	129.5
1965	98.3	2015	128.9
1970	103.7	2020	126.9
1975	111.9	2025	124.1
1980	117.1	2030	121.2
1985	121.0	2035	118.5
1990	123.6	2040	115.7

respects, its dependence on overseas sources of supply is greater than that of other advanced nations.

Figure 5.3 identifies six main factors behind the economic miracle. Although these factors apply ostensibly to the explanation of Japan's record of high-growth achieved between the early 1950s and the early 1970s, they have since continued to operate in an inter-related and complex way. In short, these factors provide the key to under-standing the economic dynamism that has prevailed in Japan throughout most of the postwar period.

5.3 HISTORICAL MOMENTUM
(Figure 5.3)

Chapters 3 and 4 have already traced the contribution made by earlier phases of development to the present character and human geography of Japan. In this section, it will be suffi-cient to look at the impact of events following the Second World War.

Shock and determination following defeat

In August 1945, Japan's economy lay in ruins. The population was thoroughly demoralised and in a state of shock following the dropping of the atomic bombs on Hiroshima and Nagasaki and the country's surrender that swiftly followed. In defeat, the Japanese people had lost face. In 1946 manufacturing production was only 17 percent of that at the start of the War in 1941, the armaments industry was dismantled, and the large commercial and industrial corporations (the *zaibatsu*), which had dominated the economic life of the country, were to be disbanded on the orders of the Allied forces. In the event, this was never enforced. Widespread human misery was the outcome of acute shortages of the basic necessities of housing, clothing and food, made worse by the sheer size of the population and the return of over 6 million Japanese from the collapsed Empire.

Yet, paradoxically, it was the shock of defeat, the loss of face and the desper-ate conditions which spurred the Japanese towards the single-minded purpose of restoring the national

growth, since Japan is well able to support its population at a comfortable standard of living, but rather about the ageing of its population. The worry centres on the future shortage of young people entering the labour pool and the need to provide for an increas-ing elderly dependent population. By 1990, the proportion of the population aged 65 and over had reached 12 percent; by 2040 it is projected to be 24 percent (Figure 5.2).

5.2 EXPLAINING THE ECONOMIC MIRACLE

The reasons behind Japan's economic success are numerous. Up to the mid-1970s, the explanation lay largely in the single-minded concentration on economic growth to the virtual exclu-sion of almost all other considerations, including matters of social welfare and environmental concern. In these other matters, Japan has lagged well behind other advanced nations. However, particularly since the 1980s, increasing attention has been given to improving the quality of living for the Japanese people and reversing environmental abuse but without losing the momen-tum of economic growth. The point has been made earlier that Japan's success is even more remarkable bearing in mind the country's meagre industrial resource base. Furthermore, despite a reasonably expansive and increasingly productive agricultural sector, Japan has to import a significant amount of its food requirements. In these

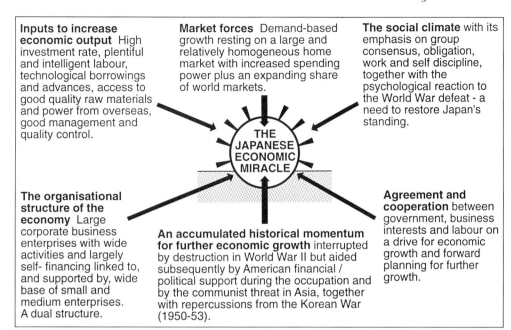

Inputs to increase economic output High investment rate, plentiful and intelligent labour, technological borrowings and advances, access to good quality raw materials and power from overseas, good management and quality control.

Market forces Demand-based growth resting on a large and relatively homogeneous home market with increased spending power plus an expanding share of world markets.

The social climate with its emphasis on group consensus, obligation, work and self discipline, together with the psychological reaction to the World War defeat - a need to restore Japan's standing.

THE JAPANESE ECONOMIC MIRACLE

The organisational structure of the economy Large corporate business enterprises with wide activities and largely self-financing linked to, and supported by, wide base of small and medium enterprises. A dual structure.

An accumulated historical momentum for further economic growth interrupted by destruction in World War II but aided subsequently by American financial / political support during the occupation and by the communist threat in Asia, together with repercussions from the Korean War (1950-53).

Agreement and cooperation between government, business interests and labour on a drive for economic growth and forward planning for further growth.

Fig. 5.3 *Factors behind the economic miracle*

economy and international respect. These objectives were to be pursued even if it meant foregoing many of the social and welfare benefits that were beginning to be enjoyed in other countries such as the UK and France. The same determination also helped to bring about a rapid decline in the high birth rate which had threatened to further increase population pressure and undermine the economic recovery. This determination was rooted in those qualities in Japanese society which have already been seen as so important in earlier periods of economic growth – consensus, a respect for hard work, self-discipline and a sense of obligation to the family, the group and the institution.

The effects of Allied occupation and aid (1945 – 1950)

As the occupying power and as a nation with vested interests in the stability of the Pacific basin and South East Asia, the USA saw the danger of leaving the power vacuum which Japan's defeat had brought. With the onset of the Cold War, the USA feared the spread of communism from the USSR and China into South East Asia. In order to stabilise the situation, to place Japan firmly in the Western camp and to quell the civil unrest simmering inside the country, the Americans began to extend aid and to introduce fundamental reforms. The

latter included the institution of democratic government, the reorganisation of education along Western lines, land reform and other measures that might aid the revival of the Japanese economy. Under the new Constitution, Japan also undertook to have no armed forces beyond the minimum needed for defence. With American protection, Japan was left free to concentrate its efforts and financial resources on economic growth.

The Korean War (1950 – 1953)

By 1950, Japan's economy had recovered to the level existing before the Second World War. The outbreak of the Korean War required a heavy commitment of American military forces to support South Korea which had been invaded by communist troops from the North. Due to its location close offshore, Japan was well placed to supply the services and backup needed by the American and UN forces. Consequently, the USA stepped up its aid programme to strengthen the Japanese economy and to get industrial production moving ahead. Reparation payments to compensate the Allied countries for the Second World War were relaxed and the disbanding of the *zaibatsu* suspended. In short, the Korean War provided a timely and powerful shot in the arm; it greatly boosted the revival of the Japanese economy.

The high-growth phase (1953 – 1973)

As a result of the stimulus provided by the Korean War, industrial expansion began to gather momentum. Profits from increased sales were invested in further industrial equipment, not only for the established basic and energy-intensive industries of steel, chemicals, engineering and shipbuilding, but also in newer durable consumer industries such as motor vehicles, televisions, transistors and office machinery. As a consequence, the industrial base gradually became more diversified. The stage was set for a phase of high growth, beginning in the late 1950s and reaching a peak in the early 1970s. During this time, GDP grew at an average annual rate of 10 percent. The industrial take-off is well illustrated by Figure 5.4.

The oil shocks, readjustment and redirection (1973 – 1990)

Japan's period of high economic growth was abruptly choked off by the 1973 Oil Crisis and the world economic recession which followed. This escalation of oil prices set by the OPEC producers, and again in 1979/80, hit Japan particularly hard since the country was so dependent on oil imports for the bulk of its energy requirements (Figure 5.1). The ensuing global recessions also adversely affected Japan's exports of manufactured goods from which much of the country's economic prosperity had been derived. But the two Oil Shocks merely hastened a process of economic adjustment which had already been set in train by increasing competition within the realms of heavy industry from cheaper producer nations, namely the newly-industrialising countries (NICs) of Singapore, South Korea and Taiwan.

Government and business circles in Japan both recognised the need to diversify the economy towards more consumer durables and information-based industries. The diversification process has certainly been widely adopted by the large industrial corporations. For example, the Ishikawajima-Harima Heavy Industries (IHI) Corporation, which had been very dependent on shipbuilding and heavy engineering, has since 1980 drastically cut production in these industries and moved into the technologically-based defence and aerospace equipment industries. More recently, it has further diversified into the service sector, embracing real estate, computer software, education and leisure activities. Emphasis has thus shifted away from the propulsive industries of the high-growth phase requiring high ratios of material and energy inputs towards energy-saving activities with low material inputs, but technologically-based and with high value-added during production. Microelectronics, biotechnology, new materials and optoelectronics figure prominently in the new industrial portfolio (Figure 5.4).

Another causal factor underlying the industrial transformation has been the revaluation of the yen, particularly against the US dollar (Figure 5.5). During the 1980s the yen doubled its value against the dollar, so ushering in what has become known as *endanka* (the era of the high yen). It has made Japanese goods much more costly overseas, and no more so than in Japan's number one foreign market place, the USA. At the same time, it has provided the opportunity for foreign manufacturers to compete more successfully against home produced goods in Japan's own domestic market. Japanese manufacturers have had to switch from

Fig. 5.4 *Changes in the value of production of major industries*

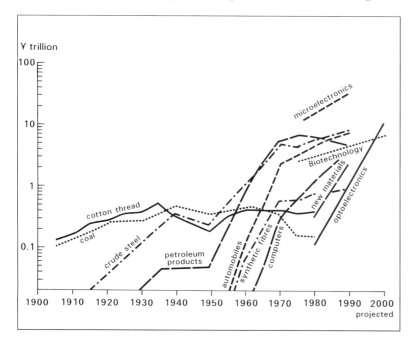

export-led growth to a massive home-sales drive. All this, together with the general affluence and high living standards of the people, has helped precipitate a general 'softening' of the Japanese economy. Manufacturing is no longer the powerhouse of the economy. Today, well over half of GDP is generated by the tertiary sector; only one-third of the workforce is engaged in manufacturing (Table 5.2).

The success of the economic restructuring is reflected in the fact that by 1990 growth in the Japanese economy had reached the 5 percent mark, a figure unsurpassed by any other advanced economy (Figure 5.1). The return to significant economic growth has been due to a variety of factors. A fall in oil prices on the world markets has been advantageous to Japan. Offshore moves such as setting up branch plants in locations where production costs are lower, and direct investment in foreign companies and institutions have played their part. At home, government efforts to stimulate consumer spending and renewed private-sector investment in technology, new products and further diversification have been significant contributory factors. However in the early 1990s, with the continued global recession the Japanese economy has relapsed into a less dynamic mode. Its financial and real estate markets have been particularly adversely affected.

5.4 MARKET FORCES (Figure 5.3)

In the West, where anxiety about Japanese market penetration has steadily increased, it is commonly believed that Japan's economic expansion has been largely due to aggressive and successful selling overseas. In fact, the expansion has been firmly rooted in the strength and buoyancy of the country's increasingly prosperous home market. For example, in 1990 only 25 percent of Japan's GNP came from the export of goods and services compared with a figure of 30 percent for the EC.

The home market

In terms of purchasing power, Japan has the next largest domestic market to

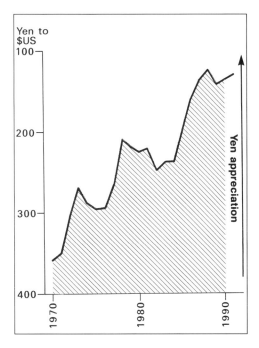

Fig. 5.5 *The appreciation of the yen against the US dollar*

Table 5.2 *Sectoral shifts in the Japanese economy (1960 – 1990)*

	Primary sector		Secondary sector		Tertiary sector	
	GDP (%)	TE (%)	GDP (%)	TE (%)	GDP (%)	TE (%)
1960	12.6	30.2	39.0	28.0	48.4	41.8
1970	5.9	17.5	43.1	35.2	51.0	47.3
1980	3.5	10.4	38.6	34.9	57.9	54.7
1990	2.8	7.2	38.4	33.5	58.8	59.3

TE = total employment

the USA. Until relatively recently, that market was to a degree protected against foreign competition. By an elaborate system of tariffs and detailed specifications for imported goods, Japanese producers and suppliers have enjoyed a much less impeded access to the domestic market place. Another obstacle for foreign companies has been the complex and fragmented nature of the internal marketing system through which foreign goods and services have to reach the consumer. It is only now, in response to severe pressure from its trading partners, that Japan is taking steps towards making it easier for foreign competitors to gain a share of its lucrative domestic market. Nonetheless, the proportion of imported goods to home products purchased by the Japanese still remains very small.

Given a sizable, assured and increasingly affluent domestic demand which is very homogenous in its make-up and historically conditioned to buy Japanese rather than foreign goods, manufacturers have been able to invest with confidence and increase their scale of operations. With the benefit of modern large-scale production techniques and its own distinctive brand of management, Japan has been able to produce goods at a cost that has made them very competitive in both the home and overseas markets. But the domestic market situation is both complex and dynamic, as are the influences upon which it depends (Figure 5.6). Whilst the home market may ultimately depend on the prosperity of the population, many products and services are not sold directly to individual consumers but to the other two sectors of the market, namely private business and government-controlled concerns of a variety of kinds. Both these sectors exercise a very important influence on the structure and well-being of the economy.

(a) The public sector market
(Figure 5.6)

The Government's share of GNP has risen since 1970 from 20 to 30 percent, an important part of it coming from increased levels of taxation which, in effect, transfer income from the private to the public sector. Government spending of that fiscal revenue is seen as one of the major pillars of present economic growth. Two of the most important areas of increased spending are education and welfare services, and private businesses helping to supply these areas are prospering (Photo 5.1). Electronics concerned with audio-visual and computing services in the case of education, and the pharmaceutical industry in the case of health care, are amongst those to benefit. Then there is the great variety of equipment, software, materials and services required by government offices at all levels from national to local. In Western countries, defence expenditure would also be high on the list, but Japan's defence expenditure is small, currently amounting to only one percent of GNP (see Chapter 12). But research into such matters as alternative energy, combatting environmental pollution, and information technology are other examples where government spending eventually increases market opportunities.

(b) The private business sector
(Figure 5.6)

In the case of private businesses, it is fairly obvious that the market for basic energy-intensive industries such as steel, petrochemicals and aluminium comes mainly from other industries which use these products as 'raw material' inputs. Iron and steel production, for example, depends on the shipbuild-

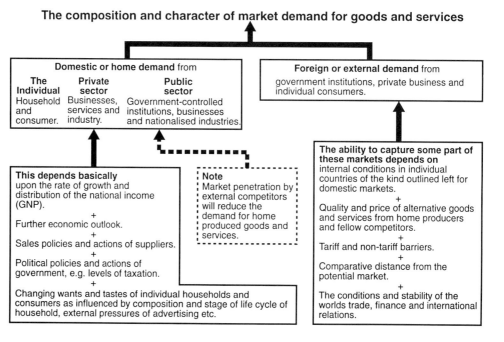

Fig. 5.6 *The composition and character of market demand for goods and services*

The composition and character of market demand for goods and services

70

ing, motor vehicle, machine-tool and construction industries for its market. The Japanese motor industry takes approximately 20 percent of the country's steel output. If there is a slump or decline in these receiving industries, then the effects repercuss through their **backward linkages**. This was well seen during the global recession of the late 1980s and the Oil Shocks of the 1970s when the demand for tankers and bulk carriers fell dramatically, not only causing a slump in the shipbuilding industry, but also contributing to a crisis in the steel industry. Since the late 1970s both industries have been the target of rationalisation and scaling down.

Dependency on other industries for a market is not limited to basic, heavy industries. One of the industries in which Japan leads the world, and which is rapidly becoming one of the country's major industries, is the manufacture of semi-conductors (microchips) in the high-tech sector (Figure 5.7). This industry supplies other manufacturers in the field concerned with such things as computers, office automation and telecommunications. Because the market for semi-conductors is rising rapidly, so funding is available from rising profits to aid research, development and investment, thereby keeping Japan at the forefront of global production.

(c) The household consumer market (Figure 5.6)

Turning now to that sector of the domestic market composed of the aggregate needs of households and individual consumers, there have been important changes in the size and character of this demand over the postwar years. As was indicated in 5.3, during the immediate postwar years the main needs were the basic ones of food, shelter and clothing. During the high-growth years of the 1950s and 1960s, as the population became increasingly affluent, so there was a boom in consumer durables – household appliances, motor cars, radios, hi-fi and televisions - which led to a marked expansion of manufacturing in these commodities. Hence, during the late 1960s and early 1970s, Japan's manufacturing base became increasingly

Photo 5.1 *Priority investment in education and the future*

diversified, shifting the emphasis away from energy-intensive industries towards a broadening range of consumer durables, a change reflected in the composition of Japanese exports (Chapter 10).

Japan's industrial base today is now being further widened by the current rapid expansion in the demand for high-tech and information-based products, both hardware and software. This is illustrated by the growth in the demand for home computers, videos and CD players (Tables 5.5 and 13.3). Whilst initially prompted by advances in technology and the popularisation of products through mass-media advertising, a considerable amount of industrial expansion today is consumer led. With real income growth in the 1990s rising faster than that of any other advanced country, this expansion is set to continue. In 1990, consumer sales in Japan rose by 9 percent, but the trend is away from the purchase of mass-produced goods towards quality products. Increasing numbers of firms are looking towards producing for the individual rather than the family.

Apart from the shift in favour of greater expenditure on labour-saving and luxury consumer goods, the other and more important shift in domestic demand has been towards those services which help raise the quality of life. So much so, that prominent Japanese researchers now talk in terms of **service-led growth** and the **post-industrial society**. This is to some extent borne out by changes in the

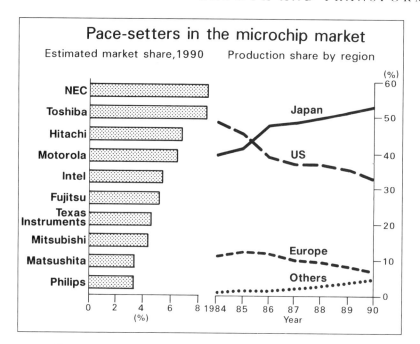

Fig. 5.7 *Japanese involvement in the microchip market*

value composition of Japan's economic structure and the sectoral balance of its employment structure (Table 5.2). Household expenditure on services has risen to around 40 percent. This increased expenditure has been particularly directed at improved housing, heating and lighting, better education for younger members of the household, travel, health care, cultural and other leisure activities. The last of these to some extent reflect an ageing population with an increasing number of retired people, but also increased leisure opportunities as the working week is shortened (Chapter 8.7).

The whole shift towards services also reflects a fundamental change in the attitudes of society, with more regard being paid to the quality of life and ways of spending income rather than the traditional obsession with work and saving. For example, there is a boom in private education, whilst, despite the high cost of housing, the Japanese household is on average now enjoying 35 percent more dwelling space than it did in 1970, as well as many more amenities within and outside the home. Small wonder, therefore, that most realms of the Japanese service sector have never had it so good, and none more so than retailing and recreation.

The overseas market (Figure 5.6)

The role of the overseas market will be

considered in some detail in Chapters 10 and 11. It will suffice at this juncture to make a few brief observations. First, it has to be said that there is some controversy surrounding the actual importance of this market so far as the 'economic miracle' is concerned. There are those who argue that Japan's post-war economic growth has been substantially export-led. In short, the overseas market has been crucial. But this does not square entirely with the trade figures. These show that for most of the high-growth phase of the late 1950s to the early 1970's Japan suffered recurrent annual trade deficits. Perversely, so it appears, trade surpluses have only been sustained during the post-1973 low-growth phase, and therefore at a time when, as has just been argued, domestic demand has become paramount. The paradox is explained, in part at least, by the restructuring of the industrial economy. The relative decline of the propulsive heavy industries of the 1960s, together with the adoption of energy-saving measures and a strategic reduction in oil-dependence, have in effect reduced imports of industrial raw materials and energy. It is this relative reduction in the volume of imports that has played a major part in reversing the balance of Japanese overseas trade.

Secondly, although the precise contribution made by exports is debatable, all are agreed that throughout the post-war period the Japanese have indulged in an aggressive and hugely successful export drive. Nothing has been left to chance. Rather, the whole business of exporting has been managed by the Ministry of International Trade and Industry (MITI) working through its network of market intelligence-gathering Japan External Trade Organisation (JETRO) offices located in all the major cities of the world.

Thirdly, from the Japanese viewpoint, the overseas market is not solely a matter of somewhere to sell goods made in Japan. Increasingly, it is seen by manufacturers as a place where goods are produced by a branch plant or subsidiary company, particularly if the location promises either lower production costs or better market penetration. Increasingly, also, Japan is looking overseas for ventures of all sorts in which to plough the huge profits of its successful economy. Japan is literally awash with surplus capital looking for secure investment opportunities.

5.5 ORGANISATIONAL STRUCTURE (Figure 5.3)

A market economy with a difference

Like Western nations, Japan is said to have a market economy in that the nature of the economy is ultimately determined by the forces of supply and demand. Ever since the Meiji Restoration, if not before, the Government has been closely involved (Photo 5.2). It has exercised direct ownership and control of certain undertakings, such as railways and telephone communications; it has had a stake in basic industries, such as steel and shipbuilding; it has been involved in close cooperation with private business corporations. So close has this involvement been that more than one economist has been led to describe Japan as a 'democratic planned economy.'

This close involvement of government has contributed in a number of ways to Japan's economic miracle. Business interests have not only been able to count on government support, but by continuous discussions at meetings set up by ministries such as MITI, they have been able to influence and be 'in the know' about official policies. Confidence to undertake long-term as well as short-term planning has been further built up through the fact that throughout the postwar period the same political party, the Liberal Democrats, has been in power. This has meant stability and a consistency of policy. The bonding of business and government has also been enhanced by the fact that many leading companies have a close tie up with influential factions within the Liberal Democratic party. It is these cosy relationships which give rise to the political scandals that frequently surface in the mass-media.

The dual structure again

Whilst this close co-operation between government and the private sector has been widely recognised as an important contributor to the Japanese economic

Photo 5.2 *The Japanese Diet – symbol of a managed market economy*

miracle, little recognition or credit has been given to another important link up within the economy. This is the cooperation between the very large industrial and trading corporations and the myriad of small- and medium-sized enterprises which support them through component supplies and ancillary services (Figure 5.8). Over 65 percent of those small firms engaged in manufacturing act as sub-contractors to the large corporations such as Mitsubishi, National Panasonic, Sony and Toyota supplying parts and components at prescribed requirements and at a very competitive price. Without this link up, it is doubtful if these large corporations could have been so successful. It is estimated, for example, that Toyota, one of Japan's most prosperous car manufacturers, relies on the inputs from no less than 36 000 small- to medium-sized companies for the production of one of its cars. Only 200 of these deal directly with Toyota, but these main suppliers have their own suppliers who, in turn, may depend on others for some of their inputs. This not only illustrates the dual structure of private business, but also the complexity of the linkages within it.

The large business corporations

These mainly comprise the *zaibatsu* and the more recent *sogo shosha* (trading houses) which provide a crucial link between the manufacturers on the one hand and their sources of supply and markets on the other. The *zaibatsu* are of several types. There are the old family corporations, like Mitsui, Mitsubishi and Sumitomo, dating back to the middle of the 19th century. Others, such as Nissan, emerged during the inter-war years when right-wing factions and the military were seeking industrial support for expansion overseas into Manchuria and elsewhere. Yet others have arisen in this century as a result of the enterprise, drive and charisma of individuals who have built up large corporations from small beginnings. Today, many of these, such as Canon, Matsushita (National Panasonic), Sony and Toyota, are household names through their brand products, not only in Japan but literally the world over.

The postwar *zaibatsu* are not the force they used to be. Indeed, this was one of the declared aims of the Allied reform programme launched in 1945. The claim that Mitsubishi 'was once a monarchy, but is now a republic' (Wilson, 1986) reflects two significant changes. First, the long-established corporations are no longer in the tight grip of their founding families. They are run by professional managers and in a much less autocratic way. Secondly, most have diversified their operations. For example, Canon, initially renowned for its cameras, now has 60 percent of its output in office equipment and is using its camera expertise in lenses to move into a variety of newer optical products. Nor is the diversification limited to the industrial field. For example, as early as the 1960s Sumitomo had moved into finance and distribution.

Two features of all these corporations help explain their immense success. First, underlying most of them is a personal drive and philosophy which permeates right through from the managing director to the shop floor. This helps give a meaning and purpose to production that goes far beyond the motive of profit maximisation. It is a vital part of Japanese management. Secondly, partly because of their diverse origins and the philosophy and drive within each corporation, there is

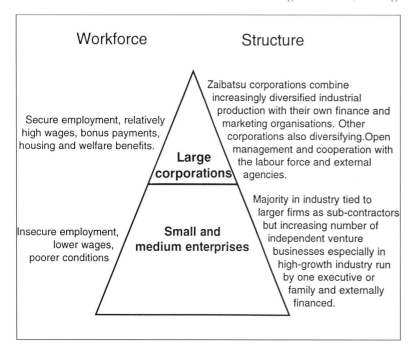

a very strong element of competition between them. Because of this competition, every corporation is well aware of the need to be efficient. Cost and quality control are fundamental to success in the market place. So too is a consciousness of the need to be responsive to changes in demand and continually to seek for technical improvement. This last has been particularly crucial in the general restructuring of the economy.

Small businesses

The small-business sector plays a more important part in Japan's economic prosperity than simply supporting the rising output from large corporations. Of the 6.5 million enterprises in Japan, 99 percent fall within this sector of small- to medium-sized businesses (i.e. employing less than 50 workers in services, less than 100 workers in wholesaling or less than 300 workers in other fields). In total, they employ some 40 million people, about 65 percent of the Japanese labour force. The sector is responsible for nearly 60 percent of manufacturing output in terms of value added. Furthermore, it is acknowledged that over the last 20 years or so, it is these businesses which have been the most dynamic in the economy, providing much of the initiative and ideas needed in the restructuring of the economy. In recognition of this, MITI has now set up a Small and

Medium Enterprise Agency to foster what are termed **venture businesses** to lead the way in new industrial areas. By this is meant not only new products, but the development of new technology and the application of automation.

Small businesses are also a vital part of the tertiary sector, most notably in retailing and wholesaling. However, it cannot be stated with confidence that their role here is as positive and beneficial. Recent surveys have shown the wholesale and retail distribution system to be behind the times, with goods on average changing hands four times before reaching the consumer. This inevitably causes delays and leads to a mark up of prices in the shops as each middleman takes his cut. Added to this, the small retailer is protected from the spread of supermarkets by a law passed in 1980.

5.6 THE QUALITY OF INPUTS
(Figure 5.3)

Labour

In the past, Japan's competitive edge in overseas markets has been largely attributed to lower labour costs. Although wage levels in the small business sector remain comparatively low, in general wages and salaries have risen appreciably since the early 1970s. They

Fig. 5.9 *Job openings and unemployment (1965 – 1990)*

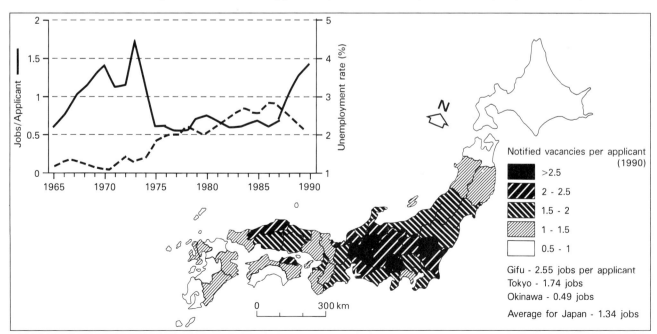

Notified vacancies per applicant (1990)

- >2.5
- 2 - 2.5
- 1.5 - 2
- 1 - 1.5
- 0.5 - 1

Gifu - 2.55 jobs per applicant
Tokyo - 1.74 jobs
Okinawa - 0.49 jobs

Average for Japan - 1.34 jobs

Table 5.3 *Sources of primary energy (percent)*

	1955	1975	1990
Coal	50.2	16.4	17.8
Geothermal	–	0.1	0.1
Natural gas, LNG	0.4	2.5	12.3
Nuclear power	–	1.7	10.3
Oil	20.2	73.3	52.1
Water	21.2	5.8	5.6
Others	8.0	0.2	1.8
Domestic	76.0	12.0	20.3
Imported	24.0	88.0	79.7

have risen at average annual rate of 7 percent, whilst productivity has increased at a rate around 1.5 percent per annum. As a consequence, Japanese labour costs are higher than in some EC countries, and appreciably more so than in the Asian NICs which are now competing with Japan for foreign markets. Where Japan scores is in the quality of its labour and the good relations that exist between labour and management. In the case of the large corporations, not only are shop-floor workers, like those higher up, better educated than in the West, but extensive vocational training is given on joining the firm. In return for loyalty, cooperation and hard work, Japanese workers have until recently been guaranteed life-time employment, an increasing wage with age, half-year sizable bonus payments and welfare benefits such as health care, leisure facilities, a good pension and, in many cases, housing. In contrast, the conditions of employment in the small-business sector have been, and remain, less good (Figure 5.8). Whilst there is now more switching of jobs and less guarantee of employment, the larger firms at least prefer to retrain rather than make an employee redundant. Consequently, even during the current recession, unemployment has remained low. At less than 3 percent, the unemployment rate has been consistently below that in most advanced economies. Indeed, one of the most pressing problems of recent years has been a shortage of labour. This has arisen because, whilst the economy has continued to expand, population growth has slowed, bringing fewer people into the labour market. In 1991 there were on average 1.4 job openings for every job-seeker; it is estimated that by 1995 there will be a labour shortfall of half a million (Figure 5.9).

Raw materials and energy

All that is necessary here is to reiterate the point made in Chapter 2, namely that Japan's poor endowment in terms of industrial raw materials and energy has resulted in a high level of dependence on overseas sources of supply. The impact of that dependence on foreign trade and Japan's balance of payments will be examined in more detail in Chapter 10. In the post-1973 era, the Japanese have contrived to reduce this dependence by industrial restructuring and by developing a new energy strategy that lowers reliance on oil, but increases the use of nuclear power, coal and natural gas, particularly in the context of electricity generation. Table 5.3 illustrates the massive switch from domestic to imported sources of primary energy that took place between 1955 and 1975, and how the balance is now being slowly reversed. Japan is also investing heavily in research into new sustainable energy resources such as geothermal power and solar energy. Certainly, a great deal has been achieved since the Oil Shocks in terms of improving the efficiency of energy use and thereby ultimately saving energy. By diversifying its primary energy budget as well as the areas from which it draws imported energy, Japan's energy supply has also been made more secure. It is markedly less vulnerable now to the price oscillations of individual fuels and the whims of individual foreign suppliers.

Investment

A relatively high rate of investment in plant and equipment, as well as in research and development, has undoubtedly been one of the reasons for Japan's postwar economic success. The ratio of investment to sales has consistently been higher than that in most Western industrial countries. Research and development expenditure during the late 1980s indicate that Japan is set on maintaining its lead (Table 5.4). In businesses of all sizes, investment is aimed at a continuous

improvement of production efficiency
and the quality of existing products
and services, whilst researching into
new ones. As regards the first of these,
investment in the automation of manufacturing processes is now given a high
priority, due to the increasing shortage
of labour.

Organisational efficiency and entrepreneurship

The emphasis in Japanese industry
throughout the postwar period has
been on high productivity, proven
quality control and prompt delivery at
competitive prices (Figure 5.10). These
objectives it largely achieves, giving its
products a keen edge both in domestic
markets and overseas. Bringing about
further efficiency and cost savings rests
very much with the managers in
consultation and co-operation with the
shop-floor workers. In addition to the
high quality and general effectiveness
of management, enterprise flourishes,
particularly in the small-business
sector, and is nurtured by government
initiatives.

5.7 THE ROLE OF GOVERNMENT
(Figure 5.3)

Changing economic policy

Whilst government economic policies
are largely implemented through
MITI and the Ministry of Finance, the
formulation of policy has rested with
the political party in power, the Liberal
Democrats. Their belief has been that
the Government should exercise
considerable guidance and influence
over what is deemed to be a market
economy. Up to the 1960s, the
Government's central concern was for
economic recovery and growth. An
important aspect of intervention was
protection of the Japanese producer
from international competition. Since
then, the nature of intervention has
been considerably modified. Its industrial priorities have become those of
encouraging restructuring and diversification, as well as helping to reduce
trade friction by ensuring that foreign
producers have unhindered access to
the Japanese market place. It has also
become more active in an international

Table 5.4 *R & D expenditure: some International comparisons (1989)*

	RRD expenditure (US $ m)	Percent of national income
Japan	79 053	3.43
USA	142 000	3.36
USSR	61 742	–
West Germany	34 467	3.70
France	22 231	2.65
UK	18 402	3.01

and diplomatic context, cooperating
with other countries to promote a freer
world trade and striving to maintain
good relations with its main economic
partners, most notably the USA. Today,
the Government is also expected to
take initiatives at home outside the
strictly economic realm. These are
more to do with improving welfare and
other public services, and reducing
environmental problems.

Government institutions

Whilst Government determines
economic policy, its ongoing relationship with the world of business is
exercised through its ministeries and
institutions (Figure 5.10). Possibly the
most influential ministry in the present
context is the Ministry of Finance,
because of its control over the national
budget and its oversight of banking,
securities, customs and tariffs. For
example, the cutting of direct taxation
under the Tax Reform Bill of 1988
significantly helped to expand
consumer spending. Since then cuts in
interest rates by the Bank of Japan
have further stimulated consumer
demand. Deregulation measures
introduced by the Ministry of Finance
have greatly facilitated the expansion of
Japanese banking and financial
activities which, in turn, have helped
promote Tokyo as one of the world's
leading financial centres.

Outside Japan, more is known of the
work of MITI. Up to the 1960s, as has
been seen earlier, its role tended to be
directive, using a 'stick and carrot'
approach to shape the growth and location of industry. Nowadays, its legal

Strong emphasis on the acquisition, analysis and rapid dissemination of information throughout the organisation, including information on competitors and possible partners.

Government support and cooperation via M.I.T.I. and other institutions with Government adopting a basic philosophy of facilitating the maximum ability of private enterprise to make the best use of market opportunities.

Strong quality control throughout all stages of production

Forward Planning allied to a relatively high level of investment in Research and Development

Detailed inventory controls

Strong links with smaller companies as suppliers of components etc. with the use of 'just-in-time techniques' i.e. cost saving by limited keeping of stocks of parts and materials through scheduling frequent deliveries from suppliers, arriving just in time to keep production rolling along smoothly.

'Enterprise' Unions cooperating with management to achieve maximum efficiency

'Commitment and Cooperation'
'A Belief in the Organisation'
'Bottom up Decision taking involving the Workforce and Management'

Thorough On-the-Job Training at all levels and 'guaranteed' employment

Seniority System - promotion based on length of service as well as merit

'Technological Targeting' with an emphasis on research and creative adaptation of techniques to ensure maximum advantage can be gained from their use. The tendency is towards incremental change in methods of production and organisation rather than sudden changes in techniques and management style. But the pace of change has quickened over the 1980s and 1990s.

Fig. 5.10 *Interlinked features characterising business organisation in Japan*

powers are much reduced and it has to rely on its influence and reasoning to persuade both industrial and commercial firms to adopt what the Government sees as an appropriate course. It says much for the staff of MITI that it continues to be a significant influence on the pattern of Japan's economic development. Most recently, it has been concerned with a diversity of tasks. These range from planning for the greater globalisation of the Japanese economy to the setting up of a joint venture between five large corporations in the development of very large-scale integrated circuits for future generations of computer.

5.8 THE CHANGING ATTITUDES AND NEEDS OF SOCIETY
(Figure 5.3)

It is clear that economic growth and social change have been involved in a reciprocal relationship. Economic growth has led to greater personal affluence. This, in turn, has stimulated the expansion of consumer durable industries and so on in an **iterative loop**. As indicated in 5.4, it was the manufacture of household appliances and motor vehicles that benefitted most from the increased consumer spending of the 1960s (Figure 5.6). Today, it is the manufacturers of high-tech products such as videos and CD-players, and of high quality, personalised luxuries

such as clothing and furnishings that benefit. Table 5.5 indicates the extent to which the potential of the Japanese consumer market has been exploited. Clearly, the considerable amount of untapped potential is good news for the Japanese consumer industries. To date, those industries have undoubtedly been greatly helped by the strong national preference to 'buy Japanese'. Maybe it is yet another form of loyalty, but unlike Western consumers the Japanese are wary of foreign products, except when it comes to buying world-renowned brand names, such as Wedgewood china, Burberry raincoats and Johnnie Walker scotch.

Another difference today is an increasing expenditure on services such as housing and leisure activities. It certainly looks as if the demand for services is set to expand still further as the average Japanese becomes more concerned with personal well-being and life-style. This, in turn, will give further momentum to the shift in the sectoral balance of the economy (Table 5.2). In a rather different vein, greater concern for the welfare of an ageing population and for the environment are examples of how changes in the attitudes of society can also impact on the allocation of public expenditure.

That completes the examination of six major factors which, in an interactive way and along with yet other factors of less weight, account for much of Japan's postwar economic success. In the remainder of this section attention now turns to four different facets of the changing face of Japan, namely the location of manufacturing, the urban system, the rural economy and regional development.

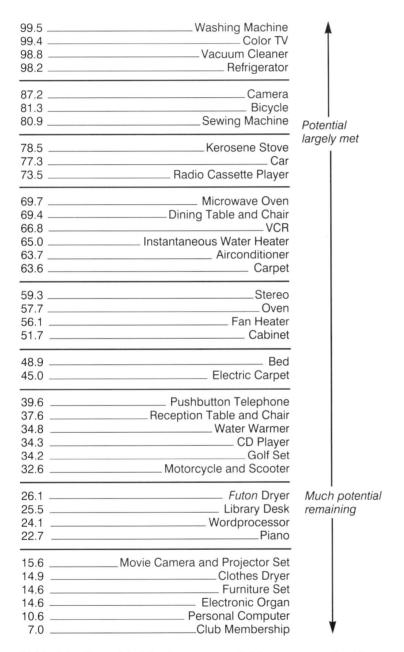

99.5	Washing Machine
99.4	Color TV
98.8	Vacuum Cleaner
98.2	Refrigerator
87.2	Camera
81.3	Bicycle
80.9	Sewing Machine
78.5	Kerosene Stove
77.3	Car
73.5	Radio Cassette Player
69.7	Microwave Oven
69.4	Dining Table and Chair
66.8	VCR
65.0	Instantaneous Water Heater
63.7	Airconditioner
63.6	Carpet
59.3	Stereo
57.7	Oven
56.1	Fan Heater
51.7	Cabinet
48.9	Bed
45.0	Electric Carpet
39.6	Pushbutton Telephone
37.6	Reception Table and Chair
34.8	Water Warmer
34.3	CD Player
34.2	Golf Set
32.6	Motorcycle and Scooter
26.1	*Futon* Dryer
25.5	Library Desk
24.1	Wordprocessor
22.7	Piano
15.6	Movie Camera and Projector Set
14.9	Clothes Dryer
14.6	Furniture Set
14.6	Electronic Organ
10.6	Personal Computer
7.0	Club Membership

Potential largely met

Much potential remaining

Table 5.5 *Potential of the Japanese market for consumer durable goods, as measured by potential already met*

6

The location of manufacturing

It has been noted in Chapter 5 that Japan is currently undergoing a prolonged transformation of its economic structure. Whilst the heavy, capital-intensive industries, such as iron and steel, shipbuilding and petro-chemicals remain important, Japan has diversified further into consumer durable industries and invested heavily in the new high-tech industries. By 1980 it was estimated that 40 percent of the workforce were already employed in information-related jobs. These are a product of the high-tech revolution, at the centre of which lies the rapid expansion of micro-electronics and related industries like mecha-tronics and bio-technology. Japan now leads the world in investment in high-tech research and development. Although the shift towards high-tech industries is likely to accelerate, other industries will remain significant (Photo 6.1). These include the now revived and reorgan-ised iron and steel and shipbuilding

Photo 6.1
Manufacturing (a) laser work in a high-tech industry, and (b) fridge-freezers, a consumer durable manufacture

industries as well as the manufacturing of machinery and consumer durables. These longer-established industries are now leaner and fitter, and the hope is that they will be able to withstand both the current global recession and increasing competition from Asia's NICs.

Given these shifts within the manufac-turing sector, it might be expected that these would be accompanied by signifi-cant changes in the overall locational pattern of industry, as has happened in the UK, the USA and other advanced countries. However, though there have been some changes, and these will be discussed shortly, the essential feature to note is that Japanese manufacturing today largely remains located where it always has been, in the Pacific Belt (Figure 6.1). Despite strenuous efforts by the Government since the mid-1960s to decentralise industry away from this heavily congested core

(a)

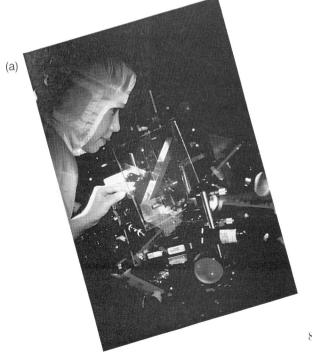

(b)

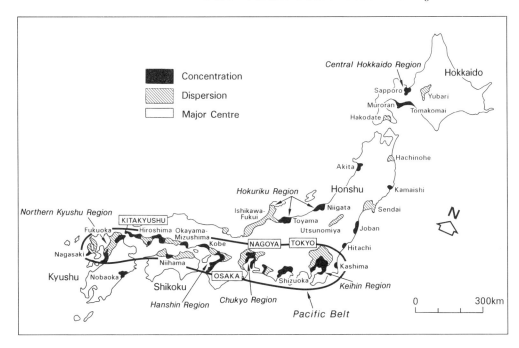

Fig. 6.1 *The distribution of manufacturing*

region, it still contains 70 percent of the country's manufacturing by value and 58 percent of manufacturing employment. There are signs that this dominance of the Pacific Belt is set to persist, as in the early 1990s the region has continued to account for an increasing share of the nation's new investment in manufacturing. The expression of this new investment is to be found in the recent industrial development taking place around and between established centres.

6.1 INDUSTRIAL CONCENTRATIONS WITHIN THE PACIFIC BELT

Much of the manufacturing within the Pacific Belt is concentrated in four major industrial nodes (Figure 6.1). The degree of concentration is clearly indicated by the regional percentage shares of the leading branches of manufacturing (Table 6.1).

The largest of these industrial concentrations is the Keihin region centred on

Table 6.1 *Regional percentage shares of selected manufactures*

Region	All manufacturing	Food	Clothing	Publishing and printing products	Chemicals and allied products	Petroleum and coal	Iron and steel	Fabricated metal	General machinery	Electrical machinery	Transport equipment
Hokkaido	1.9	8.3	1.0	2.2	6.2	3.9	1.3	1.9	0.7	0.4	0.2
Tohoku	4.1	8.5	8.2	2.9	2.7	2.4	2.1	3.6	2.3	8.5	9.9
Keihin *(Tokyo)	33.1	27.4	18.1	53.4	35.2	38.3	28.5	31.7	32.6	42.9	31.9
Chukyo *(Nagoya)	20.5	15.0	16.3	9.2	12.2	7.2	14.6	17.0	26.5	16.5	41.6
Hanshin *(Osaka/Kobe)	20.3	16.7	21.1	18.7	23.0	22.0	25.2	25.2	25.5	18.5	11.2
Inland Sea *(Hiroshima)	7.2	5.7	15.9	2.2	12.8	15.0	15.0	4.3	6.2	3.6	10.3
Hokuriku	4.0	3.8	5.0	4.5	4.2	2.6	2.3	9.3	5.4	3.5	0.6
Shikoku	2.4	3.5	7.2	1.3	3.1	4.7	0.7	2.0	2.3	1.4	0.6
Kyushu	5.6	10.9	7.3	5.3	6.1	3.9	8.5	5.2	3.9	4.7	2.5

*Main centre for the region
Note the importance of a region for a particular manufacturing sector may be assessed not only from its percentage share by value of that sector but also be comparing this with its percentage share of all manufacturing shown in the first column.

The industrial character of the major

General

The major metropolitan areas are made up of clusters of cities but each is centred on one primate city. They form giant urban agglomerations spreading out from the coast inland across some of the best of Japan's agricultural lowlands. Each contains a diverse range of industries and has a character of its own. But certain common elements can be recognised in the pattern of industry:

1. **A coastal belt of heavy industry**, much of it on land reclaimed from the sea – iron, steel, shipbuilding, oil-refining, petro-chemicals, power stations but with some areas now redeveloped for leisure, light industries and housing.

2. **Processing industries around port areas** based on food etc. coming into the country, e.g. milling, sugar-refining, paper.

3. **Inner urban areas** devoted to a range of consumer and electronics industries dominated by small businesses in which a skilled workforce is required.

4. **Larger assembly industries on the periphery** e.g. car assembly, electronics and domestic electrical goods assembly.

5. **Science parks** on the periphery in semi-rural surroundings.

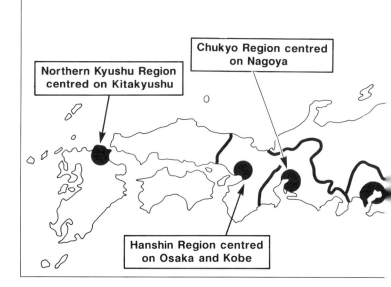

Northern Kyushu region centred on Kitakyushu

Northern Kyushu is different from the other major metropolitan areas being relatively remote from major markets, smaller and until recently less diversified, due to dependence on heavy industry, especially iron and steel but also petrochemicals and shipbuilding. Heavy industry was initially based on local coal and imported raw materials. But the coal is largely exhausted and the area suffered recession in the 1970s with the relative decline nationally of heavy industry. Despite industrial rationalisation of heavy industry, including the modernisation of steel production, this sector is likely to decline further in favour of more centrally-placed locations.

National and local government efforts plus proximity to neighbouring Asian markets are beginning to result in a more diversified industrial base modelled on the Pittsburgh (USA) re-organisation lines.

Hanshin region centred on Osaka and Kobe

Next most important region to Keihin but recently losing some importance to the Keihin region: not the same level of infrastructure.

Industrial character influenced by its earlier historical pre-eminence when Kyoto was Japan's capital and Osaka the port and gateway to the Inland Sea region.

Initially noted for fine craft industry but from 1870 heavy industry and engineering introduced in the coastal belt around the ports of Kobe and Osaka.

Light industry and electrical goods spread inland along valley of Yoda rivers, e.g. Matsushita Corporation Electronics based on Kadoma City.

Figure 6.2

nodes within the Pacific Belt

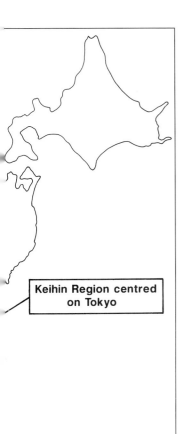

Keihin Region centred on Tokyo

Keihin region centred on Tokyo

As a capital region it contains every conceivable kind of industry. Whilst still having significant heavy industry, mainly in Chiba Prefecture and further south around Kawasaki and Yokohama, this has relatively declined. Lighter consumer industries and assembly industries have increased with the region particularly noted for the expansion of information and technologically-based industries.

Until recently most of the specialist consumer industries e.g. printing, clothing and electronic software have been in inner areas. Some declined due to a policy of redevelopment in inner areas but now once again the value of mixed inter-linked residential and small business areas is recognised e.g. southern Tokyo (Ota Ward). Close interlinkages plus sub-contracting for larger corporations are common features.

Machinery and assembly industries tend to concentrate further out to the west, e.g. in Saitma Prefecture. More recently, further dispersion has occurred.

Government has encouraged dispersion. This has also included science and research activities most notably the development of Tsukuba City, 60 km to the north-east of Tokyo.

Chukyo region centred on Nagoya

Lagged behind Keihin and Hanshin regions in importance but prospered on the basis of its historical roots of local enterprise rather than actions of large corporations from outside the region. Historically important for ceramics and textiles.

Most noted now for the Toyota Corporation's automobile manufacturing centred on Toyota City but with sub-contractors throughout the region. Toyota Corporation had its roots in the textile machinery industry.

The region is also noted for its consumer industries including textiles and clothing in the Bisal area north-west of Nagoya and ceramics and porcelain originally centred on Seto City, but is now more dispersed and diversified.

Heavy industry is of more recent origin, particularly established during the 1960s along Ise Bay, west of Nagoya, with Mitsubishi Corporation setting up a complex at Yokkaichi and others at Tokai city – now rationalised and diversified.

Tokyo and Yokohama, but the scale of industrial growth has been such that it has now spread over much of the Kanto plain (Figure 6.2). Next in size is the Hanshin region focussing on Osaka, but also including the port city of Kobe and the old capital of Kyoto. Situated between Keihin and Hanshin and sharing their markets is the third industrial region of Chukyo, with Nagoya as its focal point. Finally, there is the Northern Kyushu region, centred on the city of Kitakyushu. Not only is it separated from the other three nodes by an appreciable distance, but it is also different in character. Its industrial base is much narrower and until recently consisted mainly of heavy industry. Particularly prominent was the iron and steel industry originally established on local coal deposits which are now largely exhausted. Because of this association with heavy industry, Northern Kyushu has suffered a relatively sharp decline since the 1960s, whereas the other regions have continued to expand and prosper. More recently, attempts have been made to introduce some of Japan's newer industries and remodel the economic base along the lines so successfully employed in the steel town of Pittsburgh (USA). But perhaps more striking has been the expansion of new industry beyond the Pacific Belt and into south Kyushu, where the manufacture of semi-conductors has taken hold.

Besides these four major nodes, the Pacific Belt also contains a number of smaller industrial centres (Figure 6.1). They include the Setouchi region located on either side of the Inland Sea, taking in the centres of Okayama-Mizushima and Hiroshima on the Honshu side and Niihama in Shikoku (Table 6.1). Every kind of manufacturing is represented here, particularly the propulsive industries of the high-growth phase as well as the newer high-tech activities. Another diversified and expanding area is centred on Shizuoka. This has undoubtedly benefitted from the excellent transport links that run along the spine of the Pacific Belt providing ready access to linked activities and to the nearby major urban markets.

The forces behind the earlier concentration of economic activity within the Pacific Belt (as outlined in Chapters 3 and 4) were given added momentum during the 1950s and 1960s by the intensive national drive for economic growth promoted by the Government. The polarisation of industry was also encouraged by the swiftly expanding and increasingly affluent home market which was largely concentrated within the corridor. Continuing dependence on overseas sources of supply, both for energy and raw materials, and expansion of overseas markets maintained the premium on coastal locations which the belt was able to provide in reasonable abundance. The close linkages between long-established major industrial companies and their numerous sub-contracted small companies (supplying either parts or services) encouraged continuing locational agglomeration rather than development in wholly more distant and peripheral locations.

Economic forces such as these, together with **distance-cost** and **supply-demand** relationships, have all been well covered within the classic theories of industrial location. But the agglomeration of manufacturing also owes much to behavioural elements, including subjective judgements made at both the individual and corporate levels in the assessment of given situations and the decision-making that follows. There is growing recognition that the cumulative process which tends to pile up further economic activity in growth centres does not solely arise from the operation of economic laws. There is this vital decision-making component. Just as market demand may be regarded as stemming from individuals or groups who express a need for a product, so the decisions about how much, and where, to produce come from those who control manufacturing and business on the supply side.

Studies have revealed some interesting points about the relative way in which different things influence that decision-making. For example, an investigation of industrial growth in the four nodes, has shown that, although significant, it is not so much the variations in transportation and other costs between different locations that carry most weight. Rather, it is the speed, efficiency and dependability of input supply and marketing, together with the mental images of perceptions held of different situations, that hold sway. Because the Pacific Belt has always been the main growth area of the country, and because locations within it have remained profitable, so businesses continue to be attracted to it. Furthermore, because of the particularly close liaison between government and private enterprise in Japan, a location within easy reach of the capital is perceived to be additionally important. Finally, given the Japanese reputation for consensus and uniformity, it is not surprising that the vast majority of the decision-makers, both in manufacturing and other businesses, should regard a Pacific Belt location as the most desirable one, especially one within the vicinity of Tokyo.

6.2 MANUFACTURING OUTSIDE THE PACIFIC BELT

Most Japanese cities are involved in some form of manufacturing or another, albeit in most cases simply to supply a local market need. However, there are urban centres outside the Pacific Belt which produce goods for wider, even overseas markets. Hitachi

and Sendai in Tohoku are cases in point. Where a number of juxtaposed cities reach this kind of industrial status, then the area concerned may qualify for recognition as an industrial region. There are two obvious candidates, namely the Hokuriku district along the Japan Sea coast between Niigata and Fukui, and the area of Central Hokkaido around Sapporo (Figure 6.4).

The Hokuriku region is a much older industrial region than Central Hokkaido (Figure 6.4). It is also more diversified, combining traditional industries, such as textiles and ceramics, with an increasing number of new growth industries in the high-tech field. Improved communications across the Japanese Alps, particularly the opening in 1983 of the Joetsu *shinkansen* between Tokyo and Niigata, have done much to link the development of the Hokuriku region with that of the Keihin and the rest of the Pacific Belt (Figure 6.3). This improved connectivity has ensured many benefits, especially access to the main national markets.

Despite the completion of the Seikan rail tunnel linking Hokkaido and Honshu, and the completion of the

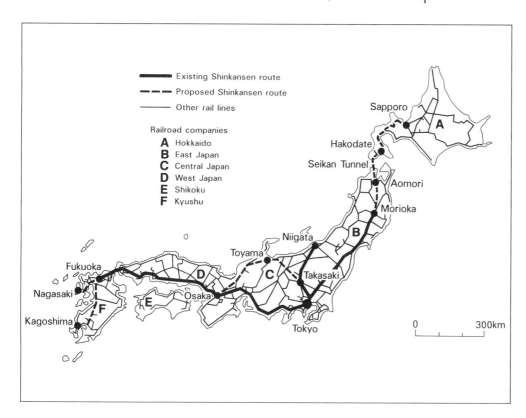

Fig. 6.3 *The shinkansen and other rail routes*

Secondary centres of manufacturing

Outside the Pacific Belt

Each centre developed independently of the main metropolitan areas being based on particular local resources, special regional skills and in some instances an advantageous location. All are now tied into the national economy and more difersified than earlier.

Hokuriku Belt

Narrow 500 km long belt and backed by steep mountains inland historically cutting it off from Pacific Belt, but now linked by *shinkansen* and motorway through mountains to the Tokyo region. Historically, specialist production of metals, cutlery, agricultural tools in the northern part and woollen fabric, lacquer and machinery to south. HEP from fast-flowing streams led to electro-chemical and metallurgical industries, e.g. aluminium. This, plus labour skills, led to modern consumer industries e.g. YKK zip factory, added to by heavy industrial complexes of the 1960s and technology industries of the 1980s.

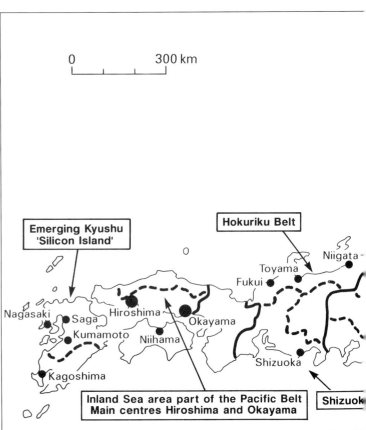

Emerging Kyushu Silicon Island

(see Figure 6.10)

Next to the Tokyo region, Kyushu has become the second largest concentration of microchip and associated technology industry. But there has also been some expansion of consumer durables in addition to long-established craft industries, e.g. Arita pottery and agricultural processing. Nagasaki, historically a main gateway to Asia, has shipbuilding , engineering etc.

Inland Sea part of the Pacific Belt
Main centres – Hiroshima, Okayama and Niihama

Industry has expanded out from the metropolitan regions to many centres in the Pacific Belt, particularly either side of the Seto or Inland Sea centring on cities such as Hiroshima and Okayama in the *San–yo* region and Niihama (Shikoku). Industry is more important on the Honshu side than in Shikoku but the latter is expanding with better access via bridge links to Honshu. In 1868 the Inland Sea belt was the most prosperous part of Japan, the Inland Sea route being the main artery of trade and close to Kyoto the political heart and cultural focus of Japan before Tokyo was established as the capital. The region was rich in resources, e.g. some copper but more importantly agricultural and textile resources – heavily

Fig. 6.4

within and outside the Pacific Belt

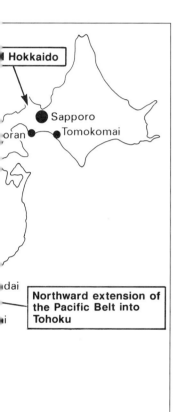

South Hokkaido

Narrowly based on heavy industry and comparatively declined in industrial importance with closure of some heavy industry because of remoteness, with industrial corporations favouring locations closer to the main markets within the Pacific Belt. Heavy industry initially developed using local coal deposits, limonite iron-ore and a coastal location. New heavy industrial complexes established e.g. at Muroran and Tomokomai in the 1960s. In the rationalisation of the 1970s and 1980s plants closed down but to some extent replaced by consumer durable and some expansion of established agricultural processing and wood industries. May be helped by recent completion of Seikan, tunnel linking it to Honshu. There is also now some development of consumer and electronic-based industries due to favourable labour costs and relatively low land prices.

Northward extension of the Pacific Belt into Eastern Japan

Eastern Japan, particularly areas adjacent to the Tokyo region, is benefitting most from the dispersion of industry. This has diversified the industrial base of main cities such as Hitachi and Sendai. Hitachi was founded by Hitachi Engineering earlier this century and is still dominated by Hitachi Corporation but now with more diversified industries – such as consumer electrical goods, cars, computer based industry. It is the largest industrial centre in Eastern Japan. Sendai was the location chosen for a heavy industrial complex in 1960 but has diversified since.

Shizuoka

Part of the Pacific Belt noted for machine manufacturing but increasingly diversified into light consumer industries – pharmaceuticals, cosmetic and electronic products – benefitting from some dispersion from nearby major industrial nodes.

populated it offered an abundant supply of labour. To its specialist industries based on craft skills – copper goods, cotton textiles, tatami matting - have more recently been added heavy industry and consumer durables, e.g. Sumitomo Corporation which originated here, Sanyo,Hitachi, Mitubishi. Hiroshima has an important motor vehicle industry, electronics and fine engineering. In the Okayama district aircraft and aerospace manufacturing has expanded. But throughout the Seto or Inland sea region as a whole industry is very diversified.

Tohoku *shinkansen* from Tokyo as far as Morioka, the Central Hokkaido region remains relatively isolated from the industrial core of Japan (Figure 6.3). The region is located in the triangular area defined by the capital city Sapporo, Tomakomai and Muroran (Figure 6.4). It remains largely dependent on the heavy, capital- and energy-intensive industries of iron and steel, shipbuilding and petrochemicals which, as has already been noted, have declined since the early 1970s. Mainly because of its peripheral location and its unfavourable image in the perception of potential investors, the Central Hokkaido region seems to have been unable to offset this decline by the growth of new consumer and technology-related industries. In this respect, it contrasts quite sharply with the Northern Kyushu region located at the opposite end of Japan.

6.3 THE DISPERSAL OF MANUFACTURING

In discussing the dispersal of manufacturing both within and beyond the Pacific Belt, two distinct components are embraced, namely (i) the relocation of an existing firm and (ii) the location of a wholly new plant arising from either the expansion of an existing business or the creation of a wholly new enterprise. In both cases, the moves are to be seen as decentralising ones, resulting in a relative shift in favour of areas outside existing industrial nodes. For example, since the late 1950s most of the larger factories in the central area of Tokyo (known as the *Ward Area*) have now been relocated elsewhere, mostly further out in the National Capital Region. In contrast, the setting up in central and southern Kyushu of 40 percent of Japan's semiconductor industry is an example of dispersal brought about by the development of new industry (Figure 6.10).

It is claimed by some that since the 1960s the industrial map of Japan has been redrawn, thereby implying a significant relocation of manufacturing. Certainly, much effort has been made to overcome the industrial congestion of the Keihin region, particularly in Tokyo. But whilst there has been some outward movement, it has been short-distanced and destined mainly for locations still within the Pacific Belt. For example, the movement of manufacturing out of Tokyo has simply generated a new industrial axis reaching northwards into Tohoku. Thus the net effect both here and in the other three industrial regions of the core has been to extend and expand rather than curtail and reduce (Figures 6.1, 6.4 and 6.5). This would seem to suggest that the forces of decentralisation are insufficiently effective to counter the

Fig. 6.5 *The continued concentration of manufacturing in the Pacific Belt*

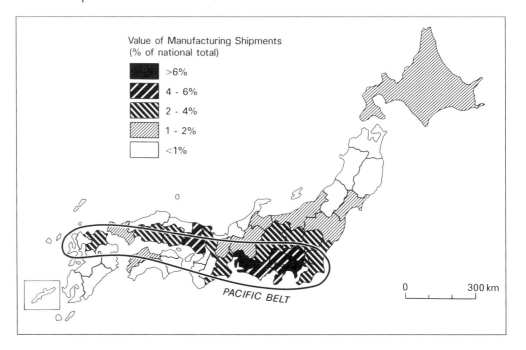

centripetal pull of established centres. In short, the peripheral regions of Japan continue to be largely unattractive to industry. Indeed, many corporations increasingly favour development of branch plants overseas rather than in the provinces, being drawn by such considerations as cheaper labour and better market penetration (Chapters 10 and 11). There is already a significant flow of reverse imports coming back into Japan from these branch plants. The flow clearly indicates the success of these offshore locations and that they are deemed to be preferable to locations in the more peripheral parts of Japan.

The limited dispersal of manufacturing that has taken place to date in Japan and other industrialised countries would seem to be the outcome of three particular factors. These need to be considered in some detail, but it must be remembered that they all operate in an interrelated and interactive way.

6.4 THE DISECONOMIES OF AGGLOMERATION

First, excessive agglomeration of economic activities creates a number of problems which lead to increasing costs or **diseconomies**. Some of them are direct economic costs to firms, such as the rise in land prices due to the shortage of, and competition for, space and the greater transport costs generated as traffic congestion becomes severe. The price of land in Japan increased sixfold between 1960 and 1970 and has continued to rise at a frightening rate. In 1991 the total value of land in Tokyo and its three surrounding prefectures was quoted as more than double that of the entire USA!

Other costs associated with over-concentration include various forms of environmental pollution. These costs are usually borne by nearby residents rather than industrial companies. However, as a result of anti-pollution laws introduced in 1967, central and local government may force firms to spend money modifying plant and equipment to lessen these dangers, so raising a firm's costs. The overloading of transport systems is one of the most serious diseconomies. Even in 1974,

the Pacific Belt was described as the 'strained heart in danger of collapse', with the average Tokyo worker having to get up at 5 am in order to commute into the central areas of the city on trains overloaded by 380 percent. In 1992 the situation remains critical, with Tokyo 'stretched just short of breaking point' and trains crowded to over 250 percent of capacity at the peak of the morning rush hour.

6.5 CHANGING LOCATIONAL REQUIREMENTS

Dispersion and decentralisation are not only induced by diseconomies. They also result from the changing locational requirements of manufacturing associated with the need to reap the benefits of **scale economies** and to capitalise on technological advances. The resulting mass-production and vertical integration of manufacturing processes into assembly lines have, in their turn, greatly increased the space requirements of many manufacturing plants. This is well illustrated by the large integrated steel works built on reclaimed land along the coast (Figure 6.6). Certainly, the search for more and cheaper space has also been an important factor encouraging the movement of consumer durable manufacturing to the peripheries of industrial nodes. The huge motor vehicle assembly plants of Nissan and Toyota, and the major factories of Toshiba, Sony and Hitachi have all taken up such locations (Figure 6.7). The growing high-tech sector is also responding in the same way since much space is required for the development of science parks to facilitate the coming together of research units and a wide range of interlinked companies.

A semi-rural location at the margins of one of the main industrial nodes offers another economy besides lower land prices. Despite automation, access to labour remains a critical consideration for many types of manufacturing, particularly the assembly-line industries. Given this need, together with the general situation of worsening labour shortages and the residential dispersal of an increasing proportion of workers

The structure and location

Japan's crude steel production (thousand tonnes)

Year	Crude steel production	Exports	Imports
1975	102 313	25 102	22
1980	111 395	24 166	696
1985	105 279	23 903	2 503
1990	110 328	23 146	6 873

World crude steep capacity (million tonnes)

Region
Western Europe
North America
Japan
Developing Countries
Others (excluding former Soviet Union)
Total

Importance

Despite some fall in output since the 1973 Oil Crisis, Japan remains a leading world producer. This reflects the continued strength of the Japanese manufacturing economy, steel production being basic to the success of other heavier industries such as engineering, construction and shipbuilding as well as to motor vehicle production. Exports, partly to supply steel for branch factories being built abroad in other parts of South East Asia, remain important but have declined in the face of competition from cheaper steel produced by NICs such as South Korea, the Philippines and Taiwan. Thus steel production is now increasingly dependent on the home market but with modernisation and rationalisation Japan is once again the world's leading producer.

Its changing structure to 1970

The development of the iron and steel industry dates from the turn of the century as the pace of Japan's industrialisation increased. With strong government involvement and financial support it continued to expand rapidly, stimulated not only by rising domestic demand but also during periods of military expansion prior to and during World War Two. Following its destruction at the time of Japan's defeat, the reconstruction of the iron and steel industry was seen as vital. Postwar it expanded rapidly, especially during the period of high economic growth of the 1950s and 1960s, again with strong government support and dominated by a few huge large corporations, such as Nippon Steel, Sumitomo Metal and Kawasaki Steel.

Japan was in the forefront of the move towards massive integrated plants during the 1960s based largely on the Basic Oxygen Steel making process and increasingly utilising fuel saving and other technological developments. But with very limited domestic fuel and iron ore resources, Japan was dependent on imports of fuel and raw materials. It also embarked on a programme of building small, electric arc furnaces for the output of special steels.

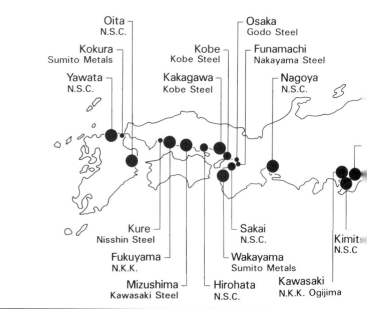

Location of Integrated Iron and Steel Works (1988

● Iron and Steel Corporation

Oita — N.S.C.
Kokura — Sumito Metals
Yawata — N.S.C.
Osaka — Godo Steel
Kobe — Kobe Steel
Funamachi — Nakayama Steel
Kakagawa — Kobe Steel
Nagoya — N.S.C.
Kure — Nisshin Steel
Fukuyama — N.K.K.
Mizushima — Kawasaki Steel
Sakai — N.S.C.
Wakayama — Sumito Metals
Hirohata — N.S.C.
Kawasaki — N.K.K. Ogijima
Kimit: — N.S.C

Rationalisation and diversification since the 1970s

Following the 1973 Oil Crisis when energy costs rose rapidly and world markets for steel failed to expand as fast as the world capacity for steel making, the Japanese iron and steel industry has undergone a period of severe rationalisation with the closure of uneconomic plants, especially in the older producing areas outside the Pacific Belt.

Production has been increasingly streamlined and employment numbers reduced with the greater use of automated methods. By the close of the 1980s, the industry had emerged out of this phase of rationalisation and in terms of costs and productivity is amongst the most efficient in the world and able to compete with the emergent steel producers amongst the NICs.

So strong has the domestic market demand been that annual production in 1990 rose to 110 million tons and the industry is in profit with increasing emphasis

Figure 6.6

of the iron and steel industry

1980	1990
223	191
156	142
126	135
33	116
15	26
533	610

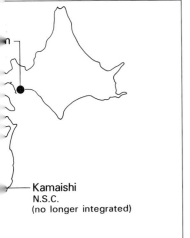

Kamaishi
N.S.C.
(no longer integrated)

oa
asaki Steel

hima
ito Metals

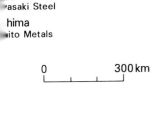

0   300 km

Source: John Sargeant,
from K. Tada, *Tekko*, 1990

placed on high-grade special steels and high value-added products such as pipes and tubes.

Despite the strength regained in steel production, all the major steel corporations have diversified their activities into other products, leisure and property ventures e.g. Nippon Steel already in engineering, chemicals and new materials is expanding into electronics, leisure, information and communication systems and bio-technology. The steel division's share of sales in 1990 fell for the first time below 50% of the total value of Company sales.

Changing locational pattern

Over time iron- and steel-making has been increasingly concentrated in the Pacific Belt, mainly at coastal locations combining the advantages of access to domestic markets, large site facilities, adequate water for cooling and other processes, deep-water access to allow import of fuel and iron ore by supertankers and bulk carriers plus access to export markets.

Stages

1. **1890s**
   Initial location was towards Japan's limited domestic sources of coal and iron ore in Hokkaido, Northern Honshu and Northern Kyushu, e.g.

   Kamaishi (N. Honshu) was based on local iron ore plus coal by sea from Hokkaido;

   Yawata (N. Kyushu) using local iron ore and coal, but later imported from China;

   Muroran – local coal and iron ore.

2. **Between two world wars 1914 – 1945**
   Surge of development at coastal sites within the Pacific Belt giving a swing away from raw materials towards market-orientation; coastal access remains significant to allow for cheap import of coking coal and iron ore from China, India and the Philippines. The Osaka-Kobe region became especially important e.g. Nippon Steel at Kimitsu.

3. **1950s and early 1960s**
   Move towards large-scale integrated coastal plants to based on expanding existing plants including Muroran and establishing new coastal plants on reclaimed land, especially in the Tokyo and Osaka regions, utilising imported fuel and raw materials from a wider area including now Australia, Brazil and Canada as well as established sources.

4. **Large-scale plants of 10 million tonnes capacity**
   To allow for economies-of-scale advantages plants built away from main industrial concentrations of Pacific Belt but (a) on reclaimed land still in proximity to Pacific Belt markets, e.g. Chiba and Kobe Bay; (b) as part of industrial combines including iron and steel, oil-refining and petrochemicals.

5. **1970s – 1980s rationalisation and modernisation with plants outside the Pacific Belt closed or cut in production**
   Concentration on plant locations which coincide with regional demand within the Pacific Belt to reduce distribution costs, e.g. Kawasaki Corporation has concentrated on its Chiba and Mizushima works whilst Nippon Steel has focussed on its Keihin and Fukuyama (Hiroshima) works. There has also been a significant development of mini-steel mills based on the electric arc furnaces meeting particular local market demands.

A case example of rationalisation

Kamaishi steel town, Northern Honshu

The Kamaishi works at the head of Nari inlet on the Sanriku coast was established in 1857 using local magnetite iron ore and imported coking coal. Nippon Steel Corporation expanded the works particularly during the 1960s when it was modernised into an integrated steel plant. But because of the recession following the 1973 Oil Crisis and overseas competition, Nippon Steel have cut back production at Kamaishi seeing the plant here as uneconomic. It is far too far from the domestic markets in the Pacific Belt and the site is not well linked to the main transport network.

Steel making has now ceased with the loss of 2 200 jobs. Only a high quality wire rod mill is left and this uses steel ingots shipped from the Kimitsu plant in the Tokyo region.

As Kamaishi has been almost totally dependent on steel and it is difficult for the Government and Nippon Steel to attract industry, the population has fallen from 92 000 to 60 000.

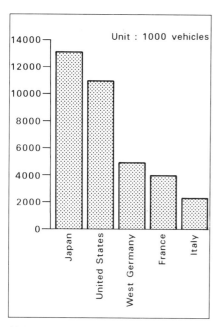

Main world producers

Overseas trade and links

Over half of Japanese production was exported in the early 1980s mainly to USA (37%), followed by the EC (19%). The proportion has now fallen due to quota measures in the main markets and increased competition from other suppliers.

But this decrease in exports has been more than offset by the setting up of branch plants overseas in different parts of the world, especially in the USA and the EC. Because of revaluation of the yen in 1985, the cost of production is cheaper overseas. In 1988 for the first time reverse imports of cars made in overseas branches came into Japan, e.g. Honda Civic cars from its Ohio plant (USA).

Increasingly Japanese corporations are also seeking co-operation and joint ventures with foreign manufacturers. Ford (USA) for example owns 25% of Japanese Mazda and the two companies have joint building ventures in Mexico and South Korea.

Co-operation on research and production due to increased sophistication and internationalisation of operations is likely to increase. Japanese car component makers are also beginning to establish parts plants near to assembly lines overseas, e.g. Toyota's suppliers are setting up in Taiwan.

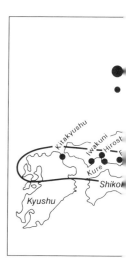

Toyota Corporation and Toyota City

General structure

Toyota, almost wholly concerned with motor vehicle production, is Japan's largest motor manufacturer with sales of $47 billion in 1989, exceeded in the world only by General Motors.

The Toyota Production System is typical of the organisation of the industry in general, the main assembly factories being supplied by thousands of subcontractors supplying the parts, most of them in close proximity. Almost all of Toyota's production is concentrated in and around Toyota City which is 90% dependent on the Corporation and now the sixth largest industrial city in Japan.

Factors underlying its location and successful development from its 1950s beginning

1. **Initial entrepreneurship** grew out of Toyota's weaving and corn industries in the area, and the later movement of the family concern into steel and aircraft manufacture. This capital and entrepreneurial basis was then used for movement into motor vehicle production in the 1950s to meet expanding market opportunities.

Nissan Corporation's cooperation with other companies overseas (1988)
% invested in company

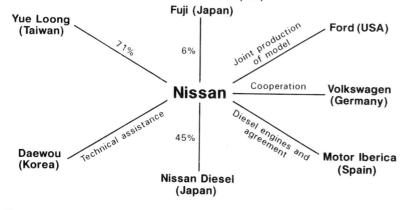

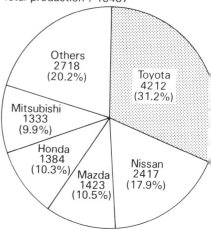

1990 production (1000 vehicle
Total production : 13487

Leading Japanese producers (1990)

2. **Commands a central position in the Pacific Belt** with excellent transport links to home market and coastal shipment points – close links to Tokyo region giving access to government departments, research and sales outlets, plus additional component suppliers.

3. **Space and facilities** for mass production encouraged by local authorities, initially centred on the small town of Koromo in the 1950s. Plenty of cheap land available, dam built for adequate water supply, parking and other facilities available. Authorities constructed new highway and rail line extended.

Figure 6.7

of the motor vehicle industry

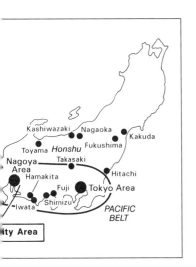

*Location of the Japanese
car industry*

Structure and locational pattern

From a relatively late start, the motor vehicle industry has developed very rapidly since the 1960s so that Japan has now replaced the USA as the world's leading producer. The bulk of the industry is concentrated in the Pacific Belt essentially because it is a market-orientated industry. Also the engineering and aircraft industries, on the basis of whose expertise and capital the motor vehicle was founded, were located in the main market areas.

As the industry moved into mass production in response to a rapidly rising and increasingly affluent home market and successful penetration of overseas markets, assembly plants have been moved to the periphery of the major built-up areas. Some of the thousands of sub–contractors to the industry have followed. But because of this close liaison of assembly plants and suppliers, any significant dispersion of the industry outside the Pacific Belt is unlikely. Investment in branch plants overseas is more likely on grounds of cheaper production costs and access to overseas markets.

Expansion of Japanese Production and Exports of Passenger Cars (1000s)

Year	Production	Exports
1975	4 568	1 558
1980	7 031	4 352
1985	7 647	5 184
1986	7 812	5 200
1987	7 891	4 984
1990	13 487	5 832

Japanese corporations are progressively establishing branch plants overseas and joint ventures with foreign companies

4. Labour force available – local labour organisations co-operative and supportive. Area previously mainly agricultural with

large adaptable labour force, which was reliable and hardworking. The Company now provides 'in house training', employment security, housing and welfare facilities. Local labour organisations are active in encouraging industry and districts amalgamated to form 'one enclosed life support system'.

5. Efficiency of large organisation – Toyota production system
Cost effective throughout, 'just in time' system of component supplies. high investment in technology and research; backing of main Japanese banks; aggressive overseas selling. There are new joint ventures overseas with General Motors (USA) and branch plants established, e.g. Kentucky (USA), Derby area (UK), Taiwan.

Honda, Nissan and Mitsubishi have the bulk of their production centred in the Tokyo region. Toyota is mainly in the Nagoya region at Toyota City and Mazda at Hiroshima.

Because of the high cost of technological developments and other increased costs, the Government, which has given significant financial support and protection to the industry now favours rationalisation into three large corporations (Toyota, Mitsubishi and Nissan). There is also pressure from the main financial banks for some rationalisation.

Home production expanded by nearly 30% between 1980 and 1990, with more emphasis on the executive car market.

*Organisational structure of
the Toyota Motor Vehicle
Industry – Toyota City Area*

■■■ Main factories
Location of
subcontracters
supplying
components

0   3 km

**Tokyo region also
supplies 30% of
components needs**

Mikawa
Line

**Further parts
suppliers in
the Nagoya
region**

Toyota
New Line

Nagoya
Line

Daijuji
Line

Tomei
Expressway

to new and ever-distant suburbs, so firms are finding it increasingly necessary to become much more pro-active in labour recruitment, to the point of being prepared to move to where the labour resides.

Whereas in the 1960s many second and third sons from rural areas migrated to become industrial workers in the Pacific Belt, the marked fall in the birth rate has stemmed this flow. Few sons of urban families these days want to go into manufacturing, as wage levels are not sufficiently high to compensate for what is regarded as lower-status work compared with white-collar occupations. But in the outer areas of industrial regions, where wage levels are generally lower, labour recruitment is found to be easier, particularly in the form of part-time working mothers and men involved in part-time farming. An added attraction in the worker's perception is that by working in these factories on the margins of the industrial regions, they are spared the expense and physical discomfort of several hours of commuting each day.

Improvement of transport networks and the general raising of accessibility are considered by many to have been fundamental to the unlocking of industrial location from its former strongholds. In this context, the extension of the expressway system, the building of the three *shinkansen* lines

and the general upgrading of suburban public transport services may be identified as key developments (Figure 6.3 and Photo 6.2). Of course, the transport improvements that made it possible to build new suburbs and dormitory towns increasingly distant from major city centres also enable the decentralising factory to maintain close contact with those linked activities remaining back in the heart of the industrial region.

6.6 GOVERNMENT INTERVENTION

Since the 1960s, the regional development policy of Japan has been directed towards achieving a more balanced distribution of industry. Whilst the emphasis was initially on relieving pressure on the main industrial cores, since the 1970s attention has also increasingly had to be given to attracting new industry to declining areas of heavy industry, particularly in Northern Kyushu and outside the Pacific Belt.

National Development Plan (1962)

In the context of industrial location, the first significant government intervention was made in the National Development Plan of 1962. This sought not only to encourage some industrial decentralisation but also to promote

Fig. 6.8 *Industrial development projects*

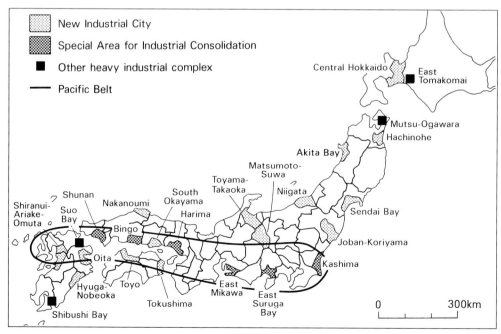

growth in lagging regions. Fifteen **New Industrial Cities** were designated as the foci for the growth of heavy, largely port-based industry (Figure 6.8). Each project involved the designation of some 1 000 ha. of land for industrial development and 300 ha. to accommodate a residential population of 200 000. Although five projects were located inside the Pacific Belt, significantly they were all established in the relatively less-developed section to the west of Osaka, particularly around the Inland Sea. The Inland Sea was able to offer sheltered deep-water anchorages, whilst reclamation of its fringing wetlands, as at South Okayama and Toyo, allowed the creation of sites for huge industrial complexes mainly concerned with the processing of imported raw materials.

The 1962 Plan also led two years later to the designation of six **Special Areas for Industrial Consolidation** (Figure 6.8). The scale of these projects was roughly that of the new industrial city. They too were largely concerned with the heavy, propulsive industries of the high-growth phase, namely iron and steel, shipbuilding, oil-refining and petrochemicals. But they were exclusively a prescription for the Pacific Belt. The schemes at Kashima, East Suruga Bay and East Mikawa were intended to achieve a degree of decentralisation by taking industrial overspill from the congested industrial nodes of Tokyo, Yokohama and Nagoya. Significantly, too, they were also intended to raise the level of industrial development in the western section of the Pacific corridor, three being located on the shores of the Inland Sea.

A third device introduced by the 1962 Plan was the **Industrial Development of an Underdeveloped Region** aimed at increasing the employment and raising the living standards of peripheral areas by means of industrial development. Inducements to factories included special depreciation allowances and exemption from local taxes. In the first five years of the scheme, no less than 150 areas were designated.

Industrial Relocation Act (1972)

The evidence suggests that individually the New Industrial Cities and Special

Areas for Industrial Consolidation were reasonably successful. For example, between 1964 and 1975 they achieved mean annual growth rates of nearly 14 percent. However, collectively they achieved little in terms of altering the fundamental distribution of manufacturing. The established industrial cores continued to grow apace. Thus in 1969, a more determined effort was initiated by the New Comprehensive Development Plan. This included ambitious proposals for environmental protection and a major expansion of the transport network (notably the construction of *shinkansen*), the latter being regarded as a vital prerequisite for industrial decentralisation.

The 1969 Plan led eventually to the 1972 Industrial Relocation Promotion Act. This set targets for the reallocation of industrial output as between the regions, the aim being to reduce the industrial growth rates in Kanto and thereby their regional shares (Table 6.2). At the heart of this part of the Industrial Development Plan was the proposal to designate 200 000 ha. of peripheral land for industrial development, mainly of a heavy calibre. Half of the land was located in coastal areas, including Eastern Tomokamai (Hokkaido), Mutsu-Ogawara (Aomori), Suo Bay (Oita) and Shibushi Bay (Kagoshima) (Figure 6.8). Table 6.2 indicates a reasonably successful start to the redistribution programme, but it might be noted that the target shares for 1975, particularly in the case of Kanto, hardly represented profound

Photo 6.2 *Aerial view of new industrial estate alongside a motorway*

	% of industrial output by value			
	Share (1965)	**Target** (1975)	**Achievement** (1975)	(1990)
Regions for decreasing share				
Kanto	35.5	35.0	34.7	33.1
Kinki	23.5	20.1	20.7	20.3
Regions for increasing share				
Tohoku	4.6	5.5	5.5	4.1
Tokai/Chukyo	16.2	17.6	16.9	20.3
Hokuriku	2.3	2.4	2.4	4.0
Chugoku	7.1	8.1	8.3	7.2
Shikoku	2.4	2.7	2.9	2.4
Kyushu	5.8	6.0	6.2	5.6
No change				
Hokkaido	2.6	2.6	2.5	1.9

Table 6.2 *Targets for the regional redistribution of manufacturing and achievements by 1975*

shifts in the overall spatial pattern. Since 1975 the regional shifts have been modest in the extreme. True that the Kanto and Kinki shares have diminished slightly, but of the regions scheduled for an increasing share, only Tokai and Hokuriku have achieved much. All the others including Hokkaido have slipped back.

The 1972 Act also designated three so-called **Departure Promotion Areas** (Tokyo, Nagoya and Osaka) from which there was to be a planned expulsion of industry. Matching them, **Relocation Reception Areas** were to be established with the intention that they would become the destinations for the 'expelled' industry, and where a variety of incentives would be offered, such as low-interest loans, tax concessions and good transport connectivity. A year earlier, the Act for the Promotion of Industrialisation in Farm Areas had been passed and this led eventually to the setting up of approximately 1 000 new medium- and small-scale enterprises for light, labour-intensive manufacturing in rural areas.

Despite this plethora of 'stick and carrot' intervention, in the event most of the proposals were only partially implemented. In part this was due to the departure of Tanaka from the Office of Prime Minister (he had been a leading advocate for the peripheral regions) and the slowing down in the economy after the 1973 Oil Crisis. But above all, it was the continued overriding momentum and pull of the Pacific Belt that largely frustrated the plans for any major decentralisation. There was also some doubt as to the strength of political will behind the various schemes. It is claimed that central government, as the supreme architect, had a vested interest in maintaining the dominance of Tokyo over the regions, and that it was subject to the persuasive influence of strong business factions still favouring investment in the Pacific Belt. Paradoxically, the heavy industrial complexes established in the periphery under the 1962 and 1969 Plans suffered relative decline during the 1980s as the iron and steel (Figure 6.6), shipbuilding and petrochemical industries sought to rationalise their undertakings in the face of falling demand and overseas competition.

Change of tack

In the late 1970s, the emphasis of government intervention changed towards an increasing concern for the depressed coalfield and heavy industrial areas. Assistance to firms willing to move to these areas was stepped up and did lead to some positive results. For example, the Nissan Motor Company established an engine factory at Kanda in an old coal-mining area of the Northern Kyushu region. In 1978 MITI identified 16 areas as being excessively dependent upon depressed industries and special government aid was given to firms locating in these. In addition, many of the large industrial corporations involved in heavy industry themselves introduced new employment opportunities to counter the growing redundancy among their workforces. Nippon Steel, for example, diversified its activities, and some of its new business ventures in electronics and information processing were located near to its ailing steel plants, as at Kamaishi in northern Honshu (Figure 6.6).

In the 1980s further emphasis was placed on accelerating regional development in order to counter the continued pull of the main industrial cores. In 1983, for example, the Law for Accelerated Regional Development introduced a new form of project involving the transfer of technology from the Pacific Belt to revitalise the indigenous enterprises of the periphery. These have been linked to the **technopolis** concept discussed more fully below. But the Government has also actively encouraged prefectural authorities to take their own initiatives. For example, in an attempt to create what it calls 'home towns', the Government has given 100 million yen to each of 3 000 towns and villages up and down the country to step up revitalisation efforts. Response from the regions has been varied. Some like Kyushu amongst the peripheral regions have been ambitious. Local and prefectural authorities there have developed a Kyushu Renaissance Plan to attract high-tech industry and to foster direct links with neighbouring Asian countries, such as Taiwan, to which they are closer in distance than to the Tokyo region. Through these links investment, technological exchanges and trade are to be encouraged.

But despite these and many other imaginative and enterprising initiatives, the immediate prognosis is that industrial development will continue to be focussed on the established industrial nodes of the Pacific Belt. Industrial decentralisation, as such, will continue to be largely a matter of removal to the margins of these cores rather than to the remoter regions which so badly need it.

6.7 THE TECHNOPOLIS CONCEPT

With the move in the economy towards the rapid expansion of high-tech and information-related industries, it is no surprise to find that the Government has pinned hopes for further industrial decentralisation on this particular sector. The expectation has been strengthened, of course, by the fact that firms in this sector require relatively little by way of material and energy inputs, and for whom transport costs are of limited concern because of the high value-to-weight ratio of their products. Furthermore, the emphasis on clean environmental conditions is an added incentive to locate outside established industrial centres.

The **technopolis** concept, which now forms the basis of the Government's current regional development programme, involves much more than just the setting up of technology-related industries in the provinces. The Government has recognised that establishing high-tech centres in the peripheral regions may be expected to lead to the revitalisation of surrounding areas, not only through the generation of additional income, but also through the diffusion of new technology into existing local industry and business.

Tsukuba Science City, located some 60 km north-east of Tokyo, begun in 1968 and still in the process of development, has together with what the Japanese have seen in other parts of the world (notably Silicon Valley, California) become the model for the new technopolis cities. Indeed, Tsukuba with its academic and research establishments (many of which have decentralised from Tokyo), its impressive array of high-tech companies and its housing and leisure facilities for 220 000 people can be regarded as Japan's first technopolis (Photo 6.3 and Figure 7.13(b)).

Under the Technopolis Policy of 1983, it is left to the individual prefectures themselves to take the initiative and apply for a technopolis designation. So much depends on local enterprise and leadership. MITI has specified that a prefecture may have only one technopolis city, that the site chosen should be

Photo 6.3 *Tsukuba Science City*

Location and locational trends

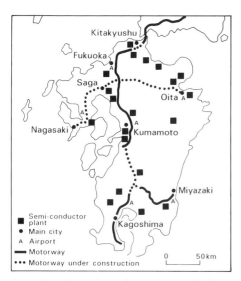

Location of semi-conductor factors in Japan

Reasons for Growth in Kyushu

1. Cheap sites available for mass production, the price of land being only 1/5th that in the Tokyo region, an important factor as e.g. Toshiba's factory covers 18 ha. including car parking, residential dormitories for workers and leisure facilities.

2. Clean air and water essential to the semi-conductor industry.

3. Until recently, a plentiful labour supply of well educated female labour – at lower cost than in the Pacific Belt.

4. Good airport, motorway and communication links back to the Tokyo region. High-value low-bulk chips can be shipped economically by air.

5. Incentives provided by local and central government to locate here – industrial estate sites available, building and other costs heavily subsidised. Drive of local officials to attract high-tech industry – e.g. Oita Prefecture is a leader in this.

6. Reputation and agglomerative advantages as high-tech industry became established – linkages etc. available.

Competing attractions of sites overseas

Japanese corporations increasingly favour branch plant sites overseas to some peripheral locations in Japan. These include sites in USA and Europe to circumvent import restrictions on Japanese imports and tap markets in these countries e.g. NEC has a factory at Roseville, California and one at Livingston (Scotland).

A significant number of plants are being established in neighbouring NICs where labour is cheaper, some production is then exported back to Japan.

Dispersion to Kyushu – the new growth centre

The growing concentration of semi-conductor and related plants in Kyushu on the periphery of the Pacific Belt has been compared to the high-technology concentration in Silicon Valley in California.

About 40% of Japan's semi-conductor industry is found in Kyushu and this includes some of the country's largest plants, e.g. NEC's Kumamoto plant and Toshiba's Oita plant. Whilst not containing a heavy concentration of R and D institutions, Kyushu has attracted ancillary industries supplying the semi-conductor industry, e.g. packaging and silicon wafer suppliers plus some marketing firms.

The strength of information-technology based industries is fundamental to the Kyushu Renaissance Plan as outlined by the Kyushu Economic Research Centre and by local governments. The twin bases of the Plan are seen as a 'Silicon Island' policy

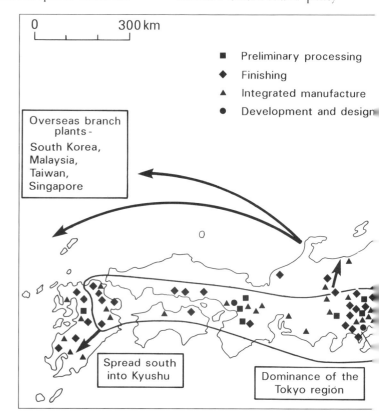

Dominance of the Pacific Belt – particularly the Tokyo region

Despite some dispersion of plants outside the Pacific Belt and overseas, the Tokyo region is dominant. Mass-production plants tend to be located towards the periphery where land is more plentiful and female labour available from nearby rural areas. Specialist chip production in smaller firms may be within the main built-up areas.

The Tokyo region has the advantages of:

1. Close contact with the main markets allowing quick response to changes in demand.

2. Proximity to the large number of public and private research institutions and also small businesses producing electronic equipment. Interlinkage is essential in a fast changing industry.

3. The largest pool of skilled workers and entrepreneurial skills.

4. Close liaison with government institutions.

Figure 6.9

in the semi-conductor industry

allied to investment and other links with neighbouring Asian countries. An indication of the significance of Kyushu's economy is that it has twice the GNP of South Korea.

Whilst Kyushu's relative importance has recently declined in favour of the Tokyo region, Kyushu is likely to continue to expand as a high-technology production area.

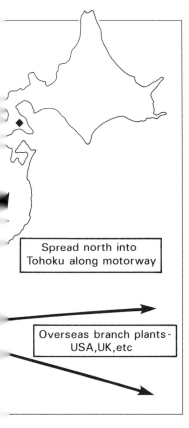

Spread north into Tohoku along motorway

Overseas branch plants – USA, UK, etc

5. Being at the centre of Japan's information flow and communication network.

6. A number of the headquarters of the large corporations involved in the information-technology industry e.g. NEC has recently built a new 40-storey head office in the centre of Tokyo.

The problem of the high cost of labour and a potential labour shortage in the Tokyo region is becoming less important as assembly lines become increasingly automated. Also the need for a clean air environment and a pure water supply can be met artificially.

Importance

High-technology industry is central to the needs of society and to manufacturing. The semi-conductor industry produces micro chips needed in high-tech products supplied to such essential areas as telecommunications, electrical consumer goods, aerospace and defence, output has expanded rapidly since the mid-1970s. Japan commands 75% of the world market for the 1 megabit chip and has the lead in the newer 4 megabit market. It is at the forefront of R and D with corporations and smaller businesses actively supported by the Government.

The world's largest semiconductor manufacturers, 1987

Name of Company	1987 Rank	1986 Rank	Revenues ($ billion)
NC (Japan)	1	1	31 993
Toshiba (Japan)	2	3	2 939
Hitachi (Japan	3	2	2 781
Motorola (USA)	4	4	2 450
Texas Instruments (USA)	5	5	2 125
Fujitsu (Japan)	6	6	1 899
Phillips – Signetics (Neths)	7	8	1 597
Intel (USA)	8	11	1 500
Mitsubishi (Japan)	9	10	1 481
Matsushita(Japan)	10	9	1 479

Output of semi-conductors in Japan

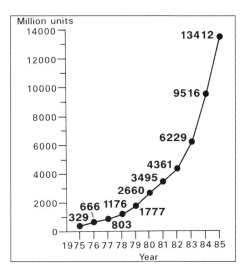

In 1984 Japanese firms invested 30% of sales revenues in large new plants which can achieve the benefits of economies of scale. Toshiba's plant at Oita (Kyushu) in the mid-1980s produced 1/3 of Japan's output of 1 megabit memory chips. Producing on such a scale, Japanese corporations can undercut many of their competitors overseas and both European and United States producers continue to lose out to Japan in the early 1990s.

Some movement of overseas competitors into Japan's Market

In response to complaints, especially from the USA, of Japan's aggressive penetration of overseas markets but protection of its own, Japan has relaxed restrictions leading to overseas corporations now having a larger share of the Japan market. In 1990 this amounted to 20% for 1 megabit chips and there are plans to establish branch plants and research institutions in Japan by overseas corporations, e.g. Texas Instruments is building a $40 million dollar research and development centre at Tsukuba. IBM has already a strong base in the Tokyo area.

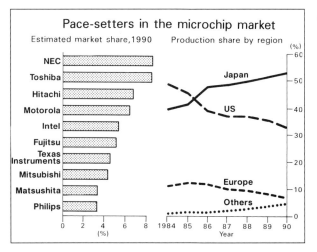

within 30 minutes reach of a major city and that it should be well connected in terms of the national transport networks (road, rail and air). Each technopolis project consists of three interlocking components, namely (i) an industrial complex made up not just of factories but also of distribution and linked business services, (ii) an academic unit comprising a university, colleges and research and development institutions, and (iii) a residential zone for the accommodation of workers and their families.

So far, 19 have been designated, but it possible that a further six may be recognised by the year 2000 (Figure 6.10). Those prefectures taking an early lead were those already involved in modern technology-based industry. These included Oita and Kumamoto in Kyushu, already a leading area of Japan's microchip industry (Figure 6.10). Those prefectures taking an early lead were those already involved in modern technology-based industry. These included Oita and Kumamoto in Kyushu, already a leading area of Japan's microchip industry (Figure 6.9). The prefectural authorities here Nagoya and already internationally renowned for motorcycles, musical instruments and home sound systems. At Nagaokoa, now linked to Tokyo by the Joetsu *shinkansen*, the technopolis designation was seen as a way of

extending a new town development project begun in the 1970s (Figure 7.13(a)).

There are already clear indications that the technopolis concept will be successful in promoting new growth areas. However, it is also becoming evident that the more successful ones will be those within the Pacific Belt and those in peripheral prefectures that happen to have good transport links with the main industrial nodes. Furthermore, the Tokyo region is already outstripping the rest of Japan in the amount and value of research and development in new materials and products, and in its share of high-tech industry.

Tokyo's attractions are overwhelming (Figure 6.9). For over a century, it has been at the forefront of the electrical engineering industry. It has the highest concentration of firms and businesses which form the main market for high-tech industries. It contains eight of Japan's universities and the greatest proportion of Japan's leading industrial research facilities. In the rapidly expanding and changing field of high-technology, prompt and sensitive response to market changes on the one hand and to advances in research on the other are vital. In addition, a location within the Tokyo region gives quick access to Government ministries and advisory institutions as well as to

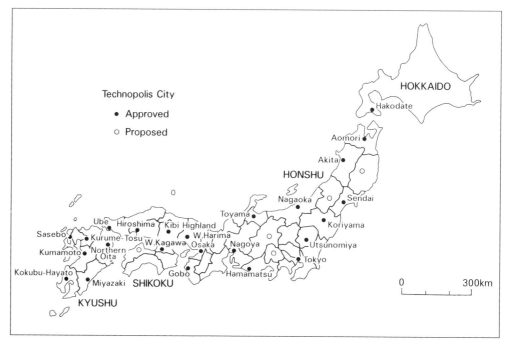

Fig. 6.10 *Technopolis cities, approved and proposed*

the best entrepreneurial skills. The emergence of Tokyo as one of the main financial centres of the world and the agglomeration of the head offices of Japan's international corporations and the Japan-based offices of other multi-nationals, such as IBM and ICI seeking to penetrate the Japanese market, add to the irresistible attraction of the Tokyo region. These pulls continue to outweigh the increasing diseconomies of the region and the decentralising efforts embodied in the Government's regional development policies.

There may be some comfort, however, in the fact that many of the high-tech industrial locations are in science parks and new cities towards the margins of the capital region and the other industrial cores within the Pacific Belt (Figure 6.9). But the role of the inner areas of these cores also remains strong. For example, many of the small factories producing printed circuits and microchips are found in the Ward Area of Tokyo. This central part of the capital also contains a major proportion of a new phenomenon known as the **system house** – the small firm engaged in the development and production of the hard and software needed to harness computers to a great diversity of operating systems (Figure 6.11). The Tokyo region has 60 percent of Japan's system houses, whilst 20 percent are in Osaka and 5 percent in the Nagoya region; in each case, they are predominantly located in inner-city areas.

6.8 ACHIEVEMENTS AND DISAPPOINTMENTS

The restructuring of Japan's industrial base has gone on for nearly twenty years now and the Government sees this as continuing past the turn of the century. It will be undertaken in response to changing market demand, the emergence of new technology and new products and the changing global economy, including fiercer competition in the international market place. Whilst perhaps the most striking feature of the 1980s and early 1990s has been the emergence of Japan as pre-eminent in a broadening range of high-tech industries, the restructuring and modernisa-

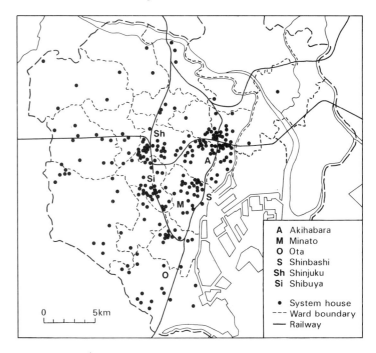

Fig. 6.11 The distribution of system houses in the Ward Area of Tokyo

A Akihabara
M Minato
O Ota
S Shinbashi
Sh Shinjuku
Si Shibuya

• System house
--- Ward boundary
— Railway

0   5km

tion of its heavier staple industries and its advances in consumer durables, such as motor vehicles and domestic electrical/electronic appliances, have been equally significant. Here concentration on the mass-consumption market is to some extent being re-oriented towards the more upmarket needs of an increasingly discerning and affluent domestic market. The steel and shipbuilding industries, much slimmed down and now more efficient using the latest technology, are once again profitable and leaders in world production.

But for all the dynamic change taking place within the manufacturing sector, the locational pattern has stubbornly refused to change to any significant degree (Table 6.2). Although new manufacturing is to be found in the Japanese periphery, very few parts of it have actually gained ground in terms of national share; most have in fact slipped back (Figure 6.12). The prognosis can only be one of continuing growth within the existing industrial cores and in adjacent areas.

What seems all too evident is that market forces remain stronger than government efforts to decentralise manufacturing. Although desirable both socially and environmentally, the attempt to achieve a more equitable distribution of industry across the country is being thwarted. Actually, it is rather more complicated than simply

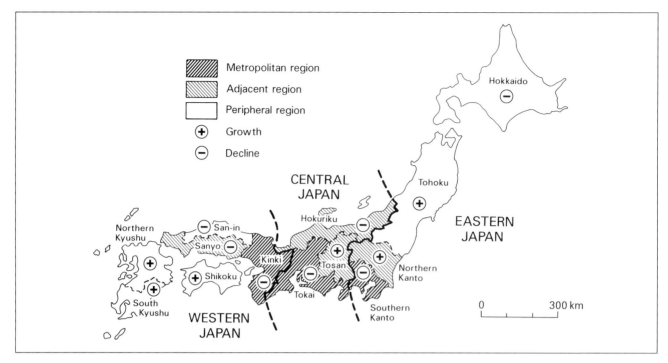

Fig. 6.12 *Changes in the distribution of manufacturing employment (1960 – 1990)*

the superiority of market forces. Despite overt and genuine government support for regional development, political factions within the ruling party are so closely allied to the huge business corporations that in reality more is being done to meet the wishes of the latter rather than the best interests of the nation. Those wishes are broadly to remain as close as possible to the Pacific Belt markets and to protect investments in real estate. Vested interests will simply not contemplate anything more than a selective, short-distance shift to the margins of the major industrial nodes. However, the negative values shown in Figure 6.12 for much of the Pacific Belt are indicative that this dispersal is highly localised. The outward limit is currently between 200 and 300 km from the centre of any one of the Pacific Belt's leading cities. That limit is determined by time-distance values and the specified need to be able, within the working day, to complete the two-way trip and yet have a reasonable amount of time for business. Clearly, the future scale of this more localised industrial decentralisation will be closely bound up with further improvements in accessibility and communications. But none of this can be expected in the foreseeable future to alter in any significant way the long-established pattern of industrial distribution in Japan.

7

C H A P T E R

The urban scene

7.1 URBANISATION AND THE MODERN URBAN PATTERN

Although towns have been important in the economic life of Japan since feudal times, even as late as 1920 only 26 percent of the population lived in urban areas (Table 4.5). But so rapid has been the pace of urbanisation since then that the proportion is now over 75 percent. In little over 50 years Japan has moved from being a predominantly rural country to become one of the most highly urbanised societies in the world. With the exception of the Second World War, urbanisation has proceeded at an unrelenting pace, the rate being particularly fast during the 1950s. Since the 1960s there has been a slight easing back (Figure 7.1). Table 7.1 serves to underline an outstanding characteristic of Japanese urbanisation, namely its very high densities. Since 1960, the Japanese Population Census has recognised what are called **densely-inhabited districts (DIDs)**. These are groups of contiguous enumeration districts within settlements which have population densities in excess of 4 000 persons per km². Although the increase in the percentage of the population living in DIDs is easing off, nearly two-thirds of the population are now crammed into such areas, which in total account for less than 3 percent of the land area.

In previous chapters, reference has often been made to the concentration of the bulk of the Japanese population in the Pacific Belt, particularly in that stretch between Tokyo and Kobe (Figure 7.2). Within that section are located seven of Japan's eleven million-aire cities. These, in their turn, are incorporated into the three main metropolitan areas centred on Tokyo, Nagoya and Osaka (Figure 7.3). Almost

	Population (m)	% of total population	% of total area
1960	40.8	43.7	1.03
1965	47.3	48.1	1.23
1970	55.5	53.5	1.71
1975	63.8	57.0	2.19
1980	69.9	59.7	2.65
1985	73.3	60.6	2.80
1990	78.3	63.2	3.20

Table 7.1 *Densely-inhabited districts (1960 – 1990)*

continuous ribbons of urban development have tended to weld these metropolitan areas into an even higher order of urban structure, linear in form and commonly referred to as Tokaido **megalopolis**. West of Kobe, three more millionaire cities - Hiroshima, Fukuoka and Kitakyushu - fall within the Pacific Belt and are the basis of two lesser metropolitan areas. Their location is such that some would regard them as

Fig. 7.1 *The urbanisation of Japan (1920–1990)*

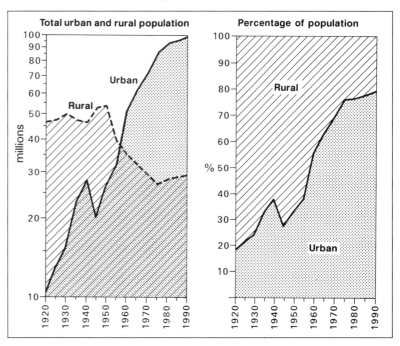

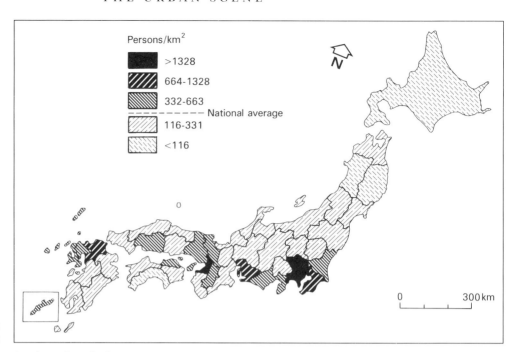

Fig. 7.2 *The distribution of population (1990)*

Fig. 7.3 *The metropolitan areas of Japan (1990)*

having already been incorporated into a Tokaido-Sanyo megalopolis. Only one of the millionaire cities lies outside the belt, namely Sapporo the capital of Hokkaido; it and the city of Sendai have become the nuclei of two more minor metropolitan areas.

Evolution of the Urban Pattern
Stage one

On the basis of the urbanisation curve

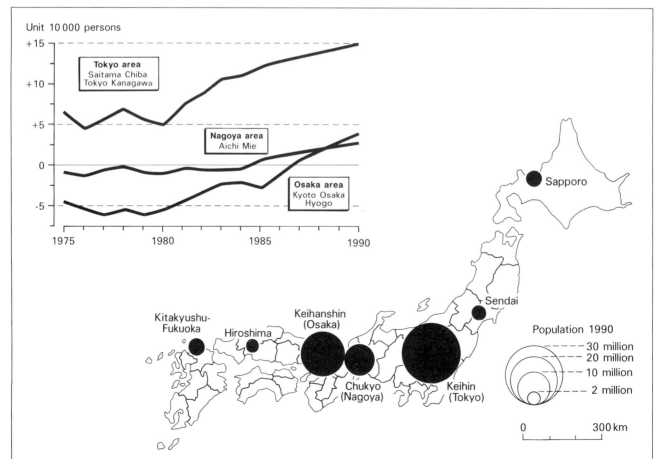

(Figure 7.1), it is possible to recognise three stages in the evolution of the urban pattern since the end of the First World War (1918) (Figure 7.4). The first stage was characterised by massive rural-urban migration and the concentration of much of the in-migration in the major metropolitan areas of Tokaido megalopolis. The acute centralisation of jobs and services and limited personal mobility gave rise to quite compact and very high density cities. The growth of lesser urban centres between the three main nodes led to the progressive erosion of green breaks and the gradual emergence of Tokaido megalopolis.

Stage two

The second stage coincides with the high-growth phase in Japan's postwar economic development, approximately from the mid 1950s to the mid-1970s (Figure 7.4). This was the time of heaviest migration into urban areas. As in the previous stage, most of this inward movement was due to the expansion of the manufacturing and service sectors (Table 5.2), the consequent rise in employment opportunities and the lure of higher wage and salary levels. Whilst disparity of economic opportunity between urban and rural areas was the main driving force behind the rapid increase in rural-urban migration, other factors were also important. Increased population pressure resulting from the postwar baby boom was one of these. Although the birth rate did fall subsequently, population increase continued since the effects of the fall were offset by the larger population base to which the rate related (Figure 4.5). Also contributing was the fact that mobility is typically greatest among the young adult cohort (i.e. 18 to 35 year olds). The postwar baby boom meant a considerable expansion of this mobile cohort in the 1960s and 1970s, and so the potential for movement to the cities continued to remain high. The Japanese experience well demonstrates the case that the pressures lying behind urban migration and growth are based on a complex set of interrelated demographic processes operating over a substantial period of time (Figure 7.5).

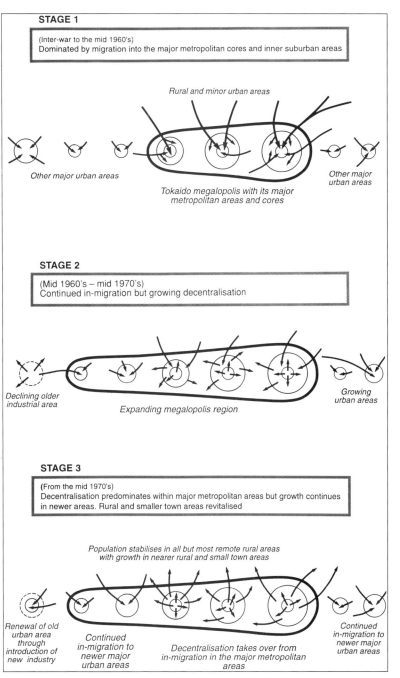

Fig. 7.4 Stages in the evolution of the urban pattern since 1918

Urban migration at this time was also influenced by a number of psychological and social factors. In the minds of the Japanese, the booming Tokaido megalopolis was not only synonymous with economic and material success in life, but also with restoration of national pride following defeat. Although close ties were maintained with the family's rural and ancestral home area, for the younger Japanese in particular, success in life was associated with Tokyo in particular. In the perception of many, Tokyo was the epitomy of material wealth and the mass-consumption

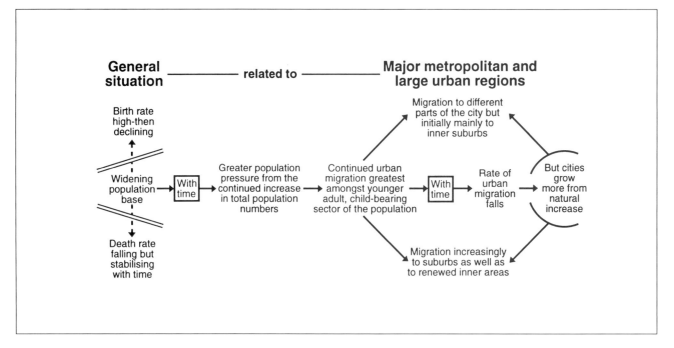

General situation —————— related to —————— **Major metropolitan and large urban regions**

Fig. 7.5 *The basic and interrelated demographic processes affecting urbanisation over time*

society; here Western influences and fashions were at their strongest; here there was greater educational opportunity and social freedom.

As for the spatial pattern of urban growth during this second stage, Tokaido megalopolis remained the prime focus (Figure 7.4). The combination of great population growth and improved mobility was to provoke a huge suburban boom and the spectacular mushrooming of the built-up area. As a consequence, the megalopolitan structure became even more tightly welded, and with a notable westward expansion along the San-yo corridor. Outside Tokaido megalopolis, a select band of freestanding cities in northern Japan, including Sendai and Sapporo, began to experience accelerating growth. At the other end of the country, stagnation in the old industrial region of northern Kyushu repercussed on the cities of Fukuoka and Kitakyushu.

Stage three

Since the mid-1970s, the rate of urbanisation has slackened off quite appreciably (Figure 7.1). Growth of the three main metropolitan areas has been intermittent and due more to natural increase than net in-migration. Indeed, out-migration has for much of the time exceeded in-migration, leading to temporary dips in the populations of the Osaka and Nagoya areas (Figure 7.3). **Decentralisation** rather than **centralisation** has become the major trend with people moving out of the congested central areas to the outer suburbs and even beyond the administrative boundaries of the metropolitan areas to rings of growing dormitory towns and settlements. Thus since the 1970s, Japan has progressed to a third stage in the evolution of urban pattern (Figure 7.4), with urbanisation being fueled by expansion of the tertiary rather than the manufacturing sector (Table 5.2).

The decentralisation taking place is essentially a decentralisation within the metropolitan areas, and should not be construed as signalling their economic decline. As the number of people wishing to live away from the main centres of employment increases, a hollowing out effect is being produced in the population density profiles of metropolitan areas, with their more central areas being denuded of residential population. Adding to the decentralisation is the fact that an increasing proportion of migrants from outside are moving directly to the outer rather than the inner suburbs. Also giving momentum is the dispersion of some manufacturing and service activities; as yet this is limited, but it is gathering pace (see Chapter 6.3).

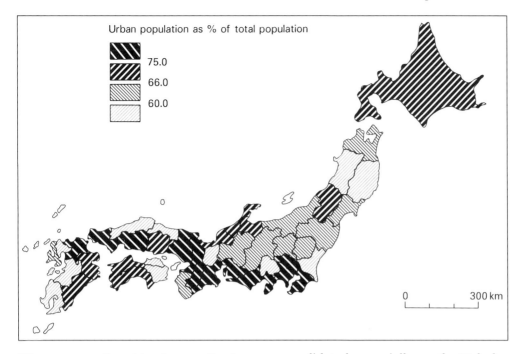

Urban population as % of total population

75.0
66.0
60.0

0   300 km

Fig. 7.6 *The distribution of urban population (1990)*

The reasons for this decentralisation tendency are numerous but one of the most important is the push factor exerted by the continuing concentration and outward spread of economic activity at the centre of the metropolitan areas. This leads to a continual rise in land prices (Figure 7.16) and increasing congestion, as well as a range of detrimental impacts on the residential environment. At the same time, the improving and extending suburban transport systems, the cheaper land for housing and the more pleasant environment further out in the suburbs and beyond are acting as pull factors. Increased leisure time due to the shortening of the working week and greater personal mobility have also encouraged a greater appreciation of access to the countryside.

At present, most decentralisation is confined to the suburbs and peripheral edges of major metropolitan areas. It is too early yet to see whether this will overspill in any substantial way to surrounding rural areas as has occurred in the USA and other Western countries. Certainly, it is extremely difficult to find any real evidence to indicate that Japan has begun to experience **counterurbanisation**. But two things do seem clear. First, that for all the decentralisation, there has been no weakening of the megalopolitan structure of the Pacific Belt. Indeed, it has become more

consolidated, especially on the Tohoku side of Tokyo and in the San-yo section beyond Kobe (Figure 7.4). The Pacific Belt is remarkably well defined by degrees of urbanisation well above the national average (Figure 7.6). Secondly, many smaller cities outside the Pacific Belt, particularly the prefectural capitals, are enjoying rising prosperity and indeed are growing at a faster rate than the core cities. This characteristic will be discussed in more detail in Chapter 9, as will the issue of whether or not this current decentralisation is to be seen as a core-periphery spread effect.

Before moving on to examine the character of the present urban system, attention needs to be drawn to some very recent signs of revival in the inner suburbs. Here residential renewal and the improvement of the living environment appear to be changing the residential preferences of some people. Perhaps it is a weariness of commuting and a desire once again to live close to work and services that is bringing about this counter-movement. It remains to be seen whether this centripetal movement heralds the beginning of a new and fourth stage in the evolution of the urban pattern.

7.2 THE URBAN HIERARCHY

Before the onset of rapid urbanisation, most towns and cities were seen

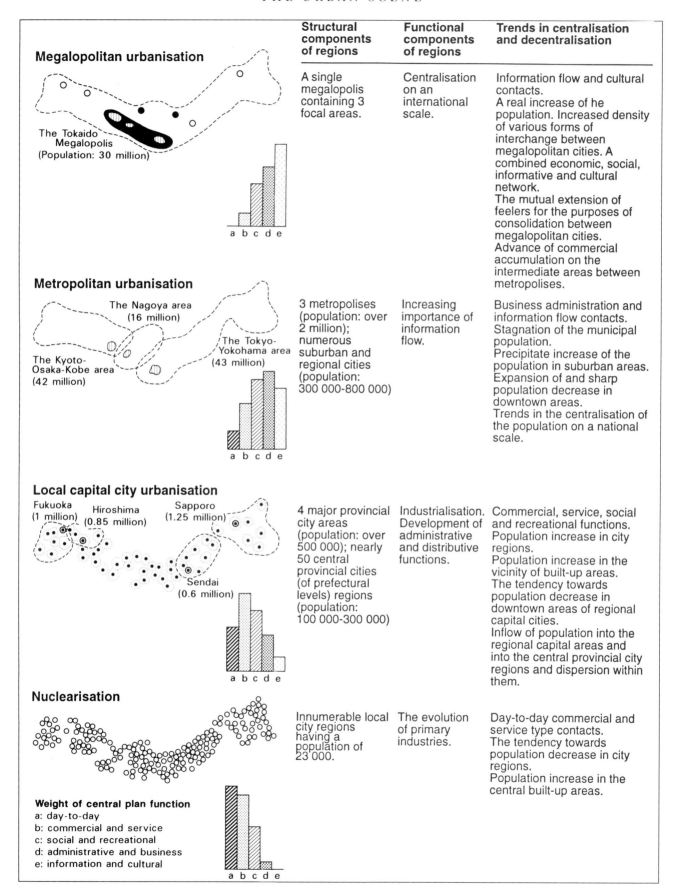

Megalopolitan urbanisation

The Tokaido
Megalopolis
(Population: 30 million)

a b c d e

Metropolitan urbanisation

The Nagoya area
(16 million)

The Tokyo-
Yokohama area
(43 million)

The Kyoto-
Osaka-Kobe area
(42 million)

a b c d e

Local capital city urbanisation

Fukuoka
(1 million)   Hiroshima
(0.85 million)   Sapporo
(1.25 million)

Sendai
(0.6 million)

a b c d e

Nuclearisation

Weight of central plan function
a: day-to-day
b: commercial and service
c: social and recreational
d: administrative and business
e: information and cultural

a b c d e

	Structural components of regions	Functional components of regions	Trends in centralisation and decentralisation
Megalopolitan urbanisation	A single megalopolis containing 3 focal areas.	Centralisation on an international scale.	Information flow and cultural contacts. A real increase of he population. Increased density of various forms of interchange between megalopolitan cities. A combined economic, social, informative and cultural network. The mutual extension of feelers for the purposes of consolidation between megalopolitan cities. Advance of commercial accumulation on the intermediate areas between metropolises.
Metropolitan urbanisation	3 metropolises (population: over 2 million); numerous suburban and regional cities (population: 300 000-800 000)	Increasing importance of information flow.	Business administration and information flow contacts. Stagnation of the municipal population. Precipitate increase of the population in suburban areas. Expansion of and sharp population decrease in downtown areas. Trends in the centralisation of the population on a national scale.
Local capital city urbanisation	4 major provincial city areas (population: over 500 000); nearly 50 central provincial cities (of prefectural levels) regions (population: 100 000-300 000)	Industrialisation. Development of administrative and distributive functions.	Commercial, service, social and recreational functions. Population increase in city regions. Population increase in the vicinity of built-up areas. The tendency towards population decrease in downtown areas of regional capital cities. Inflow of population into the regional capital areas and into the central provincial city regions and dispersion within them.
Nuclearisation	Innumerable local city regions having a population of 23 000.	The evolution of primary industries.	Day-to-day commercial and service type contacts. The tendency towards population decrease in city regions. Population increase in the central built-up areas.

Fig. 7.7   *The four orders of the urban hierarchy*

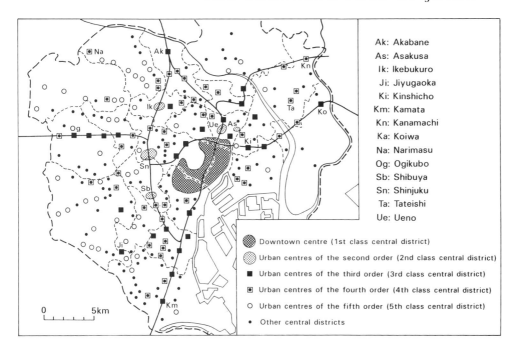

Ak: Akabane
As: Asakusa
Ik: Ikebukuro
Ji: Jiyugaoka
Ki: Kinshicho
Km: Kamata
Kn: Kanamachi
Ka: Koiwa
Na: Narimasu
Og: Ogikubo
Sb: Shibuya
Sn: Shinjuku
Ta: Tateishi
Ue: Ueno

Downtown centre (1st class central district)
Urban centres of the second order (2nd class central district)
Urban centres of the third order (3rd class central district)
Urban centres of the fourth order (4th class central district)
Urban centres of the fifth order (5th class central district)
Other central districts

Fig. 7.8 *The central-place hierarchy of the Ward Area, Tokyo*

primarily as **central places** serving surrounding rural hinterlands. Whilst this urban-rural relationship remains the essential function of the smaller urban centres of less than 30 000 people, the larger towns and cities within the urban hierarchy are much more concerned with the more specialist functions which are either an integral part of industrialisation or exist to service the needs of urban populations and institutions. With three-quarters of the population now living in an urban environment, the earlier central place function that bound urban and rural areas has become submerged beneath a web of inter-city relationships. As a consequence, it becomes possible to recognise an **urban hierarchy** of four orders of centres differentiated on the basis of both the scale of economic activity present and the relative weighting of functions (Figure 7.7).

At the bottom of the hierarchy are the fourth-order or small local cities, usually with populations less than 30 000 (Figure 7.7). These are largely concerned with the provision of goods and centralised services for a surrounding rural area. The third order comprises the prefectural capital cities, with populations falling mainly within the 100 to 300 000 range. Administration is clearly a prominent aspect of a well-developed central place

function. In addition to high-order services, these capitals are found to be involved, to varying degrees, in both manufacturing and tourism. Amongst the ranks of prefectural capitals there are cities like Fukuoka, Hiroshima, Sendai and Sapporo which are additionally important in a regional sense because of their size and national status as industrial and business centres.

The next order is made up of the three main metropolitan areas of Tokyo-Yokohama, Nagoya and Osaka-Kyoto-Kobe which effectively carve Japan into three unequal territories (Figure 7.7). Besides providing very specialist services within the contexts of industry, business, administration and information services which are marketed over large areas of the country, they also function as central place systems in their own right. Within them, it is possible to recognise a hierarchy of centres ranging from the central business district down to a local shopping centre (Figure 7.8).

Such has been the dynamism and outward growth of these three metropolitan centres, together with the intensity and scale of the interchanges between them in the form of goods, information and people, that they have simply become components of an even higher-order of urban structure – Tokaido megalopolis (Figure 7.7). Its arteries are the fast and efficient

Photo 7.1 Fast, efficient transport – the key to the creation of Tokaido megalopolis

transport links provided by the *shinkansen*, the Tomei expressway and inter-city air services, and all manner of modern communication media (Photo 7.1). Its existence bears testimony to the fundamental division of Japan into a core and periphery.

7.3 THE STRUCTURE OF CITIES

Models used to describe city structures in Western countries are of only limited use when it comes to analysing Japanese cities. Beyond recognising areas largely devoted to industrial or commercial usage, and the density gradient that runs from those inner areas of compact, older housing to extensive suburban sprawl towards the city margins, Japan's urban scene defies generalised description.

There are a number of reasons for this. First, there are the diverse origins of urban centres, ranging from castle towns, ports and staging posts to religious and cultural centres. The very fact that each town and city tends to have had a unique history inevitably adds to their diversity. The actual built-up area has been made more disparate by its frequent destruction and subsequent rebuilding after earthquakes, floods and fires. Since most buildings

were and still are constructed of wood, the Japanese city has always been particularly vulnerable to these kinds of hazard. Intensive bombing of Japan's major cities during the Second World War also led to the destruction of much of the built-up area. Thus, whilst the gridiron pattern of streets may remain to distinguish the older parts of the city from later accretionary growth, of the older buildings it is only the more sturdily built temples, shrines and castles that remain. Most of the fabric of the Japanese city today dates from the postwar period. Adding still further to the apparent chaos and randomness has been the absence of effective planning, particularly during the boom years of the high-growth phase when little was done to curb the suburban explosion.

Small wonder, therefore, that Japanese cities appear as formless sprawls. It says a lot when the capital city is justifiably described by a Japanese writer as 'an organic blob . . . Razed to ashes in the Great Kanto Earthquake of 1923 and again in the bombing of 1944–45, this great brainless amoeba licked its wounds and rebuilt itself in the same formless pattern evolved since the days when everything centred round the castle, namely a ripple of broken rings rolling out across the Kanto plain from Tokyo Bay in the general direction of Mt Fuji'.

Photo 7.2 *Aerial view of the Imperial Palace and environs*

7.4 PATTERNS OF COMMERCE

The spatial distribution of commercial land uses is perhaps the aspect of the structure of the Japanese city about which generalisations may be made. In all towns and cities it is possible to recognise a **central business district** (CBD) and distributed around it within the confines of the built-up area a hierarchy of lesser central places of varying complexity (Figure 7.8).

Within the CBD, there is a fine spatial sorting of different types of business, reflecting differences in their precise locational requirements and their bidding power on the land and property markets. Amongst the specialised quarters within Tokyo's downtown area, which pivots around Tokyo Station, mention might be made of Ginza with its impressive array of expensive stores, the Marunouchi district with its company headquarters, insurance and banking. Around the Japanese Diet there is the Kasumigaseki district with its agglomeration of government ministries and departments, whilst ranks of international hotels overlook the grounds of the Imperial Palace which remains the symbolic centre of modern Tokyo (Photo 7.2)

A wholesale resort to vertical development is the conventional way of maximising the limited amount of space available. The omnipresent earthquake hazard does not appear to have discouraged Japanese developers, but no less impressive in the case of many of Japan's larger cities is the scale of development underground. In central Tokyo, it is increasingly commonplace to find two or more levels of development below the surface. Shops, eating places and bars, together with carparks and pedestrian ways, are the leading 'mole' land uses. The resort to both upward and downward development is greatest in a growing number of highly prestigious downtown redevelopment schemes to be found in Tokyo and the other leading cities. In central Tokyo, noteworthy projects include the Grand Yaesu Underground Town and the Ark Hills Complex, a 24-hour business centre.

During the postwar period, most of the downtown areas of major cities in Japan have been redeveloped, but the few remaining areas of narrow streets and wooden buildings, with their shops and discrete bars, are becoming increasingly popular amongst the most affluent and discerning shoppers. Shintomachi, only a few minutes walk away from the Ginza in Tokyo, is a case in point. These older shopping areas are of a more intimate scale and offer a pleasant change from the concrete-clad

Figure 7.9 *Ancient and modern – an artists view of Tokyo*

Photo 7.3 *Shinjuku business centre, Tokyo*

blocks which make up much of modern Tokyo and other large cities (Figure 7.9).

In the case of Tokyo, the next order down the commercial hierarchy is made up of quite prestigious business centres which have been deliberately created in the postwar period to relieve some of the acute congestion of the downtown area (Figure 7.8). These include Shinjuku, Shibuya, Ikebukuro and Ueno, each strategically located adjacent to one of the major terminals of the suburban rail network, and thus ensured of a high degree of accessibility. These second-order centres are readily discernible by their clusters of high-rise buildings (Photo 7.3). They contain high-order specialist services ranging from large department stores and headquarter offices to international hotels and expensive restaurants. Leisure and entertainment are recognised as important activities, so that each centre has its *sakariba* or entertainment quarter of bars, *pachinko* (pinball) parlours and *love hotels*. The last arise partly from the lack of privacy for most young couples at home and for business people to offer their clients all manner of hospitality.

Down the hierarchy, the CBD is succeeded by the large suburban centres located towards the margins of the city (Figure 7.8). These third-order centres act as reception areas for the lower-orders of service progressively removed from the CBD. They also develop as important centres in their own right, being patronised by customers who are drawn from areas beyond the city boundary, but who are increasingly deterred by traffic congestion from travelling into the CBD for the more routine shopping. Below these enhanced commercial nodes are the smaller centres, largely concerned with retailing and found in two type locations, namely around suburban railway stations and in the cores of old settlements which have been engulfed by the spread of the built-up area. Finally, at the bottom of the hierarchy, are the small clusters of shops, usually at street corners, which serve the immediate neighbourhood with low-order convenience goods.

It is in its commercial structure that the Japanese city bears the closest resemblance to its Western counterpart, but with one notable exception. What are still largely absent are the edge-of-town and out-of-town hypermarkets and superstores. This is mainly because much of the retailing in Japan remains in the hands of small family concerns and legislation has until recently protected the small retailer. However, since 1990 legislative controls have been loosened and there are now active plans for hypermarket-type developments. One of the first to be completed is on the outskirts of Hiroshima; this comprises two large stores, 180 speciality shops and amusement facilities. Perhaps it is indicative of the slow take-off of out-of-town shopping in Japan that in its first year of operation sales in this centre were between 10 and 15 percent below expectation.

7.5 INDUSTRIAL AREAS

Since the Second World War, the intra-urban pattern of industry has become more complex. Not only has heavy industry been intensified and extended at established coastal sites, including

Photo 7.4 *A large complex of heavy industry built on reclaimed land*

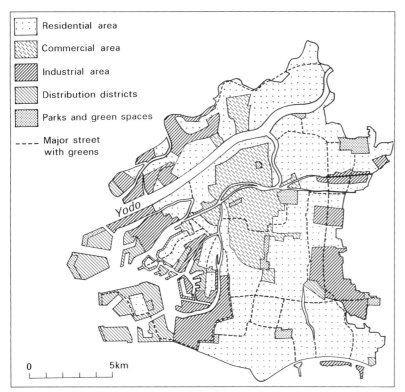

Fig. 7.10 *The land-use pattern of Osaka*

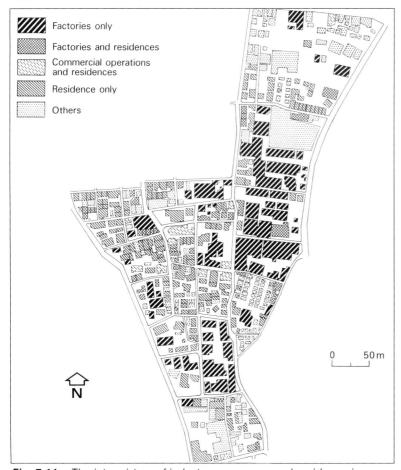

Fig. 7.11 *The intermixture of industry, commerce and residence in Higashi-tateishi*

for example chemicals, steel and heavy engineering along the shores of Tokyo Bay between Tokyo and Yokohama, but new industrial complexes have been established. The latter are frequently in areas where previously little industry had been present, and have often involved extensive reclamation of offshore areas to provide the large sites that are needed. This has occurred for example around the eastern shores of Tokyo Bay in Chiba prefecture and also around parts of Osaka and Kobe bays (Photo 7.4). Such developments have been partly a response to the need for more sites close to the points where raw materials are imported and finished goods exported. But they are also encouraged by the need of heavy industry for large level sites and plentiful water supplies. Almost inevitably the location of these new heavy industrial complexes tends to be marginal to the built-up area (Figure 7.10).

Whilst the areas of heavy manufacturing are entirely given over to industry and can therefore be clearly classified as industrial zones, this is not the case with much of the light industrial development. Light industry is mainly in the hands of family concerns and consists of small factory premises intermixed with housing (Figure 7.11). The location is typically inner city. Until relatively recently, these inner industrial zones have been slow to change. The tendency has been for existing factory buildings to be adapted to accommodate new processes and products such as electrical and electronic components. Although most of these inner areas contain a considerable variety of industries, for historical reasons certain districts within them have become noted for particular manufactures. For example, the Yao district in south-east Osaka is noted for brushes and Higashi-Osaka for metals.

Small-scale industry has tended to remain in inner urban areas partly because close linkages between firms and the horizontal organisation of much of the manufacturing require close contact and therefore the juxtaposition of factories. There is also a heavy reliance on the skilled labour living nearby. Furthermore, there is also a need for light industrial firms to locate close to wholesale and retail outlets in and around the CBD. Small producers often need to meet orders at short notice and respond quickly to changing fashions; this is especially true for the clothing and furniture industries. The characteristic close association of producer, wholesaler and retailer is well illustrated by the location of the handbag industry in Tokyo (Figure 7.12). Another industry reliant on close links with its market is the printing and publishing industry. It tends to be highly localised in areas close to the offices of government and large corporations, both of which supply many of its orders. Again, such is the specialised and rushed nature of some of the customers' requirements that close contact is vital.

For all the persistent concentration of light industry in inner-city areas, it has to be pointed out that industrial estates are beginning to make an appearance. Indeed, prefectural and local government authorities are increasingly combining a policy of renewing the old areas of mixed industrial and residential development with the building of industrial estates in the suburbs or at the city margins. The challenge in such renewal programmes is to ensure that factories remain accessible to labour. It is for this reason that there have materialised a few schemes involving the relocation of both factories and their workers. For example, metal toy and clothing manufacturers have removed en bloc from the Joto area of inner Tokyo into purpose-built premises and housing in the North Kanto area.

The new light industrial estates are by no means completely occupied by firms which have decentralised from the inner-city. Many of the premises are taken up by new enterprises developing in response to growing and changing consumer demands. Typical industries include the manufacture of household consumer durables such as electrical appliances and furniture. The rapid expansion of the motor vehicle industry has also led to the development of modern large-scale assembly plants. Because of their need for spacious sites, a location on the urban-rural fringe has been sought, where land values are lower. But many of the

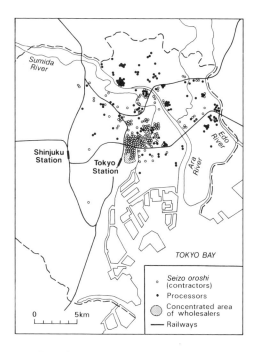

Fig. 7.12 *The distribution of the handbag industry in Tokyo*

small-scale component suppliers remain in inner areas.

The latest greenfield development has been that of science parks and campus sites for high-tech industries. These are located close to a university or research institution in areas which have good transportation links and which are deemed to offer an attractive working and residential environment. Significant here are the technopolis projects (Chapter 6.7) which have been grafted onto a select number of cities scattered throughout Japan (Figure 6.10). Nagaoka in Niigata is one such example, but undoubtedly the best known venture of this kind is Tsukuba Science City located some 60 km outside Tokyo (Figure 7.13).

Thus, there are signs that the intra-urban pattern of industry is becoming more open and that the decentralisation of light industry from its inner-city strongholds is beginning to gather some pace.

7.6 RESIDENTIAL STRUCTURE

As has already been noted, the susceptibility of wooden buildings to destruction by earthquakes, floods and fire, as well as intensive bombing during the Second World War, have meant that many older housing areas have been broken up by later and often

Fig. 7.13(a) *Nagaoka technopolis and (b)Tsukuba Science City*

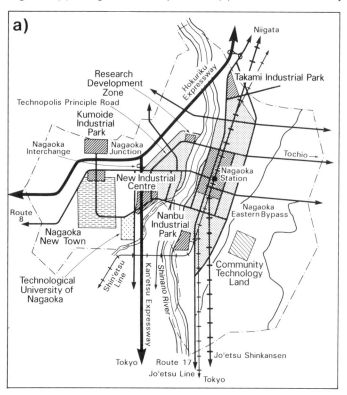

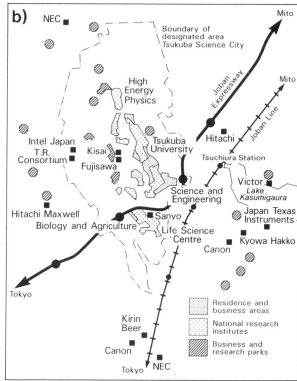

Fig. 7.14 *Urban renewal schemes in the Ward Area of Tokyo*

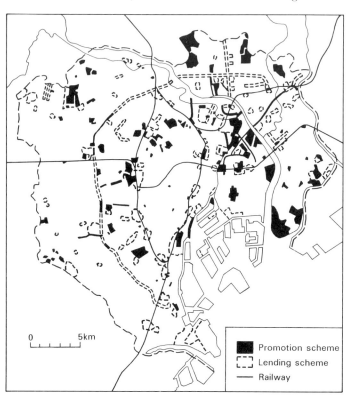

piecemeal redevelopment. Less than ten percent of the housing in Japan today was built before the Second World War. Also contributing to the newness of the housing have been the postwar programmes of planned renewal (Figure 7.14). Up to the 1970s, these were mainly concerned with lowering residential densities by removing a proportion of the existing residents to new housing in the outer suburbs and dormitory settlements beyond. Often the strategy was to make more space for non-residential activities. However, more recently, as in Western countries, planning policy has begun trying to retain the existing population and to attract younger people back by refurbishing the most rundown areas of inadequate housing. The net result of all this are inner-city areas characterised by housing which is very mixed in terms of age, mode, condition and amenities. The only common characteristics are the high densities and a predominance nowadays of apartment blocks over individual dwellings.

Broadly speaking, the residential areas show a gradient of declining density with distance from the city centre (Figure 7.15). Further out, the overriding impression is one of residential sprawl. This was very much the outcome of a suburban housing boom which has lasted four decades, and

Tokyo : 2 km Square in 15-20 km Distance Band

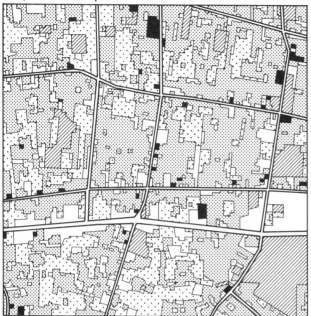

Tokyo : 2 km Square in 30-35 km Distance Band

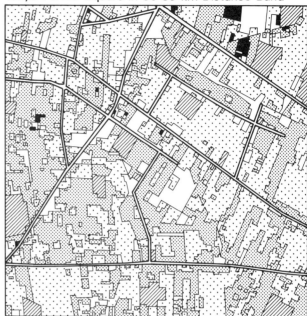

Tokyo : 2 km Square in 40-45 km Distance Band

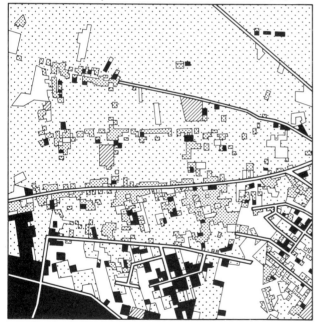

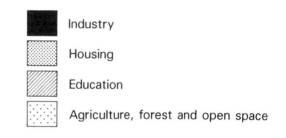

■	Industry
▦	Housing
▨	Education
⸭	Agriculture, forest and open space

0   1500 metres

during the first two of which there was a total absence of effective planning control. Adding to the chaotic pattern has been the fact that much of the land at the urban margins is held in small plots by individual landholders. Thus when it comes to development, land is acquired in piecemeal fashion and the resulting built-up area assumes a distinctly patchy appearance with residual plots of agricultural land encapsulated within it.

The direction of urban sprawl has largely been influenced by transport lines leading from town and city centres. Initially, development along main roads is ribbon like, but this soon gives way to a tangential spread of housing. In contrast, railway stations tend to provide the nodes for growth of a more accretionary kind. Added to these two recurrent and essentially spontaneous patterns of residential development, there are planned

Fig. 7.15 *The decreasing density of residential development with distance from central Tokyo*

Detached, middle-class housing

Luxury apartments

Traditional buildings in Kyoto

Municipal flats in Tokyo

Photo 7.5 *Different residential landscapes with social connotations*

housing projects which represent a determined attempt to bring some rationale and order into the suburban spread. These projects, particularly those undertaken by what was the Japan Housing Corporation, include the provision of shops, as well as schools, medical centres and community facilities. Unfortunately, it is only in recent years that any attempt has been made to introduce employment in the form of light industry and services. As a consequence, the bulk of suburban residents are forced to commute on what during rush hours are manifestly overloaded transport systems.

Residential space is very limited in Japan. For example, the average dwelling size in Tokyo is a mere 50m²; nationally the figure is 90m². The key factor is the acute shortage and consequent expense of building land (Figure 7.16). The cost of housing in Japan is between five and eight times the average annual income of the prospective occupier compared with three to five times the average income in the UK and USA. Despite this, slightly over 60 percent of Japan's housing is owner-occupied. It is part of government policy to encourage more owner-occupation and financial incentives are being offered to first-time buyers. In its time, the Japan Housing Corporation did much to raise home ownership. Today, the responsibility rests with

various housing loan and housing development corporations.

The rented sector is still dominated by housing owned by private landlords. In fact, 25 percent of all dwellings fall in this category. The Government actively encourages private developers to build housing for letting, most often in the form of *danchi* or apartment blocks. Prefectural and local government authorities are also disposed to lend developers money at favourable interest rates in an effort to increase the privately-rented housing stock. Many younger married couples now prefer to rent privately rather than be tied to company housing, which currently accounts for 6 percent of the housing stock.

At present, compared with the UK, municipal housing represents a small proportion of the total housing stock (6 percent), but the percentage is rising as part of the effort to combat Japan's severe housing shortage. Although some municipal or council housing has been provided since as early as 1919 as part of a basic welfare programme for the poorest section of society, it is only since the Public Housing Act of 1951 that the Government has extended the provision of such housing to both low- and middle-income households. Today, public housing is of comparable standard to that provided in the private sector.

Table 7.2 Class perceptions of Japanese households (1990)

Perceived social class	% belonging to
Upper	0.5
Upper middle	6.7
Middle middle	52.1
Lower middle	28.5
Lower	8.8
Don't know	3.4

It is claimed that Japan is a highly egalitarian society. In the circumstances, one might expect the residential areas of the Japanese city not to show the same degree of social segregation as is encountered in Western cities. Whilst the Japanese perception is that the bulk of them belong to the middle class, there is nonetheless a spatial sorting of residents (Table 7.2). Here, as elsewhere, it is mainly on the basis of occupation and income. The distinctions between owner-occupation and tenancy, and between housing rented from employers, private landlords and local councils are significant in the social geography of the city (Photo 7.5). So too is the popular perception and evaluation of different residential areas and the considerable variation in the size and price of owner-occupied housing. But the social mosaic of the Japanese city tends to be rather more mixed and abrupt. Certainly, it is difficult to discern the broad sectors and concentric rings stressed in models of the Western city.

7.7 SOCIAL PATHOLOGY

Table 7.3 looks at change in the housing stock over a 25-year period. Two conclusions are to be drawn, namely how bad housing conditions were even during the high-growth phase, and how much has since been achieved by way of general improvement. But despite the progress, housing continues to rank as the top social problem confronting urban Japan today. The problem is multifaceted, but essentially spirals from the acute shortage and high cost of decent owner-occupied housing and the severe restriction

Table 7.3 Changing housing conditions (1963 – 1988)

	1963	1968	1973	1978	1983	1988
Floor space per dwelling (m²)	72.5	73.9	77.1	80.3	85.0	89.9
Persons per dwelling	4.7	4.2	3.6	3.6	3.4	3.3
Owner-occupied (%)	64.3	60.3	59.1	60.4	62.4	61.3
With flush toilet (%)	9.2	17.1	31.4	45.9	58.2	65.0
With bathroom (%)	59.1	65.6	73.2	82.8	88.3	91.2
Wooden (%)	86.2	76.9	66.5	56.2	46.1	41.3

which these characteristics place on access to it. The inevitable spin-off is discrimination in all sectors of the housing market; relatively few households escape unscathed. The issue is further discussed later in this chapter (7.8.) and again in Chapter 13. But what about those other ills that seem to afflict contemporary urban society worldwide, such as ethnic segregation and crime? How does Japan fare?

As for ethnic segregation, it has to be said that there are less than one million foreigners living in Japan. Of these, something in excess of 80 percent are Koreans who came to the country either as willing migrants or forced labourers during the 35 years (1910 – 1945) that Japan annexed Korea. Only a small number of these people have been granted Japanese citizenship; the vast majority are classified as 'resident aliens'. Discrimination against the Koreans has prevailed not just in housing, but also in employment and marriage, and yet has not give rise to inner-city race riots or anti-immigrant thuggery. That may perhaps be explained by the fact that the Korean community is not growing in size and that most of its members are culturally fairly well integrated.

More remarkable is the discrimination against the *burakumin* (or outcastes), because these people are ethnically indistinguishable from ordinary Japanese. The discrimination has a long history dating back to the times when Buddhist taboos banned from normal society all those people engaged in what were deemed to be 'unclean' occupations, such as animal slaughtering, leather working and well digging. Today, there are estimated to be about two million members of the *burakumin* community, many of them living in the Osaka area. Although granted full legal rights in the reforms of the Meiji Restoration, most are still confined to ghetto districts and socially they are still ostracised. By comparison, the general situation of the other two minorities identifiable within Japanese society, the Ainus and the Okinawans, cannot be considered problematic in the present context.

When it comes to law and order, the Japanese record is quite outstanding.

'Picture a country where you never need to count your change; where the streets are free from litter, the walls free from graffiti; where no one feels compelled to vandalise public telephones; where people visit sports grounds not to engage in tribal warfare but to cheer good play; where there are no muggings, no skinheads, no hippie convoys, no recreational brawls on Saturday nights; where policemen are affable and courteous, and the pistols they carry are only fired a couple of times a year by the entire force' (Tasker, 1987).

This is a fair description of the present condition of Japanese society. Its law-abiding nature is emphasised by the international comparisons in Table 7.4. This highly laudable state of affairs no doubt stems in part from the Japanese wish to conform and the fear of losing face. Japan is a 'shame culture', in that behaviour is not regulated by individual conscience but by public acceptance. This does not mean however that the Japanese are complete angels. Crimes against people and property may be out, but attitudes

towards *ura* (private) crimes, such as tax evasion and ticket fraud, are often quite different. Perhaps the most widely known symbol of lawlessness in Japan is the *yakusa*, the syndicates of gangsters, the *zaibatsu* of the underworld. They tend to make their livelihood out of the *ura* needs of modern society – prostitution, pornography and debt collecting, but not as yet drugs. They also provide a range of corporate services, from fixing annual general meetings to persuading reluctant sellers to sell.

Finally, two other facets of the social pathology requiring a brief mention are poverty and suicide. The former exists, but on a limited scale. However, it cannot be said with any confidence that the welfare systems of Japan are effective in netting and helping those with the greatest needs. A relatively high rate of suicide may be seen simply as a symptom of a pressured and competitive society, which is none more so than in the city (Table 13.4). However, it may be that there is also a a difference in the perception of suicide rooted in Japanese culture.

7.8 TOKYO – JAPAN'S NUMBER ONE URBAN PROBLEM

Like so many that have achieved the status of **world city**, Tokyo has been the victim of its own success. The huge spread of the built-up area generated by its booming economy has given rise to a whole series of problems. These range from acute traffic congestion to the shortage and great expense of housing, from environmental pollution to great personal stress. In addition to these internal problems, Tokyo's success has given rise to external costs. Immediately, outside the built-up area, these include the rapid erosion of Kanto Plain's stock of good agricultural land and excessive pressure on rural recreational amenities, as well as environmental pollution on a wider spatial scale. Further afield, there is the imbalance within the Pacific Belt caused by Tokyo's eccentric location at one end of the corridor. Then there is perhaps the greatest cost of all, namely the huge **backwash effect** unleashed by Tokyo. Tokyo's growth has had a

Table 7.4 *The law-abiding Japanese: some international comparisons*

	Japan	UK	USA	W Germany
Murders per 100,000 people	1.5	2.8	8.3	4.5
Rapes per 100,000 people	1.7	8.8	33.7	11.0
Robberies per 100,000 people	1.9	44.6	213.8	48.1
Arrest rate (% of crimes)	60.0	37.0	20.0	46.0
Policemen per 100,000 people	182.0	251.0	254.0	314.0
Lawyers per 100,000 people	10.0	94.0	194.0	61.0

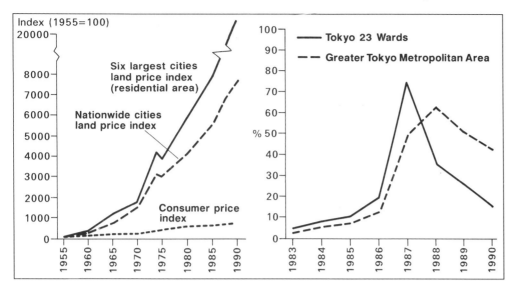

Fig. 7.16 *Rising land prices in (a) Japan and the six largest cities (1955–1990); (b) Tokyo ward Area and Metropolitan Area*

debilitating impact on much of the rest of the country, particularly on areas outside the Pacific Belt. In short, the more it has succeeded, the more deeply ingrained has the **core-periphery** structure of the country become.

Defining Tokyo

One difficulty that confronts any discussion of Tokyo is the very basic one of actually defining and delimiting it. There are several different Tokyos. First, there is what is called the *Ward Area* or *Tokyo-ku* (Figure 7.17). This is very much the historic nucleus and is equivalent in scale to Central London, except that it contains a huge residential population of over eight million. Then there is the area of Tokyo Prefecture, more commonly referred to as the *Tokyo Metropolitan Government area*. This is probably the most widely-accepted definition of Tokyo. It contains nearly 12 million people. Because of the prefecture's rather linear form, it certainly does not contain the whole of what might be recognised as Tokyo's continuous built-up area. Because it cuts a sort of transect, the Tokyo Metropolitan Government area also includes some rural areas to the west of the city.

If continuity of the built-up area is taken as the main criterion for defining modern Tokyo, then it becomes necessary to embrace a huge crescentic area of urban development wrapping around the shores of Tokyo Bay (Figure 7.17). What is delimited is a

vast conurbational structure which includes at least two other major, once-separate cities, namely Yokohama and Kawasaki, as well as a number of lesser cities to the east. This area of continuous urban development is probably best referred to as *Tokyo metropolis*. With a population approaching 25 million, it is arguably the largest city in the world. Tokyo metropolis is not to be confused with the *Tokyo Metropolitan Area* which is officially defined as including the prefectures of Tokyo, Chiba, Saitama and Kanagawa.

Fig. 7.17 *The National Capital Region and its subdivisions*

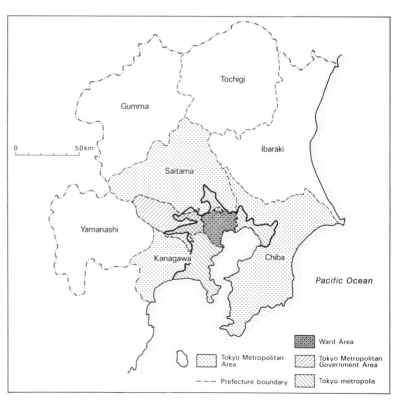

Finally, it is necessary to draw attention to what is called the *National Capital Region* (NCR) (Figure 7.17). This was first defined in 1956 when it became clear that any planned solution of the problems of Tokyo metropolis would involve an area reaching well beyond the then limits of the built-up area. In fact, the NCR comprises eight prefectures and reaches out to some 150km from the centre of Tokyo. In 1990 the region contained a population of nearly 40 million, a little short of one-third of Japan's total population.

Why does Tokyo continue to grow?

Tokyo's history is a very long one. Since the 17th century it has enjoyed almost uninterrupted growth and prosperity, and none more so than during the postwar period. Much of its success is to be explained by the simple fact that has been the capital city for well over 300 years, and the economic heart of the country for rather longer, growing on a balanced mix of manufacturing, commerce and government. Today, Tokyo is well over twice the size of Yokohama, Japan's second largest city; truly, it is a **primate** capital city.

'Tokyo is not only the political and economic center of the country, but also its window on Western culture, with all the glamor that entails. The home of the media, publishers and universities, the city has a cultural authority that provincials respect ... Tokyo is not just a place to work. People are drawn to the city because they want to enrich their lives' (Katayama, 1989).

This quotation neatly summarises the continued attraction of Tokyo, but it also begins to highlight a new contributory factor, namely the **internationalisation** of the city. It is something which has emerged mainly since the 1980s as Japan has begun to show an increasingly higher profile in the international scene, particularly in the management of the global economy. Since the 'Yen Crisis' of 1987, and with the deregulation of financial services and other commercial activities, Tokyo has developed as an international centre. Today, it is the third largest financial centre in the world. Its stock market dealings are anxiously watched by countries around the world. A location in Tokyo has now become essential for Japanese and overseas banks and securities corporations alike, as well as for a whole range of other financial services. As a result, the demand for office space in the core of Tokyo has escalated and outstripped supply. In 1987, land prices in central Tokyo increased by 75 percent (Figure 7.16).

Apart from the rising importance of Tokyo as a financial centre, other Westernising influences have brought added growth. The wave of leisure and service development which swept the USA and Western Europe 20 years ago is only just gathering momentum in Japan. The great increase in restaurants, bars and takeaways with different national flavours is evidence of this, as is the proliferation of Western-style entertainment and the development of 24-hour service outlets. For example, Tokyo now has over 150 theatres; there are fashion houses of international repute and luxury goods drawn from all over the world are readily available. All this simply serves to fuel the attraction of Tokyo, especially to the younger generations. Certainly, with their great affluence, the Japanese are already proving to be voracious consumers of non-essential goods and services.

Planning Tokyo

In this section, attention will be confined mainly to the planning strategies which have been pursued during the postwar period to deal with the internal problems created by Tokyo's growth. Discussion of the strategies which have sought to address the external problems is to be found in Chapters 6 and 9.

It was in 1956 that the Japanese Government decided the time had come to make an intervention on behalf of a Tokyo running out of control. The NCR was designated and an NCR Commission charged with the task of devising a master plan to guide the growth of Tokyo over the next ten years. It took two years to prepare the plan, closely moulded on the Abercrombie Plan for Greater London (1944). In the event, it was shortly to

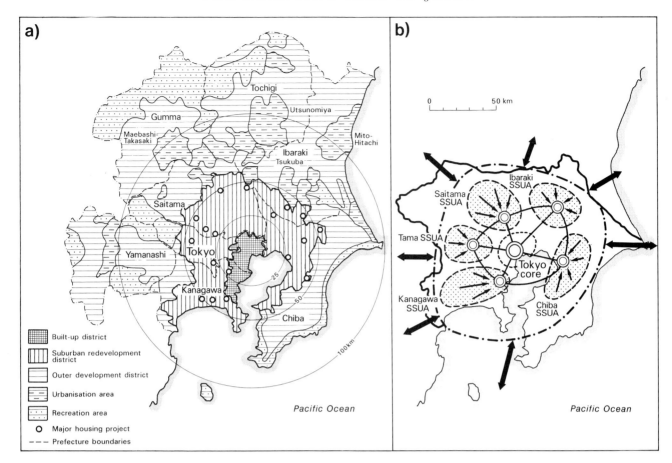

prove wholly ineffective, and unable to cope with the mounting scale of Tokyo's growth. Tokyo was bound within an absurd tightly drawn green belt which, due to the lack of development control, promptly burst under pressure and was quickly built over. Only some of the satellite towns beyond the green belt survived.

As a consequence, a new and more realistic master plan was called for in 1966, to take into account the accelerating rate of growth and to bring about some sort of compromise between the need for Tokyo to be allowed to to fulfil its capital city function and the need to solve the problems of congestion generated by that function. The Second Master Plan was first implemented in 1968. The Plan was a composite one, involving a different strategy or programme of action for each of three subdivisions of the NCR (Figure 7.18a) (Table 7.5).

Implementation of this Plan was somewhat handicapped by a lack of commitment on the part of involved parties and by the delay in giving the

NCR planners the legal powers necessary to put the plan into effect. However, there were some achievements, most notably the restructuring of the core (as evidenced by new business centres such as Shinjuku, Shibuya

Fig. 7.18 *Plans for the National Capital Region (a) the Second Master Plan (1968); (b) the current strategy*

Table 7.5 *Summary of objectives of the Second Master Plan (1968)*

Subdivision	Objectives
The core	1. Selective decentralisation – removal of 'non-pivotal' functions (manufacturing, distribution, higher education, etc.). 2. Restructuring - creation of new business nodes to relieve pressure on downtown area. 3. Improvement of accessibility. 4. Public nuisance abatement. 5. Residential renewal and lowering of densities.
The suburban ring	1. Tighter control over location and standards of new housing. 2. Provision of better infrastructure. 3. Improving the quality of the residential environment.
The outer development district	1. Development of reception area function. 2. Concentration of new growth in 'urbanisation areas'. 3. Protection and encouragement of agriculture. 4. Promotion of recreation and tourism.

Photo 7.6 *Large-scale waterfront projects, Tokyo Bay*

and Ikebukuro), improved accessibility, a higher standard of suburban development and a limited amount of decentralisation to some of the **urbanisation areas**. In fact, essentially the same objectives were to be pursued by the ensuing Third Basic Development Plan (1977).

Currently, development in the NCR is being directed by the Plan for the Remodelling of the Greater Tokyo Region, first published in 1983 (Figure 7.18(b)). In this fourth plan, renewed efforts are being made to loosen the overall metropolitan structure. The aim is now to establish five **self-sustained urban areas** (SSUAs) out in the Outer Development District as defined in the Second Master Plan, thereby creating what the planners call a 'multi-satellite complex'. The hope is that these five areas will prove powerfully attractive to employment, services and people currently located in Tokyo proper, and therefore engender the required amount of decentralisation. Hopefully they will serve to counter some of the inherent magnetism of the core of the NCR.

In terms of implementation, current investment appears to be favouring the two waterfront SSUAs of Chiba and Kanagawa (Figure 7.18(b)). This is partly to be explained by the availability of land that was reclaimed but never used and by the vacating of waterfront sites as a consequence of industrial restructuring. The argument that the use of reclaimed land reduces the loss of all too precious farmland further inland is a persuasive one provided one does not look too closely at the actual costs of creating land by artificial

means. Amongst the waterfront schemes currently under way, perhaps the most notable are the Minato Mirai 21 project in Yokohama, the Makuhari project in Chiba and Tokyo Teleport Town (Photo 7.6). The last of these, in fact, will occupy an artificial island.

Intractable problems

Presumably it is to the credit of these four development plans for the NCR that Tokyo has continued to both grow and prosper. Without them, and the intervention of planning at a more local level, it is conceivable that Tokyo would have ground to a halt long ago, overwhelmed by chaos and congestion. At least, the great metropolis remains in reasonable working order. However, it has to be said that today's Tokyo is not really the Tokyo envisaged in those plans. It is still irrefutably a very strong-centred metropolis. How to reduce the magnetism of the core and to create a looser structure remains an unresolved issue.

As a consequence, other internal problems remain as well as the wider repercussions of a buoyant and primate Tokyo discussed elsewhere. Housing is set to persist as the priority issue, both here in Tokyo and elsewhere in urban

Japan. The most immediate aspects of the problem are availability, size, price and amenities. Given the acute shortage of land, the average size of dwelling in Japan is always likely to lag behind that in other advanced countries, whilst housing costs may be expected to consume a larger proportion (13 percent) of disposable income. A concerted effort to reduce the housing shortage in Tokyo may be expected to calm the inflation of house prices. So, too, would a bursting of what an increasing number of people see as the **property bubble**. This perception is based on the conviction that there is a conspiracy to maintain prices at an artificially high level. Whilst most Japanese homes are bursting with consumer durables (e.g. TVs, videos, refrigerators), 35 percent of them still do not have exclusive use of a flush toilet, and ten percent have no bathroom (Table 7.3). The percentage figures may be expected to be higher in Tokyo.

Outside the home, the built environment still leaves much to be desired. The visitor is struck by the lack of local recreational and amenity space, the pace, noise and stress of the Japanese urban life style, as well as what the Japanese themselves refer to as *uglification* – garish advertising, poor drainage, the lack of greenery and street clutter in the form of posts, cats-cradling overhead wires and kerbside parking. Clearly, much has yet to be achieved in terms of improving this aspect of the urban scene.

7.9 A COUNTERBALANCE TO TOKYO – INTERNATIONAL-ISATION OF OSAKA AND THE KANSAI REGION

Reference has already been made to the serious core-periphery imbalance caused by Tokyo at a national level, and this will be examined in more detail in Chapter 9. At the meso-scale, it is clear that within the confines of the Pacific Belt a whole range of problems arise from the location and sheer mass of the Tokyo Metropolitan Area. It is very much off-centre and causes the balance of the linear corridor to tip overwhelmingly to the east. To redress the situation, the best hope lies in encouraging growth in the Kansai region with its metropolitan area incorporating the cities of Osaka, Kyoto and Kobe.

Between 1965 and 1985 the Osaka Metropolitan Area suffered a relative decline in prosperity. Osaka was superseded by Yokohama as the second largest city, whilst the area's shares slipped to only 20 percent of Japan's manufacturing, 10 percent of its financial transactions and less than 15 percent of its population. Since the mid-1980s, however, 23 massive development schemes have been launched in the hope of reversing the tide of fortune and making this metropolitan area an internationally-important business centre.

Internationally, the most important step to date is the construction of the new Kansai international airport on reclaimed land. Alongside this, Osaka Prefecture is trying to attract companies to the new 318 ha complex of Rinku Town. It is unlikely that Japanese corporations will decentralise their headquarter offices away from Tokyo, but hopefully they and overseas companies will set up branch offices. The other prestigious development is Kansai Science City which is set to achieve for Western Japan what Tsukuba Science City is already doing for Eastern Japan. The intention is that it will be more diversified than Tsukuba, including not only scientific and research institutions, but also bodies concerned with the advancement of culture and the humanities. It will also contain a significant amount of housing to allow for community development.

At present, there seems to be every chance that as a result of these and other ambitious proposals the Osaka metropolitan area will come to assume the role of a second international gateway to Japan. There is a real chance that it will act to some extent as a countermagnet to Tokyo and thereby serve to reduce the imbalance within the Japanese core. Internationally, the emphasis will be on strengthening trade and other links with neighbouring Asian countries and Australasia. To this end, a Pacific trade centre and a free-trade zone are being set up.

CHAPTER 8

The rural scene and its economy

8.1 URBAN-RURAL INTERACTION AND INTERDEPENDENCE

It is difficult to dissociate Japan's countryside, both spatially and socio-economically, from its urban counterpart. Despite growing planning measures to check urban sprawl, urban usages continue to consume valuable agricultural land and raise land prices. Industry and urban-type jobs have diffused into rural areas in all but the remotest corners of Japan, the outcome of conscious policies on the part of both private firms and government. Business interests are now being drawn to rural areas by the benefits of lower land and labour costs. The Government sees this dispersion to rural areas as a way of relieving the growing pressures in cities and of helping to keep people in the countryside. By boosting the opportunities to gain income from non-farm employment, so one of the main attractions drawing people to towns and cities, namely higher wages, is effectively reduced.

Today, the interdependence of town and country in Japan has become quite complex. Urbanising influences now affect rural communities in ways other than the recruitment of labour. The permanent migration of members of rural households into towns and cities has gathered such momentum during the postwar period that there has been a considerable breakdown of traditional family life. Diffusion of urban values and the urban life style into the countryside has brought a more materialistic outlook. These changing values, in turn, repercuss on rural customs, most notably diluting the mutual obligation and cooperation so fundamental to the unity and stability of life in hamlets and villages. Improved transport and accessibility,

more leisure time and greater disposable income place another pressure on the rural areas as increasing numbers of urban dwellers take weekend breaks and annual holidays in the countryside. These urbanising influences are most intensely felt in areas nearest to the leading cities and decrease with distance to give rise to an urban-rural continuum (Figure 8.1). But the ripple effects are now being experienced even in the more remote mountainous and peripheral areas of Hokkaido, Shikoku and southern Kyushu, whether it be the exodus of young people or the periodic influx of urban-based tourists.

This use of the countryside to meet the needs of urban dwellers has also caused significant deterioration of the rural environment, a feature common to all advanced countries. It varies from unsympathetic new building to the excessive trampling of fragile mountain and coastal habitats. Intensified agricultural practices have had undesirable effects. For example, the much greater use of fertilizers, pesticides and water have led to the pollution of river and lakes and a serious lowering of groundwater levels.

So important is this urban-rural interaction, particularly the impact of the former on the latter, that recent studies of Japan's rural geography have sought to analyse the character of its remaining rural space in terms of the type and scale of the urban elements that it contains. Most agree that, of all the intrusive urban elements, the most critical is the varying character and mix of employment. Thus the scheme in Table 8.1 covers the transition from rural areas distinguished by varying levels of commuting to nearby towns and cities, through areas marked by different degrees of reliance on farming and

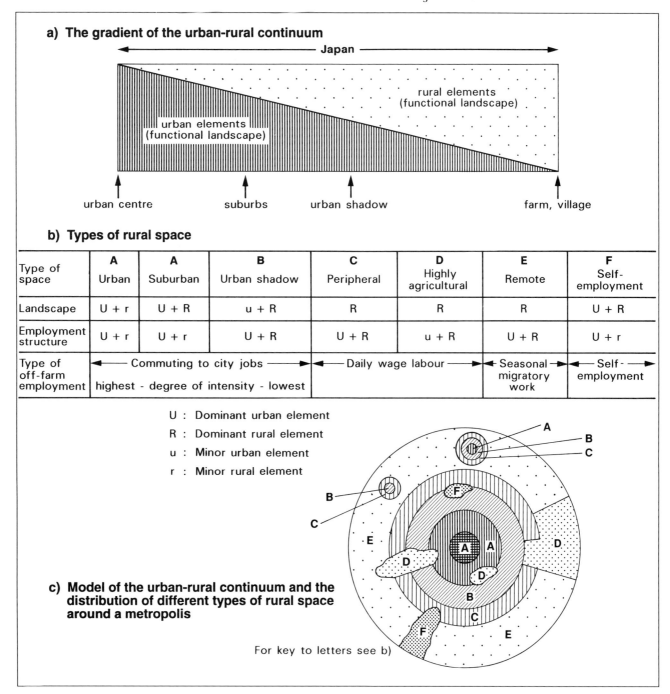

a) **The gradient of the urban-rural continuum**

Japan

rural elements
(functional landscape)

urban elements
(functional landscape)

urban centre   suburbs   urban shadow   farm, village

b) **Types of rural space**

Type of space	A Urban	A Suburban	B Urban shadow	C Peripheral	D Highly agricultural	E Remote	F Self-employment
Landscape	U + r	U + R	u + R	R	R	R	U + R
Employment structure	U + r	U + r	U + R	U + R	u + R	U + R	U + r
Type of off-farm employment	← Commuting to city jobs → highest - degree of intensity - lowest			← Daily wage labour →		← Seasonal migratory work →	← Self-employment →

U : Dominant urban element
R : Dominant rural element
u : Minor urban element
r : Minor rural element

c) **Model of the urban-rural continuum and the distribution of different types of rural space around a metropolis**

For key to letters see b)

Fig. 8.1   The urban-rural continuum

different types of self-employment, to the really remote rural areas almost wholly devoid of in-situ employment opportunities.

8.2 THE FARMING SCENE

The discussion so far has been urban-based with emphasis placed on the increasing effects of urbanising influences on rural areas. However, it needs to be stressed that the rural economy, and the social and economic environment in which it operates, provide much more than space and a change of scene for the urban dweller. Indeed, the contribution of rural Japan to the well-being of the country as a whole is vital. Its contribution is not to be measured just in terms of its generation of GDP or its creation of jobs, but rather by the actual importance attached to the rural sector by both the Government and the people, largely in the context of food supply.

Table 8.1 *Types of rural space in Japan (after Yamamoto and Tabayashi)*

Types of employment structure					Farming	Types of rural spaces
	Type and intensity of farm income supplementation					
	Main jobs	Husband	Wife	Son		
A Intensive A commuter type	Commuting to city jobs. Managing apartment houses and parking lots, etc.	●	●	●	A few intensive horticultural operation vs many extensive field crop operations.	A Urban rural space A Suburban rural space
B Commuter type	Commuting to city jobs.	●	▲	●	Middle = scale rice farming or field crop farming	B Urban shadow rural space
C Daily wage labour type	Daily wage labour in construction or part-time jobs in factories	✳	✳	●	Small = scale subsistence rice and field crop farming	C Peripheral rural space
D Agricultural type						D Highly agricultural rural space
D_1 Viable farming	Daily wage labour	✳		●	Large scale dairy and beef cattle farming. Intensive vegetable and fruit growing	D_1 Highly agricultural rural space (viable farming)
D_2 Viable farming with migratory wage labour	Seasonal migratory wage labour in construction	❏		●	Large = scale rice monoculture	D_2 Highly agricultural rural space (viable farming migratory wage labour)
D_3 Subsistence farming with daily wage labour	Daily wage labour in construction	✳	✳	★	Subsistence farming. Combination of rice, some cash crops and livestock	D_3 Highly agricultural rural space subsistence farming, daily wage labour)
D_4 Subsistence farming with migratory wage labour	Seasonal migratory wage labour in construction	❏	✳	★	Subsistence farming. Combination of rice, some cash crops and livestock	D_3 Highly agricultural rural space subsistence farming, migratory wage labour)
E Migratory wage labour type						E Remote rural space
E_1 Non-technical	Seasonal migratory wage labour	❏	✳	★	Subsistence farming. Rice and field crop farming	E_1 Remote rural space (non-technical migratory wage labour)
E_2 Technical		❏	✳	★		E_2 Remote rural space (technical migratory wage labour)
E_3 Depopulation		❏	✳	★		E_3 Remote rural space (depopulation) migratory wage

Table 8.1   *continued*

	Types of employment structure				Farming	Types of rural spaces
	Type and intensity of farm income supplementation					
	Main jobs	Husband	Wife	Son		
F Self-employment type						F Self-employment rural type
F₁ Recreation	*Minshuku* operation	✻	○	○		F₁ Self-employment rural space (recreation)
F₂ Technical	Fishing	○		★	Subsistence farming. Rice and field crop farming	F₂ Self-employment rural space (fishing)
F₃ Depopulation	Weaving, Chinaware making, Wood-work, etc.	○	○	★		F₃ Self-employment rural space (domestic industries)

● Full-time and stable   ▲ Full-time and unstable   ✻ Part-time and unstable

❏ Seasonal migratory and unstable   ○ Self-employment, seasonal and stable   ★ Outflow

Agriculture, the mainstay of the rural sector, now contributes less than three percent of GNP and provides work for less than ten percent of the labour force. Throughout the postwar period, the Japanese Government has been intent on raising the level of food self-sufficiency. In pursuit of this objective, Japan has stood guilty of protecting its own agriculture in the arena of inter-national trade (Figure 8.2). The foreign view is that Japan's concern about agricultural self-sufficiency verges on paranoia, and that in a world of grow-ing economic interdependence there are few risks attached to a heavy reliance on imported food supplies. Attention is also drawn to the inescapable fact that the physical environment imposes real limits on Japan's ability to feed itself (Chapter 2). Certainly it can be shown that Japanese self-sufficiency has declined since 1970 and that compared with other advanced countries it now pitches at a relatively low level (Figure 8.3).

The Government has another vested interest in looking after the rural popu-lation of Japan, particularly the farm households. Because of the outdated nature of constituency boundaries, the ruling Liberal Democratic party is dependent on the rural voter for its parliamentary majority. In fact, 48 percent of the votes keeping the party in power come from the countryside. Despite the rapid and continued urbanisation which has occurred during the postwar period, constituency representation has not changed since 1948 when there were many more people in rural areas. Rural populations are now over-represented in Parliament by a factor of about four to one, whilst the block lobbying power of *Nokyo*, the agricultural cooperative, is a formidable influence. Government support for the rural sector of the economy through a variety of interven-tions has been fairly successful in main-taining this alliance between farming households and the ruling politicians. But it is now being threatened as the Government seeks to improve the effi-ciency of the agricultural industry by enlarging farm holdings and placing more emphasis on full- rather than part-time farming. All this is being undertaken because Japan is being forced to open its doors to imported foodstuffs. In the circumstances, if Japanese agriculture is to survive then it has to become much more competent

Fig. 8.2 *Cartoon illustrating the Japanese view that they are not the only state seeking to protect domestic agriculture*

and competitive.

However, it is not simply a matter of the Government being unduly influenced by the rural community. Agricultural links underpin the very fabric of Japanese society. Most older and middle-aged Japanese living in cities still regard their roots as being in rural areas. Indeed, many retain ownership of the old family agricultural holding for its monetary value

Fig. 8.3 *Changes in calorific self-sufficiency: some international comparisons*

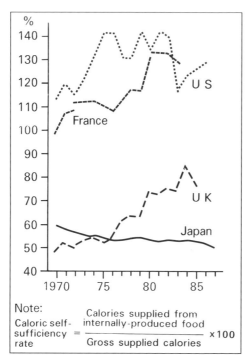

Note:

$$\text{Caloric self-sufficiency rate} = \frac{\text{Calories supplied from internally-produced food}}{\text{Gross supplied calories}} \times 100$$

and because the spirits of the family ancestors are associated with it. Many also look forward on retirement to returning to the countryside and the old family home. There is much in Shintoism and Buddhism that subconsciously draws the Japanese back to the natural environment and their rural roots.

If the free play of market forces was permitted, the majority of Japanese farmers would probably be driven out of business and the whole structure of Japanese agriculture changed. As it is, despite some postwar reform, agriculture remains dominated by inefficient family farms, averaging little more than 1 ha in size, largely run on a part-time basis, with the main income of the household now coming from non-farm sources (Table 8.2). The real picture of farming today is significantly different from the long-held popular image of Japan as the classic example of efficient, intensive high-yielding farming. Furthermore, despite government support for domestic agriculture, as pointed out earlier the extent of Japan's self-sufficiency has declined over recent years (Figure 8.3). Although Japan remains virtually self-sufficient in rice and nearly so in vegetables, fruit and dairy produce, food production has not kept pace with the demands of a growing and increasingly urban population (Table 8.3).

Today, Japan is the world's largest net importer of food by value. Economically, it would make sense to liberalise agricultural trade, freely letting in rice from the USA, Thailand and Burma, grains, beef and citrus fruits from Australia and the USA, and meat and dairy produce from Australia and New Zealand. But until Japanese farming can stand on its own feet against imported foodstuffs, pursuit of a more liberal agricultural trade policy is likely to be both reluctant and slow, despite international pressures to the contrary. For all the outward political posturing, historical and other in-built circumstances may be expected to continue to work against the further reforms needed to achieve the goal of an efficient and highly productive farming industry. Meanwhile, the Japanese people remain willing to spend a higher proportion of their disposable income (18 percent) on food than do families in other advanced countries.

8.3 MAJOR HUMAN INFLUENCES ON AGRICULTURE

A variety of influences have been at work over the postwar years bringing about changes in the nature and struc-

Table 8.2 Full- and part-time farming households (1960 – 1990) (000s)

	Full-time households	Part-time households (main income from farming)	Part-time households (main income outside farming)
1960	2 078	2 036	1 942
1970	831	1 802	2 709
1980	623	1 002	3 036
1990	592	531	2 712

ture of Japanese farming, but these need to be set in the context of the country's physical geography (Chapter 2). With less than 15 percent of the land available and suitable for farming, and given the increasing harshness of the climate northwards, the potential for agricultural expansion is modest, to say the least. Postwar change in Japanese agriculture has probably been most affected by (i) government intervention and the way in which farming households and rural communities have reacted to this, and (ii) a range of other external influences, particularly technological developments and market changes (Figure 8.4).

Government intervention (Figure 8.4)

In respect of agriculture, the Japanese Government is currently well and truly

Table 8.3 Japan's food demand and supply (000 metric tons)

	Domestic Production (A)	Foreign Trade		Domestic Consumption (B)	Self-Sufficiency Ratio (%) (A/B)
		Imports	Exports		
Cereals	11 731	27 662	0	39 565	30
Rice*	10 347	50	0	10 499	99
Wheat	985	5 182	0	6 204	16
Maize (Corn)	28	20 343	0	20 355	0
Beans	455	4 682	0	5 236	9
Vegetables	16 235	1 502	2	17 735	92
Fruit	5 214	2 638	46	7 829	67
Meat	3 565	1 514	6	4 949	72
Eggs	2 417	45	0	2 462	98
Cows Milk	8 135	2 175	1	10 222	80
Fish and Shellfish	11 120	3 310	1 647	13 341	83
Fats and Oils	2 364	506	198	2 689	88
Soy Sauce	1 225	0	8	1 215	100

*Although producing a rice surplus, the small import relates to varieties of rice that cannot be grown in Japan; hence the self-sufficiency ratio of less than 100.

caught on the horns of a dilemma. Up to 1960, the emphasis was on land reform and the protection of agriculture from overseas competition. This led to the creation of an industry dominated by small holdings and part-time farmers, and was manifestly inefficient. Since 1960, in the face of growing external pressures to liberalise agricultural imports, together with the rising costs of protecting the small, part-time farmer, the Government has become increasingly aware of the need to enlarge the scale of farming to make agriculture more efficient and better able to survive unaided.

Government intervention in Japanese agriculture has taken many forms. The following account merely examines what have been the two most important.

Land reform

The land reforms initiated immediately after the Second World War under the supervision of the USA were primarily aimed at abolishing the oppressive landlord tenant system. About half the country's farmland had been worked under that system. The 1945 Land Adjustment Law enabled the State to buy up all the land of absentee landlords and all land in excess of one hectare in the case of farm holdings occupied by a resident landlord. The land was then sold on either to sitting tenants or to men demobilised from the armed forces. In the case of the ten percent of farmland remaining in tenancy, rent in kind was abolished and a carefully controlled cash rent substituted. Security of tenure was also safeguarded.

Although the amount of farmland that could be held by an owner-occupier was subsequently raised in 1952 from one to 12 ha. in Hokkaido and to five hectares elsewhere, the land reforms were to have a lasting effect on the structure of postwar agriculture. Whilst greater productivity was encouraged because farming households were now largely working for themselves, a system of small holdings was created with many of those holdings fragmented into dispersed fields (Photo 8.1). Clearly, such a system has seriously hindered the creation of the larger farm units needed to take advan-

Fig. 8.4 *The interplay of influences affecting the character of agriculture*

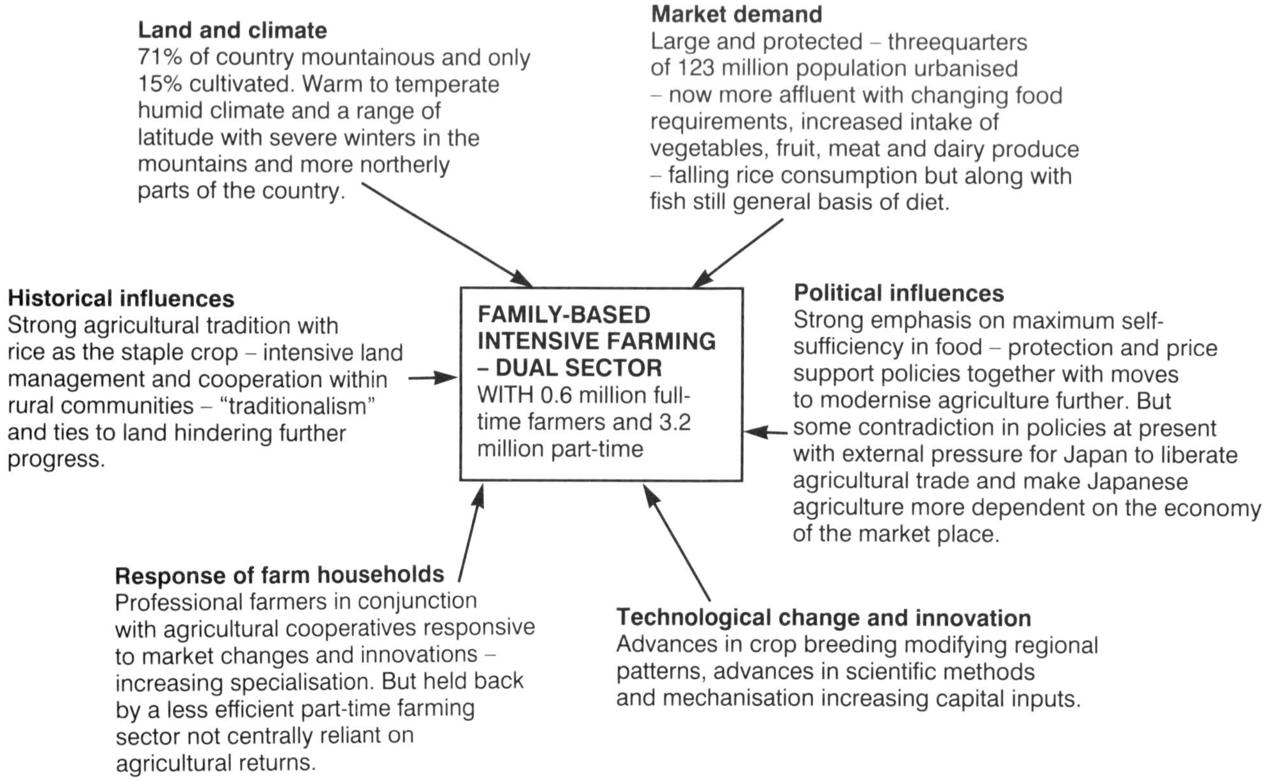

Land and climate
71% of country mountainous and only 15% cultivated. Warm to temperate humid climate and a range of latitude with severe winters in the mountains and more northerly parts of the country.

Market demand
Large and protected – threequarters of 123 million population urbanised – now more affluent with changing food requirements, increased intake of vegetables, fruit, meat and dairy produce – falling rice consumption but along with fish still general basis of diet.

Historical influences
Strong agricultural tradition with rice as the staple crop – intensive land management and cooperation within rural communities – "traditionalism" and ties to land hindering further progress.

FAMILY-BASED INTENSIVE FARMING – DUAL SECTOR
WITH 0.6 million full-time farmers and 3.2 million part-time

Political influences
Strong emphasis on maximum self-sufficiency in food – protection and price support policies together with moves to modernise agriculture further. But some contradiction in policies at present with external pressure for Japan to liberate agricultural trade and make Japanese agriculture more dependent on the economy of the market place.

Response of farm households
Professional farmers in conjunction with agricultural cooperatives responsive to market changes and innovations – increasing specialisation. But held back by a less efficient part-time farming sector not centrally reliant on agricultural returns.

Technological change and innovation
Advances in crop breeding modifying regional patterns, advances in scientific methods and mechanisation increasing capital inputs.

tage of postwar technological advances and scale economies.

Slowly, the Government has come to recognise the need to work towards an average farm holding of 10 ha. Table 8.4 clearly shows that there is still a long way to go. Holdings today average only 1.15 ha., making them among the smallest in the world. In fact, over much of Japan the percentage of holdings under 0.5ha. actually increased between 1960 and 1990. Only in Hokkaido, where holdings are distinctly larger anyway, has there been any significant increase in average size. Achievement of this much needed land reform has not been helped, of course, by the Government's vested interest in safeguarding the rights of part-time farmers occupying those very small holdings created under the 1945 land reform measures.

Failure to increase the size of farm holdings, together with the rising costs of production, have also contributed to the creation of an agricultural sector increasingly dominated by part-time farmers (Table 8.2). Off-farm employment has long been a feature of the Japanese rural economy and way of life. Today, 70 percent of farming households gain the major part of their income from outside farming. However, despite this, these part-time farmers firmly still regard themselves as 'farmers who work' not 'workers who farm.' This view is part of a deeply entrenched ideology which is at variance with the economics of the market place.

Protection and subsidies

Throughout the postwar period, Japanese agriculture has enjoyed a high degree of protection from the competition of cheaper imported foods. It has also benefitted from subsidies and price support measures. All these interventions have had the effect of sheltering the less efficient, part-time farming households. They have also encouraged farmers to persist with rice production when in fact the demand for rice has fallen in favour of other foodstuffs, such as meat, fruit and dairy produce. As rice surpluses have mounted, so the Government has been increasingly faced, not only with the costs of subsidies and price support measures, but also of storage. Up to 15 percent of the annual agricultural budget has been spent on storage alone. Ultimately, of course, all these costs are passed onto the consumer

Photo 8.1 *Cultivation of small fields in fragmented holdings*

Table 8.4 *Changes in the size of farm holdings (1960 – 1990) (ha.)*

	No. of holdings	<0.5	0.5 - 1.0	1.0 - 2.0	2.0 - 3.0	>3.0
			(percent of all holdings)			
Japan, except Hokkaido						
1960	5 823	39	33	24	3	1
1970	5 176	39	31	25	4	1
1980	4 542	42	29	22	5	2
1990	3 739	42	28	21	6	3
Hokkaido			**<1.0**			
1960	234		26	11	14	49
1970	166		22	8	9	61
1980	120		19	8	8	65
1990	95		18	6	6	70

either directly through inflation of the price of rice or indirectly through raised taxes. Understandably, there is growing resentment, particularly among urban consumers, even though it can be demonstrated that the area of rice production was cut back by 36 percent between 1965 and 1990 and that price support has been reducing by five percent per annum.

Technological progress (Figure 8.4)

Of all the technological advances applied to Japanese agriculture during the postwar period, four may be singled out for special mention. First, there have been the large-scale public works concerned ostensibly with better irrigation and improved water control. One relatively simple innovation here has been the use of intermediate ponds to raise the temperature of water before flooding the paddyfields. This has increased both the rate of plant growth and yield of rice.

Secondly, in Japan as elsewhere in the world, mechanisation has played its part. This has proved to be a mixed blessing, because if anything it has increased the amount of time that farmers can afford to devote to off-farm employment. Mechanisation has been particularly significant in rice cultivation (Photo 8.2). Statistics show that the percentage of input costs accounted for by machinery and implements doubled from 14 to 30 percent between 1965 and 1990. Factory

farming techniques are now widely used in the rearing of poultry and pigs and in dairying. Thirdly, mention must be made of the development of new and more productive strains of both crops and livestock better able to flourish in the harsher conditions of northern Japan. Finally, there has been a number of advances all to do with improving crop production, including the use of vinyl and polythene sheeting to protect and nurture crops, as well as increased use of artificial fertilizers, herbicides and fungicides.

Much of the diffusion of the new technology has been through local agricultural cooperatives (the *nokyo*) and their extension services, whilst much of the required capital has been obtained in the form of government grant aid. However, it is only the full-time sector that has reaped the benefits in the form of increased profitability. In the part-time sector, capital investment in mechanisation and other forms of new technology is still not being covered by revenue output. Hence the **vicious downward spiral** continues to drive farmers to seek supplementary sources of income.

Changing market demand (Figure 8.4)

Whilst agricultural diversification has been encouraged by postwar government policies, the make-up of Japanese agricultural output has also been crucially affected by changes in the level and character of market demand. Despite a slowing down in the rate of natural increase, population numbers have continued to rise leading to an increased overall demand for food. This demand has become all the more noticeable as the population has become increasingly urban. In the immediate postwar years, most evident was the raised demand for staple foods such as rice, vegetables and fish. But as the population has become more affluent and open to Western influence, diets have changed becoming essentially more varied. Much more meat, dairy produce and fruit are now being consumed. In recent years, particularly amongst the younger generation, American fast foods have become increasingly popular and

fashionable as the spread of burger bars and doughnut shops in the cities clearly indicate (Photo 8.3).

These changes in eating habits have been met by a significant rise in the level of food imports, with the USA as the leading supplier. This, in turn, has caused the Government to redouble its efforts to diversify farming in such a way that the demand for many of these new foods might be satisfied from domestic sources. Paradoxically, although agriculture is now becoming more diversified at a regional level, there is a growing tendency towards specialisation in certain types of agricultural production at the level of the individual farm. The nature of the specialisation depends on such factors as location, market accessibility and environmental conditions. Near cities, the specialisation has tended to be in horticultural and dairy products; in the warmer areas of southern Japan it has been in fruit and early vegetables, whilst in Hokkaido it has been in root crops and beef. Specialisation, if it is to be profitable, requires among other things expertise, capital investment and great efficiency. In these things, again the full-time farmers has been much better placed than the part-timers.

8.4 THE REGIONAL DIVERSITY OF AGRICULTURE

Having looked at the forces affecting the changing structure and productivity of Japanese agriculture during the postwar period, attention now turns briefly to its regional pattern. Although rice remains the dominant crop and is grown over virtually the length and breadth of the country, the varied

Photo 8.2. The mechanisation of rice cultivation

Photo 8.3 Fast food fever

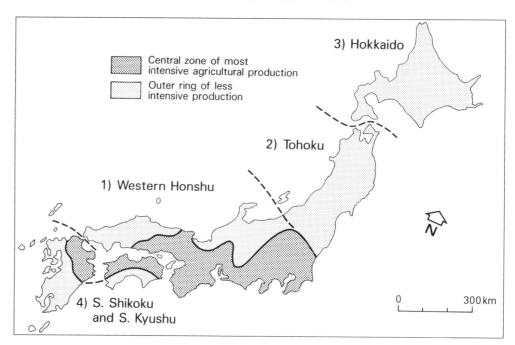

Fig. 8.5 *The major agricultural divisions*

terrain and significant climatic differences, together with the legacy of different regional traditions in farming, have meant that there has always been considerable regional differences in the pattern of agriculture (Figure 8.4). If anything, the postwar trend has been for this regional differentiation to increase.

Out of the regional diversity and complexity, it is possible to think broadly in terms of dividing Japan into a central zone of intensive agricultural production surrounding the major metropolitan market areas and an outer zone of less intensive, but nonetheless specialised commercial production (Figure 8.5).

The central zone (Figure 8.5)

Because of ready market access and the character of demand, much of the lowland near the cities of the Pacific Belt is given over to highly intensive production of vegetables, salad crops, soft fruit, flowers, meat and dairy goods. Dairying is particularly important around Tokyo, with some of the activity actually taking place within the suburbs. Here is the greatest concentration of vinyl-covered crops and greenhouses; the prefectures of Aichi, Shizuoka and Okayama account for over 60 percent of Japan's greenhouses. Stall-fed cattle and factory-farmed poultry and pigs are

other manifestations of the intensity of farming. However, rice is still significant, principally grown by part-time farmers on small paddy strips.

Further south in the Pacific Belt, where winters are milder and winter sunshine hours relatively high, crops can be grown throughout the year. Typical winter crops include vegetables (lettuce, cabbage, cucumber and melon) grown in the paddy fields, soft fruit (strawberries, table grapes) and some tree fruits (persimmon, mandarin oranges). Above the lowlands on the rising land of the diluvial terraces, tree fruits are widely grown where mulberry and tea bushes once flourished. Whilst relentless urban sprawl throughout the central zone continues, this is to some extent compensated by the reclamation and subsequent intensive farming of wetlands and diluvial uplands (Figure 8.6).

The outer ring (Figure 8.5)

The outer ring may be subdivided into four broad zones.

First, there is the western Honshu zone along the Japan Sea coast and separated from the Pacific Belt by the mountainous interior. This is one of the main granary areas of Japan with much of the alluvial lowland dominated by commercial rice-growing. However, the severity of the winter,

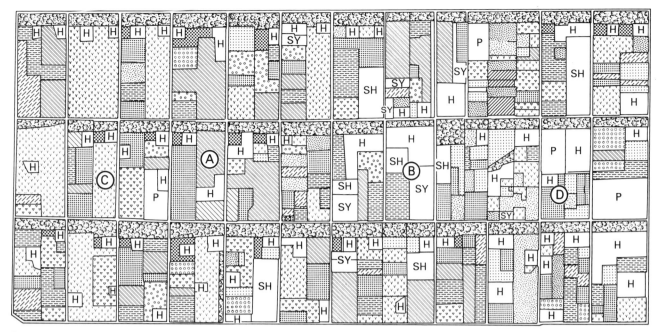

Land use on part of the Kushibiki Area – 1983

Arable land

░	Wheat and barley	▒	Upland rice	▨	Sorghum and millet
▽	Mulberry	▨	Italian rye grass	▒	Waste land
▒	Orchard and chestnut	▓	Garden cultivation	▒	Radish
▨	Oats	▒	Windbreak woodland	▒	Other vegetables
▽	Nursery and garden trees	▒	Swedish turnip	▒	Harvested field

Other land use

H	Housing lot
SH	Stock-house
SY	Stock-yard
P	Public facilities
(A)	Case farms

Changes

The area is on the old alluvial plain of the Arawaka River. It was originally communal grass and woodland but 500 hectares were reclaimed after World War Two and divided into 242 parcels for settlers. Initially, it was farmed for local food needs with such crops as upland rice, wheat, barley, millet and sweet potatoes. But under the postwar advances in agriculture significant changes occurred. By 1970 the major part of farm output was being sent to nearby urban markets. Vegetables had become the dominant crop combined with cereals and mulberry trees for silk production. But some farmers had introduced dairying as the area was within the Tokyo 'milkshed' area. Cattle were stall tethered and fed on turnips, rye grass and oats grown on the cultivated area.

The dual structure of agriculture

By 1983 half of the households had shifted to part-time farming, reflecting the difficulty in making very small holdings viable and the growing opportunities for a higher income outside of farming. Holdings in this part-time farming sector now averaged approximately 1 ha. Up to half is used for vegetables for domestic consumption; there is an increasing tendency for the remainder to be leased out to neighbouring full-time commercial farmers.

These full-time farming units are larger being between 2 and 3.5 ha. and additional land was rented. Holdings have become more specialised in line with national trends.

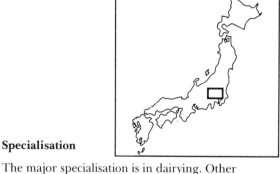

Specialisation

The major specialisation is in dairying. Other specialisations include cattle fattening, pig rearing, poultry, garden tree growing (horticulture) and vegetables reflecting ready access to the Tokyo region's markets.

An illustration of a viable commercial holding is the largest dairy unit in the area; it has 105 dairy cows kept under cover and stall-fed. The feed comes partly from corn, clover, Italian rye grass grown on 1.5 ha. of the holding and on 2.0 ha. of rented land and partly from feed concentrates and roughage straw purchased through the local agricultural co-operative. Such intensive dairying requires a comparatively large labour input – five members of the household working full-time.

Fig. 8.6 *Case study of the Kushibiki reclamation area (Saitama), 1983*

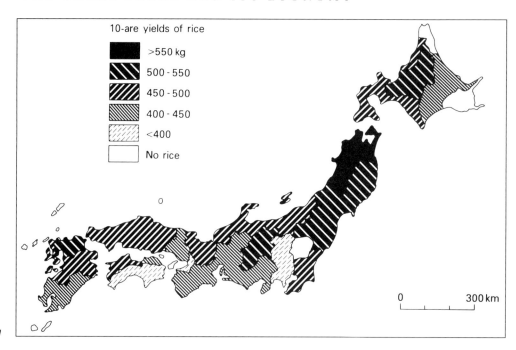

Fig. 8.7 *Rice production*

with its heavy snowfalls, allows only one crop to be grown a year.

The second zone covers the Tohoku region of northern Honshu. This is without doubt the rice bowl of modern Japan, with over 40 percent of the farmland given over to paddy rice, average yields in excess of 50 kg per ha. and rice accounting for over 40 percent of farm sales (Figure 8.7). However, as improvements in transport have opened up the area to the markets of the Pacific Belt, there has been a drive to reclaim more land, especially wetlands, for agricultural use. Apple and other orchards, together with vineyards, are evidence that crop production here is becoming more diversified, a trend reinforced by the expansion of beef and dairy production in the uplands (Figure 8.8).

Hokkaido constitutes the third zone. The character of agriculture here differs markedly from that in the rest of Japan having more similarities with commercial farming in Western Europe (Figure 8.9). Of all the agricultural regions of Japan, it has probably benefitted most from the postwar changes in the Japanese diet. The increasing taste for meat, dairy products, root vegetables and beer (much of it brewed in Sapporo from island-grown barley) all involve branches of agricultural production which have come to prosper in Hokkaido. Equally, however, perhaps

more than any other part of Japan, its farming prosperity is under threat from agricultural imports, particularly from Australia, New Zealand and the USA. As the drive to liberalise trade in foodstuffs gathers pace, so Hokkaido farmers are made vulnerable by their relative high production costs.

The final zone of the outer ring, at the other extremity of Japan, comprises the southern parts of Shikoku and Kyushu. Being in the sub-tropical part, farming systems are less threatened by the liberalisation of agricultural trade, with the possible exception of citrus growing. One particular advantage of this zone is that its warm climate allows double-cropping, either of rice alone or a combination of summer rice and winter vegetable or cereal (Figure 8.10). Fruit-growing is an important part of the agricultural economy, as is the growing of vegetables such as aubergines, tomatoes and peppers. By Japanese standards, much of the farming is fairly efficient, with quite extensive mechanisation reducing the traditionally high labour input.

8.5 FROM FISH EXPLOITATION TO FISH FARMING

With 29 000km of coastline giving access to once rich fishing grounds, Japan's exploitation of those marine resources within its immediate reach

Northern Honshu agricultural change (1952–1990) in the Shiwa area of Iwate prefecture – rice remains the basic crop but with diversification into intensive livestock production, mushroom cultivation and apple growing

From a situation in which 38% of the 820 households were part-time farmers, the number by the early 1970s had increased to 84%. But the Shiwa Agricultural Co-operative was actively engaged in maintaining the number of households in farming. Holdings range in size from 0.5 to 3 ha.

Three-quarters of the area is upland, left as woodland or pasture; the remainder is alluvial lowland drained by the Takima river. Irrigated rice is therefore still the main crop though environmental conditions, including a temperate climate and rainfall with summer maxima, are conducive to a variety of crops and livestock production.

Extension and increased intensity of rice growing

In keeping with northern Honshu trends, but against national trends, rice area has increased. Between 1952 and 1973 it increased from 730 ha. to 1215 ha., yields rose by 44% and income from ¥100 to 660 million.

Influences promoting this:

(a) Extension of rice land by reclamation of rough grazing and by irrigation through the construction of the Sonnoika dam with government advice and financial support, but under the direction of the Shiwa Agricultural Co-operative.

(b) Greater rice production encouraged by the high price for rice guaranteed under the Government's food control system.

(c) Higher yields due to better hybrid strains of rice, greater capital inputs and improved methods helped by the Co-operative and nearby University Agriculture Research Institute – better drainage, deeper ploughing, regularisation of shape of paddy strips to allow for more mechanisation. Between 1952 and 1973 the mechanisation input rose 5% to 20% of total input costs, whilst the number of labour hours was reduced by 40%. There has been a great increase in fertiliser usage, green manuring with crop waste being combined with increased input of chemical fertilisers. The new hybrid rice strains have also required better water control and careful use of herbicides to control weeds and pests.

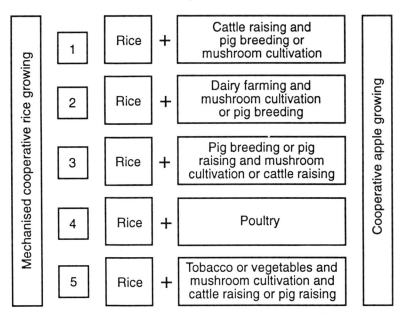

Future modes of household farming in Shiwa illustrating different combinations of crops and livestock

The economic development plan for Shiwa instigated in 1964, continuing the 'industrialisation' of farming and increasing farm incomes through diversification of production by the introduction of new cash crops and greater emphasis on livestock production

The stages of implementation were the dissemination of ideas, choice of a future mode of farming and implementation. Producer associations were formed and provided with credit and advice together with purchasing and marketing through the Co-operative.

Mushroom-growing is the most important cash cropping, introduced as there is a good urban market demand, it took up little land and employed family labour in the slack winter months. Apples, tobacco and vegetables (cucumbers and lettuce) were marketed nationally.

Livestock-rearing and dairying were supported by the Cooperative's own Niiyama Ranch with access to improved pastures and winter fodder. The smaller farmers went in for pig production. Poultry is less popular as egg prices fluctuate. Despite these moves a greater share of income is from non-agricultural sources.

Fig. 8.8   *Case study of agricultural change in the Shiwa area (Iwate)*

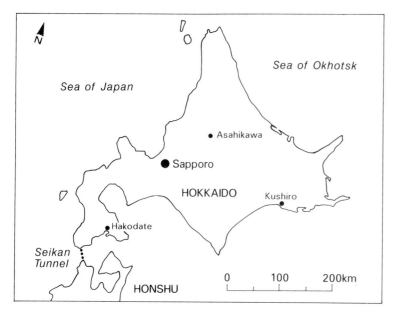

Late development

With a severer climate than the rest of Japan and remote from the main populated region, Hokkaido was not developed for agriculture until the 1920s and 1930s. Now it is one of Japan's most important agricultural regions and the only one still with substantial land available for clearance e.g. 50 000 ha. of forested land in eastern Hokkaido recently cleared for dairying.

A distinctive agriculture character

Cool humid temperate climate favours a Western European pattern of agriculture – the region accounts for 35% of Japan's dairy output.

Though rice is important especially on the Ishikara Plain, Hokkaido is also noted as a mixed farming region with holdings significantly larger than in the rest of Japan, commonly 25 to 30 ha. in size. Sugar beet, potatoes, various kinds of beans, wheat and barley are important along with livestock production including cattle and horse rearing.

Food-processing industries

The nature of farm output, together with the considerable distance from the main urban market, have encouraged the development of a wide range of food-processing industries. One of the most famous of these is the brewing industry centred in Sapporo.

Market access

Sapporo, with one and a half million population, offers a large urban market resulting in horticulture, market gardening, dairying and 'factory farming' of pigs and poultry in nearby rural areas.

The opening of the Seikan rail tunnel connecting Hokkaido to mainland Honshu is likely to increase the importance of the region's farming, especially as it specialises in agricultural products for which there is an expanding market.

Distinctive also in having a high proportion of full-time commercial farming households

The emphasis is on economic efficiency and responsiveness to market changes, as illustrated by the Kirihata's household farm near Asahigawa City. It is a mixed farm of 20 ha. with the emphasis on dairying. Because of the severe winter conditions, cattle must be stall fed for 6 months of the year. Thus 12 ha. are under grass and legumes to make silage for cattle feed. The remainder is under rice, wheat, potatoes and sugar beet. Because of the Government land diversion scheme, the rice area is being reduced.

Markets are Sapporo for potatoes, a local processing factory for the sugar beet and the milk is bottled and marketed via the local co-operative.

Fig. 8.9 *Case-study of farming in Hokkaido*

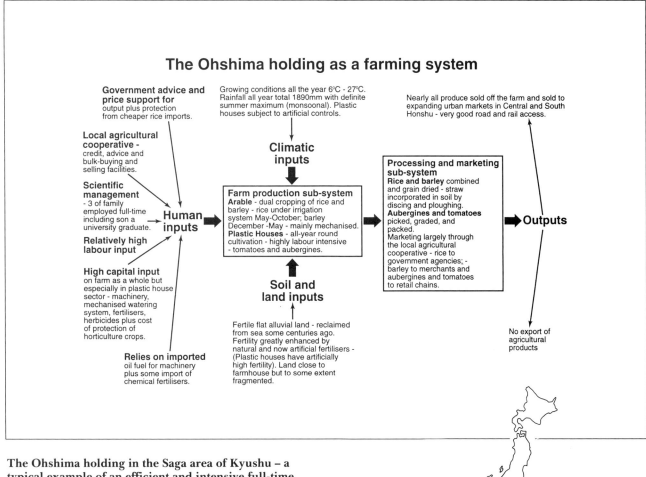

The Ohshima holding as a farming system

Government advice and price support for output plus protection from cheaper rice imports.

Local agricultural cooperative - credit, advice and bulk-buying and selling facilities.

Scientific management - 3 of family employed full-time including son a university graduate.

Relatively high labour input

High capital input on farm as a whole but especially in plastic house sector - machinery, mechanised watering system, fertilisers, herbicides plus cost of protection of horticulture crops.

Relies on imported oil fuel for machinery plus some import of chemical fertilisers.

Human inputs

Growing conditions all the year 6°C - 27°C. Rainfall all year total 1890mm with definite summer maximum (monsoonal). Plastic houses subject to artificial controls.

Climatic inputs

Farm production sub-system
Arable - dual cropping of rice and barley - rice under irrigation system May-October; barley December -May - mainly mechanised.
Plastic Houses - all-year round cultivation - highly labour intensive - tomatoes and aubergines.

Soil and land inputs

Fertile flat alluvial land - reclaimed from sea some centuries ago. Fertility greatly enhanced by natural and now artificial fertilisers - (Plastic houses have artificially high fertility). Land close to farmhouse but to some extent fragmented.

Nearly all produce sold off the farm and sold to expanding urban markets in Central and South Honshu - very good road and rail access.

Processing and marketing sub-system
Rice and barley combined and grain dried - straw incorporated in soil by discing and ploughing.
Aubergines and tomatoes picked, graded, and packed.
Marketing largely through the local agricultural cooperative - rice to government agencies; - barley to merchants and aubergines and tomatoes to retail chains.

Outputs

No export of agricultural products

The Ohshima holding in the Saga area of Kyushu – a typical example of an efficient and intensive full-time family commercial enterprise, combining cereal growing with specialised horticulture under glass

The Ohshima household own 3.5 ha. which have been in the family for a number of generations. As is customary in Japan, the eldest surviving son inherited the holding. He currently works it with the help of his own elder son who has a degree in agriculture and the son's wife who is also a graduate.

Approximately two-thirds of the holding is under cereals with rice as the summer crop followed by barley as the winter crop. The other third is covered by plastic housing in which aubergines and tomatoes are grown as profitable high-value cash crops. In contrast, rice and barley are only profitable because of government price support. Without this, the present high capital input costs now involved in cereal-growing could not be covered and some of the cultivated land would probably be given over to specialised vegetable production.

The organisational structure of the farm holding and the input and output flows associated with it are summarised above.

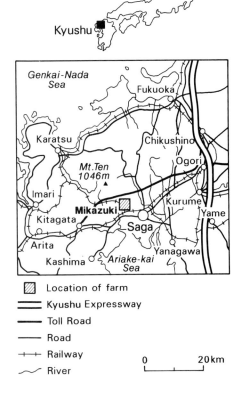

Kyushu

Genkai-Nada Sea

Fukuoka

Karatsu

Chikushino

Ogori

Mt.Ten 1046m ▲

Imari

Kurume

Yame

Mikazuki

Kitagata

Saga

Arita

Yanagawa

Kashima

Ariake-kai Sea

▨ Location of farm
═ Kyushu Expressway
▬ Toll Road
─ Road
+++ Railway
∿ River

0   20km

Fig. 8.10 Case study of farming on the Saga plain (Kyushu)

Table 8.5 *Imports of seafood (1970 – 1990)*

Year	Value (¥ bn)
1970	94
1975	355
1980	684
1985	1 096
1990	1 518

have until relatively recently been more than adequate to meet the needs of its population. Fish has always been Japan's main source of protein. Most of the fish has come from coastal waters, but a significant amount has also been taken from rivers, lakes and ponds. Yet the relative importance of marine foods in the general diet of the Japanese has radically altered since the 1970s. The decline has been the result of, on the one hand, the continued rise in population and a change in the type of seafood demand and, on the other, increasing problems of supply. Despite the fact that nearly 60 percent of Japan's protein demand is now satisfied by meat and other sources, the country can no longer meet the demand for fish and other types of seafood. Although it remains the most important fishing nation in the world, with annual catches through the 1980s generally steady at around 12 million tonnes, Japan is now the largest

importer of seafood. Such imports come mainly from the USA, South Korea, Taiwan and China which together supply one-third of Japan's consumption, whereas until 1971 Japan had been a net exporter (Table 8.5).

Problems of the fishing industry

The fishing industry, and as a consequence the many fishing ports around the Japanese coast, faces serious problems (Figure 8.11). Many fishing enterprises are in serious debt. The first major blow came with the Oil Shocks which led to substantial increases in fuel costs. Unfortunately, these additional costs were not adequately passed on to the consumer. The decision not to do so was taken in the light of (i) consumer resistance to rises in fish prices and (ii) the already declining demand for the more common fish as diets changed and meat supplies became more plentiful. That miscalculation has since come home to roost as fishing has simply become uneconomic. Secondly, the growing pollution of coastal waters during the high-growth phase caused by the discharge of rapidly increasing amounts of industrial and domestic waste had an adverse effect upon fish stocks, particularly in the Inland Sea. The scale of the pollution was high-

Fig. 8.11 *The location of fishing ports and markets*

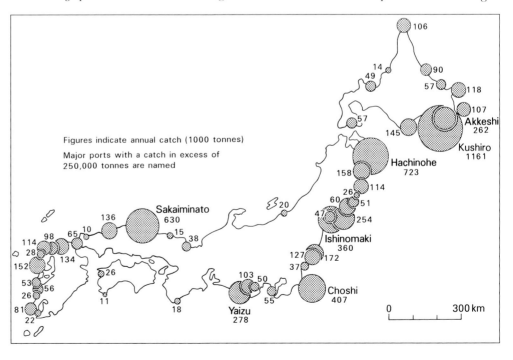

Figures indicate annual catch (1000 tonnes)

Major ports with a catch in excess of 250,000 tonnes are named

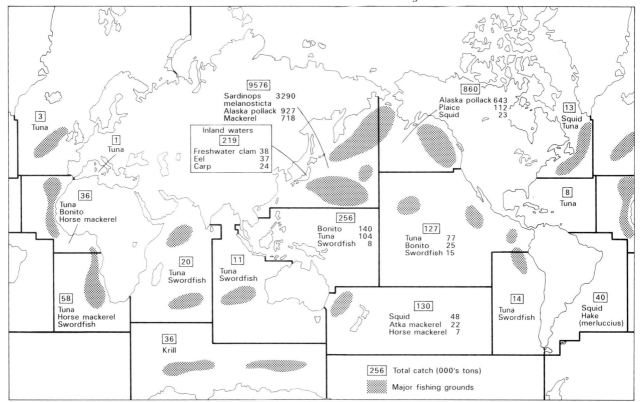

9576
Sardinops   3290
melanosticta
Alaska pollack   927
Mackerel   718

Inland waters
219
Freshwater clam 38
Eel   37
Carp   24

860
Alaska pollack 643
Plaice   112
Squid   23

3
Tuna

1
Tuna

13
Squid
Tuna

36
Tuna
Bonito
Horse mackerel

8
Tuna

256
Bonito   140
Tuna   104
Swordfish   8

127
Tuna   77
Bonito   25
Swordfish 15

20
Tuna
Swordfish

11
Tuna
Swordfish

58
Tuna
Horse mackerel
Swordfish

130
Squid   48
Atka mackerel 22
Horse mackerel 7

14
Tuna
Swordfish

40
Squid
Hake
(merluccius)

36
Krill

256   Total catch (000's tons)

      Major fishing grounds

lighted by the dramatic **red tide** phenomenon. Although various measures have been taken since 1972 to reduce the pollution of rivers and coastal waters, the problem persists. Thirdly, overfishing has occurred in inshore waters as the fishing industry has sacrificed sustainable exploitation for short-term profits. As a consequence, marine stocks have become seriously depleted and food chains profoundly disrupted.

Fishing in more distant waters has been dealt two body blows in addition to that of rising operating costs. Japanese fishing fleets had increasingly sought to meet the growing gap between supply and demand by fishing beyond their territorial waters, often in the fishing grounds of other nations, as well as in international waters (Figure 8.12). But the establishment of 300 km offshore fishing zones in 1977 has drastically reduced the catches Japan has been able to take from further waters. Bilateral agreements have had to be negotiated and fees paid for the right to fish inside the limits of other countries. But gradually the permitted quotas have been either reduced or stopped altogether. This is reflected in the fact that pelagic catches today are only half of what they were in 1975.

In addition, like other fishing nations, Japan has been seriously affected by the rising international concern over the depletion of the oceans' resources due to unsustainable exploitation. The wholesale adoption of factory methods of fishing and the cruelty of some aspects of fishing have also sparked criticism. These three issues have been highlighted in the media coverage given to whaling where Japan is seen as a prime culprit. The moratorium on whaling imposed by the International Whaling Commission has had a severe impact on the traditional small whaling ports. Krill and tuna fishing using factory methods are also now the subject of discussion for possible international control. Most recently, in 1991, a ban was imposed on drift-net fishing in international waters, to which Japan reluctantly agreed despite the detrimental effects on the economy of fishing ports, especially in northern Japan.

A final problem which needs to be identified, but requiring little explanation, is that of an ageing labour force. Fishing, like farming, is finding it increasingly difficult to recruit younger people. Failure to resolve this problem will certainly hasten the demise of the fishing industry.

Fig. 8.12 *Japan's fishery production, by area*

Location of Karakuwa township and fishing ports on the Sanriku coast

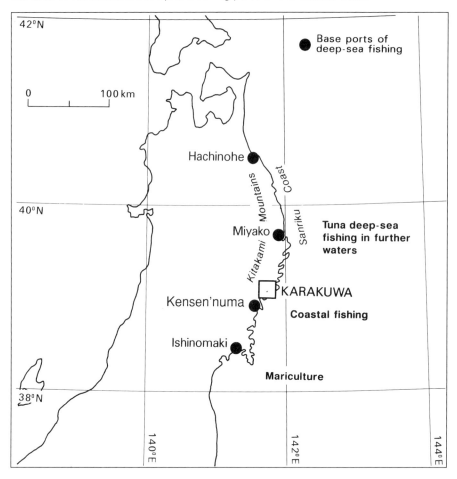

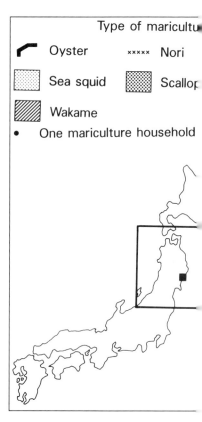

Location of Activities

Initially based on fishing villages within the Karakuwa township. But as the scale of fishing in further waters developed, especially after the Second World War, the deep-sea fishing fleet transfered to Kensen'numa which had better boat-yard

Mariculture expansion

From the 1950s mariculture was established as a right for existing households. This is mainly run by the head of the household, with younger male members away most of the year with the tuna fishing fleet.

Oyster-farming and sea-weed (*wakami*) collection are traditional activities but a rising market has led to diversification with squid and scallops now also farmed. Operating costs have increased but increased prices have continued to mean good profits.

Table 1 *Number of fishing establishments by types of fishery*

Types of fishery	Number
Mariculture	184
Nori	0
Oyster	59
Wakame	125
Scallop	0
Boat fishing	164
Less than 1 ton	93
1 – 5 ton	30
5 – 20 ton	22
20 – 50 ton	0
50 – 100 ton	7
100 ton and over	12
Set net	11
Total	359

Figure 8.13

Case study of fishing ports on the Pacific Coast of Honshu

and other facilities. This is now Japan's main centre for the deep-sea tuna fishing fleet.

Coastal fishing by small family concerns remains based in the villages of Karakuwa township.

The distribution of mariculture is influenced by favourable environments and tradition. Oyster beds are mainly located in the sheltered bay area behind the tip extending southward from the Karakuwa Peninsula.

Distribution of mariculture areas and households in Karakura township

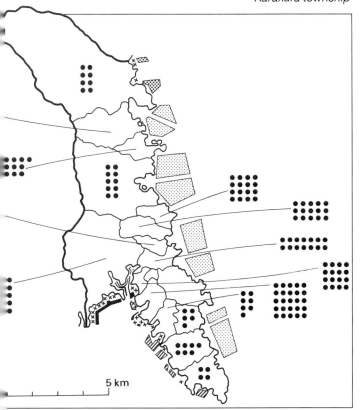

Factors affecting growth and dependency on fishing

1 Very restricted land area for cultivation, only five percent of township area.

2 Backed by mountains inland, therefore looks to the sea as a resource.

3 Access to rich coastal fishing grounds and resources further afield.

4 Sheltered inlets and bays suitable for mariculture.

5 Historical tradition of fishing going back to the 17th century, therefore accumulation of expertise.

6 Postwar growth in markets for quality fish and seafood in which fishing ports in area have specialised – deep sea tuna, line fishing and mariculture, especially of oysters.

7 Capital investment – support of fishing co-operatives and government.

8 Improved transport to main urban markets mainly by road.

Table 2 *Number of fishing households by extent of dependency on fishery*

	1978	1983
Exclusively engaged in fishery	24	38
Mainly engaged in fishery	149	158
Partly engaged in fishery	203	159
Total	376	355

Structure of the fishing industry in Karakuwa township

Over half of total income is from fishing, including mariculture, giving households greater prosperity than in nearby non-fishing townships. But there is an increase in part-time businesses traditionally combining fishing with farming, fish processing and packing; nowadays increasingly combined with leisure and service-related occupations.

From Edo period to after the Second World War traditional dependence on skipjack and line fishing continued, though some oyster mariculture begun in 1930.

After the Second World War continuation of coastal fishing by small boats but increasingly a dual structure developed of:

(a) tuna line fishing in further waters

  – mainly younger male members of households for 8 months to 1 year at sea – high wage income;

(b) expanding mariculture frequently run by the household head.

Table 3 *Number of fishing households by side-businesses and by extent of dependency on fishing*

Side business	Mainly engaged in fishing	Partly engaged in fishing
Agriculture	118	138
Fish processing	2	6
Lesiure fishing or seasonal	7	11
Others	17	23
Wage work for fishing	47	156
Wage work for other than fishing	63	113

Table 8.6 *Production of cultivated seafood (1970 and 1990)*

Sea		1970	1990
		(000 tons)	
Fish	Yellowtails	43	154
	Sea bream	0.4	46
	Mackerel	–	7
Shellfish	Oysters	191	256
	Scallops	6	180
	Prawns	0.1	3
Seaweed	Laver	231	403
	Wakame	76	108
Freshwater			
Fish	Eels	16	34
	Trout	9	16
	Comon carp	4	15
	Sweet fish	3	11

Changes in popular taste and their impact

Since the 1960s, there has not only been a levelling off in the demand for fish in favour of meat, but also a significant shift away from the ordinary cheaper fish, such as mackerel and pollack, that once figured so prominently in the traditional Japanese diet. Instead, a sophistication of eating habits has led to a marked rise in the demand for higher-priced fish, such as sea bream, salmon and yellow-tail tuna, and other seafoods, most notably shell-fish. The greatly increased popularity of eating out, particularly in *sushi* bars and fish restaurants, has also played its part in changing popular tastes and therefore the type of fish and seafood in demand. Since supplies from Japan's territorial waters are insufficient, there are only two ways in which this change in demand can be met. These are by importing those seafoods, hence the marked rise in imports (Table 8.5) and by fish-farming (Photo 8.4).

Farming the waters

The move away from fish catching to fish cultivation, or to be more precise **aquaculture**, should in theory help to solve a number of the problems currently facing the Japanese fishing industry, particularly the over-exploitation of its in-shore waters, falling pelagic catches and the changing demand for seafood.

Although freshwater aquaculture is undertaken on some of the rivers and lakes, as well as in artificial ponds and tanks, the bulk of Japanese fish farming is increasingly coastal or in-shore (Figure 8.13). **Mariculture**, as it is called, involves the cultivation of both fish and other marine products such as oysters, scallops and seaweed (a traditional and popular part of the Japanese diet). Mariculture is nothing new. Oyster-cultivation and the production of pearls was begun in the 17th century. The cultivation of laver, carp and eels became important in the early 20th century. By 1940, fish-farming in both sea and freshwater environments produced about 100 000 tons of food products annually. This has expanded rapidly during the postwar period, and now accounts for over 25 percent of all the fish and other seafoods consumed in Japan.

Today, the largest fish-farming sector is that concerned with the breeding and fattening of yellow-tail tuna, mainly in the calmer bays of the Japan Sea coast and in the Inland Sea (Table 8.6). Highly lucrative shellfish culture is also important in the latter, as well as in northern and southwestern Japan. One very positive outcome of mariculture has been the need to reduce drastically pollution levels in in-shore waters. As that challenge has been met for

Photo 8.4 *A modern maricultural plant*

localised fish-farming ventures, so it has yielded wider benefits. It has become possible to contemplate restocking large expanses of coastal water, and so begin the slow process of bringing them back to something like their former productivity. Steps are already being taken to breed young stock of such species as sardines, mackerel and calamari (a kind of squid) and releasing these in open water. Although these are no longer popular eating, the rising catches are being processed to make cattle feed, as well as fish meal and paste. Another benefit is that they form the basic food for many of the larger and higher-priced species that are now being farmed, most notably the yellow-tail tuna. There is also the prospect that their abundance will once again attract into in-shore waters sought-after fish such as sword-fish, bonito and salmon.

It is quite clear that modern aquaculture requires much investment in research, new technology and expensive equipment (Photo 8.4). It also requires the cooperative efforts of many people and different interest groups; it critically needs young minds receptive to new ideas and procedures. There can be no doubt that aquaculture is going to play an increasingly important part in the feeding of the Japanese to compensate for the declining contribution made by fish taken from international waters. But the transition from traditional fishing to fish cultivation is not going to be easy. The Government has recognised this and has already identified nearly 3 000 coastal settlements for particular help and financial support.

In the past, coastal settlements have combined fishing with farming to allow households to eke out a living. With the increase in leisure time and the growth in tourism and water-based recreation, many fishing ports are now being encouraged to participate in these new activities in order to remain economically viable. This involves providing accommodation, building marinas, as well as promoting sports fishing, surfing and sea-bathing. It remains to be seen how compatible such things are with both the traditional fishing economy and the new-style aquaculture.

8.6 FORESTRY

Forests cover approximately 60 percent of the land area and Japan is one of the largest consumers of wood products, especially paper for print. Throughout the postwar period demand has expanded markedly. It might have been expected, therefore, that commercial forestry would have expanded in response to this demand. Such was the case through the 1950s and 1960s, but since then production has declined and the industry has become depressed. In 1981, Japan was 36 percent self-sufficient in its wood products needs, since when the figure has fallen to under 30 percent. Although in 1990 2.5 million households derived some form of income from forestry, only 100 000 people were employed on a regular basis. The remainder derived the greater part of their employment and income from farming.

Given the high percentage of land under forest cover, it is strange that there have been few government initiatives to expand forestry and cut down on costly imports of wood products. The explanation has several elements. For one thing, much of the forest is unsuitable for commercial exploitation. Distance from the major markets combined with the difficult mountainous terrain make lumbering an expensive operation. Since the 1960s, the costs of production have risen faster than the market price of wood. The situation has been made worse for the Japanese producer by the import of cheaper wood products from abroad. A further problem has been labour recruitment. Most forest workers are over 50 years of age, with the younger members of forestry households preferring to take less strenuous, higher status and better paid jobs away from the remote forested areas.

The demise of the forestry industry is also to do with an important change of government policy towards Japan's forests. Today these are no longer seen as primarily sources of timber but as part of the national heritage to be managed rather than exploited (Figure 8.14). Much of the productive forest occurs in areas designated as national parks and contains protected species of

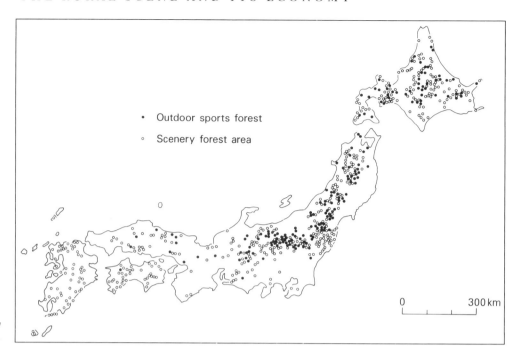

- Outdoor sports forest
- Scenery forest area

Fig. 8.14 Designated forest areas

wildlife. Moreover, these forests are increasingly seen as 'breathing spaces', as areas of recreation for a largely urban population looking for ways of escaping the stress of modern city living. It is no coincidence that the National Forest Service Special Laws of 1978, which reorganised the management of forest areas, came into being at the same time as two other changes began to make their impact. These were the upsurge in public concern for the environment and the increase in leisure time which provided people with the opportunity to enjoy the national parks. Furthermore, increased car ownership and improved public transport made many of these areas much more accessible.

For the mountain villages traditionally dependent on farming combined with forestry work, the changes have had serious consequences, particularly since they were already declining as younger people left. Those villages must now look for alternative sources of income and this increasingly means tourism and recreational activities. The problem is that, although such new activities may help the villages to survive economically, their character is likely to change and bring about the end of the traditional closely-knit rural community. Such demise is also being hastened in those settlements accessible from the major cities as second-home

buying gathers pace.

Forest areas with commercial potential are scattered throughout the uplands of Japan, but to date exploitation has been mainly concentrated in the Tohoku region of Honshu and in Hokkaido. The concentration here is partly due to climatic conditions favouring both coniferous and deciduous tree growth, but it is mainly the result of a deliberate planting of these areas during the Edo period (1615–1867). This was undertaken in order to supply the growing market for timber as industrialisation and urbanisation began to take off. For mountain villages here, as in other parts of Japan such as the Central Alps, forestry has long been one of the most important activities alongside various timber-processing industries, most notably charcoal burning. Up until the late 1950s, charcoal remained a major fuel.

Today, Japan's forest areas are divided into national and private forests, with the former accounting for nearly 60 percent of the total forest area and the latter supplying almost double the amount of lumber (Figure 8.15). In both sectors, there has been a switch to forest conservation and management, with an active regeneration programme being pursued. Selective felling has now replaced clear felling and is practised alongside both natural and artificial regeneration. As a consequence, the 1990 figure of 24.6 million ha. of forest shows a very slight increase over the 1960 figure. Japan uses its domestic timber mainly for housing construction and needs around the home. Japanese homes have traditionally been built of wood, but the proportion of wholly wooden houses among newly-built residences has declined as high-rise developments have become common. In 1970, 60 percent of all new dwellings were built of timber; that figure has now declined to 40 percent. A small amount of domestic timber is used to make plywood and chipboard, but Japan's very large consumption of paper and paper board is largely met from imports (Table 8.7). Also worth mentioning in the context of timber consumption is the huge daily throw-away by homes, bars and restaurants of wooden chopsticks which are only used once.

8.7 THE INTRUSION OF LEISURE AND TOURISM

Farming, fishing and forestry have traditionally provided the economic base for rural areas, but as was discussed in 8.1 the diffusion of urban influences and of non-agricultural employment into the countryside has been going on for a long time. What has emerged is a sectoral interdependence between manufacturing and farming, with the latter in certain places keyed in with part-time fishing or forestry. However, just as service activities have taken on a dominant role in the urban economy, so leisure, recreation and tourist-led service development are beginning to exert a very strong influence in rural areas. This has particularly gathered momentum since the 1960s as both the Government and the public at large have begun to wake up to the importance of leisure. Introduction of the two-day weekend has led to a better balance of work and leisure, whilst increased disposable income has meant more money available to spend on recreational pursuits, be it golf, skiing or a short stay at a hot spring resort. Certainly, the popular image of the Japanese as a workaholic population has to be revised. It would seem that

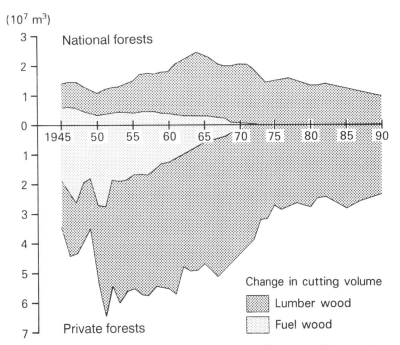

Fig. 8.15 Changes in timber extraction from national and private forests (1945 – 1990)

Japan is about to make the transition from Stage Two to Stage Three in the model of leisure development, with leisure education beginning to add a new dimension (Table 8.8).

Whilst the numbers of Japanese going abroad is increasing, in 1990 amounting to about 10 million, the percentage figure of 8 percent pales when compared with figures of 17 and 48 percent for the USA and UK respec-

Table 8.7 Consumption of timber and paper (1990)

	Lumber (000m³ per capita)	Plywood (000m³ per capita)	Paper and paper board (kg per capita)
Japan	0.31	0.07	205
USA	0.55	0.09	311
Canada	0.85	0.08	236
EC	0.17	0.01	146

Table 8.8 The model of leisure development

Stage	Social stage	Lifestyle	Type of leisure
1	Pre-industrial society	Working and saving	Recreation
2	Industrial society	Having and consuming	Recreation + amusement
3	Post-industrial society	Being and self-development	Recreation + amusement + education

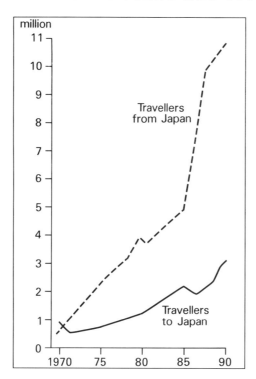

Fig. 8.16 *Inbound and outbound tourists (1970 – 1990)*

tively (Chapter 11) (Figure 8.16). This partly reflects the fact that on average the Japanese worker takes only seven days holiday leave a year outside public holidays – too short for a trip abroad. Similarly, though the number of foreign tourists coming to Japan has significantly increased, the impact of the three million overseas visitors outside Tokyo and the cultural heart of the country is very limited (Table 8.9) . Certainly, their importance for rural areas is as yet insignificant except in certain favoured locations such as Okinawa.

In rural areas, the impact of greater leisure and tourist activities comes on the whole from short visits (day and weekend excursions) and trips associated with popular festival dates and the established holiday periods, such as

Table 8.9 *Origins of inbound tourists (1990)*

	%
South Korea	27
USA	18
Taiwan	16
UK	6
China	3
Philippines	3
West Germany	2
Canada	2
Malaysia	2
Australia	2

Golden Week (late April – early May). In 1990, it was estimated that the Japanese made over 315 million leisure/tourist trips, spending over ¥15 trillion. But the bulk of this trip-making was in family or group outings during Japan's 12 national holidays. In Golden Week alone, 17 percent of the population travelled. However, relatively little of the tourist expenditure benefitted rural areas, since much of the trip-making was within the Pacific Belt and the most popular visits were to exhibitions and theme parks, temples and shrines (Figure 8.17). Rather more benefit comes earlier in the spring from the *hananu* or cherry-blossom viewing parties which follow the cherry-blossom 'front' as it advances northwards across Japan. The small spas and hot-spring resorts of rural areas continue to be as popular as ever, particularly given improved accessibility and greater personal mobility. So too are the 'soaphouses' with their hostesses (*geisha* girls are now virtually a thing of the past). Horror stories about the AIDS epidemic in the resorts of Bali, Thailand and the Philippines have persuaded many men to abandon overseas pleasure trips in favour of what are perceived to be 'safer' indulgences in Japan.

On top of these traditional ways of spending leisure time, there has since the 1960s been a rapid expansion of Western-style recreational pursuits – sports activities of different kinds, scenic viewing with some hiking, the development of seaside resorts with bathing and other water-based activities, and more recent still the growing popularity of winter sports, especially skiing in the Japanese Alps and Hokkaido. In some areas, these have been superimposed on the traditional leisure-trip activities. It is the impact of these newer activities on rural economies and communities which needs now to be explored.

Impact on rural areas close to cities

In those rural areas close to the major cities, the effect of recreation and tourist activities is felt in two ways. First, there is the taking up of land previously used for agriculture, and secondly the overtaking of farm income by income derived from providing

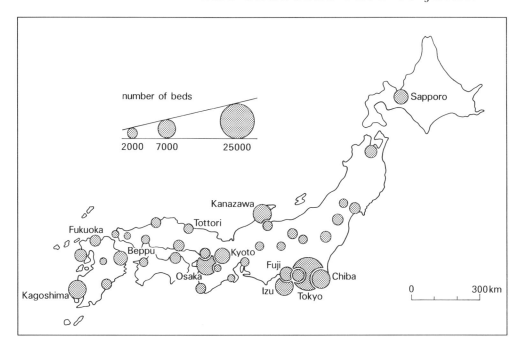

Fig. 8.17 The distribution of major resorts on the basis of accommodation capacity

leisure services.

Particularly noteworthy in the former context are the very large areas being devoted to theme parks. This began in 1983 with the creation of Tokyo Disneyland on the shores of Tokyo Bay near Urasayu (Chiba) and covering 83ha. of land. Today, there are over 20 theme parks established in different parts of the country. Whilst some like Tokyo Disneyland are mainly on land reclaimed or earlier industrial use, others have consumed large tracts of farmland (Photo 8.5). Research has shown that these parks have a cumulative causation effect leading to further investment in related services and activities. It is estimated, for example, that Tokyo Disneyland has stimulated some Y500 billion of additional investment, including five large hotels and better transport links. There can be no doubting that these theme parks generate considerable income in what may be described as urban fringe areas, but equally they threaten much environmental damage and the breakdown of rural communities.

Less spectacular but equally important has been the expansion of recreational activities. For example, some 20 to 30km to the west of Tokyo small farms previously devoted to growing fruit, vegetables, cut flowers and potted plants for the capital's market have turned over to the provision of a wide range of sports and leisure activities

(Figure 8.18). These include golf ranges (golf courses are prohibitively expensive), tennis courts, *pachinko* parlours, restaurants and saunas. Although most of the clientele is made up of Tokyo residents, people are also drawn from more distant rural areas.

Impact on more remote rural areas

Further away from the immediate influence of major cities, the expansion

Photo 8.5 Tokyo Disneyland

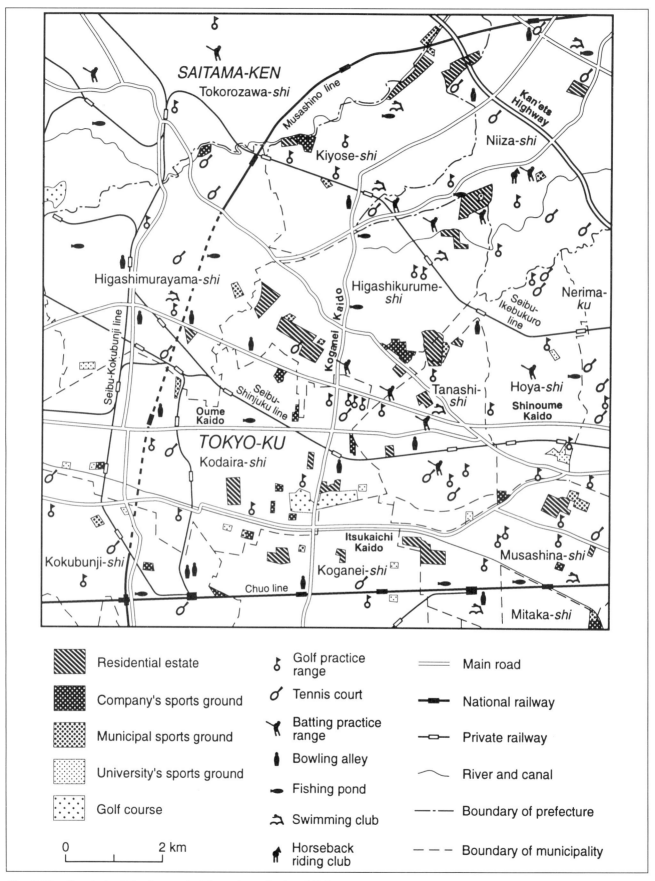

Fig. 8.18 *Sports facilities in a part of the outer suburbs of Tokyo*

of recreation and tourism is reflected in the resort boom of mountain and coastal areas catering both for the daytripper and increasingly the week-end and weekly visitor. In addition, in these remoter areas where land costs are low considerable investment is being made in the construction of golf courses. Another growing phenomenon is the second home to which the more affluent city workers escape at weekends. As in Western countries, this has had a disturbing effect on land and property prices as well as on the social structure of affected communities. A classic example is provided by the second-home developments in Yuzawa (Niigata). However, local economies have benefitted from the bourgeoning of *minshuku* (bed-and-breakfast places), souvenir shops and visitor-related employment.

The development of resort areas in highland, coastal and other attractive rural areas has gathered further impetus from central and prefectural government efforts to promote regional development through the medium of tourism. Since 1987, when the Law for the Development of Comprehensive Resort Areas was enacted, prefectures have been designating huge recreational districts, each more than 1 500km^2 in extent, and drawing up plans for the development of facilities at specified centres. Once approved by central Government, implementation of the proposals benefits from various concessions such as tax refunds and low-interest loans. As of 1990, 20 such resort areas had been approved, with another 20 awaiting ratification. In total, they account for 16 percent of Japan's land area.

The idea of using the leisure and recreation expenditures of urbanites to revitalise depressed rural areas is eminently appealing – in theory, at least. In practice, however, some problems have already emerged. To begin with, there is the feeling that too many resorts of the same type are being developed. Most coastal resorts have marinas and golf courses, whilst mountain ones are largely concerned with winter sports, but also have their golf courses. Because of the nature of the facilities offered, the business of the new resorts is almost inevitably uneven and seasonal. There is concern that many of the younger generations are proving to be more attracted to the theme parks and recreational areas close to the urban fringe, whilst older people still prefer to go on group visits to established hot spring resorts and shrines (Photo 8.6). Thus, at present, supply in these new resort areas exceeds demand. In addition, there are the detrimental effects of the new developments. These include the escalation of land prices which, in turn, tend to put the squeeze on farming and

Photo 8.6 *Hot sand therapy at Ibusuki, Kyushu*

Tourism in the Shima Region

The development of multi-purpose tourism in the coast area of the Shima Region (Kinki)

Initially coastal settlements were based on fishing and farming; scenery, coastal inlets and sandy beaches attracted visitors by the 1920s as railways and excursion routes developed, making the area accessible to urban populations from the Osaka and Kyoto areas.

Fishing and farming activities have been increasingly modified to allow the development of the seasonal tourist industry. Females are mainly in charge of services and accommodation and men of transport, marine excursions and the preparation of seafood; e.g. fishing boats used for tourist trips in the morning and fishing in the evening. Rice transplanting and harvesting times have beem modified to avoid peak visitor times.

Distribution of tourist areas and development of transportation

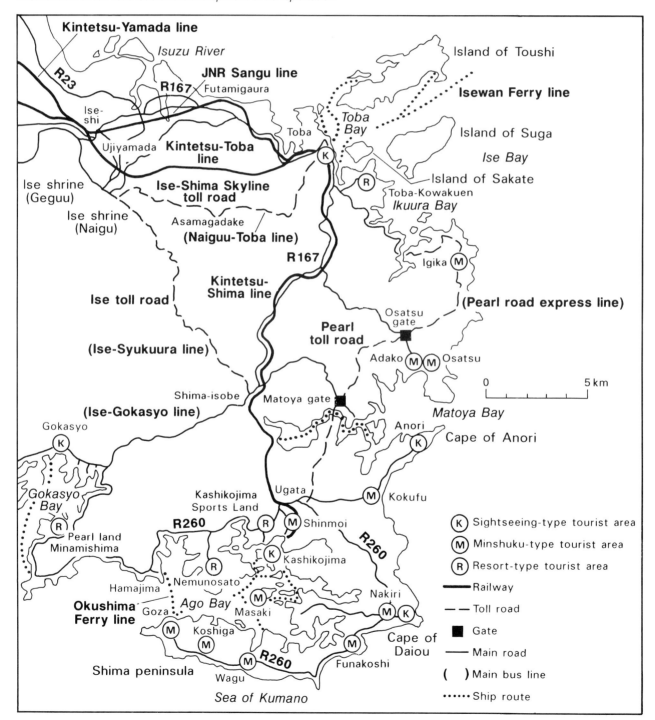

Figure 8.19

Types of tourist area in the coastal region of the Kinki District.

Type of tourist area	Main tourist attractions	Main tourist facilities
Sightseeing-type tourist area (K)	seaside landscape	inn, hotel
Shifting to resort-type tourist areas	seaside landscape sea bathing place (one or both)	inn, hotel, field sports facilities
Resort-type tourist area (R)	seaside landscape sea bathing place	hotel, rental villa, field and marine sports facilities
Minshuku-type tourist area (M)	sea bathing place	*minshuku**
Sightseeing and resort complex type tourist area (K R)	sea landscape sea bathing place	inn, hotel, rental villa, land and marine sports facilties
Sightseeing and *minshuku* complex type tourist area (K M)	sea landscape sea bathing place	inn, hotel, *minshuku*
Minshuku and resort complex type tourist area (M R)	sea landscape sea bathing place	*minshuku,* hotel, rental villa, land and marine sports facilities
Sightseeing, resort and *minshuku* complex type tourist area (K R M)	sea landscape sea bathing place	inn, hotel, *minshuku* rental villa, land and marine sports facilities

Note: K, R, M in table correspond to map
Minshuku – private and guest house accommodation

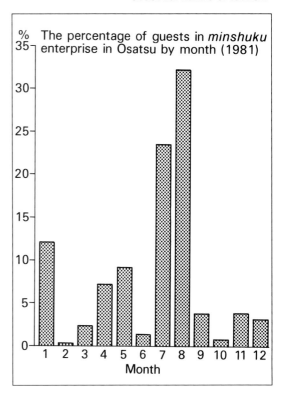

Seasonal nature of tourism

The percentage of guests in *minshuku* enterprise in Osatsu by month (1981)

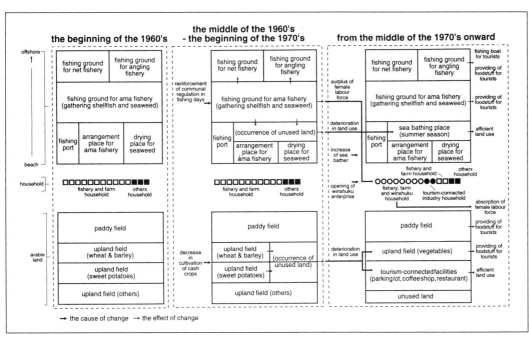

→ the cause of change   → the effect of change

Evolution of a mixed economy based on the development of tourist facilities alongside fishing and farming. Tourist facilities include – bathing, beaches, sightseeing, boat and fishing trips and good seafood plus hotel and guest house accommodation.

Development based on –

1 Natural resource attractions.

2 Local organisation of tourism backed by government financial support.

3 Adequate infrastructure.

4 Growing reputation for tourism.

forestry, and the environmental damage caused by construction of the required physical infrastructure – new roads, water supply and sewage disposal.

What is becoming increasingly evident, therefore, is that the speculative development triggered by the 1987 Law threatens to overwhelm the basic economic and social fabric of much of the countryside and to inflict irreparable environmental damage. But is this the cost of putting new life back into rural areas or is it possible to arrive at a more moderate and balanced mode of development? There are some signs that central and prefectural government are now beginning to ease back in the development of resort areas, trying to achieve a better matching of supply and demand and a better integration of the new tourism with the local economy. An illustration of how this can be achieved is to be found in the controlled and steady growth of coastal tourist areas in the Kinki district serving the very large urban populations of Osaka and Nagoya (Figure 8.19). Here the provision of coastal facilities has been carefully planned and controlled since the 1960s in reasonable harmony with the rise in demand. Certainly, the worst excesses of the speculative element have never arisen.

8.8 THE CHALLENGE

The problem confronting rural Japan today poses two related questions – how best to revive the rural economy and community, and how best to absorb the ever-spreading and infiltrating urban influences? It is clear that the traditional countryside will change irrevocably as urbanisation and modernisation processes diffuse further afield into the remoter and more peripheral parts of Japan. The challenge is to harness that change in such a way that there is still a viable economic role for the traditional activities of farming, fishing and forestry. Agriculture should be left to find its own niche in the market place. Continued government support on the grounds of national self-sufficiency is no longer tenable. If there is to be government intervention, then it would be better directed towards achieving a sustainable utilisation of fish and forest resources.

To these three traditional activities, new ones need to be added. These should not be confined merely to the provision of those services and facilities demanded by today's tourism and recreation; some modern manufacturing might also be sought. These economic goals then need to be fused and harmonised into a broader package which promises two things, namely a good quality of life for the local people and conservation of the natural environment. Achievement of the first will no doubt help persuade rural inhabitants to stay put and hopefully attract others in, whilst the second will safeguard what nurtures the most potent of today's urbanising influences, recreation and tourism.

9 *Recent trends in regional development*

9.1 THE CORE-PERIPHERY PATTERN OF HIGH-GROWTH JAPAN

It has been established in preceding chapters that the Japanese **space economy** – that is, the distributions of industrial development, GDP-generation, urbanisation and other facets of economic development – are very uneven. In fact, today's space economy shows the classic core-periphery structure, as it has done so for much of the country's history (Figure 4.10). The greater part of Japan's economic effort and prosperity has become concentrated in a relatively small part of the national territory, the **core**. In comparison, the remainder of Japan, the **periphery**, appears distinctly disadvantaged and second-class. Its share of national productivity is disproportionately small compared with its share of the national territory.

The distribution of population density is probably one of the best single indicators of the overall pattern of the space economy. Figure 9.1 shows the spatial imbalance typical of the core-periphery structure at a significant time in the postwar evolution of the Japanese space economy. In 1970, Japan was at the peak of the **high-growth** phase. Sixteen of the 47 prefectures showed mean population densities equal to, or greater than, the national average of 281 persons/km². Most striking was the confinement of these above-average densities within the Pacific Belt running along the southern coastlands of Honshu, extending westwards from Tokyo and spilling over onto northern Kyushu. The linearity of the core is one of its most unusual features; cores by definition are normally thought of as being circular in shape. Another noteworthy feature which persists today is the

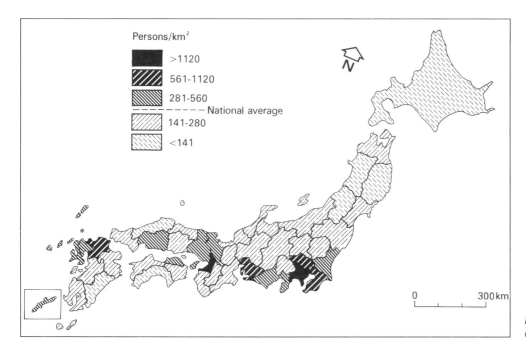

Fig. 9.1 *The distribution of population (1970)*

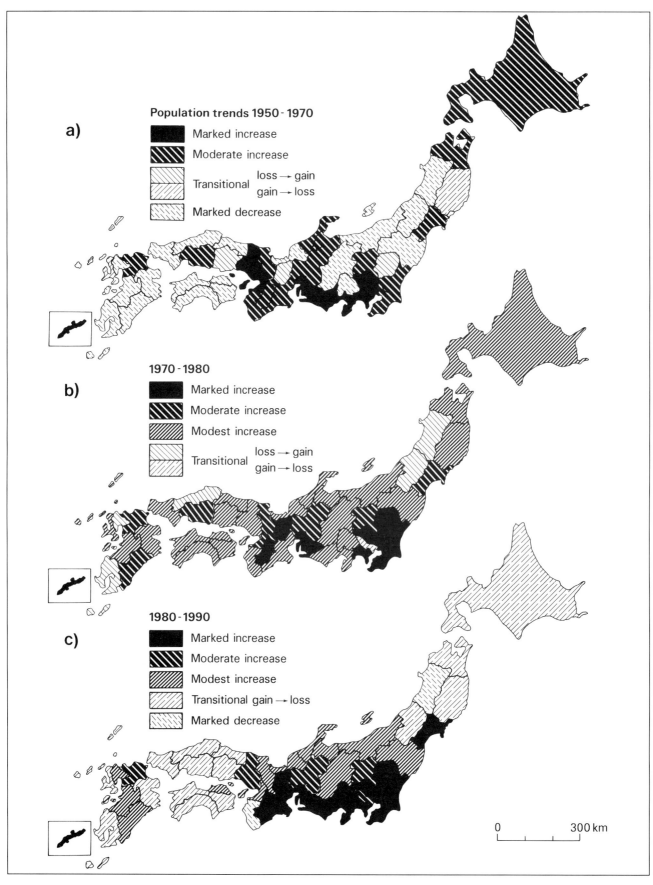

Fig. 9.2 *A summary of population trends (a) 1950-1970, (b) 1970 – 1980 and (c) 1980 – 1990*

uncvenness of development within it. At least four distinct nodes are in evidence along the corridor. From east to west, they are the urban agglomerations, the so-called metropolitan areas centering on (i) Tokyo-Yokohama, (ii) Nagoya, (iii) Osaka-Kyoto-Kobe, and (iv) Kitakyushu-Fukuoka (Figure 7.3).

Given this definition of the core, by implication the Japanese periphery may be defined as broadly comprising Hokkaido, northern Honshu, the interior mountains and Japan Sea coastlands of central and southern Honshu, Shikoku and the southern two-thirds of Kyushu (Figure 4.10). Over quite large areas, population densities in 1970 were less than half the national average (Figure 9.1).

The summary of population trends shown in Figure 9.2(a) indicates consolidation of the core, in demographic terms, during the period 1950 to 1970. The prefectures falling within the 'marked increase' category are those which for at least three of the four five-year intercensal periods recorded a rate of population growth above the national average ('moderate growth' is defined as persistent increase, but at a rate mainly below the national average). The **backwash** or draining effects of the core's development is clearly seen, in that sizable areas of the periphery showed a recurrent loss of population, particularly the 'backside' of Honshu, Shikoku and much of Kyushu. But not all parts of the periphery suffered in this way. Indeed, select areas appear to have been in rather better heart, as, for example, Hokkaido (under the stimulus of a succession of government development programmes) and certain parts of Honshu which were beginning to emerge as centres of industrial development, such as Hachinohe (Aomori), Sendai (Miyagi) and Hokuriku (Toyama and Ishikawa).

In the remainder of this chapter, the aim is to analyse what has happened to the core-periphery structure since 1970, which is taken as the benchmark of the high-growth phase. Has the advent of a prolonged period of 'low growth' altered the basic pattern in any way? Have the industrial restructuring (examined in Chapter 6) and the

urbanising influences (examined in Chapters 7 and 8) in any way altered the developmental gap between core and periphery through their progressive colonisation of remoter rural areas? If changes are found to have occurred in the geographical pattern and balance of the space economy, do these changes mirror what is anticipated in the models of regional development theory? And, does current regional theory fully explain these changes?

9.2 CHANGING NATIONAL PATTERNS SINCE 1970

The first task is to establish the extent to which the basic pattern of the Japanese space economy has changed since 1970. The pattern will be investigated in terms of five different criteria: population growth, net migration, GDP growth, urbanisation and prefectural capital city primacy.

Population growth

Figures 9.2(b) and (c) summarise population trends during two decades. During the 1970s there is clear evidence of population growth in the core, particularly around Tokyo, Nagoya and the Hanshin centres of Osaka, Kyoto and Kobe. However, looking at the situation for the country as a whole, it would seem that 1970 was something of an important turning-point in the demographic fortunes of many prefectures. Whilst 20 prefectures lost population between 1965 and 1970, only five did so between 1970 and 1975 and only one between 1975 and 1980. Indeed, for the first time in the postwar period, all parts of the Japanese periphery sustained an increase in population for at least five years. Thus, despite continuing increments of population in the linear core (with the notable exception of Tokyo prefecture which actually lost population), the signs at the end of the 1970s were of a shift towards a more open, more uniform pattern of population change than hitherto. The basic question arises – did this change in the pattern of population growth mark the beginnings of a **spread effect**, in which

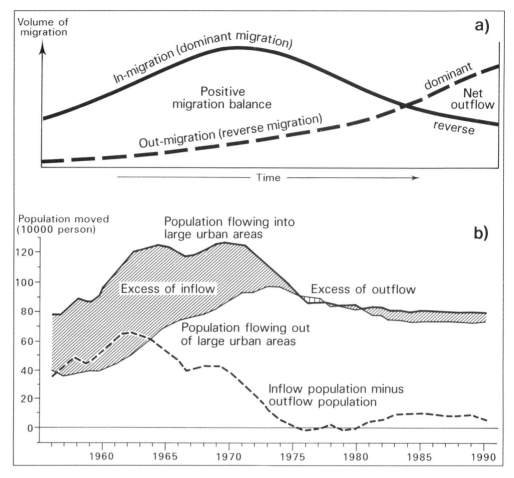

Fig. 9.3 *The changing balance between dominant and reverse migration: (a) the model and (b) the Japanese experience*

growth would be transmitted from the core to adjacent parts of the periphery?

The question is partly answered by Figure 9.2(c) which clearly shows that during the 1980s most parts of the periphery returned to a situation of population decline. The only exceptions were the extreme south of Tohoku, the Japan Sea coast of central Honshu and parts of southern Kyushu. However, the outstanding feature of the 1980s was the re-emphasis of population growth in the core, particularly in the eastern section between Tokyo and Osaka. The picture is clearly one of growth polarising around the major cities in the form of suburbs and dormitory settlements reaching ever further out into the countryside. The combination of above-average rates of population growth in the core and widespread population loss in the periphery leads to the conclusion that **backwash** has once again became the dominant process of the space economy. In retrospect, the demographic events of the 1970s may now be seen as nothing more than a temporary relapse

in the long-term advance of the core at the expense of the periphery.

Net migration

Population change is the outcome of two components, natural increase and net migration. In the context of this analysis, it is important to establish the scale and character of the latter, since the movement of people may be taken as an indicator of backwash and spread effects. Migration is rarely a wholly one-way traffic; most often, there will be movements in both directions between any two places. Thus, migration is to be seen as having two components: a larger flow, referred to as the **dominant migration** and a lesser flow in the opposite direction, known as **reverse migration** (Figure 9.3).

Figure 9.3(a) models the postwar experience of many core regions in developed countries, with a fundamental change taking place in the balance of inward and outward movement. A phase in which the dominant migration was inwards and the migration balance positive has been succeeded by one in which there is increasing net outflow. Research has clearly shown that in Japan's case the dominant migration during the 1950s and 1960s was towards the core and that, by comparison, reverse migration from the core to the periphery was extremely weak (Figure 9.3(b)). However, during the early 1970s the situation began to change, in that the volume of dominant migration began to slacken off, whilst reverse migration steadily strengthened. For a while, in the mid-1970s, there was in fact a net outflow from the major urban areas of the core. Since 1980, however, the situation appears to have stabilised somewhat with the persistence of a small positive migration balance.

Taking a rather broader view, and looking at trends in migration balances at a prefectural level over a 20-year period, the situation in the core might at first sight seem confusing with apparently contradictory trends being shown (Figure 9.4). However, the significant point is that Tokyo prefecture experienced a persistently negative migration balance, whilst in Osaka and Kyoto prefectures the balance changed from gain to loss. All this supports the point made in Chapter 7.1, concerning the onset of decentralisation from these three leading cities. The fluctuating balances of Aichi and Hyogo prefectures, dipping from gain to loss and back, also suggests a temporary surge of outward movement from the cities of Nagoya and Kobe respectively. Consistent with this idea of a growing tide of out-migration from the largest cities are the persistently positive migration balances of those prefectures around Tokyo and adjacent to Osaka and Kyoto. Similarly, the shift to migration gain in Gumma and Yamanashi prefectures, both within commuting reach of Tokyo and Yokohama respectively, supports the idea of outward-moving ripples of suburbanisation.

As for the periphery, only one peripheral prefecture, Miyagi, achieved a turnaround in its migration balance from loss to gain. But here and there, notably in southern Kyushu, northern Shikoku and along the Japan Sea coast, some prefectures showed a migration balance fluctuating from loss to gain and back.

The main conclusion to be derived from Figure 9.4 is that there is no evidence of a significant spread effect from core to periphery. The volume of reverse migration may have increased during the two decades, but peripheral migration balances are still negative and the dominant migration remains from periphery to core. The more conspicuous outward movement during these two decades was the

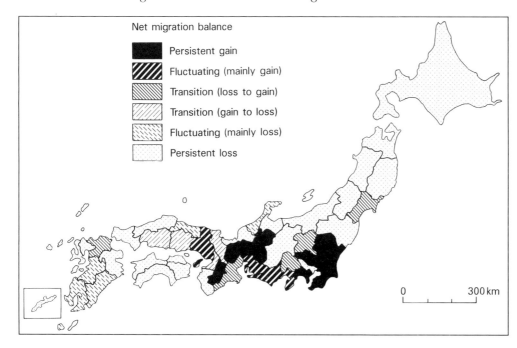

Net migration balance

- Persistent gain
- Fluctuating (mainly gain)
- Transition (loss to gain)
- Transition (gain to loss)
- Fluctuating (mainly loss)
- Persistent loss

0   300 km

Fig. 9.4 *The changing pattern of net migration (1970 – 1990)*

short-distance dispersal of people living in the largest cities towards the suburban margins and dormitory settlements beyond.

Gross Domestic Product growth

Of the many measures that might be used to monitor the changing pattern of economic productivity within Japan none is better than Gross Domestic Product (GDP) at a prefectural level. As a measure, it has the advantage of taking into account all three major economic sectors. In the following analysis, two snapshots have been taken – one in the late 1970s and the other in the late 1980s (Figure 9.5). In both cases, the mean annual rate of growth in GDP in each prefecture over a period of three years is compared with the national average. A fourfold classification is derived using the mean and plus and minus one standard deviation. It is assumed that spread effects would be indicated where peripheral prefectures showed rates of GDP growth above the national average.

Figure 9.5(a) shows the situation at a time when Japan was suffering from the two Oil Shocks, and yet there was a surprising amount of above-average growth in many parts of the periphery – Hokkaido, Miyagi (northern Honshu), in the Hokuriku district, in northern Shikoku and over much of Kyushu (particularly in Oita prefecture). However, remote parts of the periphery, such as stretches of the Japan Sea coast of Honshu, southern Shikoku and the extreme south of Kyushu are shown to have been significantly lagging in terms of growth. In contrast, it is interesting to note that, with the exception of Kyoto, the highest rates were not experienced by prefectures containing the leading cities of the core. By far the most impressive concentration of such growth occurred within the orbit of Tokyo, but towards the margins of the National Capital Region (NCR). This would suggest a localised spread effect, of growth rippling out from the capital.

Figure 9.5(b) paints a generally gloomier picture, with Japan well entrenched in its low-growth mode. The national mean annual rate of GDP growth was one percentage point lower than it had been a decade earlier. The situation in the periphery appears rather mixed. Although there was growth throughout the periphery, in many parts it was growth at a rate below the national average and substantially below what had previously prevailed. Hokkaido appears to have slipped in growth terms, as also the Japan Sea coast of Tohoku and southern Kyushu. Some compensation was to be found in isolated pockets of peripheral growth as along the Japan Sea coast of southern Honshu (Ishikawa and Tottori prefectures), eastern Shikoku (Kagawa and Tokushima) and eastern Kyushu (Oita). Perhaps more surprising was that the San-yo section of the linear core beyond Kobe continued to show only modest growth. As in the 1970s, the NCR remained the number one growth area, except that the growth now also involved the more central prefectures (Saitama, Tokyo and Kanagawa) and spilled westwards (Shizuoka) towards Nagoya. The overall impression, therefore, is that whilst the core, especially its eastern section, remained as dynamic as ever, there were a few emerging growth points within an otherwise lagging periphery.

Urbanisation

The next measure to be used in this analysis is the degree of urbanisation. It is a good measure because, given the multi-dimensional nature of the process, it takes into account significant demographic and economic aspects of development. In the case of the latter, it reflects the relative importance of manufacturing and services in the overall economy. For the purposes of this exercise, as in Chapter 7, the degree of urbanisation is measured in terms of the percentage of a prefecture's population which is city-living, a city (or shi) being generally defined as a settlement with a population greater than 30 000 persons.

Looking at the pattern of urbanisation in 1970, and focusing on those prefectures recording values in excess of the upper quartile (i.e. more than 68 percent urban), it does not require too much imagination to pick out the linear

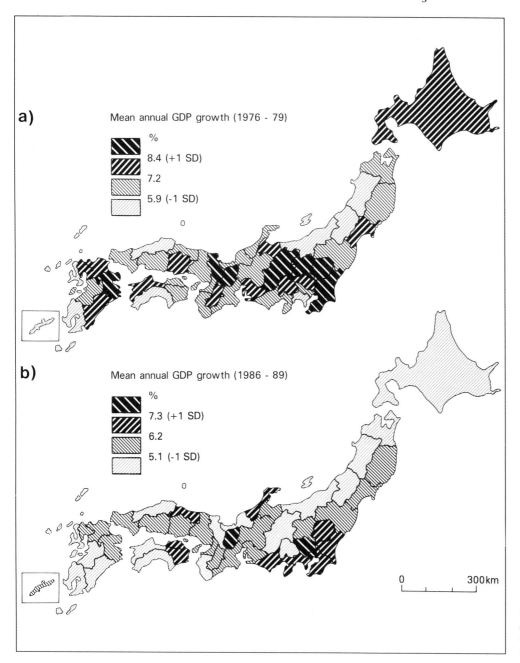

Fig. 9.5 *The changing patterns of GDP in (a) the late 1970s, and (b) the late 1980s*

core (Figure 9.6). All but one of the prefectures showing this high degree of urbanisation fell within the corridor. The one exception was Toyama, part of the Hokuriku industrial region on the Japan Sea coast. But the occurrence of prefectures with values within the upper quartile range was hardly confined to the core at all. Quite clearly, extensive tracts of the periphery had already achieved significant levels of urbanisation. What needs to be pointed out, however, is that these prefectures were not necessarily highly and widely urbanised in quite the same sense as many of the high-scoring core

prefectures containing Japan's leading cities. In these more peripheral locations, the high values tend to reflect the existence in those prefectures of an all-dominating, primate capital city set in a relatively sparsely populated context (see next section). The rather inhospitable and thinly-populated prefecture of Ishikawa on the Japan Sea coast is one such example, with its long-established capital city of Kanazawa accounting for over half the prefecture's urban population. So the distinction to be made is broadly between the rather widespread, comprehensive urbanisation typifying the core and the highly-

163

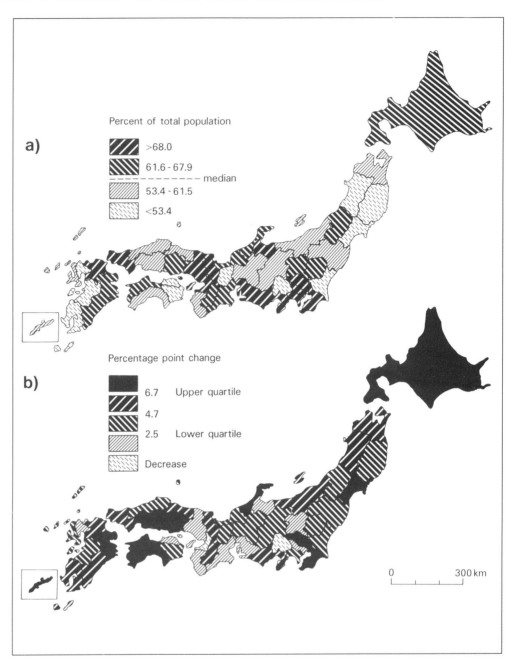

Fig. 9.6 (a) The distribution of urban population (1970); (b) change in urban population (1970 – 1990)

localised urbanisation more characteristic of peripheral prefectures.

What has happened since 1970? Figure 9.6(b) shows percentage point changes in the degree of urbanisation. There is some evidence of further urbanisation within the core, as for example around Tokyo, in the rural break between Yokohama and Nagoya, between Osaka and Kyoto and, perhaps more significant, a firmer definition of the western end of the core corridor between Kobe and northern Kyushu. Two prefectures actually experienced a decline in the degree of urbanisation, but for different reasons. In the case of Osaka prefecture, it was due to the decentralisation of population away from Osaka city and into adjacent prefectures. In Yamanashi's case, it was more a case of people moving away from that prefecture's small cities and into the nearby major cities of the core. But the feature of greatest importance shown by Figure 9.6(b) is the quite substantial increase in the level of urbanisation in the periphery, notably in Hokkaido, northern Honshu, along sections of the Japan Sea coast, in parts of Shikoku and southern Kyushu. Certainly, this evidence may be taken

Fig. 9.7 *The capital city primacy multiplier*

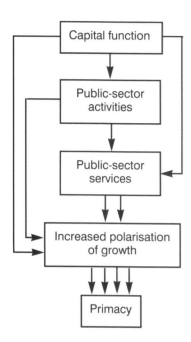

as a signal of peripheral economic development, at least in the sense of shifting the emphasis away from agriculture towards city-based manufacturing and services.

Prefectural capital city primacy

Mention was made a little earlier to one of the characteristics of Japan's urban geography, namely the **primacy** of many of the prefectural capital cities. The system of government in Japan means that much of the day-to-day running of the country is conducted at a prefectural level. One immediate consequence is the generation of considerable amounts of public-sector employment, most of which is concentrated in the prefectural capital cities. This agglomeration of public-sector employment, in its turn, has a markedknock-on effect (Figure 9.7). It encourages the polarisation of a wide diversity of private-sector employment of a tertiary and quaternary calibre. The net result of this cumulative causation is to inflate the significance and status of the prefectural capital cities in the Japanese urban system. In arithmetic terms, the size of the capital size is more than twice that of the second-ranked city. In short, the government arrangements encourage the prefectural capitals to assume a degree of primacy, to stand literally head and shoulders above the rest of the prefectural urban system. In 1970, for example, in nine of the prefectures, the prefectural capital city accounted for over one-half of the total urban population, a situation most commonly, but not exclusively, encountered in those prefectures containing the largest cities (Figure 9.8(a)). The prefectural capitals of Shikoku and Hokkaido are an obvious exception (Photo 9.1). Looking further down the scale, there were a further 23 prefectures where the capital city accommodated more than 30 percent of the urban population. The prefectures figuring in this category were certainly by no means all highly urbanised, this being the case with the peripheral prefectures in Kyushu and along parts of the Japan Sea coast of Honshu.

Turning to Figure 9.8(b), it is apparent that in all but 13 of the prefectures, the capital city increased its share of the urban population. Most of these exceptions were the prefectures containing the largest cities of the core, most notably Tokyo, Yokohama (Kanagawa), Nagoya (Aichi), Kyoto and Osaka. Two peripheral capitals also fell in this category, namely Kanazawa (Ishikawa) and Sendai (Miyagi). Another interesting feature revealed by Figure 9.8(b) is the occurrence of the highest percentage point changes (i.e. the greatest increases in primacy) in two type locations: in the less-developed parts of the core corridor (Shizuoka, Okayama and Hiroshima) and in most parts of the periphery. The increase in Hokkaido, Shikoku and Kyushu were particularly marked. What this evidence confirms, therefore, is the occurrence of growth in the periphery and the increasing polarisation of that growth around the prefectural capital cities.

9.3 CORE-PERIPHERY CHANGES

Pulling together the five strands of evidence considered during the preceding section, as well as relevant observations made in the preceding three chapters, it is possible to derive the following conclusions about changes in the core-periphery structure of Japan between 1970 and 1990. The demographic evidence of popula-

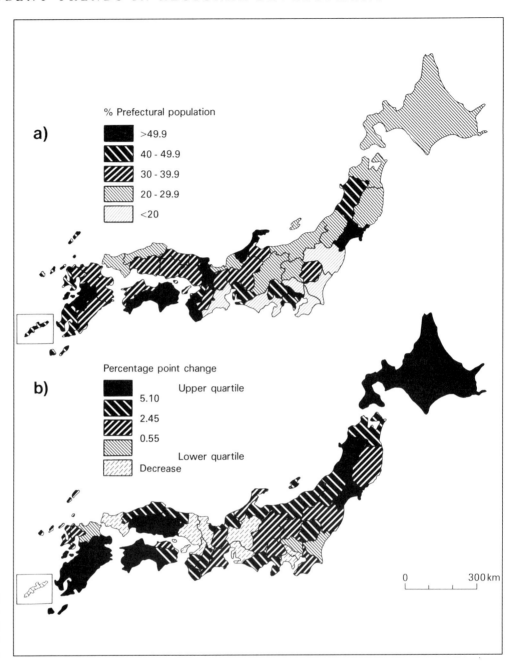

Fig. 9.8 (a) Prefectural capital primacy 1970); (b) change in prefectural capital primacy (1970 – 1990)

tion change and net migration suggests that, although there was a temporary respite in the 1970s, the developmental gap between the core and the periphery may well have continued slowly to widen (Figures 9.2 and 9.4). The core may still be gaining ground seemingly at the expense of the periphery. Despite the growing volume of reverse migration, there is nothing to support the idea that spread effects may have already set in. But whilst the periphery may have slipped even further behind in population terms, at least there was some economic growth. Indeed, the analysis of GDP growth revealed the existence of some possible growth points within favoured parts of the periphery (Figure 9.5). The last two analyses throw some light on the nature of this peripheral growth, such as it is. The rising levels of urbanisation suggest that there has been some displacement of farming by the expansion of manufacturing and tertiary services (Figure 9.6). The analysis of prefectural capital city primacy clearly indicates that the development has such has been very much focussed on the capital cities of the periphery (Figure 9.8). It may well be the case, therefore, that these cities are

Photo 9.1 *Sapporo, one of the primate capitals of the Japanese periphery*

exerting their own local backwash effects. They have been drawing their growth from adjacent rural areas and smaller urban centres within their administrative orbits.

The whole question of possible changes in the balance between core and periphery and the developmental gap that separates them may be pursued further and perhaps more precisely. Using measures broadly similar to those already considered, taken mainly from the Japanese Census, it is possible to monitor the general performance of the core in a national context. This is simply done by calculating the core's share of national phenomena at five-yearly intervals. The basis of the argument is simply that that any increase in the core's share can be taken as indicating a widening of the developmental gap.

Before embarking on this analysis, however, it is first necessary to delimit in precise terms the extent of the Japanese core. Where one draws the boundaries is a potentially contentious matter, since there is likely to be much disagreement as to which prefectures are included and which are thought to lie outside. Everyone would agree about including prefectures like Tokyo, Kanagawa, Aichi, Kyoto, Hyogo and Fukuoka, but what about the prefectures, such as Mie, Nara, Shiga and Yamaguchi which link them together to form the continuous corridor? Rather than become embroiled in a prolonged debate, for the purposes of this analysis, the core has simply been defined in terms of 17 prefectures (Figure 9.9). In doing this, one important point is acknowledged, namely that the extent of the core may well have increased during the 30 years. It is conceded, for example, that there has been a westwards extension of the core corridor from Kobe to Fukuoka, encouraged no doubt by the completion of that stretch of the Tokaido *shinkansen* in 1975. It is interesting to reflect that this area was the original core region at the beginning of the Tokugawa period (see Chapter 3).

A fundamental point to be borne in mind when looking at Table 9.1 is that

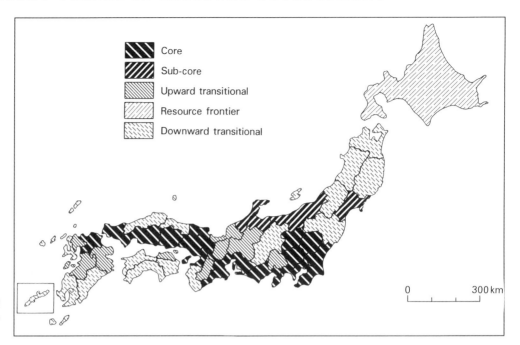

Fig. 9.9 *The regional development pattern (1990)*

the 17 prefectures of the core account for only 25 percent of the national territory. The fact that only one of the percentage values dips below 60 percent is, in itself, a clear marker of the degree of polarisation and the extent to which the core dominates the space economy. The picture given by Table 9.1 is rather clouded, but it would seem that two broad observations might be made. First, there does not appear to have been any substantial change in the overall balance of the core-periphery structure during this 30-year period. In other words, there are no clear indications of a spread effect really getting under way. Secondly, all the measures do indicate a slight wavering in the dominance of the core. But there is little consistency in the actual timing, except that in general it appears to have happened in the second half of the period. Only one measure, the percentage of GDP, shows a consistent decline in the core's

share over the last 20 years.

Returning to the indicators discussed in 9.2, three significant features of the core itself are revealed. First, there is the unevenness of development within it (Figure 9.5). The Tokyo region represents the dominant and eccentrically located node, whilst the section west of Kobe remains relatively undeveloped. Secondly, in the eastern section, there is firm evidence that the largest cities are beginning to experience decentralisation (Figures 9.4 and 9.6). But it would seem to be an outward movement of residential population rather than a serious dispersal of high-order urban functions (see Chapter 7). Some of this urban growth may be overspilling into adjacent peripheral prefectures, such as Fukushima and Yamanashi, and may in fact represent an incipient spread effect. Thirdly, the nature of developments within the western section of the core bear a fairly close resemblance to what is happening in the periphery, namely rising levels of urbanisation and an increasing polarisation of growth in the prefectural capital city (Figures 9.6 and 9.8).

9.4 EXPLAINING PERIPHERAL GROWTH

Although the conclusion has been reached that there has been little if any change in the overall distribution of

Table 9.1 *Some indices of the status of the Japanese core (1960–1990)*

	1960	1965	1970	1975	1980	1985	1990
			(percentage share of national total)				
Total population	60.6	58.9	61.4	62.3	64.7	62.9	63.4
Preferectural in-migration	75.4	74.6	75.0	70.4	70.1	71.1	70.7
Urban population	65.7	67.5	68.9	69.3	69.1	65.1	66.9
GDP	71.5	71.7	72.5	71.0	68.0	69.7	69.4

growth in Japan during the last four decades, the plight of the periphery has not been one of total gloom and despondency. Indeed, the analyses of GDP growth and urbanisation have indicated the occurrence of pockets of hope – prefectures and cities which have been doing rather better than the peripheral average. It may well be that these represent important growth-points in the making; nodes that will play a crucial part in triggering a general raising of the fortunes of the Japanese periphery. Given their possible future role, it is important that the reasons for this localised peripheral growth are understood and seen in the context of regional development theory.

As regards the relationship between what has been observed as happening in Japan and what is stated in regional development theory, it would seem that during the 1970s and 1980s Japan started to graduate from Stage 2 to Stage 3 of Friedmann's development model (Figure 9.10). Although the national core remained strong and unchallenged, there slowly began to emerge this small number of peripheral growth-points – sub-cores of increasing status. The slowness of the transition is possibly partly the result of the core's shape and internal pattern. Its linearity, the off-centre location of its major nucleus, and the discontinuous nature of growth along its length have left plenty of space for 'in situ' growth. In short, there has been more scope for accommodating growth than had the core been circular in shape and tightly wrapped around by the periphery.

Spread effects

So how has this peripheral growth come about? Is it because Japan is approaching the stage in the development of its space economy where, at a national level, spread effects begin to outweigh backwash and there is decentralisation (Figure 9.11)? The body of evidence considered in this analysis does not lend much support to this explanation. At most, what can be detected are some localised **upward transitional areas** immediately adjacent to the the more dynamic and congested parts of the core (Figure 9.9). The peripheral prefectures of Yamanashi, Gifu, Nara, Shiga, Kagawa, Saga and Oita probably represent a small number of locations where core growth has simply overspilled or rubbed off. But what about the growth in prefectures, such as Miyagi in Tohoku and Niigata, Toyama and Ishikawa along the Japan Sea coast? These are effectively detached from the core? It is probably safest to regard these as defining two sub-cores, Sendai and the

Stage 1. Relatively independent local centres; no hierarchy. Typical pre-industrial structure; each city lies at the centre of a small regional enclave.

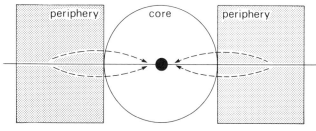

Stage 2. A single strong core. Typical of period of incipient industrialisation; a periphery emerges; potential entrepreneurs and labour move to the core, national economy is virtually reduced to a single metropolitan region.

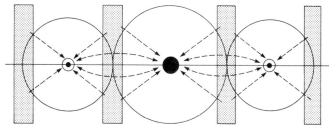

Stage 3. A single national core, strong peripheral sub-cores. During the period of industrial maturity, secondary cores form, thereby reducing the periphery on a national scale to smaller intermetropolitan peripheries.

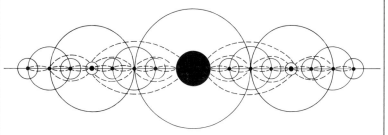

Stage 4. A functional interdependent system of cities. Organized complexity characterised by national integration, efficiency in location, maximum growth potential.

Fig. 9.10 Friedmann's development model

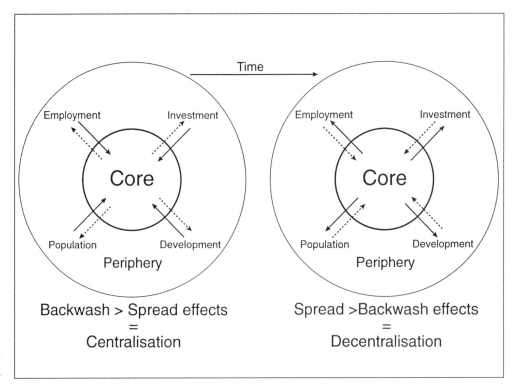

Fig. 9.11 *Model of the changing balance between core and periphery*

Hokuriku region, which have developed during the postwar period in response to government direction and improved accessibility.

Government intervention

Earlier chapters have revealed that the Japanese space economy has been the target of considerable government intervention aimed at correcting core-periphery imbalance. The four national plans adopted since 1962 have all striven in various ways to spread growth more evenly across the country. Certainly, a number of the peripheral growth areas coincide with locations chosen by the Japanese Government for special development. For example, the growth sustained in central Hokkaido, at Sendai (Miyagi), Niigata and Toyama-Takaoka can be linked to their designation as New Industrial Cities in the early 1960s. Likewise, growth at Toyo and Tokushima (Shikoku) and at Oita (Kyushu) no doubt springs in part from their status, established in 1969, as Special Areas for Industrial Consolidation (Figure 6.8). It was concluded in Chapter 6 that these attempts and the more recent technopolis projects, whilst they have undoubtedly brought new manufacturing to the periphery, have achieved little in terms

of altering the long-established regional shares of manufacturing.

But perhaps potentially the most effective intervention yet made by the Japanese Government has been its financial support of major transport developments. The three *shinkansen* emanating from Tokyo have contributed much (Figure 6.3). The Tokaido *shinkansen* has helped to extend the core corridor westwards to embrace northern Kyushu; the Joetsu *shinkansen* to Niigata has provided a boost to the Hokuriku district, whilst the Tohoku *shinkansen* has done much for Sendai and for bringing northern Honshu and Hokkaido 'closer' to the core. Less spectacular, but no less important in terms of improving accessibility, have been the belated upgrading of the trunk railway system and the construction of an expressway network reaching out to the periphery (Figure 9.12). Much has also been done to overcome the insularity of the periphery. Kyushu is now directly linked to Honshu by road and rail tunnels. The Seikan Tunnel, the longest tunnel in the world and opened in 1989, now provides a direct rail link to Hokkaido, whilst in 1990 the first of three separate 'island-hopping' bridge links planned for Shikoku and Honshu was completed (Photo 1.11). One can only admire these ambitious civil

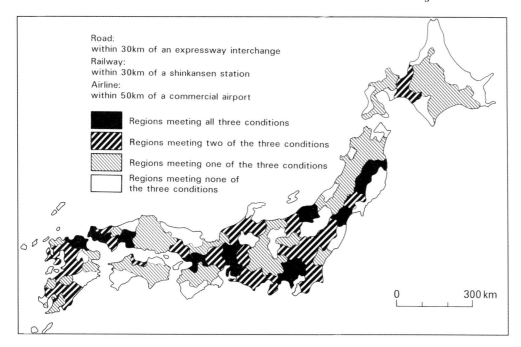

Road:
within 30km of an expressway interchange
Railway:
within 30km of a shinkansen station
Airline:
within 50km of a commercial airport

■ Regions meeting all three conditions

▨ Regions meeting two of the three conditions

▨ Regions meeting one of the three conditions

□ Regions meeting none of
the three conditions

0   300 km

Fig. 9.12 Accessibility of transportation

engineering projects – no challenge seems too great. Quite clearly, although late in coming, these island links and the general improvement of the transport infrastructure promise much for the periphery, if only because they all serve to reduce its fundamental weakness – its inaccessibility.

Resource frontier role

One possible explanation of peripheral growth offered by regional theory is that continuing growth in the core generates demands that the core itself cannot fully satisfy. Indeed, the traditional role of the periphery and of **downward transitional areas**, is that of having their resources exploited for the benefit of the core. But this is not sufficient to qualify as, what theory calls, **a resource frontier**; the area has to be one where new resources are being discovered and exploited. The part of the periphery which comes closest to that rather more exacting definition is Hokkaido, by virtue of the fact that much of it is still at the pioneering stage. During the postwar period, it has done much to satisfy the changing eating habits of the urbanites of the core (see Chapter 8). Hokkaido has become important for the growth of temperate cereals and root crops, as well as for livestock-rearing and dairying. The great potential of the island within the realms of tourism has also

begun to be exploited as the traditionally workaholic Japanese gradually gain a taste for leisure. It has much wilderness to offer; it has a rapidly-developing winter sports industry and many hot-spring resorts It is perhaps this tourist element of Hokkaido's economy which has benefitted most from the general improvements in accessibility just discussed. It now has an international airport, a direct rail link to Tokyo and good expressway connections interrupted only by the efficient ferry services between Aomori and Hakodate. Clearly, these improvements have facilitated the resource-frontier role as a whole.

Prefectural initiatives

Whilst there is irrefutable evidence of increased resource exploitation in much of the periphery, and localised upward transition in some areas immediately adjacent to the core, there are also certain types of recent growth that cannot be explained in this way or in terms of the impact of government intervention. For example, much of Kyushu is rapidly gaining the reputation of 'sunrise' or 'sunbelt' island. Old cities such as Kagoshima, Kumamoto and Oita are fast becoming important centres of high-tech industry, marketing their output internationally rather than nationally (Figure 6.9).

It is developments such as these that lead us to consider the possibility that there may have been a fourth trigger mechanism playing a part in stimulating peripheral growth, a mechanism that could well be unique to Japan. Unlike the previous explanations, this one develops from the idea that the stimulus may have come from within, rather than from outside, the periphery. So what is the mechanism, what is the evidence for it and why might it have occurred in Japan? The answers to all three questions are to be found in the prefectural system of government and in the postwar reform of that system. As a result of the latter, prefectures now enjoy a greater degree of autonomy. In practice, this means that any prefecture – whether it be in the core or the periphery – has the opportunity and the incentive to pursue its own economic ambitions. They are even encouraged in these matters by central government.

It has already been pointed out that the prefectural system has encouraged the primate growth of prefectural capital cities (9.2). It has also been shown that much peripheral growth has become polarised in these capitals. In addition to all this, it can be demonstrated that some of the more ambitious and enterprising prefectural governments have deliberately promoted their capital cities above and beyond the normal level of polarisation. They have done much, largely through investment in basic infrastructure, to make their capitals attractive to the propulsive high-tech industries and to high-order quaternary activities. This is well demonstrated by Sendai, the capital of Miyagi, which now merits the status of sub-core (Figure 9.9). Investments made there include the construction of a major airport, a subway system, expressways and business parks, as well as the encouragement of R and D links between industry and the science departments of its prestigious Tohoku University.

Unfortunately, this particular growth mechanism appears to have one serious snag. In the short-term, these artificially nurtured capital cities have been creating their own local backwash effects rather than attracting growth from the core. In other words, they have tended to grow, initially at least, at the expense of lesser urban centres and rural areas within their administrative orbits. They have created their own peripheries.

The challenges

Clearly, much has yet to be done if Japan is to realise the basic aim of all its postwar national plans, namely to achieve a much more equitable spatial distribution of growth. Stage 4 of Friedmann's model, with its promise of national economic unity and territorial justice, remains a long way off (Figure 9.10). Japan continues to be characterised by a two-class spatial society, of the 'haves' and 'have nots', of the core and the periphery. Reducing, if not eliminating, this distinction at a national level is seen to be a major challenge. No less critical, however, is the need to overcome the primacy and dominance of the prefectural capital cities located in the periphery and to encourage a spread effect from these mini growth-points to even less-developed parts of the periphery – the truly downward transitional areas (Figure 9.9).

But what should the Government's strategy be? Should it allow the national core and the prefectural capitals of the periphery a free rein in the hope that, as the model seems to promise, eventually they will generate spread effects which reduce core-periphery imbalances? Or should there be even more decisive intervention of a corrective kind? No matter what the answers to these questions might be, one is bound to ask whether the ideal of even growth is really attainable. Surely, the geographical reality is that, since no two places are alike in terms of resource potential, there will always be an unevenness in regional development. No matter how hard a government might strive to the contrary, the spatial patterns of development and economic wealth will always show the existence of cores and peripheries at a range of scales.

The new Japanese empire: face regained

10 Overseas trade

$$\text{C H A P T E R}$$

10.1 NO NATION IS AN ISLAND

The poet John Donne, writing at the turn of the 17th century, stated that "No man is an island, entire of itself." Whilst that comment is no less true today, it applies as much to human groups as it does to individual people. For example, it is virtually impossible for the small ethnic minority of some inner-city area to isolate itself completely from the rest of the urban community around it. Contact is inevitable through such day-to-day activities as work, shopping and education. Similarly, at the other end of the scale, rarely is it possible for a nation to seal itself off entirely from the rest of

Fig. 10.1 *The growth of the Japanese Empire (1861 – 1945)*

the global community. Self-imposed isolation is simply not a viable option for any nation with ambitions in terms of economic development and political survival. The reasons for this will be explained in more detail shortly. For the moment, it is sufficient to say that, since no country possesses all the resources necessary for balanced development, there will, to varying degrees, be a dependence on overseas trade to make good what is lacking. Similarly, few countries are able properly to defend themselves in military terms. The need for collective security and to deter potential aggressors will most likely lead to the formation of defensive pacts with other countries.

This idea that no nation is an island has a particular relevance in the case of Japan. First, and most obviously, because of its location offshore from the Asian continent, Japan literally is an island nation. Secondly, because it is a nation born from the political welding together of some three thousand islands. In this sense, then, Japan is a supreme example of a nation of islands.

Thirdly, as was indicated in Chapter 3, for some 250 years (spanning from the early 17th century), Japan lived in self-imposed isolation. In that time, two particularly noteworthy things happened. Japan gained in terms of national unity, but it lost in terms of technological and economic progress. Whilst it closed its doors to the rest of the world, great strides were being taken in the West. Amongst these were advances in agriculture and industry which, in turn, gave rise to large-scale urbanisation. Progress in military technology (in armaments and warships), coupled with the needs of expanding industrial economies (raw materials, food and markets) had led some countries, notably Britain, France and Spain, gradually to acquire large overseas empires. Indeed, by the mid-19th century, Japan itself was under threat as a potential colony. The history of Japan during this time, then, clearly highlights the two main costs of isolation. Not only did Japan lag increasingly behind the leading nations of the global community, but its ignorance of new technologies (economic and military) made it increasingly vulnerable to annexation by those countries – its very survival as a nation became threatened.

Between the Meiji Restoration (1868) and the end of the Second World War (1945), Japan made strenuous efforts to catch up with the West, particularly so far as industrialisation and military know-how were concerned (Chapter 4). The expansion of industry created demands for fuel and raw materials which could no longer be met entirely from within Japan's boundaries. As a result, Japan turned her attention more and more to overseas sources of supply. An increasing population needed to be fed. The poor productivity of Japanese agriculture likewise led to a search overseas for much-needed foods such as rice and soya. But rather than seek these things through the peaceful medium of trade, Japan sought to acquire the overseas areas that produced them. The first major annexation was of Taiwan (1895); this was followed by Korea (1910) and Manchuria (1932). By the early 1940s, the Japanese Empire accounted for a very large area of East and South East Asia (Figure 10.1). Clearly, Japan quickly discovered the benefits to be gained from ceasing its insular existence. By the adoption of a more outward looking perspective, and through its economic and military strength, Japan soon became one of the world's leading powers.

10.2 THE POSTWAR EXTERNAL GEOGRAPHY

Comprehensive defeat in the summer of 1945 saw the end of Japan as a major military power. However, some 45 years on, Japan is back as a leading figure on the world stage. But this time, its status derives almost exclusively from its economic achievements. Today, a whole range of measures all indicate that the Japanese economy is second only to that of the United States in terms of its wealth and strength (Table 1.1). The postwar recovery of Japan, particularly of its economy, has been truly miraculous (Chapter 5). Success has been closely tied to the gradual emergence of what is best described as an ever-growing **external geography**. The Japanese economy reaches out to an increasing number of countries. Through the vital linkages of trade, investment and aid, the economy draws more and more of its energy and growth (Figure 10.2). They tap the world of economic opportunities (Photo 10.1). Through them, Japan has become the focal point of an economic system which extends well beyond its shores. Indeed, this external geography now embraces much of the globe. Its emergence simply reflects what have become outstanding characteristics of the Japanese economy today, namely a high degree of **internationalisation** and a progressive move offshore. Japan now commands a new empire, an economic one, and in so doing has regained face in the eyes of the global community.

Fig. 10.2. *Components of Japan's external geography*

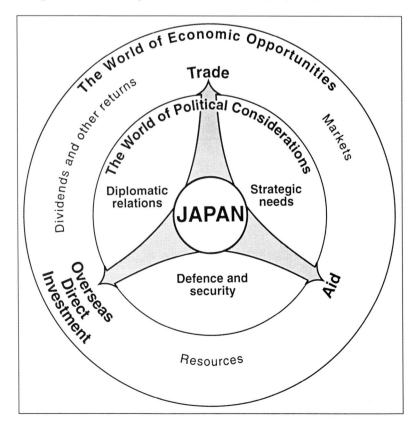

London Road site, Reading University, owned by a Japanese company

Japanese development worker discussing a rice project in Zambia

Loading containers for export

Photo 10.1 *The three overseas links – trade, investment and aid*

Of the three life-support systems which maintain this external geography, trade has been, and remains the most important (Figure 10.2). Above all else, the expansion of the economy has required huge imports of energy and industrial raw materials and massive exports of manufactured goods. A similar two-way traffic is evident under the heading of **overseas direct investment** (Chapter 11). An increasing amount of Japanese investment is moving offshore as Japanese firms set up affiliated companies overseas. At the same time, foreign companies are investing in Japan, particularly in its manufacturing. Under the heading of Official Development Assistance (ODA) Japan provides aid in the form of loans, grants and technical assistance to help the development process elsewhere in the world (Chapter 12). The benefits to be reaped from this apparently charitable activity are far more than just the interest paid on loans. They are to do with rather more pragmatic matters, such as ensuring the future supply of raw materials and creating markets for Japanese goods.

Thus, by these various offshore activities, the economic life of Japan has become closely interwoven with the economic life of much of the globe. But it is necessary to understand that success in this external geography depends upon two basic things. First, there are the 'ups' and 'downs' of the world economy. No country is so strong that it is completely immune from these influences. Inevitably Japan, like all other countries, has experienced cycles of boom and recession. No matter how productive and competitive a nation's industry, recession still means reduced demand, and reduced demand means reduced sales and profits.

Secondly, international economic cooperation of all kinds requires a secure political environment. This is absolutely vital if it is to flourish. Whenever there is instability in any part of the globe or whenever Japan's relationships with another country become strained in some way or another, there is the likelihood that trade will become disrupted, investment confidence lost and the will to lend assistance weakened. For these reasons, the success or otherwise of the three economic linkages depends heavily on the Japanese Government and the policies it pursues in such vital areas as international diplomacy, defence and security (Chapters 12 and 14). The number one priority is to maintain friendly international relations on the widest possible front. This need for a peaceful scenario clearly reinforces the notion than no nation can afford to be an island.

Finally, it needs to be stressed that

what is shown by Figure 10.2 applies not just to Japan. It provides a model for most countries. No matter whether they are classified as **developed** or **developing**, most countries are involved in trade to some degree. If they are not overseas investors themselves, then most countries will certainly be the target for foreign investment. Whilst, so far as aid is concerned, if they are not recipients, then most countries will be donors.

10.3 THE POSTWAR GROWTH OF OVERSEAS TRADE

Overseas trade is a two-way traffic. It can be seen as satisfying two broadly different needs of a country. On the one hand, it can provide those requirements which are not sufficiently available from within the national borders. On the other hand, it can make available to others those things which are surplus to a nation's needs. Viewed in this way, then, trade may be seen as allowing sales of the latter to be used to buy the former.

For any country, the most critical aspect of trade is the balance between what it sells (**exports**) and what it buys (**imports**). The more exports exceed imports, the more favourable the trade situation, that is the greater the profit margin. However, it needs to be remembered that there are two types of trade: (i) trade in commodities (e.g. food, minerals, manufactured goods and (ii) trade in services and capital (e.g. tourism, banking, insurance). The former is strictly known as **visibles trading** and the latter as **invisibles trading**. In each instance, the difference between exports and imports gives rise to the **balance of trade** or **trade balance**. However, the combined balance of trade in both visibles and invisibles is referred to as the **balance of payments**. The discussion in this chapter is largely confined to the trade in commodities, but in the last section some consideration will be given to invisibles trading and the overall balance of payments.

Figure 10.3 shows the growth in the value of Japanese visible exports and imports during the postwar period. So great has been the expansion that it has

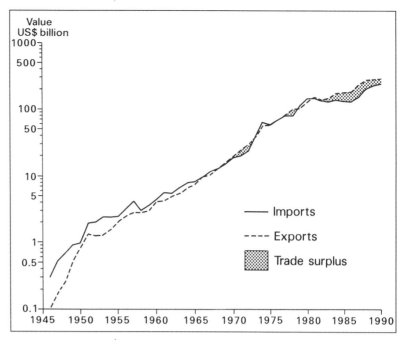

Fig. 10.3. *The growth of visible trading (1945 – 1990)*

been necessary to use a logarithmic scale in the construction of the graph. The value of total trade (exports plus imports) increased by more than 250 times between 1950 and 1990. However, it needs to be stressed that both this multiplier and the graph overstate the true increase in the volume of trade, because neither take into account the great inflation of prices that has occurred. Nonetheless, it can be seen from Table 10.1 that today Japan ranks as the third largest exporting country, accounting as it does for nearly ten percent of all the world's exports. As regards imports, it lies further down the rankings, with only a six percent share of the global total. The encouraging outcome of this stronger showing in terms of exporting is that Japan enjoys a favourable balance of trade. In 1990 that **trade surplus** was valued at $64 billion, having apparently peaked in 1986 at $83 billion. The only other major economy to achieve a notable surplus was West Germany ($74 billion). In the same year, the USA and UK suffered **trade deficits** of $108 billion and $31 billion respectively.

10.4 IMPORTS

Let us now look separately at the two components of visibles trading, starting with imports. For all its success in terms of trade, there is no denying that Japan

Table 10.1 *Shares of world trade for selected countries (1989)*

	World exports (%)	World imports (%)
Japan	9.1	6.7
France	5.9	6.1
UK	5.0	6.3
USA	12.1	15.7
W Germany	11.3	8.6

has had to rely heavily on imports in order to satisfy a range of basic needs, from food to industrial raw materials, from energy to certain types of manufactured goods. It is interesting to note how the percentage composition of imports has changed during the post-war period (Figure 10.4).

The commodity group which has most influenced the changing percentage values is mineral fuels (oil, gas and coal) (Figure 10.4). Of the three constituent fuels, crude oil has been by far the most significant. In the early postwar, the decision was taken that much of Japan's energy need should be satisfied by imported crude oil. At this time, oil was readily available on the world market and at a very cheap price (about $3 per barrel). The rise in the percentage importance of mineral fuels from the early 1950s through to the early 1970s simply reflects the steadily increasing reliance of Japan on overseas sources of crude oil and coal. However, the marked rise in the

percentage figure during the 1970s and up to the mid-1980s reflects the impact of the two Oil Shocks (1973 and 1979/80). During this time, the cost of a barrel of crude oil increased by more than 10 times. It was this inflation of oil prices rather than increased oil consumption that caused mineral fuel to account for nearly half of all imports by value in 1980.

Since 1980, the proportional importance of mineral fuels has fallen by over a half (Figure 10.4). This has been due partly to a subsequent substantial reduction in oil prices; in fact, they fell by about one half during the second half of the 1980s. The percentage decline also reflects that, since the first Oil Crisis, Japan has made considerable progress in two vital directions. First, it has greatly increased the efficiency with which it uses fossil fuels. Secondly, its total energy requirement is now much less dependent on oil (Chapter 5.6). Alternative sources of energy now play a larger part (Table 5.3). Although most of these alternative sources still have to be imported (coal, liquid petroleum gas and liquid natural gas), they are relatively cheap and therefore do not over inflate the percentage importance of mineral fuels in today's import ledgers.

Looking at the other commodity groups in Figure 10.4, it will be noted that as the mineral fuel figure increased, so the percentage values for foodstuffs and for raw materials tended to fall. Equally, it will be seen that these two commodity groups appear to have recovered slightly with the recent marked fall in the mineral fuel percentage. All these reciprocal shifts simply attest to the general 'weight' (volume multiplied by unit value) of mineral fuels in Japanese imports and the disturbance that this 'weight' has had on the rest of the imports table. But other factors have also been at work. For example, the persistence of import quotas on a range of foodstuffs and the increased productivity of Japanese agriculture have combined to reduce the volume of food and drink imports (Chapter 8). However, the recent removal of those import quotas may have played a part in helping to reverse the downward trend. Similarly, as the emphasis of Japanese industrial

Fig. 10.4 *The changing composition of imports (1950 – 1990)*

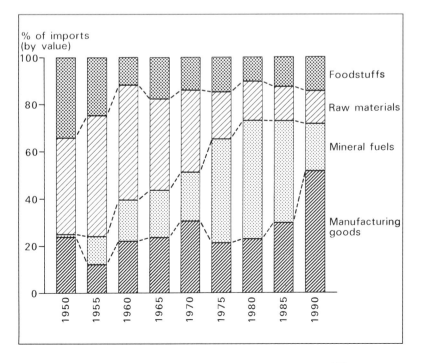

production has shifted from textiles (with its high dependence on imported fibres) through heavy industries (relying on cheap imported ores and fuel), and so to the present modern consumer and high-tech industries (with their much smaller material requirements), so the relative importance of raw materials has declined (Chapter 6).

Perhaps the most surprising fact to emerge from Figure 10.4 relates to the remaining major commodity group. It is truly remarkable to find that nearly half of the imports of the world's leading manufacturer are today made up of manufactured goods. What could Japan possibly need that she cannot make for herself? Unfortunately, detailed information about the composition of such imports is hard to come by. The largest single category is referred to as 'machinery and equipment'. Accounting as it does for nearly 30 percent of all imported manufactured goods, it includes such things as factory machinery, electrical appliances, transport equipment (aircraft, motor vehicles and ships) and precision instruments. Next come chemicals which make up about 15 percent of imported manufactures. Overall, it would seem that more than half of all imported manufactures fall in the broad class known as **capital goods** – equipment and processed materials used in the production of other manufactured goods. In other words, far from competing against and displacing Japanese goods, a significant proportion of these imports is actually being used to support Japanese manufacturing output. Of the **consumer goods**, textile products (largely clothing) and processed foods dominate the **non-durable** sector, whilst motor cars account for 25 percent of imported **consumer durables**, followed by toys and musical instruments (20 percent). A growing proportion of these inward shipments of manufactured goods are **reverse imports** – that is, goods made by Japanese branch plants overseas. For example, one of the most recent reverse imports into Japan are Nissan cars made in North East England.

Today Japan draws just over half its imports from the First World (Figure 10.5). Here, North America supplies a quarter of Japan's needs (mainly machinery and equipment, foodstuffs and raw materials). The second ranking of Europe (largely the EC) is to be explained mainly in terms of the supply of manufactured goods. It is interesting to note that the North American share has been reduced by nearly one half during the postwar period, whilst Europe has trebled its share. The latter is partly explained by the enlargement of the EC's membership and by the bloc's general disposition to trade with Japan. Japan looks to the Third World mainly for mineral fuels and raw materials, drawn largely from South East Asia and the Middle East. During the 1970s there was a major oscillation in the relative importance of the First and Third Worlds as sources of Japanese imports. A sudden rise in the Third World's share showed the impact of the massive surge in oil prices during the two Oil Shocks. Equally, the return of that share to its earlier level reflects the availability on today's world market of cheaper supplies of crude oil.

Looking at the catchment of imports in a little more detail, Table 10.2 shows the dominance of the USA. Significantly, though, the US share has shown a steady decline. This is to be explained largely in terms of the US ceasing to be an oil exporter and Japan striving to reduce its reliance on

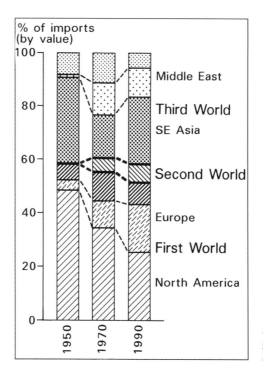

Fig. 10.5 *The changing geographic origins of imports (1950 – 1990)*

Table 10.2 *Top ten suppliers of Japanese imports in 1955, 1970 and 1990*

Rank	1955		1970		1990	
			(percentage of total imports by value)			
1.	USA	31.3	USA	29.4	USA	22.3
2.	Australia	7.2	Australia	8.0	Australia	5.3
3.	Canada	4.4	Canada	4.9	China	5.2
4.	Saudi Arabia	3.9	Indonesia	3.4	Indonesia	5.0
5	Malaysia	3.7	West Germany	3.3	South Korea	5.0
6.	Philippines	3.6	Philippines	2.8	West Germany	4.9
7.	Mexico	3.4	USSR	2.5	Canada	3.6
8.	China	3.3	Saudi Arabia	2.3	Taiwan	3.6
9.	India	3.3	Malaysia	2.2	France	3.2
10.	Taiwan	3.3	UK	2.1	UK	2.2
		67.4		60.9		60.3

imported food. Australia, a source of coal, metal ores, wool and foodstuffs, has maintained a second place in the rankings. But its share has slipped as Japan's industrial restructuring has reduced the demand for the first three commodities. Although Japan has sought to reduce its overall energy dependence on crude oil since 1973, it has also sought to diversify its sources (i.e. to draw its oil supply from more countries). There are clear risks attached to being over-dependent on a few countries for such a vital resource. Thus two non-Middle Eastern oil-producing states, namely China and Indonesia, are found in the present ten top rankings. However, both countries also supply other commodities. China exports coal and textiles in significant quantities, and Indonesia hardwoods and vast amounts of natural gas.

Three countries, South Korea, Taiwan and former West Germany, appear in the top ten rankings largely by virtue of their success in exporting manufactured goods to Japan (Table 10.2). On the face of it, it would seem that these countries are beginning to outplay Japan at her own game. The rise of South Korea has been particularly spectacular. It has proved itself to be a highly successful seller of a wide range of manufactures, from ships and machinery to electrical goods and textiles. Finally, the fact that Canada has appeared in the rankings for all three sample years merits a mention. It has maintained a fairly consistent percentage share of Japanese imports, providing a variety of primary commodities, including foodstuffs, timber, metals and coal.

10.5 EXPORTS

In the view of most of Japan's trading partners, it is her postwar record of achievement as an exporter that draws much more attention than her performance as an importer. This bias is understandable if only because, whilst the value of imports grew by a factor of 241 between 1950 and 1990, exports increased by a factor of 350. Perhaps it is because of this superior performance that some economists regard the whole of Japan's postwar economic growth as having been 'export-led'. The growth in exports is claimed to have been the 'engine' or generator of economic expansion. However, there are others who hold the view that exports have simply been the 'handmaiden' of economic growth. In other words, it is economic expansion that has given rise to increasing volumes of trading, particularly of exporting. Despite this division of opinion, all are agreed that successful exporting has played an integral part in Japan's emergence as an economic superpower.

The commodity structure of Japanese exports has shown three significant changes during the postwar period (Figure 10.6). First, there has been a marked slide in the importance of textiles. The decline has been even greater than that shown, for in the mid-1930s textiles accounted for nearly 60 percent of all Japanese exports. Secondly, this decline appears to have

Photo 10.2 *Nissan cars being loaded for Export to Europe from Kita kyushu*

been more than compensated by the expansion of shipments of machinery and equipment which now represent almost 75 percent of all exports. Within this very broad commodity group, machinery and electrical goods each now account for about one quarter, whilst over one third is made up of transport equipment, these days motor vehicles rather than ships (Photo 10.2). Figure 10.7 clearly indicates that vehicles and their diverse components accounted for five out of the ten top export items in 1990. Also noticeable is the rising importance of high-tech products, such as semi-conductors (microchips) and computers (data processors), and a range of consumer durables other than motor vehicles. Table 10.3 shows the rising volume of Japanese overseas sales of a sample of such goods. Thirdly, the relative rise and fall of both chemicals and metals and metal products reflect the changing fortunes of particular Japanese industries, namely oil-refining and iron and steel production.

Looking at the general distribution of Japanese exports, the Third World (i.e. Asia, Latin America and Africa) held a slight edge over the First World during the 1950s and 1960s (Figure 10.8). It was hardly surprising that Japan should direct its marketing of a whole range of manufactured goods towards what were largely non-industrialised countries. Significant, too, was the fact that Japan was exporting capital rather than consumer goods to these countries. Such goods were vital if industrialisation was to be encouraged in the Third World. Equally, the prevailing low levels of personal affluence meant a very limited market for consumer goods.

After some oscillation between 1960 and 1980, the balance of Japanese exporting has now swung decisively in favour of the First World (Figure 10.8). It is ironic that Japan's greatest exporting today involves shipping manufactured goods (largely consumer durables) to the opposition, her industrial rivals in North America and Western Europe. That point is driven home by Table 10.4. Here it will be seen that the great majority of the ten largest consumers of Japanese exports in 1990 were either long-estab-

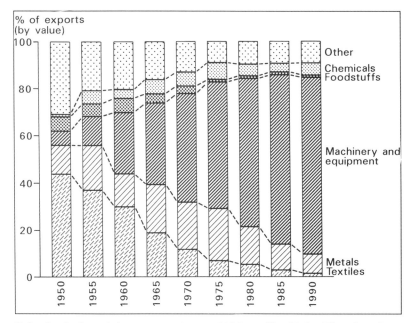

Fig. 10.6 *The changing composition of exports (1950 – 1990)*

lished industrial states (e.g. USA, former West Germany and the UK) or newly-industrialising economies (e.g. South Korea, Taiwan, Hong Kong and

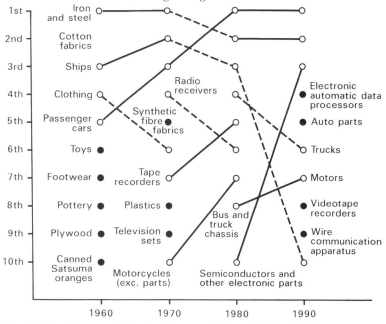

Fig. 10.7 *Changes in the top ten export items (1960 - 1990)*

Table 10.3 *Japanese exports of selected consumer goods (1960 – 1990)*

	TV sets (000s)	VTRs (000s)	Motor vehicles (000s)	Cameras (000s)
1960	45	–	39	–
1965	1 457	–	202	–
1970	5 355	–	1 096	2 811
1975	5 798	–	2 602	5 133
1980	9 479	3 444	6 119	11 098
1985	14 827	25 475	7 199	14 142
1990	7 598	26 465	6 165	21 411

Fig. 10.8 *The changing geographic destinations of exports (1950 – 1990)*

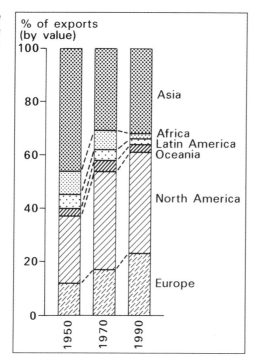

above the rest, namely the USA. Its position as the number one consumer of Japanese exports has gone from strength to strength during the postwar period. Today, its share has risen to almost one-third.

10.6 TRADE BALANCES

It is now necessary to take an overview of Japan's trading situation and that of its trading partners. In Figure 10.9, Japan's annual trade balance has been plotted as a percent of total trade (i.e. exports plus imports). Expressing data in this way eliminates the effects of inflation which has prevailed throughout the postwar period. The graph shows two significant features.

First, Japan's terms of trading have shown a marked improvement. For the first 20 years after the end of the Second World War, Japan suffered a recurrent trading deficit. However, since 1965, annual surpluses have not only become increasingly common, they have increased in size. So far, 1986 seems to have been the peak year in terms of the trade surplus, but more noteworthy is the fact that exports have exceeded imports in every year since 1980. It seems strange that trade surpluses should only become a regular occurrence during the current 'low-growth' phase. Why were they not achieved throughout the preceding much more dynamic phase? This is a intriguing but complex question. The explanation is more to do with imports than exports. It is to be found in the fact that the propulsive industries of the day consumed large quantities of imported raw materials and imported fuel. An undervalued yen made those imports relatively expensive.

Secondly, whilst the trading curve on Figure 10.9 shows a general upward trend, the progress seems to have been somewhat faltering. What can be clearly seen as impacting on the curve is a series of **business cycles**, an alternation of booms and slumps with a frequency of about five years. These cycles have characterised Japan's postwar economic development. As such they give the lie to the popular misconception that Japan's economic advancement has been one of

Singapore). Together, these two different market places accounted for some two-thirds of all Japan's exports. The former, with its high levels of personal affluence takes mainly consumer durables, whilst the latter opts for those capital goods necessary to support further industrialisation. Japan's success in both markets clearly attests to its skills in industrial efficiency, competitive pricing and aggressive marketing. As these industrial countries have moved up the league table of importers of Japanese goods, so some of the Third World representatives have been displaced altogether. But, as with imports, there is one country which has stood head and shoulders

Table 10.4 *The top ten consumers of Japanese exports in 1950, 1970 and 1990*

Rank	1950		1970		1990	
			(percent of total exports by value)			
1.	USA	22.1	USA	30.7	USA	31.3
2.	Pakistan	6.2	South Korea	4.2	West Germany	6.2
3.	Hong Kong	6.0	Hong Kong	3.6	South Korea	6.1
4	Indonesia	5.2	Taiwan	3.6	Taiwan	5.4
5	Thailand	4.8	China	2.9	Hong Kong	4.6
6.	Taiwan	4.3	Canada	2.9	UK	3.8
7.	South Africa	3.3	West Germany	2.8	Singapore	3.7
8.	UK	2.9	UK	2.5	Thailand	3.2
9.	Australia	2.6	Thailand	2.3	Australia	2.4
10.	Philippines	2.4	Philippines	2.3	China	2.3
		59.8		57.8		69.0

uninterrupted progress. From Japan's point of view, her present trading situation is clearly a good one. But the harsh fact of trading is that one nation's success is usually gained at another's expense.

At present, Japan trades with just over 90 countries. Of these, only 12 percent are involved in what might be described as a reasonably balanced trading with Japan, where imports and exports are roughly equal. Of her top 30 trading partners which are shown on Figure 10.10, only Malaysia, Mexico and the Philippines fall in this category. Japan suffers a trading deficit with only 30 percent of her partners. Almost without exception, these are developing countries supplying either mineral fuels or raw materials. The only developed countries to fall in this category are Australia, New Zealand, Canada, South Africa, Italy and Switzerland. Clearly, the first three fit the same mould; they are providers of primary commodities. Japan enjoys trade surpluses with more than half of her partners. Even more reassuring is the fact that falling within this group are her biggest partners. Most notably, there is the USA, which totally dominates the trading scene, together with former West Germany, the UK and France, which are also high-volume markets for Japanese consumer goods.

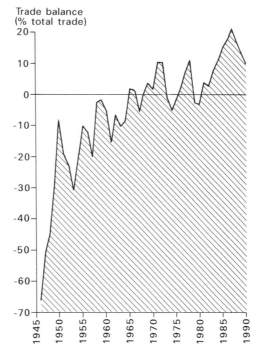

Fig. 10.9 Japan's balance of trade (1946 – 1990)

Also in this grouping are four of Asia's NICs, South Korea, Taiwan, Hong Kong and Singapore, which need capital goods such as machinery.

10.7 TRADE WITH THE USA

Having made some general comments about the postwar growth of Japanese foreign trade – its changing com-

Fig. 10.10 Japan's top thirty trading partners

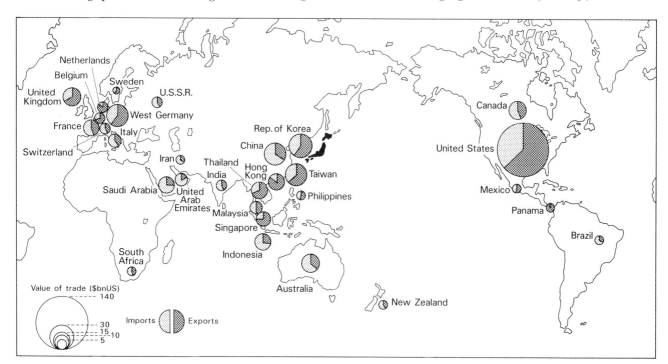

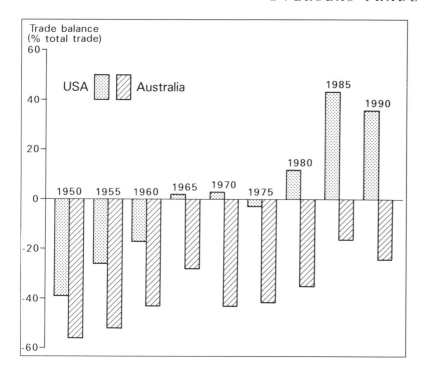

Fig. 10.11 *Japan's changing trade balances with the USA and Australia (1950 – 1990)*

position, balances and geographic directions – let us now consider briefly Japan's trading with two of her partners, the USA and Australia. Although both are developed countries, they differ sharply in terms of the balance of their trade with Japan, its volume and composition.

The USA is unchallenged as Japan's number one trading partner. It is the destination for about one-third of all Japan's exports, and it supplies nearly a quarter of all imports (Tables 10.2 and 10.4). Clearly, these figures indicate a very close interdependence which is unrivalled by any other trading nations. In some respects, this closeness in foreign trade is not surprising, bearing in mind that for most of the postwar period the USA has deliberately 'courted' Japan. It has seen the existence of an economically-strong and Western-oriented Japan as a vital part of the American defensive

strategy for the Pacific region (Chapter 12). Japan has certainly enjoyed a special relationship with the USA. In the very early postwar years, it benefitted from American aid, and for rather longer from the **special procurements** arrangements.

Figure 10.11 summarises much of what needs to be known about trade between Japan and the USA. The main point is that there has been a complete reversal in the balance of trade between them. Up until the early 1960s, the USA enjoyed a trading surplus on its Japanese account, albeit a diminishing one. The Nixon Shock of 1971 and the 1973 Oil Crisis were mainly responsible for the temporary recovery evident in the 1975 figures. Since then, the trading situation has deteriorated badly for the Americans. In 1990, the trading deficit was equivalent to roughly 25 percent of total trade. Table 10.5 highlights the principal commodities involved in that trade. Exports from the USA appear to mainly either primary products (both agricultural and industrial) or manufactured goods (notably aircraft and office machines). Exports from Japan are dominated by manufactured goods; the machinery and equipment category includes electrical goods, electronic equipment and motor vehicles.

The key question in this case-study is clearly, how has this dramatic reversal of the trade balance come about (Figure 10.11)? At least seven contributory factors can be identified.

First, as a broad observation, the point might be made that much of the USA's postwar economic effort has been directed towards the needs of defence and international political influence. Japan's efforts have not been thus deflected; it has single-mindedly pursued the goal of maximum economic growth. Secondly, there has been little government intervention in the American economy. By comparison, the Japanese Government has been highly active in terms of promoting industrial development and foreign trade. In this sense, the American economy has been much more of a market economy. Thirdly, and following on from this, the tradition of American companies has been to favour overseas

Table 10.5 *The principal commodities traded between Japan and the USA (1990).*

Exports	%	Imports	%
Motor vehicles	27	Machinery and equipment	29
Office equipment	10	Foodstuffs	23
Scientific and optical equipment	5	Chemicals	11
Electronic	4	Timber	6
Iron and steel	3	Mineral fuels	4

direct investment rather than direct exporting.

The superior productivity and competitive pricing of the Japanese manufacturing has been a fourth major factor tipping the trade balance in Japan's favour (Figure 10.11). Fifthly, the US embargo on oil exports in the in the early 1970s, together with the great improvements in Japanese agriculture, have effectively reduced the volume of American exports to Japan and thereby helped to widen the trade gap. Sixthly, the Americans claim that for most of the postwar period the Japanese yen has been significantly undervalued against the American dollar (Figure 5.5). In a nutshell, with an undervalued currency exports may appear attractively priced, and imports rather expensive. In other words, the currency situation, by encouraging exports and discouraging imports, makes for a favourable trade balance. Finally, the Americans frequently claim that Japan's trading success has been achieved, in part, by unfair means and practices. These accusations are examined in more detail in 10.9. For the moment, however, it is not too difficult to understand the frustration and humiliation experienced by the Americans as they slip increasingly into the red with their number one trading partner. The feelings are perhaps intensified by the fact that, in GNP terms at least, Japan is an inferior economy.

10.8 TRADE WITH AUSTRALIA

Australia is one of a fairly exclusive group of countries that still enjoys a trading surplus with Japan. During the early postwar period, trade between the two countries was very slow to recover to what it had been before the Second World War. This was due partly to the bitter feelings which Australia harboured toward Japan as a result of the Japanese treatment of Australian prisoners of war. It was also due to the fears of Australian manufacturers that trading with Japan would drive them out of business. However, during the 1950s the Australians gradually came to realise that an industrially expanding Japan represented a huge potential market for Australian primary products, both agricultural and industrial. Clearly, if Australia was to tap that market, then it would have to open its doors to Japanese manufactured goods. Thus, in 1957 a trade agreement between the two countries was signed.

Since then, trading has gone from strength to strength, to the extent that Japan now surpasses the USA as Australia's chief trading partner. Essentially, Japan has really taken up the trading niche left by the UK as it gradually turned its back on what had been the British Empire and joined the European Community. Today, Japan consumes just over a quarter of all Australia's exports, and supplies just under a quarter of its imports. But whilst Japan figures very prominently in Australian trading ledgers, Australia is less conspicuous in the Japanese ledgers, with a 2 percent share of Japanese exports and a five percent share of imports (Tables 10.2 and 10.4). As regards the latter, Australia ranks as Japan's second largest supplier.

Japanese imports from Australia are dominated by primary products, namely industrial raw materials (notably iron and non-ferrous ores), fuel (coal and liquid petroleum gas) and agricultural commodities (beef and wool). During the late 1960s and early 1970s, there was a remarkable expansion of Australian iron production and much of the output was destined for Japan. However, with the restructuring of the Japanese industrial economy that followed the 1973 Oil Crisis, so Japan's imports of iron ore have tended to decline. As for the other principal imports from Australia, shipments of beef and coal (steam rather than coking) have continued to increase in recent years, whilst shipments of wool have fallen as the Japanese textile industry continues to decline.

Until the late 1960s, Japanese exports to Australia were dominated by textile yarns and fabrics, a fact which highlights the strange plight of Australia, namely that a developed country so rich in industrial raw materials (including wool) should be so poor in manufacturing. As the Japanese textile industry has declined, so motor vehicles have become the main export (accounting for about a third of all exports to Australia), followed by a widening range of consumer products, particularly electrical appliances and electronic equipment.

Figure 10.11 shows the trade balance as a percentage of the total volume of trade between Japan and Australia. Clearly, throughout the period, the balance has been in Australia's favour. Up until the mid-1980s, the general picture was one of a decline in that balance, but since then there have been clear signs of a recovery in Australia's favour. It is ironic to note that in the context of trading with Japan, Australia finds itself in much the same predicament as the Third World. Like countries as far apart as Brazil, Mexico, Zimbabwe, Saudi Arabia and Indonesia, Australia is cast in the role of a provider of raw materials and a consumer of Japanese manufactured goods. From the Australian viewpoint, that predicament is acceptable so long as the Japanese industrial economy requires large quantities of raw materials and fuel. It would be even better if the Australian farmer were to be allowed freer access to the Japanese food market. For the Japanese, a major current concern is that many of the consumer goods which it has supplied over recent decades are now being produced at competitive prices by Asia's NICs. Although, with a population of only 17 million, Australia represents a modest consumer market, it is nonetheless one which the Japan would prefer not to lose. To do so would throw into even greater deficit its trading with Australia.

10.9 TRADE FRICTION

In the eyes of some of her trading partners, Japan's trading success has not been achieved by wholly legitimate means. Over the years, accusations have been made about her indulging in 'unfair trading practices.' Such accusations have been voiced most loudly and most often by those countries which, like the USA and the UK, suffer increasing deficits in their trading with Japan. The feelings of resentment which have arisen on both sides give rise to what is commonly referred to as **trade friction**. While her partners feel that Japan does not always abide strictly by the rules of international trade, Japan's perception is that her image is being deliberately smeared and that her partners are trying to cover up for their own inadequacies. The critical questions, then, are these: do these accusations of unfair trading have any substance? If so, is Japan the only guilty country?

The general view of economists and economic historians is that the accusations made against Japan did have substance during the 1950s and early 1960s. At this time, the Japanese Government exercised strict control over foreign trade and exchange dealings. They did so in order to protect Japanese farmers and manufacturers on the home market and to strengthen the ability of the latter to compete and sell abroad. A number of different ploys was used. For example, there was tax discrimination in favour of exports – a Japanese manufacturer stood to gain (i.e. pay less tax) if a product was sold overseas rather than in Japan. This was reinforced by a sort of dual pricing system, whereby the Japanese consumer paid more for the same product as the overseas buyer. In effect, home sales 'subsidised' exports. There was also organised **dumping** of Japanese goods abroad – that is, getting rid of excess production (of textiles, TV sets, steel and motor vehicles) by selling it overseas priced at, or even below, production cost. At the same time, restrictions on imports, by means of strict quotas and raised customs dues, made it difficult for foreign farmers and manufacturers to gain access to the Japanese market place.

It is widely thought that perhaps the greatest boost to the Japanese export drive, at least up to the early 1970s, was provided by the careful maintenance (by the Government and the leading banks) of an undervalued Japanese currency, particularly against the US dollar. As such, it may been seen as having helped to maintain the competitive edge of Japanese products in terms of their selling price overseas. However, it needs to be stressed that an undervalued currency is bad news for imports; it means a reduced purchasing power. So given the level of importing required by the Japanese economy as a result of its need for energy and raw materials, maybe the benefits of a 'cheap' yen in the context of exporting were in effect cancelled out by its costs in the context of importing. Between 1950 and 1970, the value of the yen against the US dollar was in fact pegged at the fixed rate of 360 yen. Since then, however, the value of the yen has increased by three times (Figure 5.5). As this has happened, so far as overseas trade is concerned, it would seem that the currency scenario has been completely reversed. Whilst it might be seen as favouring imports, it has certainly made export sales much more difficult.

Since the mid-1960s, Japan claims to have gradually introduced a whole series of what are called **trade liberalisation** measures. These include **voluntary export controls**, whereby Japan has agreed to restrict the volume of certain exports. Initially, the control was applied to textiles, but subsequently extended to steel, chinaware, motor vehicles and most recently to microchips and electronic equipment. At the same time, Japan claims to have introduced a series of **market-opening measures**. In practice, this has involved gradually removing most, if not all, of its restrictions on foreign imports. So the Japanese feel that they have done much to improve the situation. Perhaps reflecting this is the fact that the sorts of complaints heard today are slightly different. They focus mainly on two aspects. First, on the fact that Japanese manufacturers enjoy cheap credit from banks in support of exporting, and secondly on the persistence of what is called **administrative guidance**. The latter refers to a whole range of regulations and administrative procedures which apply to foreign imports. There are stringent safety tests to be passed; there is much niggling red tape to deal with, and so on. They certainly cause much irritation and frustration; the net effect is to hinder (not prevent) the entry of goods into Japan.

It has to be said, however, that Japan believes some of its partners have not been entirely blameless when it has come to unfair trading. Over the years,

Japanese products have been the discriminated against in the most overt manner, as by the USA, France and Italy, to name but three guilty parties. These and other countries, most of them like Japan members of the General Agreement on Tariffs and Trade (GATT), have threatened Japan with **protectionism** – that is, literally to put up the shutters to Japanese goods. The Japanese perception of the EC is well summed up in the description 'fortress Europe' (Figure 10.12). Although the Japanese say little about the protectionism inherent in the Common Agricultural Policy (because they too are keen to protect their farmers from foreign competition), they do feel bitter about the strict quotas which have long been placed on imports of Japanese cars and on the overt attempts to keep Japan out of Europe's consumer electronics market. Japan also believes that government subsidies, such as those given in the past to the UK steel, shipbuilding and motor vehicle industries, provided those industries with an unfair advantage over their Japanese counterparts which received no such help.

Of course, it is possible to explain Japan's success in international commodity trading, particularly in the 1980s and 1990s, in terms other than a

Figure 10.12 *Cartoon of Fortress Europe (Times, 6th August, 1991)*

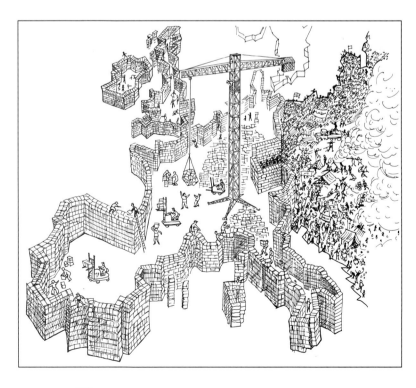

an increasing strain on the international relationships of supposedly friendly nations.

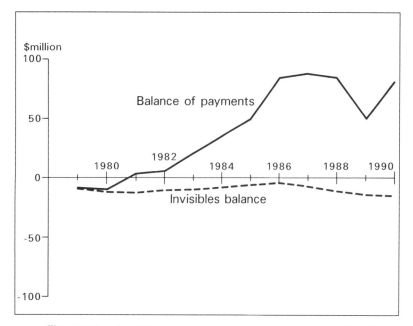

Fig. 10.13 *Japan's balance of payments (1979 – 1990)*

10.10 INVISIBLES TRADING AND THE BALANCE OF PAYMENTS

Finally, this discussion of Japan's trade needs to be broadened to take account of invisibles trading. The point to be made, and one that is stressed time and time again by the Japanese when the annual commodity trade figures show yet another huge surplus, is that no such surplus is to be found in its trade in invisibles. Indeed, throughout the postwar period, Japan has suffered a recurrent deficit. In 1990, the deficit amounted to over $22 billion, when the greatest losses occurred under the headings of transportation, travel and royalties (see Chapter 11.7), and the only major aspect in the black was the income from overseas investments (see Chapter 11.5). In the same year, the USA and the UK showed overall surpluses of $19 billion and $14 billion respectively.

However, the significant observation to be made from Figure 10.13 is that the recurrent annual deficits in invisibles trading have been progressively dwarfed by increasing surpluses in commodity trading. The former is now equivalent to little more than 10 percent of the latter. Because of this, Japan's overall international balance of payments has since 1980 shown an increasingly healthy surplus. In 1990, this amounted to nearly $36 billion. This was only surpassed by the former West Germany, which enjoyed a balance of $44 billion. The USA and the UK suffered negative balances of $92 billion and $23 billion. Such figures clearly signal Japan's success as a trading nation. This one aspect of its external geography has enabled Japan to create much wealth and a formidable global reputation.

resort to unfair practices. Certainly, there is plenty of evidence to support the Japanese view that its trading success derives from such things as (i) the superior efficiency and productivity of its manufacturing, (ii) its shrewdness in seeking out cheap and reliable overseas supplies, and (iii) its effective overseas marketing and salesmanship. In the last two contexts, much credit must go to JETRO. With offices in most major cities of the world, JETRO has served as a vital intelligence-gathering machine. It has sought out overseas sources of supply and overseas market opportunities. The collected information has been relayed back to the Ministry of International Trade and Industry (MITI) in Tokyo, analysed and the results passed onto Japanese manufacturers and trading companies for them to take appropriate action.

Thus, it may well be the case that those trading partners who complain most vocally about Japanese trading practices do so to cover up their own lack of competitiveness, be it as producers, buyers or sales promoters. But no matter what the reasons might be for the Japanese trade surplus, it seems clear that imbalances in the trade between Japan and many of her partners will persist. In the particular cases where the imbalance favours Japan, the heat is unlikely to be taken out of trade friction. For certain, the climate of accusation and counter-accusation seems set to continue, thereby placing

11 Overseas direct investment

11.1 WHAT IS OVERSEAS DIRECT INVESTMENT ?

Overseas direct investment (ODI) describes the various ways in which businesses from one country gain entry to, and become involved in, the business life and markets of another. Since the investment is being made by private-sector firms, ranging in size from the small family business to the huge Japanese conglomerates, like Hitachi and Mitsubishi, the dominant driving force is profit-taking. This motivation can take a number of different guises. These include the chance of gaining direct access to lucrative foreign markets, particularly where trade friction exists, as in the USA. Seeking out new sources of energy and raw materials, particularly oil, gas and iron ore, is another motivation, as is also the chance to exploit the secure investment opportunities offered in stable countries such as the UK. Foreign investment may be encouraged as governments at various levels offer incentives in order to bring new life into lagging regions, as in the peripheral regions of the European Community (EC).

Just as the specific motivations of ODI are varied, so too are its forms. To simplify the situation, perhaps to a dangerous degree, in the following analysis Japanese ODI is assumed to embrace three main types. First, there is the setting up of **affiliated businesses** (branch plants and subsidiaries) by Japanese parent companies. The former are largely to do with manufacturing, as for example the Sony and Hitachi plants in South Wales (Photo 11.1), whilst the latter generally are perhaps less directly controlled by the parent company and are rather more involved in the tertiary sector.

Secondly, there is the so-called **joint venture**, a sort of partnership between a Japanese and a foreign company. Notable examples include the Rover-Honda collaboration to make cars in the UK, and Olivetti's venture with Sanyo and Mitsui to manufacture and sell fax machines. Most of these ventures involve the transfer or exchange of technology. In other instances, they involve the transfer of what are called **managerial resources**. This term includes such things as knowledge and experience in production methods, personnel management, the procurement of raw materials and sales. Thirdly, there is that investment which literally involves Japanese companies and business institutions acquiring major holdings in foreign companies and institutions. The purchase of substantial amounts of **equity** (i.e. shares) allows the Japanese company a high degree of direction over the way in which foreign businesses are run. In some cases, the level

Photo 11.1 Sony branch plant in South Wales

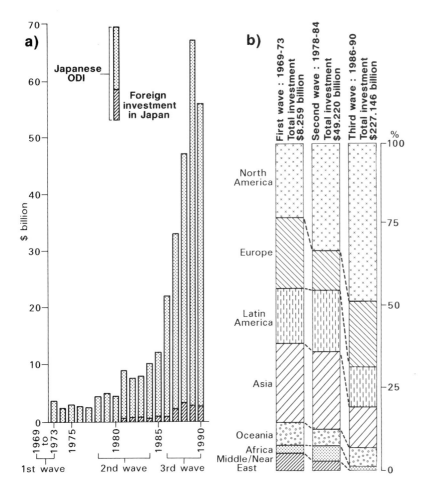

Fig. 11.1 *The growth of Japanese ODI (1969 – 1990)*

of Japanese investment is overwhelming; for example, Fujitsu now has an 80 percent holding in Britain's largest computer maker, ICL.

There are other characteristics of ODI which need to be identified early on. For instance, it should be understood that ODI is an accumulating process. New investments are made each year, and these are added to the investments made in previous years, thereby creating what is known as **cumulative ODI**. Then there is the 'import' aspect of ODI in that the 'export' of investment capital produces a return flow of profits and dividends. Furthermore, some investments are made for a fixed term – it may be for 5 years, 10 years or for very much longer. On maturity, (i.e. when the fixed term has expired), the initial investment capital joins the return flow to the investor country. So the amount of cumulative ODI at any one time is the outcome of the two processes of investment and withdrawal. Finally, it should be pointed out that there is another way in which ODI is a two-way traffic. A significant

number of the countries in which Japan invests are themselves investors in Japan. So, as with trade, a vitally important aspect of ODI is the overall balance of the bilateral investment flows. For example, how does the amount of Japanese investment in the UK compare with the UK's investment in Japan?

11.2 GROWTH AND GEOGRAPHICAL DISTRIBUTION

It was not until 1951, well after the end of the Second World War, that Japan was allowed to resume making overseas investments. At first, the volume of investment grew very slowly; between 1951 and 1973 cumulative ODI amounted to only $10 million. Up until 1969, all private-sector foreign investment was strictly controlled by the Japanese Government. As controls were gradually relaxed, so Japanese ODI began to take off, generating the so-called 'first wave', which was abruptly dissipated by the 1973 Oil Crisis (Figure 11.1(a)). Since then, the amount of new investment has increased nearly 30-fold from $2.4 billion in 1974 to over $67 billion in 1989. Two further waves of accelerating investment may be recognised on the rising curve, namely between 1978 and 1984, and after 1986. The 1990 figure of $57 billion (15 percent down on 1989) suggests that the 'third wave' may now have passed.

The significance of the 1973 Oil Crisis in the context of ODI is that it persuaded the Japanese, not only that they should rethink their wholly energy strategy (Chapter 6), but that it was imperative to reduce its dependence on Middle Eastern oil. New sources had to be found elsewhere. Japan had to be prepared to take initiatives and to make sizeable investments in oil exploration projects in various parts of the world, particularly in those developing countries, such as Indonesia, Mexico and Nigeria, which had the right geological structures but lacked the capital and technical know-how to undertake the exploratory work themselves.

During the 1980s, other specific motives, such as those briefly mentioned at the beginning of the chapter, have encouraged the continuing rise in ODI. These will be examined in more detail later. However, at this stage, one overriding factor should be identified, namely the unremitting success of the Japanese economy. This has generated new capital and thus greatly increased the funds available for investment. Japan has literally become awash with money looking for secure investments. As the investment opportunities within Japan itself have been taken up, so the investor's search has had to turn increasingly overseas.

As each successive wave of Japanese ODI has involved ever larger sums of money, so a significant change has occurred in the geographical pattern of investment (Figure 11.1(b)). During the first wave, slightly more than half of the investment was made in the Third World, particularly in Asia. During the second wave, that division as between the First and Third Worlds remained much the same, but within the former there was a significant change in the percentage allocations to North America and Europe. In the third wave, the allocation of ODI has been overwhelmingly to the First World, with North America increasing its share to almost one half. Table 11.1 shows the top 15 recipients of Japanese ODI in 1990. It is relevant to note that eight of the rankings were occupied by developed countries (with the USA way ahead at the top), together with three NICs.

The shift in the general direction of new investment is explained largely in terms of a change in the Japanese perception of its own needs and overseas opportunities. During the 1970s, Japanese ODI was concentrated on resource development and labour-intensive manufacturing (e.g. textiles) in developing countries (Photo 11.2). Investment was drawn in these directions by (i) Japan's need for basic resources, not just oil, but food and minerals, (ii) the availability of very cheap labour, and (iii) the rise in the value of the Japanese yen which so raised the price of goods made in Japan that poorer countries were unable to buy them. By setting up branch plants in developing countries, and using cheap local labour, so Japanese companies were able to produce goods at prices that could be afforded by Third World buyers. In addition to these three factors, there has been the impact of government intervention. Throughout the 1950s and 1960s, but decreasingly in the 1970s, the Japanese Government strictly controlled and directed overseas investment. Its top priority at that time was to seek out new sources of energy and industrial raw materials. The Government view was that such a search was best conducted in the Developing World.

During the 1980s, however, with the relaxation of government direction, Japanese investors began to see a rather different set of overseas business opportunities. Two of the prime targets today are the more advanced types of manufacturing and the financial institutions of industrialised countries. Several factors help to explain this shift. The Developing World is increasingly perceived to be a high-risk area for investment, as more and more developing countries have become wary about having their resources exploited by foreigners. Political instability and increasing Third World debt have also encouraged this perception. Another part of the explanation is to be found in Japan's embarrassingly large trading surpluses with many developed countries and the need to ease simmering trade friction. As will be illustrated in more detail in one of the following case-studies, manufacturing Japanese goods in the country where they are to be consumed is a simple but effective

Table 11.1 *The top 15 recipients of Japanese ODI (1990)*

		% total
1.	USA	45.9
2.	UK	12.0
3.	Australia	6.4
4.	Netherlands	4.8
5.	Hong Kong	3.1
6.	Panama	2.4
7.	France	2.2
8.	West Germany	2.2
9.	Thailand	2.0
10.	Indonesia	1.9
11.	Canada	1.9
12.	Singapore	1.5
13.	Malaysia	1.3
14.	Switzerland	1.1
15.	Brazil	1.1

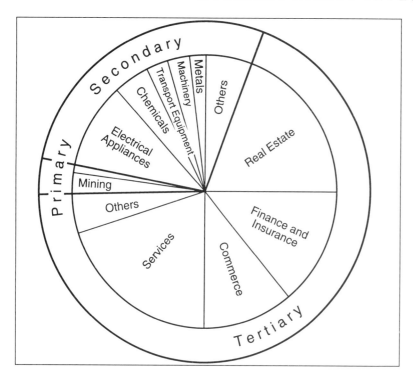

Fig. 11.2 *Sectoral allocation of new ODI (1990)*

way of reducing the actual import of Japanese goods and therefore of reducing trading imbalances. In short, such ODI is being use to achieve what from the Japanese viewpoint is **export substitution**; Japanese exports are being replaced by locally-made Japanese products. Finally, it is necessary to note that Japanese ODI has gradually assumed a broader perspective; Japan has come to realise that investment opportunities overseas are not confined just to mining and manufacturing.

11.3 THE SECTORAL ALLOCATION OF INVESTMENT

That last point requires that the distribution of Japanese ODI is now analysed in another way; not geographically, but in terms of economic sectors. Figure 11.2 shows that today mining (i.e. resource exploitation) accounts for a very small proportion of cumulative ODI (only 7.5 percent). Over half of that is concerned with mineral exploitation in various parts of Asia. Perhaps rather more surprising is that only a little more than a quarter of Japanese cumulative ODI is in manufacturing; nearly half of that is located in North America and a quarter in Asia. The investment in manufacturing falls

broadly into two types. That in Western Europe and the USA is mainly concerned with building factories producing consumer goods, mainly to ease trade friction (Figure 11.3), whilst that in Asia is motivated by labour shortages and soaring wages in Japan.

Four types of manufacturing seem to be favoured (Figure 11.2). In order, they are electrical appliances, chemicals, transportation equipment (mainly motor vehicles) and machinery. What is being backed, therefore, is a mix of both capital and consumer industries. However, the outstanding feature of Japanese ODI today is the supremacy of the tertiary or service sector, accounting as it does for nearly two-thirds of new ODI. Here, three specific categories of activity are much in evidence, namely real estate, finance and insurance, and commerce. As regards all three, Europe and North America are the chief target areas. The large 'services' category is a rather catch-all one embracing a diversity of activities which are predominantly business-related.

Figure 11.4 gives a slightly different view. It looks at cumulative investment in three sample years during the 1980s, and deals separately with manufacturing and non-manufacturing (i.e. primary and tertiary activities). So far as manufacturing is concerned, the picture is one of declining investment in textiles, chemicals and metals, compensated by growth particularly in electrical appliances and transport equipment. In the non-manufacturing sectors, it is clear that there was a considerable reduction of investment in mining and commerce. This was counteracted by a significant rise in investment in finance, insurance and real estate. During the decade, the proportion of Japanese ODI invested in the tertiary sector rose from two-thirds to nearly three-quarters. This clearly runs contrary to the popular belief that Japanese ODI is preoccupied with manufacturing.

11.4 FOREIGN DIRECT INVESTMENT IN JAPAN

At the global scale, Japan along with the EC and USA emerges as a major

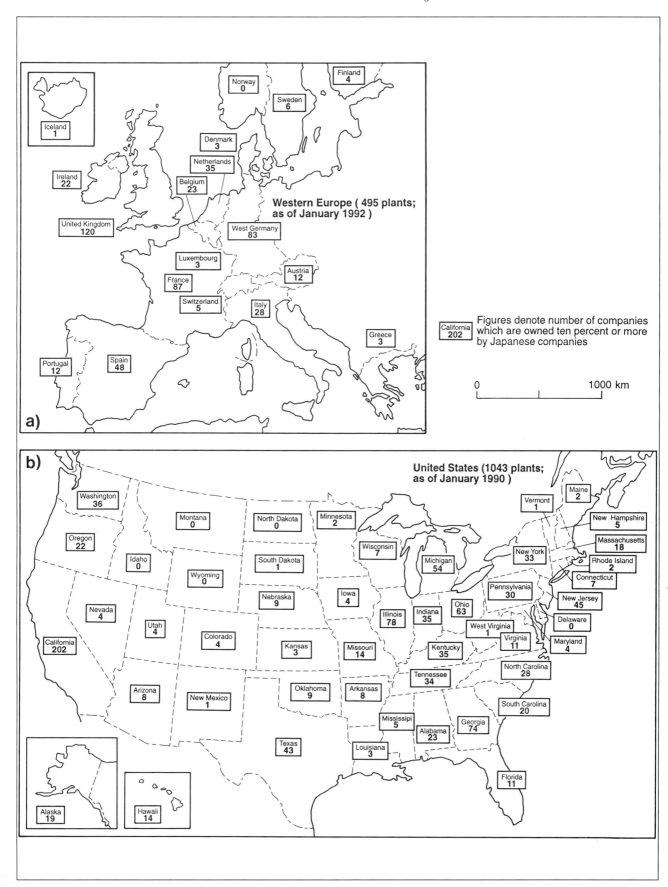

Fig. 11.3 *The distribution of Japanese manufacturing companies in (a) Western Europe and (b) the USA*

a) Manufacturing

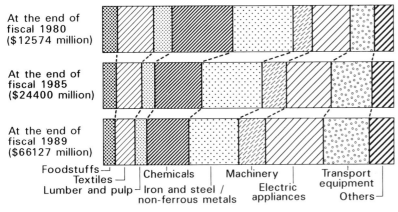

At the end of
fiscal 1980
($12574 million)

At the end of
fiscal 1985
($24400 million)

At the end of
fiscal 1989
($66127 million)

Foodstuffs
Textiles
Lumber and pulp
Chemicals
Iron and steel /
non-ferrous metals
Machinery
Electric
appliances
Transport
equipment
Others

b) Non-manufacturing

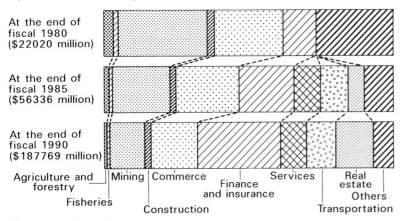

At the end of
fiscal 1980
($22020 million)

At the end of
fiscal 1985
($56336 million)

At the end of
fiscal 1990
($187769 million)

Agriculture and
forestry
Fisheries
Mining
Construction
Commerce
Finance
and insurance
Services
Transportation
Real
estate
Others

Fig. 11.4 *Changes in the sectoral allocation of cumulative ODI during the 1980s*

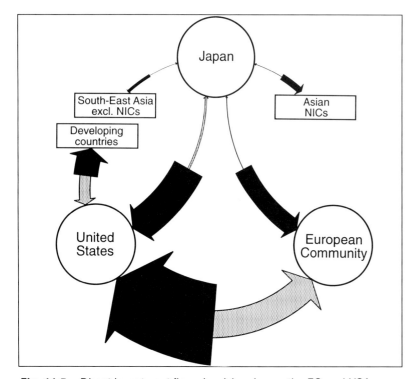

Fig. 11.5 *Direct investment flows involving Japan, the EC and USA*

node in the network of investment flows (Figure 11.5). At each node, there is a two-way but unequal movement of investment. Japan is clearly to be seen as a net exporter. Although there has recently been a slight acceleration in the amount of foreign investment moving into Japan, in 1990 that 'import' only totalled just over $3 billion. Of the $18 billion of cumulative ODI made in Japan during the period 1950 to 1989, over half was invested between 1987 and 1990 (Figure 11.1(a)). But the inward movement of capital from some 15 countries pales into insignificance compared with Japan's own ODI. In fact, in 1990 new ODI in Japan was equivalent to only one-twentieth of Japan's own overseas investment. Clearly, as in trade, a mammoth imbalance exists (Table 11.2). The outflow of investment exceeds the inflow by a factor of at least 15.

Between 1950 and 1986, over two-thirds of foreign investment was in Japanese manufacturing; more recently this has contracted slightly (Figure 11.6). An analysis of factories owned by foreign-affiliated companies shows the top five industrial activities to be, in order, chemicals, electronics and electricals, general machinery, pharmaceuticals and metals (Figure 11.7). Unfortunately, the conventional categories used in the collection of industrial data conceal what is the real focus of interest for foreign investment, namely high-tech activities such as the manufacture of microchips and microprocessors, new materials and advanced communications equipment. The Japanese Government, as well as many prefectural governments, have been keen to encourage foreign investment in these high-tech fields. Important in this respect have been the **technopolis** projects and their associated incentives and concessions (see Chapter 6.7). Figure 11.7 also shows the distribution of foreign-owned factories. With the exception of Hokkaido and Hyogo, the prefectures appearing to be most successful in terms of attracting foreign factories are those within easy reach of Tokyo, be it by *shinkansen* or expressway.

Although manufacturing is the dominant focus of foreign investment,

Figure 11.6 clearly indicates that the tertiary sector has gained ground in recent years. Commerce, business services, banking and insurance have all increased their share. Investment in Japanese real estate is a newcomer and already has nearly achieved a nine percent share. Inevitably, the distribution of this tertiary sector investment shows a pattern of polarisation in Tokyo and the other leading cities of the Pacific Belt.

Foreign investment in Japan is dominated by the USA; it accounts for nearly 60 percent of all investment (Figure 11.7). A long way behind comes a small group of investor countries in Western Europe comprising Denmark, France, Germany, the Netherlands, Sweden, Switzerland and the UK. Outside Europe and North America, the only other countries with anywhere near comparable shares are Australia and Hong Kong.

11.5 JAPANESE ODI IN THE FIRST WORLD: THE UK EXPERIENCE

A European focus

Of the $200 billion of Japanese ODI made since 1951, roughly three-quarters has been made in the First World,

Table 11.2 *Japan's two-way cumulative ODI with leading industrial countries (1989).*

	Japanese ODI ($ bn) A	ODI in Japan ($ bn) B	A/B
USA	104.4	7.9	13.2
UK	15.8	0.6	26.3
West Germany	3.4	0.7	4.9
France	2.9	0.2	14.5
TOTAL	253.9	15.7	16.2

and of this two-thirds (about $100 billion) ended up in the USA. By comparison, investment in the EC has been relatively small (a mere $30 billion). What is quite clear is that when the Japanese Government made the decision in the 1970s to persuade companies to direct more of their investment to the Developed World, it was the USA which immediately benefitted rather than Europe or Australasia. However, whilst during the 1980s the EC's share showed a modest increase (it currently stands at a little less than 20 percent), the proportion coming to the UK rose considerably. Today, the UK is the second largest recipient of Japanese ODI, in 1990 enjoying a 12 percent share (Table 11.1). It accounts for approximately a third of all Japanese ODI entering the

Fig. 11.6 *Sectoral allocation of foreign direct investment in Japan (a) 1950 – 1986, (b) 1987–1990*

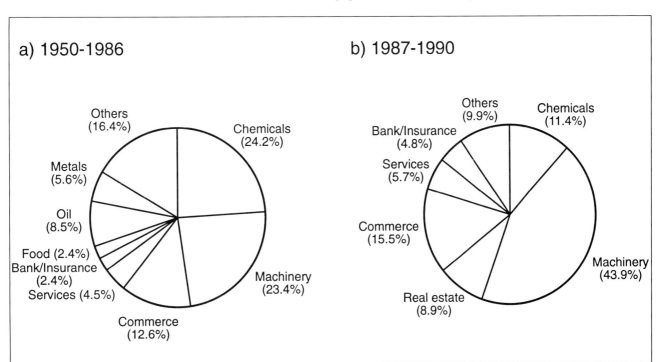

a) 1950-1986

Others (16.4%)
Chemicals (24.2%)
Metals (5.6%)
Oil (8.5%)
Food (2.4%)
Bank/Insurance (2.4%)
Services (4.5%)
Machinery (23.4%)
Commerce (12.6%)

b) 1987-1990

Others (9.9%)
Chemicals (11.4%)
Bank/Insurance (4.8%)
Services (5.7%)
Commerce (15.5%)
Machinery (43.9%)
Real estate (8.9%)

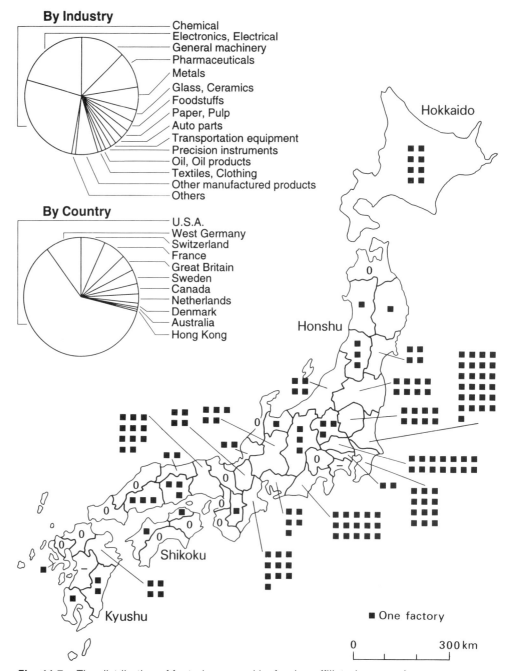

By Industry

- Chemical
- Electronics, Electrical
- General machinery
- Pharmaceuticals
- Metals
- Glass, Ceramics
- Foodstuffs
- Paper, Pulp
- Auto parts
- Transportation equipment
- Precision instruments
- Oil, Oil products
- Textiles, Clothing
- Other manufactured products
- Others

By Country

- U.S.A.
- West Germany
- Switzerland
- France
- Great Britain
- Sweden
- Canada
- Netherlands
- Denmark
- Australia
- Hong Kong

Hokkaido

Honshu

Shikoku

Kyushu

■ One factory

0   300 km

Fig. 11.7 *The distribution of factories owned by foreign-affiliated companies*

Community. An obvious question, therefore, is why this apparent preference for the UK rather than the Netherlands, Luxembourg or Germany, to name but its nearest rivals?

Basic dimensions

In answering this question, it is first necessary to make a few broad observations about the nature of Japanese investment in the UK. First, it should be remembered that the setting up of branch plants and subsidiaries and other forms of ODI is only one part of total Japanese investment in the UK. It accounts for about 25 percent of that investment. Something like 65 percent takes the form of **portfolio investment**, mainly involving the acquisition of securities and bonds. Secondly, and not unrelated, statistics suggest that Japanese investment is overwhelmingly aimed at the tertiary sector, possibly as much as 80 percent of it (Figure 11.8). Finance and insurance accounted for over half of Japan's cumulative ODI in

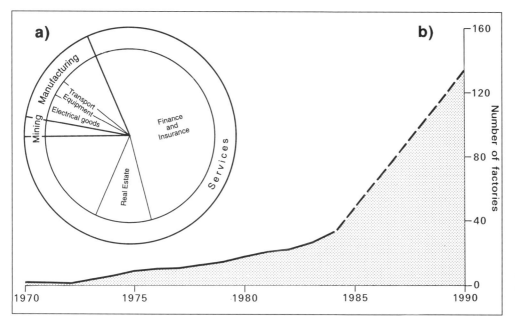

Fig. 11.8 *Japanese ODI in the UK (a) by sector; (b) factory growth (1970–1990)*

1990; manufacturing's share was a little under 15 percent, the mere tip of the iceberg.

Clearly, these figures about the sectoral allocation of Japanese ODI contradict the bias of reporting in the mass-media which tend to see the 'Japanese connection' almost exclusively in industrial terms. They are also inclined to give the impression that the British market is being swamped by consumer goods made in Japanese branch plants located in the UK. The fact of the matter is that of all the 'Japanese' goods being sold on the British market, only about ten percent are actually manufactured in the UK. So penetration of the UK market is still largely being achieved by direct exports.

Finally, there are two aspects of the overall capital flows between Japan and the UK where the balance tips in the latter's favour. First, there is the transfer of royalties and fees which are paid on patents, copyrights and technological know-how. These payments are part of invisibles trading. Rather interestingly, and again possibly contrary to popular thinking, the figures indicate that the net flow of technology has been from the UK to Japan rather than vice-versa. Secondly, and much more significantly, there is the aggregate situation with regard to capital flows. These are referred to as either **capital exports** or **long-term capital flows**. They take into account

all forms of investment movement, including ODI; they are a vital part of invisibles trading and therefore crucial to the balance of payments. For a long time, the long-term capital flows between Japan and the UK have been greater in the direction of Japan, but that imbalance increased decisively during the late 1980s (Table 11.3). The movement of Japanese funds into the UK has been largely in the form of portfolio investment. However, when it comes to the returns on investment payments (investment income), Table 11.3 suggests that Japan's investments in the UK are currently yielding proportionately better profits than the UK's in Japan.

Table 11.3 *Capital exports between Japan and the UK (1985 – 1989)*

Year	Long-term capital flow ($million)		Investment income payments ($million)	
	Japan to UK A	UK to Japan B	UK to Japan C	Japan to UK D
1985	6 984	11 597	2 782	3 712
1986	14 946	13 490	4 198	4 866
1987	11 697	20 189	7 270	8 162
1988	16 322	22 579	10 677	12 969
1989	17 082	97 376	14 482	18 305

Services

Within the tertiary sector, portfolio investment (that is buying shares in British businesses) is a very important component, but many affiliated companies concerned with finance, insurance and real estate have also been set up. The attractions of the UK service sector appear to be (i) London's continuing reputation as one of the world's leading financial and business centres, and the desirability of maintaining a presence in the capital, (ii) the political stability of the country, (iii) the integrity and reliability of its public institutions (such as the Stock Exchange, the Bank of England and the legal system) and (iv) the soundness of the real estate market. These and other qualities have combined to make the UK an appealing proposition for the massive funds, both corporate and personal, which, because of limited opportunities in Japan, are forced to look elsewhere for a safe, but reasonably lucrative investment haven. Whilst most investors are keen to maximise their profits, at the end of the day the key requirement is one of minimised risk. The security of the UK draws the inherently cautious Japanese investor, as does the strength of the yen against the pound sterling, still one of the leading global currencies. Similarly, the UK investor's perception of Japan is that it represents a safe haven.

Manufacturing

Although investment in manufacturing is only a small part of Japanese ODI in the UK, it is worth briefly looking at some of its characteristics. This will also help to shed some light on why the Japanese appear to prefer the UK to other member countries of the EC as an investment location.

Today, there are close to 150 Japanese branch plants and subsidiaries in the UK, employing something in the order of 25 000 people. In addition, there is a growing number of joint ventures. The first direct investment in British manufacturing was made in 1969. The record during the 1970s was one of a slow but steady rise (Figure 11.8). During the 1980s, however, particularly in the second half of the decade, the number of Japanese affil-

iates increased at an accelerating rate. This surge is largely explained by the need on the part of the Japanese producer to establish a presence within the EC before the end of 1992 when trade between member countries became completely free of restrictions and when it became rather more difficult for other countries to trade with the Community. In short, better be within than without. Hence also the high ranking of the Netherlands, France and Germany in the 1990 distribution of Japanese ODI (Table 11.1). The shrewdness of the Japanese strategy was well demonstrated in 1991, when the EC decided to freeze the number of cars imported from Japan (then 1.23 million a year) until the end of 1999. However, it is estimated that Japanese car plants in the Community will raise their production to 1.2 million cars a year by the turn of the century from a figure of 250 000 in 1991.

These Japanese manufacturing concerns show that a number of recurrent structural characteristics are apparent. First, the affiliated companies are small in payroll terms. Less than ten employ over 1 000 people; these include GCE-Hitachi, Sony, NEC and Nissan (Photo 11.1). Secondly, the emphasis of production is very much on consumer goods. The product range is quite diverse; it is far wider than the popular perception of just cars, computers and domestic appliances. The manufacture of zip fasteners, spectacle lenses, fishing tackle, fire alarms and chairs for hairdressing salons illustrates this diversity. Thirdly, despite this overall product diversity, most Japanese companies are highly specialised to the extent of being single-product concerns. Fourthly, the output of most of the factories is not sold exclusively in the UK. The export, or rather the reverse import of Nissan cars made in the North East of Britain to Japan is somewhat exceptional. However, what is much more evident is that many of the Japanese affiliated companies in the UK supply both the UK and the European markets. So the UK is cast in the role of an offshore production base. Presumably it has been chosen for this role because it enjoys good access to the major centres of consumer demand scattered throughout the EC. Equally, the economics are such that (i) it is preferable to have production concentrated in one location rather than proliferate the number of branch plants so that there is one in each country, and (ii) it is cheaper to supply the European market with locally-produced goods rather than export directly from Japan.

Why the UK ?

The last general point raises, in a more specific way, the broad question posed earlier – why locate the production base in the UK? In its time, the relative cheapness of British labour, as compared with that in other 'core' countries of the EC, has been significant. The distribution of Japanese affiliated factories in the UK provides another clue in that there is a clear tendency for them to set up in **assisted areas**, most notably in South Wales. In short, the Japanese have taken advantage of a whole range of financial incentives offered, not just by the British Government and by local authorities, but also by the EC as part of a programme of aid for its peripheral regions. By setting up in assisted areas, and therefore being seen as helping to reduce high levels of unemployment, Japanese companies have been able to neutralise instinctive feelings of resentment towards incoming foreigners. Equally, the Japanese have understood that a labour force which lives under the constant threat of unemployment is going to be more disposed to adopt the rigorous work practices for which the Japanese are famous.

Surveys amongst Japanese companies have also revealed that, when it comes to choosing between the UK and continental Europe, the location decision-making has been influenced by language and other cultural factors. It is interesting to note that of all the European languages, the Japanese feel that they can cope most easily with English. Their perception tends to be that the British are most like themselves, in terms of their attitudes and how they go about things.

In summary, then, the Japanese

interest in British manufacturing is to be explained in terms of (i) cultivating the UK as an offshore production base for the wealthy consumer markets of Europe, (ii) getting a good toehold in the EC before 1993, (iii) benefitting from various governmental incentives, (iv) doing business in a 'sympathetic' country, and (v) reducing trade friction, to some extent, by substituting locally-made products for direct exports.

11.6 JAPANESE ODI IN ASIA

The dominance of North America and Europe in the global distribution of Japanese ODI is readily explained. What seems curious, however, is Japan's relatively limited investment in its own backyard. Although Asia's percentage share rose steadily during the 1970s and 1980s, even today its collective share, 17 percent, is less than half the US figure and is only marginally larger than the European share (Figure 11.1). The smallness of that figure should not be taken as meaning that Asia has little to interest the Japanese investor. Far from it, for as will be demonstrated shortly, Asia has much to offer which is rather different from the sorts of investment opportunity found in the First World.

Background

It would be fair to say that Japan has been somewhat cautious about seizing these opportunities in Asia for historical reasons. During the Second World War, most countries of Asia were occupied by Japanese troops and annexed to the Japanese Empire. Bitter war-time memories of ruthless exploitation, wholesale destruction and human atrocities mean that even today there still persists a degree of anti-Japanese feeling. The Japanese, for their part, have been sensitive to this resentment and investment has proceeded in a cautious manner less they be accused of attempting a second takeover – this time by economic rather than military means. Nonetheless, since 1983, Japan has replaced the USA as the single largest investor in the Asian Pacific region.

199

Fig 11.9 *Japan's stake in Asia: (a) affiliated companies and total employees (1990); (b) total expenditure (1979 – 1989)*

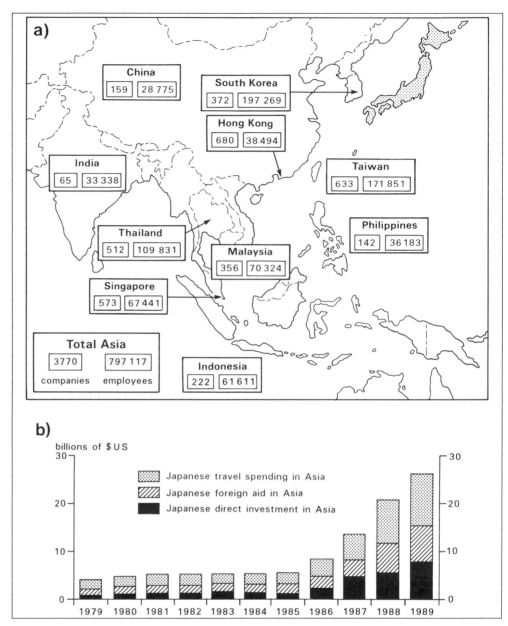

Geographical distribution

Figure 11.9(a) shows the distribution of Japanese ODI in the late 1980s in terms of affiliated companies and their number of employees. At that time, there were nearly 4 000 such companies employing about 800 000 people. Table 11.4 perhaps gives a more comprehensive picture, since the figures for new investment in 1990 include portfolio investment. What needs to be remembered, however, is that direct investment is but one of three major dimensions of Japan's stake in Asia, accounting for slightly less than one-third of its total expenditure (Figure 11.9(b)).

The distribution pattern at a national level is conditioned above all by three motives underlying Japan's ODI in this part of the globe, namely its need (i) to acquire raw materials and energy, (ii) to take advantage of lower industrial production costs, and (iii) to set up the infrastructure necessary for trade (banking, insurance and distribution services) (Table 11.4). To a lesser extent, the distribution is influenced by the pattern of perceived investment risk which, in turn, is largely conditioned the pattern of political stability. Investment tends to be deterred where the political future appears unduly uncertain. This would clearly be a factor in the present relatively low

Table 11.4 *Japanese ODI in Asia (1990)*

	$ billion
Hong Kong	1.79
Thailand	1.15
Indonesia	1.11
Singapore	0.84
Malaysia	0.73
Taiwan	0.45
South Korea	0.38
China	0.37
Philippines	0.26

ranking of China and the Philippines.

Primary commodities

The exploitation of raw materials and energy accounts for about a quarter of Japan's ODI in Asia (Photo 11.2(a)). The raw materials are broadly of two kinds, namely vegetable and mineral. As for the former, Japan's huge demand for hardwood has certainly been responsible for the clearance of much tropical rainforest, particularly in Malaysia and to a lesser extent in Indonesia, Taiwan, the Philippines, Thailand and Burma. The supply to Japan of rubber (mainly from Malaysia and Thailand) and raw cotton (mainly from China and India) are two other raw materials in this first category that have received backing from the Japanese investor. Mineral resources vital to Japan's industry that have attracted investment attention include iron (Pakistan and the Philippines), tin (Malaysia and Indonesia), nickel (Indonesia and the Philippines) and bauxite (Australia, India, Indonesia and Malaysia). However, the prime target of Japanese ODI within the primary sector has been the exploitation of crude oil and natural gas, as part of Japan's efforts since the 1973 Oil Crisis to reduce its energy dependence on Middle Eastern oil. In this context, it is Indonesia, Malaysia and China which have received the closest attention.

Manufacturing

Close to a half of Japanese ODI in Asia is to do with the promotion of manufacturing. Four types of industry are conspicuous, namely the manufacture of (i) electrical goods, (ii) metals, (iii) chemicals and (iv) motor vehicles (Photo 11.2(b)). Japanese investment appears to have been driven by four considerations.

First, Japanese ODI has sought to take advantage of Asia's undoubted

Photo 11.2 *Japanese involvement in (a) resource exploitation, (b) manufacturing and (c) transport*

Electrical goods

Rubber tapping in Malaysia

Japan Air Lines

resource of cheap labour. From the Japanese viewpoint, this has become a very significant factor cost as the high cost of labour at home threatens to reduce the competitiveness of its industries. Secondly, much of that cheap labour is being used to assemble parts made in Japan into finished goods which are then exported to European and North American markets. In this respect, the experiences of the UK and many Asian countries are similar; all are being exploited as offshore production bases. All are being used as a sneaky way of getting around any import quotas that might be imposed on goods made in Japan. Japanese companies, such as Sony and Sanyo, admit that between 80 and 90 percent of their offshore production in Asia is aimed at Europe and North America. Thirdly, by encouraging industrialisation in these countries Japan has a captive market for its own manufactures of machinery and other types of capital good.

In general terms, investment in support of the first three industrial motives has been mainly focused on Hong Kong, Singapore, South Korea and Taiwan. Between 1975 and 1990, due largely to Japanese capital and technology, industrial exports from these economies increased by over ten times.

Finally, some of the industry being supported by Japanese investment exists principally to supply Japanese manufacturers with refined raw materials such as iron and steel, non-ferrous metals, chemicals and textiles. In general, it the less-developed countries, like Indonesia, the Philippines and Thailand, which have been the main targets of such investment. In encouraging such industries, the Japanese have been accused of exporting some of their 'pollution industries'.

Infrastructure

The two main objectives of Japanese ODI discussed so far, namely the exploitation of resources and the promotion of offshore manufacturing, have involved huge expenditures. But both have required that a third type of investment be made, namely one to ensure that the resulting commodities (raw materials, energy, industrial parts and finished goods) are moved, efficiently and economically, to their markets. In the context of Asia's developing countries, this has meant, in physical terms, the construction of roads, railways, ports and airports (Photo 11.2(c)). In business terms, it has meant the setting up of collection and distribution networks, providing banking, insurance and other commercial services. Probably as much as 20 percent of Japanese ODI in Asia has been concerned with this task of creating the infrastructure necessary for trade. The Japanese have not been keen to leave these key matters to the governments of the countries concerned.

Concerns

These three areas of Japanese investment in Asia have not been without their problems. For example, Japanese-backed resource development seems to have caused something of a nationalistic backlash. The developing countries of Asia have become much more protective and convinced that resource exploitation really should be left to them rather than to foreigners. The same sorts of worries surface as in connection with trade. There are two specific concerns. First, that there is too much Japanese involvement and direction, that the business life of Asian countries is becoming too infiltrated by the Japanese. Secondly, that the transport systems, which have emerged as a result of Japanese help, are designed to benefit Japanese investments rather than necessarily meet the developmental needs of the host countries. Countries, like Indonesia and Thailand, also frequently complain that Japan remains only a partially opened door, and that it is still very difficult to export to Japan those agricultural products (rice and fruit) which they can produce at very competitive prices.

So far as Japanese investment in manufacturing is concerned, the criticisms tend to revolve around the observation that Japanese involvement is too capital-oriented and that there has been too little transfer of technology and marketing know-how by Japanese firms. Despite their investment in what are essentially labour-intensive industries, Japan's ODI in Asia is criticised for not creating enough employment. The number of locally-recruited employees in Japanese firms as a proportion of the total workforce is surprisingly low. In Indonesia, that number represents a mere 0.1 percent of the total labour force; in Thailand and South Korea the percentages are 0.3 and 0.7 respectively.

All in all, the popular image of Japan in Asia is increasingly one of a self-seeking, exploitive nation concerned only with satisfying its own needs and promoting its own best interests. The opinion is widespread that Japan should be rather more humanitarian and less hard-headed in its dealings with those developing countries in its own backyard. Whilst one sympathises with such views, one also has to spare a thought for the Japanese. Given that Japan is the successful and therefore dominant economy, it is natural that its partners should harbour feelings, both imagined and real, that they are the victims rather than the beneficiaries of Japanese investment.

In the circumstances, it is difficult for Japan to put a foot right. At times it is faced by contradictory criticisms. For example, on the one hand Japanese capital is accused of dominating the economy of the Asian Pacific region, whilst on the other it is criticised for being too small in amount to play a substantial part in the industrialisation of host countries. Japan's share of total ODI in the region is not overwhelming and averages about 30 percent. This means that by far the greater part of an Asian country's foreign investment comes from non-Japanese sources. Yet even at a level of 30 percent, Japanese ODI is playing a catalytic role in the general development of the Asian Pacific region, particularly its industrial sector. Indeed, so effective has it been in this respect that there has emerged this breed of 'tigers', the NICs, who are already seriously challenging in those industrial fields where Japan has reigned supreme for much of the post-war period. It would be wholly understandable for the Japanese to claim that they are now paying the price for being too helpful, as Hong Kong, Singapore, South Korea and Taiwan threaten in a range of industries from the manufacture of steel, ships and chemicals to motor vehicles, domestic electrical goods and microprocessors. Furthermore, the real maverick among these Asian economic powerhouses, Taiwan, has even emerged as a serious rival in terms of regional offshore investment. In this respect, it was significant that in 1989 Taiwan dislodged Japan as the major foreign investor in the Philippines and Indonesia and ranked ahead of Japan as the second largest overseas investor in Malaysia and Thailand. Taiwan is certainly proving to be a highly ambitious new player in the Asian offshore investment business.

11.7 THE JAPANESE TOURIST ABROAD

Strictly speaking, tourism is a vital part of invisibles trading. However, with over ten million tourists travelling abroad each year, and the number continuing to increase, such an exodus might be seen as a form of Japanese capital export or overseas investment (Figure 11.10(a)). This is particularly so given the Japanese tourist's reputation as a high-spender. A host of benefits ensue tourist expenditure (Figure 11.9(b)), the most basic of which are the support of a diversity of jobs throughout the tourist and travel industries and a good supply of yen currency. Other bonuses include high occupancy rates in expensive hotels, much business for airlines and coach operators, buoyant sales of more costly souvenirs and patronage of a range of personal services.

Figure 11.10(b) shows the growth in Japanese overseas tourism between 1970 and 1990. Two features are noteworthy, namely the depressive effects of the two oil crises and the great take-off in numbers in the second half of the 1980s. The latter would seem to have been the outcome of a number of factors, including rising levels of personal affluence, the overriding strength of the yen against nearly all currencies, the prevalence of a less insular outlook amongst the Japanese and a government programme to encourage travel abroad. The USA is the top destination, followed by a number of Asian Pacific countries

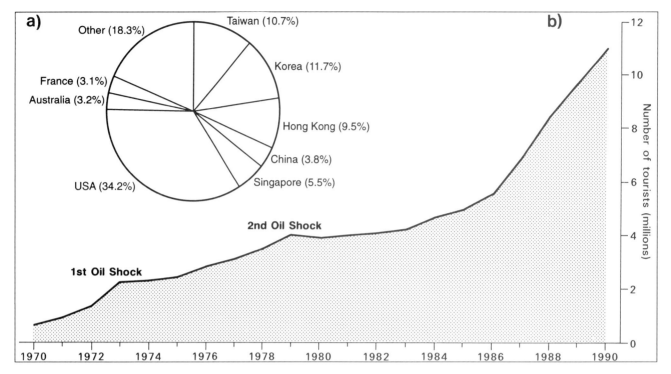

Fig. 11.10 *The growth and destination of Japanese overseas tourism (1970 – 1990)*

(Figure 11.10(a)). The popularity of these geographically close countries is partly explained by the fact that the average Japanese trip abroad lasts a mere five days. One investment outcome of this tourism is that travel abroad does lead in a small number of cases to the private acquisition of real estate, mainly for either vacational use or for retirement. In this context, the Australian Gold Coast has attracted growing interest.

Analyses of Japanese overseas travellers in terms of age and sex highlight the general preponderance of male travellers, except in the 20 to 30 age-range. The popularity of foreign travel with women in their twenties is intriguing. Is it really that they are the more adventurous sex at this age? Or is it to do with Japanese society stereotyping behaviour, along the lines that women who wish to travel overseas should do so before rather than during marriage, and that men in their twenties should be pursuing their early careers in earnest? In much the same way, Japanese convention seems to require that today's newly-wedded couples should honeymoon overseas.

Finally, it is necessary to make the obvious observation that overseas tourism has a flip-side. As with trade and ODI the reciprocal flows are imbalanced in that Japanese outbound tourists outnumber foreign inbound visitors by nearly four to one (Figure 8.16). The fact of the matter is that, for all its dynamism and undoubted scenic and cultural attractions, Japan is for the majority a very expensive tourist destination, given the strength of the yen on the foreign currency exchanges. The number of visitors to Japan is probably also depressed by perceived difficulties with the Japanese language and cultural customs. Nonetheless, although relatively small in number, these overseas visitors to Japan represent yet another international capital flow, yet another strand in the complex external geography of Japan.

12

Aid and defence

The external linkages considered so far in this section have been wholly economic in character (Figure 10.2). Although the two relationships to be examined in this chapter are of a rather different calibre, they do nonetheless both have significant economic connotations. The motivation to become a donor of aid is usually thought of as arising from humanitarian concerns. However, in practice, foreign aid is often about improving economic well-being and promoting development in less fortunate nations. Furthermore, it may be observed that donor nations are not averse to deriving economic benefits for themselves should the opportunity arise. Whilst Japan acknowledges its moral obligations to extend various forms of assistance to the Developing World, examination of its aid programmes reveals a distinct element of self-interest. But Japan is certainly not alone in this respect.

In comparison, defence is an even more egocentric linkage. Here the basic motivation is one of self-preservation. But the precise defensive arrangements made by a country, both in terms of military equipment and international pacts, are also influenced literally by its vested interests, both at home and abroad, and the wish to protect these in the most effective way possible. Clearly, in Japan's case, there is much to be safeguarded.

12.1 OFFICIAL DEVELOPMENT ASSISTANCE

Growth

The aid which the Japanese Government extends to the Developing World is referred to as Official Development Assistance (ODA). Its origins trace back to the reparations payments that Japan was required to make as a condition of its surrender in 1945 and as set out in the 1951 Peace Treaty. Basically, these payments were compensation for the destruction and suffering caused by the Japanese during the Second World War, particularly in the developing countries of South East Asia. Reparations payments started in 1954 and were concluded in 1977. In 1958, Japan began its own voluntary aid programme, with the launch of what was called **loan aid** or **yen loan**. So Japanese ODA was born.

In monetary terms, there has been an impressive rise in the amount of ODA. Even allowing for the effects of inflation, there would appear to have been two waves of accelerated expenditure, in the late 1970s and the late 1980s (Figure 12.1). Between 1985 and 1988,

Fig. 12.1 *The growth of Japanese ODA (1970 – 1990)*

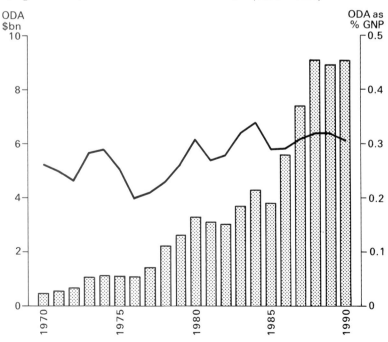

Table 12.1 ODA spending by leading donor nations (1990)

	$ million	Share of GNP (%)
USA	11 366	0.21
Japan	9 069	0.31
France	6 571	0.55
Germany	6 320	0.42
Italy	3 395	0.32
UK	2 647	0.27
Netherlands	2 592	0.94
Canada	2 470	0.44

it more than doubled. On the face of it, Japan would seem to compare very favourably with its fellow donor nations (Table 12.1). But what has to be pointed out in Japan's case is that the increased level of funding has only minimally exceeded the overall expansion of the Japanese economy. The proportion of GNP spent on ODA appears to have stagnated recently at around the 0.3 percent mark. Viewed in this way, Japan shows one of the lowest levels of expenditure among the leading donor nations.

Table 12.2 helps to put ODA expenditure into the broader perspective of what the Japanese refer to as **economic cooperation**. Three distinct flows or sectors are shown. **Official flows** are

overseas investments made by the Government; ODA is seen as accounting for an increasing share. The remaining official flows are made up of things, like export credits and ad hoc payments to multilateral institutions, which also have an air of aid about them. **Private flows** are those overseas investments made by companies, individuals and non-government organisations; these are clearly dominated by ODI, that is essentially company investment (see Chapter 11). **Voluntary flows** largely comprise financial contributions made mainly by individuals to international or multilateral organisations, such as the Red Cross and UNESCO. It also includes private donations to disaster appeals. The points to be emphasised in Table 12.2 are (i) that ODA has progressively dominated official flows, and (ii) that in the late 1980s the value of ODA became outweighed by the sums involved in ODI.

Components

Table 12.3 shows ODA to have two main components – **bilateral** and **multilateral aid**. The **bilateral aid** accounts for about three-quarters of all ODA. This type of aid involves Japan entering into arrangements with individual countries on a one-to-one basis. It comprises two sectors – grants and loans. The latter, the outgrowth of yen loan, is the larger in terms of the sums involved. Not only do the loans have to be repaid within an agreed period, but they also require the payment of interest. By comparison, the grant sector would appear to be a much less commercial, more philanthropic type of aid, involving as it does the provision (usually with strings attached) of capital and of technical assistance. **Multilateral ODA** covers the aid which Japan provides through the medium of a third party, like the United Nations Organisation, the World Bank and various regional development institutions, such as the Asian Development Bank, the African Development Fund and the Inter-American Development Bank. It too comprises two sectors, namely grants (usually of capital) and capital subscriptions to organisations of the type just mentioned.

Table 12.2 Japanese economic cooperation (1970 – 1989) ($ billion)

Year	Official flows			Private flows			Voluntary flows	ODI/ ODA
	Total	ODA	ODA(%)	Total	ODI	ODI(%)		
1970	1.15	0.46	40.0	0.67	0.27	40.3	–	0.6
1975	2.52	1.15	45.6	0.36	0.27	75.0	0.01	0.2
1980	4.78	3.30	69.0	1.96	1.57	80.1	0.03	0.5
1985	3.50	3.80	108.6	7.65	6.17	80.7	0.10	1.6
1989	10.51	9.00	85.6	13.50	11.29	88.1	0.11	1.3

Table 12.3 The sectoral breakdown of ODA (1989)

	Sector		Value ($billion)	Percentage of ODA
Bilateral ODA	1. Grant aid		3.04	33.9
		A. Capital	1.56	
		B. Technical assistance	1.43	
	2. Loans		3.74	41.7
Multilateral ODA			2.19	24.4
Total ODA			8.97	100.0

In the remainder of this discussion, we shall be concerned only with bilateral ODA, because it is in this rather than in multilateral ODA, which works through a third party, that we can best detect Japan's own objectives and inclinations in the field of foreign aid. The data used in the analysis of the current situation will be that for 1989 rather than for 1990, when the general pattern of disembursement was seriously disrupted by the 'freezing' of ODA to one of the leading receiving nations, China (see 12.3).

Geographical distribution

In 1989 Japan extended bilateral ODA to over 130 countries around the world. Table 12.4 analyses its geographical distribution in terms of five groupings of country based on the general level of development. What is noteworthy in these snapshot figures for the 1980s is that the **least-developed countries** (LDCs) received a small but increasing share. The next grouping up the development scale, the more numerous **low-income countries**, appears to have fared proportionately well. Above them, the **middle-income countries** appear to do have done particularly well in the early 1980s, bearing in mind that their general level of need is likely to be less than the two lower groupings. The diminishing allocation to the NICs is hardly surprising, since most of these are now well able to stand on their own feet.

Analysis of ODA allocation at a continental scale shows Asia to be the prime target accounting for just over 60 percent. In 1970, however, that share was over 90 percent (Figure 12.2). Next in the rankings comes Africa. It has taken an increasing share, but in 1990 that portion was still only of the order of ten percent. Table 12.5 sharpens the spatial focus and analyses the distribution in terms of the top ten countries for a sample of years during the 1980s. Particularly impressive here is the sudden appearance of China. It was not in the 1980 rankings, but by 1985 it had come to occupy a position at the top of the league table (see 12.3). Also worthy of note is the high ranking of four of the member states of the Association of South East Asian Nations (ASEAN) - Indonesia (the largest recip-

Table 12.4 Allocation of bilateral ODA, by development grouping (1981 – 1989)

Grouping	1981 (%)	1985 (%)	1989 (%)
OPEC	0.7	0.8	0.4
NICs	15.6	2.9	3.6
Middle-income	31.9	32.9	16.1
Low-income	34.8	45.3	57.4
Least-developed	12.8	12.7	15.0

ient of all on the basis of aggregate figures for the 1980s), the Philippines, Thailand and Malaysia.

Sectoral allocation

An analysis of the purposes to which aid is put reveals yet another significant difference between ODA and ODI. Whilst both types of economic cooperation are concerned with the promotion of development, Figure 12.3 shows that

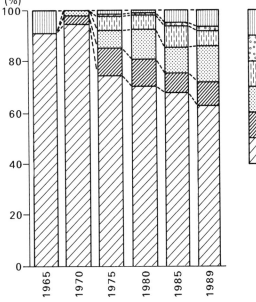
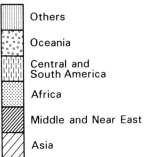

Fig. 12.2 The changing geographical distribution of bilateral ODA (1965 – 1989)

Table 12.5 The ten leading recipients of bilateral ODA (1980 – 1989)

	1980	%	1985	%	1989	%
1.	Indonesia	17.9	China	15.2	Indonesia	12.7
2.	Bangladesh	11.0	Thailand	10.3	China	11.7
3.	Thailand	9.7	Philippines	9.4	Philippines	8.0
4.	Burma	7.8	Indonesia	6.3	Thailand	6.8
5.	Egypt	6.3	Burma	6.0	Bangladesh	5.7
6.	Pakistan	5.7	Malaysia	4.9	India	3.9
7.	Philippines	4.8	Bangladesh	4.8	Pakistan	3.4
8.	South Korea	3.9	Pakistan	3.6	Burma	3.3
9.	Malaysia	3.3	Sri Lanka	3.3	Sri Lanka	2.4
10.	Sri Lanka	2.3	Egypt	2.9	Malaysia	1.6

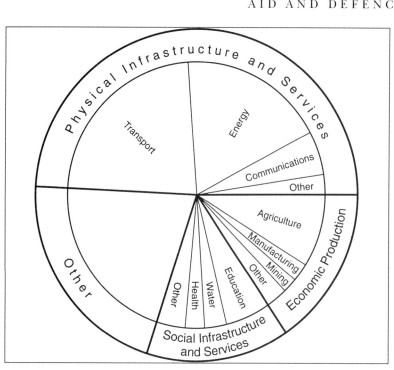

Fig. 12.3 *Sectoral allocation of ODA (1989)*

only 15 percent of bilateral ODA is directly concerned with the promotion of economic production, and that within this sector there is rather more concern with agriculture than with manufacturing. By far the most important target for bilateral ODA is the physical infrastructure and services sector, accounting for almost one-half of total expenditure. The main beneficiaries are, in order, transport (road, rail and port construction), energy (electricity generation) and communications. Also conspicuous is the social infrastructure sector involving the provision of welfare services such as education, medical care and water supply. Collectively, these account for 14 percent. Certainly, one of the impressions gained from this sectoral allocation is that of support for those things most likely to help improve the basic quality of life. Equally, there is the inescapable impression, particularly in the overwhelming size of the physical infrastructure sector, that the Japanese Government is backing projects that ultimately support Japanese private-sector investments.

12.2 ODA AND ASEAN

The origins and aims of ASEAN

The Association of South East Asian Nations (ASEAN) was established in 1967 at a time of great political instability in the region caused largely by the gradual withdrawal of European colonial rule and the rampant spread of communism. The original members were Indonesia, Malaysia, the Philippines, Singapore and Thailand, but in 1984 they were joined by the newly-independent Brunei (Figure 12.4). Table 12.6 shows the sharp contrasts that existed between the original member countries at the time of ASEAN's inauguration, particularly in terms of population, economy and level of development, with Indonesia and Singapore representing the extremes.

Besides promoting regional peace and stability, the objectives of ASEAN included accelerating economic growth, social progress and cultural development, and providing mutual assistance in terms of education and technical training. It may be claimed that today Japan and ASEAN have a special relationship which has grown out of the ASEAN-Japan Forum set up in 1977.

Allocation of ODA

In 1990 ASEAN accounted for 30 percent of bilateral ODA. Figure 12.5 monitors change in Japanese aid over three decades in terms of its composition and allocation to member countries. As regards the former, it is clear that as the relative importance of grant aid has fallen so loan aid has increased; technical assistance has shown a steady rise. In short, the emphasis appears to have changed from straight giving to aid that has to be repaid with interest.

Although ASEAN is a collective organisation, when it has come to the disbursement of bilateral ODA, it has been undertaken on the basis of separate transactions with each of the member countries. At this level, Figure 12.5(b) shows a very uneven allocation. Although Indonesia remains the largest single recipient, its overall share has shown a steady decline; so too has that of the Philippines. But as these two countries have faded somewhat, Malaysia and Thailand have increased their share, particularly the latter in the 1980s. Given Singapore's superior level of development, and Brunei's great oil-based riches, it is hardly surprising that

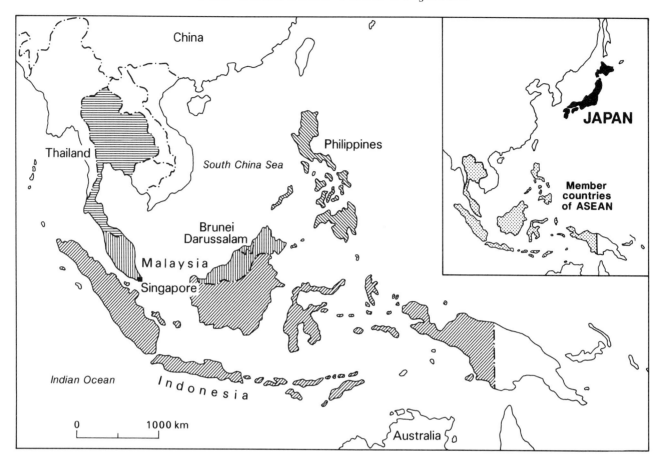

they have taken only a miniscule share of bilateral ODA.

Looking at the sorts of activities and projects which have been supported by ODA in Indonesia and the Philippines, many might be seen as broadly related to resource exploitation. Electricity generation, road building, port development, airport modernisation and communications network schemes have been conspicuous. As is the case elsewhere, loan aid provides the main support for such infrastructural projects. In contrast, grants rather than loans back the more humanitarian and welfare-oriented undertakings, such as irrigation and flood control projects, the construction of hospitals and medical centres, and the setting up of training programmes. It is these types of scheme which promise more immediate benefit for the poorer people; it is a pity that there are not more of them. In Thailand, ODA appears to have a much more distinctly rural or agrarian flavour, as illustrated by village electrification, irrigation and fertilizer

Fig. 12.4 *The member countries of ASEAN*

Table 12.6 *Selected indices for ASEAN countries (1967)*

	Indonesia	Malaysia	Philippines	Singapore	Thailand
Population					
Size (million)	111	10	35	2	33
Density (km²)	58	31	116	3 367	64
Life expectancy years	47	64	58	68	56
Literacy (%)	57	58	81	72	56
Economy					
GNP per capita ($)	100	280	160	570	130
Average annual GNP growth (%)	nd	2.8	0.8	nd	2.4
Primary sector(% total employed)	68	81	58	9	82
Urban (%)	17	27	33	100	13

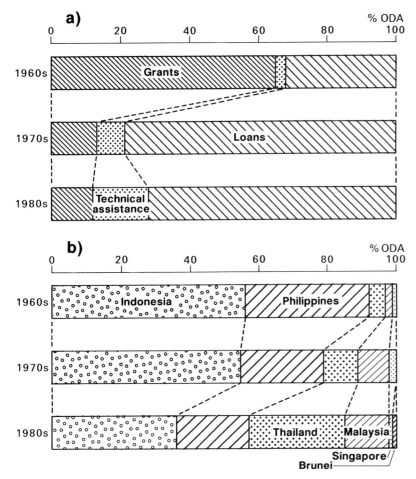

Fig. 12.5 *Changes in bilateral ODA to ASEAN: (a) by type and (b) by country*

documents around the time ODA was launched clearly spell out the underlying philosophy.

'The keynote of Japan's ... policy for economic cooperation must be to contribute to the promotion of economic development for the less-developed countries in the spirit of international cooperation on the one hand, and to the expansion of Japan's export markets as well as for securing Japan's import markets for essential raw materials on the other.' (Department of Foreign Affairs, 1958).

'From the long-run viewpoint of Japanese economic development, it is indispensable for Japan to increase exports of machinery and to secure enough stable sources of raw materials for expanding the scale of the Japanese economy. For this purpose, it is necessary for Japan to take an active part in developing less-developed countries, which are suffering from a shortage of capital and technology, but which have a willingness to develop their abundant natural resources.' (Department of Foreign Affairs, 1961).

No one can accuse the Japanese of hypocrisy, but there are many around the globe, particular other donor nations, who wish that Japan was pursuing a policy of international assistance based less on self-centred pragmatism. Two related changes even in the emphasis of this economically-oriented aid might go some way to achieving a mode of development better suited to the immediate needs of developing countries: (i) to support rural rather than industrial development and (ii) to give a much higher priority to raising the living standards of the poorest people, particularly peasant farmers.

(2) Interestingly, the governments of ASEAN are not heard to complain too much about the economic thrust of Japanese ODA, for economic development is what ASEAN sets as its own top priority. However, ASEAN has been heard to criticise Japan on three counts. First, that Japan is not providing enough ODA in the form of technical assistance and vocational training. Secondly, that so far Japan has done little to help weld member countries into a really cohesive bloc. Instead,

production projects. There is also evidence of rather more support for ventures of a broadly educational and training nature. Given Malaysia's quite longstanding ambitions to become one of Asia's NICs, it is hardly surprising to find ODA largely targeted at creating the infrastructure necessary for industrialisation, from power generation to the opening of research centres, from port schemes to advanced skills training.

Review

Three broad observations may be drawn from this analysis of Japanese aid to ASEAN. As such, they probably hold true for other parts of the Third World currently receiving bilateral ODA.

(1) It is all too easy to be critical of Japanese aid for its economic orientation and its bias towards loans rather than grants. To be fair, however, the Japanese have always openly admitted their essentially pragmatic and material approach. Two quotations from official

Japan has sought only to develop bilateral trade between itself and individual member countries. Thirdly, it is claimed that Japan still does not allow some of ASEAN's primary products, particularly agricultural commodities, open access to its market. The same also applies to much of the output of ASEAN's labour-intensive industries. Market-opening, it is thought, would provide an immense boost to the development of ASEAN; the cost to Japan would be no more than what it is prepared to spend on ODA.

(3) Japan has always been frank as to its objectives within the context of aid, but has the time not come for more enlightened attitudes and greater magnanimity to prevail? Supporting the development of other countries is highly laudable, provided development is recognised as being a multi-dimensional process. It derives from economic progress, yes, but development is also about improving the welfare and well-being of ordinary people, raising the quality of life and broadening horizons. Japan, as the most powerful and wealthy nation in this part of the world, is now well past the point where it needs to be constantly protecting and promoting its own economic interests. Its success now requires that it faces up to new responsibilities and accepts the obligation to do more for the collective good of others in a whole range of fields, not just in the economic. An obvious step here is for Japan to change the aid-mix of grants and loans more in favour of the former. That would certainly help reduce both the exploitive aspect of ODA and the millstone of Third World debt.

12.3 ODA AND CHINA

A chequered history

Of all the countries in the Pacific region with which Japan has links of some sort of another, none is more critical and intriguing than the People's Republic of China. Japan and China stand as the two giants of Asia – Japan by virtue of its economic wealth and influence, China because of its geographical size and immense population. Both countries proudly symbolise two fundamentally different ideologies, capitalism and communism. The links between the two countries date back many centuries. Important aspects of Japanese culture came from China. Historically, the relationship has fluctuated between peaceful co-existence and outright hostility.

At present, the relationship between the two countries appears to be in transition from military confrontation towards a mood of reconciliation and cooperation. It is not an easy transition because there are many people alive in China today who remember Japan's annexation of the Chinese province of Manchuria in 1930 and its occupation of much of the rest of the country during the Second World War (Figure 10.1). Bitter war-time memories endure, often kept alive by the Chinese propaganda machines. However, for all the political posturing, there are some signs of an improving relationship, such as an increasing amount of bilateral trade, rising levels of Japanese ODI and a growing flow of aid from Japan to China. The last two are truly remarkable, bearing in mind that both imply that, if it has not won the day, then certainly capitalism has the upper hand. It must be difficult for the party faithful in China to accommodate this possible interpretation.

It was during the so-called 'Era of the Four Modernisations' (1976–80) that China first nervously opened its doors to Japanese ODI. Bilateral ODA was not agreed until 1981, in which year aid to the value of $28 million was granted. By 1989, the value had increased to $832 million (Figure 12.6). Between 1982 and 1987 China was the top recipient of bilateral ODA (Table 12.5), but its percentage annual share slipped from 15 to 10 percent (Figure 12.6). Since 1988, it has been displaced by Indonesia as the top recipient, whilst the events of Tianamen Square in 1989 caused all aid to, and ODI in, China to be 'frozen' as part of a coordinated international protest. Whilst aid has since been resumed slowly (with

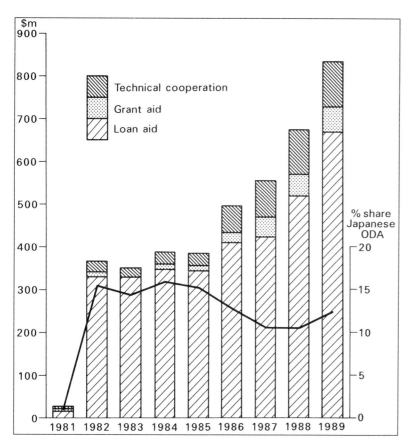

Fig 12.6 *Disbursements of Japanese bilateral ODA to China (1981–9)*

tially increasing energy supplies. Coal and oil are two Chinese commodities which also happen to greatly interest the Japanese. Japanese technical assistance has been almost wholly concerned with the modernisation of Chinese factories.

The little grant aid forthcoming so far is the only aspect of ODA which has not been directed towards economic objectives (Figure 12.6). Instead, it has paid for such things as building and equipping hospitals, supplying library equipment and educational aids. At present, Japan is by far the largest donor of aid to China; it provides something in the order of 80 percent of all received aid. The obvious questions are, what does Japan want from China, and what does China want from Japan? These questions need to be addressed in terms broader than just bilateral ODA.

An intriguing relationship

Initially, the answers lie in the physical closeness of the two countries and the fact that each appears to be able to offer what the other lacks. In strictly economic terms, it may be said that Japan looks to China first and foremost as a huge and untapped market, mainly for its manufactured goods. To a lesser extent, Japan looks to China as a nearby source of oil and coal. Tapping these resources would certainly help Japan achieve the target of diversifying the sources of its energy. China looks to Japan for, above all else, technology. In the Chinese view, Japanese goods are, by comparison, a very secondary requirement, and if China is to buy, it should be capital goods rather than consumer goods.

Beneath these basic needs on both sides, there are some complex undercurrents. For example, Japan is anxious to see China maintain its economic progress because, in its view, a prosperous China is more likely to buy Japanese goods. In contrast, China's view is that economic progress will mean that it can increasingly satisfy its own needs. Indeed, China is very ambitious to become a major industrial power in its own right. It is already actively seeking out future markets for its products, not in Japan of course, but

effect from July, 1990), the confidence of the Japanese investor in China remains seriously shaken.

Composition and allocation of ODA

Approximately 80 percent of the ODA extended to China has been in the form of loan aid (Figure 12.6). The great bulk of this has been used to finance infrastructural developments, such as the building of a freeport on Hainan Island, installing a modern communications system, extending and electrifying the railway network, building HEP stations and so on. In this respect, the picture is very similar to that of ASEAN. In addition to bilateral ODA, inter-bank loans have been agreed between the Export-Import Bank of Japan and the Bank of China. These, loans, like yen loan, have been essentially long-term and low-interest, but they have been used for slightly different purposes. To date, they have financed three oilfield development projects and the opening of eight huge coal mines. The current Chinese plans for greatly increasing agricultural and industrial output by the turn of the century depend critically on substan-

rather in the Third World and, up until recently, elsewhere in the Second World. Another example of the under-tow is provided by China's necd for technology. It was this need that, in the first instance, persuaded the Chinese to open their doors to Japan. China would see itself as deriving long-term benefit from this import of technology. In the short-term, however, China is having to pay a high price, in the form of large loans with interest payments attached, the loss of all too scarce foreign currency and a growing Japanese presence in the country. But by literally letting the Japanese in, the Chinese economy is being infiltrated by an alien influence which it cannot entirely control. In short, the Chinese are inevitably losing some of their autonomy.

Japanese willingness to trade and aid has an important political motivation. The Japanese Government recognises that its own future security is closely tied up with the general well-being of China. Up until the advent of *glasnost* in the late 1980s, both countries felt threatened by the former USSR. The view had prevailed that a modernising and prospering China easing back from hard-line communism was more likely to be able to stand firm against the Soviet Union. Since then, of course, the Second World scenario has changed almost beyond all recognition, but this does not seem to have changed the Japanese conviction that it should seek to develop the best possible rela-tionships with its neighbouring giant.

From the Chinese viewpoint, becoming a recipient of ODA and ODI from capi-talist Japan has clearly posed some ideological problems. Attention has been deflected by placing an emphasis on pragmatic considerations such as the nearness of Japan, their common cultural roots and the tendency for both peoples to think in the same general way. Those Chinese people, who still harbour resentment towards Japan as a consequence of the Second World War, seem able to rationalise their acceptance of Japanese aid and investment by seeing both as wartime reparations. Indeed, accepting these things from Japan is found to be far easier than receiving them from two of its neighbouring NICs, South Korea

and Taiwan. The former because of the Korean War (1950-53), when China backed North Korea's invasion of the South, and the latter because it was the refuge for people who fled mainland China to escape the spread of com-munism during the late 1940s.

One final comment on the Sino-Japanese relationship involves making the point that, in the extreme case, Japan could do without China. China has nothing to offer that Japan cannot find elsewhere, except the tantalising prospect of a huge consumer market. China has only a short-term need for the sort of technology and machinery that Japan is able to provide. There does not seem to be quite the same degree of reciprocity here as compared with that between Japan and ASEAN. Thus, it is possible to appreciate from these two case-studies that Japanese ODA has been stimulated by a different balance of motives. In the case of ASEAN, the considerations are first and foremost economic; they are to do with securing sources of supply and markets and ensuring both for the future. With China, political considera-tions are paramount and relate more to maintaining security and stability in the Asian Pacific region. Security and stability are, of course, a necessary scenario if the Japanese economy is to sustain continuing expansion and rising prosperity. Mention of security provides a neat cue for now consider-ing the defence linkage in Japan's external geography.

12.4 JAPAN'S STRATEGIC LOCATION AND GLOBAL SECURITY

It is widely recognised that the preva-lence of a largely uninterrupted global peace for nearly 50 years has been an important factor in Japan's postwar economic progress and to the exten-sion of the three external linkages of trade, direct investment and aid (Figure 10.2). In some respects, Japan has been a somewhat passive partner in the maintenance of global peace and security. This has been the case princi-pally because the conditions of various treaties have required that Japan should forever renounce the sovereign right to wage war and that it should rearm only in a self-defensive capacity. In addition, the Japanese have placed high priority on regaining face in the eyes of the global community. Almost inevitably, this has meant maintaining a low profile and a degree of neutrality in the various localised disputes which have punctuated postwar history, from the spread of communism in South East Asia to the recurrent troubles in the Middle East.

But Japan has not been able to detach itself completely from global politics of a more offensive kind. The reason simply lies in Japan's strategic location vis-a-vis the two global power blocs of the postwar period up to the early 1990s, the former USSR and the USA (Figure 12.7). It was the West's appreciation of that location in the early days of the Cold War that was initially to hasten Japan's postwar recovery. It was realised that an economically-strong Japan clearly aligned with the West would be an important chess-piece in terms of its global strategy to halt the spread of communism in the Pacific region. Thus shortly after the end of the Second World War, the USA and its allies decided that, rather than extract their pound of flesh from defeated Japan, they should instead encourage recovery and development. The shrewdness of that decision was to be quickly proven within five years of the end of the Second World War,

when communist North Korea invaded the South. During the Korean War, Japan proved its value as an offshore military base and a bastion of capitalism standing firm against an expansive communism.

Let us take a closer look at the strategic aspects of Japan's location in terms of conventional warfare. There are two basic dimensions, namely its location off the eastern seaboard of the CIS and the communist states, North Korea and China, and the great latitudinal range of the islands that make up the Japanese archipelago (Figure 12.8). At its nearest, Japan is only some 200km from the mainland of Asia, where the Tsushima and Chosan Straits separate it from the Korean peninsula. In terms of latitude, Japan stretches for almost 4 000km. Thus it effectively screens and contains a very long stretch of the east coast of Asia. In naval terms, this means that from Japan it is possible to command the entry of shipping into and out of a number of seas formed by macro-embayments of the coast. From north to south, these are: (i) the Sea of Okhotsk – since the loss of the Kurile islands, control of access to the CIS coast has been less complete (see 12.6); (ii) the Sea of Japan – Japan is able to seal off a significant part of the CIS coast and all of the North Korean East coast; (iii) the Yellow and East China Seas – a long stretch of the North

Fig. 12.7 *Collective security arrangements in and around Japan*

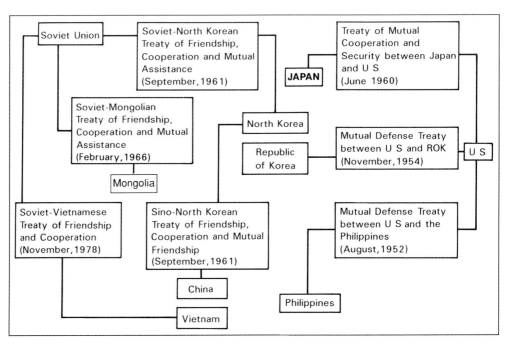

China coast is almost completely sealed off by the Ryukyu islands, except for the Formosa Straits which separate Taiwan from China.

In terms of the deployment of conventional air and land forces, Japan offers immense potential, again principally because of its locational qualities and its latitudinal extent. Japan's location is such, therefore, that it provides three key military opportunities, namely (i) control over vital CIS and Chinese shipping lanes, (ii) a forward base from which to launch direct attacks on the Asian mainland, and (iii) an offshore base for servicing a mainland military presence (Figure 12.8).

One might be forgiven for thinking that, given the advanced military technology of nuclear weapons and long-range guided missiles, that there might have been some devaluation of Japan's strategic significance. There is little evidence, however, to indicate that the USA is any less interested in Japan today, in a military sense, than it was 30 or 40 years ago. For all the modern weaponry and the end of the Cold War, military strategists on both sides have, up to the early 1990s, continued to scheme in terms of conventional forces. The massive deployment of military might in and around Japan clearly attests to the strategic significance of the Asian Pacific in the perception and evaluation of both the capitalist and communist blocs (Figure 12.9).

12.5 SECURITY ARRANGEMENTS WITH THE USA

Japan's current security arrangements date from the two treaties which were hurriedly drawn up shortly after the outbreak of the Korean War in 1950 – the Treaty of Peace (1951) followed by the Treaty of Security (1952). Both were concluded to ensure that Japan became part of the Western alliance and that Japan's location and resources could be used to support the US and UN defence of invaded South Korea.

The Treaty of Security established three vital principles: (i) that Japan should forever renounce war as a

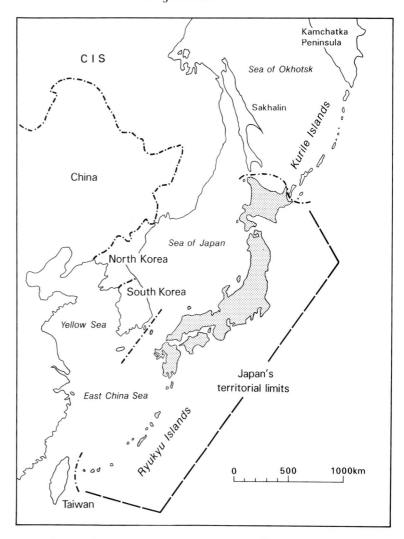

Fig. 12.8 *The strategic value of Japan's location*

sovereign right – in short, Japan was not permitted to take offensive military action; (ii) that the national defence of Japan should derive from security arrangements with the USA – the latter was to be cast in the role of 'minder', and (iii) that the Americans should have the right to station their armed forces in Japan. Such forces were to be permitted on Japanese soil for three purposes: (i) to allow the USA to contribute to the maintenance of peace and security in the Western Pacific region; (ii) to suppress large-scale civil war or internal disturbances in Japan – a sign of the uncertainty which surrounded postwar Japan, and (iii) to help safeguard Japan's security from outside attack. Thus it was that for more than 25 years, Okinawa was requisitioned as a sovereign base for American troops.

During the early 1950s, as a result of the ever chilling Cold War between the

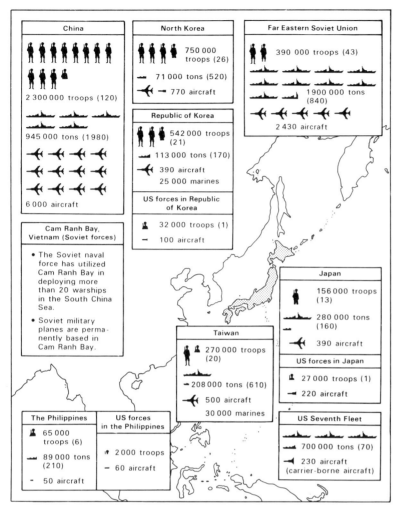

Fig. 12.9 *The deployment of armed forces in and around Japan*

reasonable sense of security and stability in Japan. That, in its turn, has been significant in terms of creating the right sort of climate for Japan's economic success.

12.6 THE SOVIET THREAT

It has to be pointed out that there have been times during the postwar period when, for all the American protection, the Japanese feared invasion by the former Soviet Union. That fear had its roots partly in Soviet treachery in the closing days of the Second World War. In 1941 Japan and the USSR had signed a neutrality pact, but on the 8th August, 1945, just as Japan was about to surrender to the Western allies, the Soviet Union declared war on Japan. Between the 8th August and the 3rd September, Soviet forces invaded Japan and occupied southern Sakhalin and the Kurile Islands (Figure 12.10). The troops of the Commonwealth of Independent States (CIS) are still there. The islands nearest to Japan are now occupied by massive military installations.

With the Soviet military presence literally within a few kilometres of Hokkaido, it is small wonder that the Japanese have felt threatened. The Japanese have consistently made the return of the **Northern Territories** (the islands of Etorofu, Kunashiri, Shikotan and the Habomai group) a condition of any peace treaty agreed with the Soviet Union. Their case has been that these islands were never part of the Kuriles and were clearly signalled as belonging to Japan in the 1951 Peace Treaty (Figure 12.10(a) and (c)). Given the undoubted strategic significance of these islands, particularly in terms of their control over access to and from the Sea of Okhotsk, the Soviet Union steadfastly refused. With no peace treaty in sight even during the closing days of the USSR, all that both nations managed to achieve was the 1956 joint declaration which terminated the state of war between them and restored diplomatic relations. It remains to be seen whether that situation will change with the CIS (see Chapter 14.1).

During the 1970s and 1980s, Japanese

USA and the USSR, it was agreed by the Western powers that Japan should assume rather more responsibility for its own defence. Although still sheltering under the American defence umbrella, from 1954 Japan was permitted to build up its own self-defence force. As a consequence, a degree of rearmament was initiated but only for use in a defensive capacity.

In 1960, a new security agreement was concluded between Japan and the USA. Among the changes introduced was the ending of America's policing role in Japan and a greater say for Japan in the use of the American bases and the troops stationed there. But the most important outcome was the reaffirmation of America's protection of Japan; any attack on Japan would be regarded as an attack on the USA. The significance of these bilateral defence arrangements, which persist today, should not be under-estimated. They have undoubtedly served to create a

fears of the former Soviet Union were heightened by a massive build-up of seemingly offensive forces in the Soviet Far Eastern Region. What were the Soviet intentions? Were they really contemplating taking Japan? It is not possible to say with any certainty. It might have been the former USSR that felt threatened by the closeness of Japan and its availability to the Americans as a launching pad for military operations. In which case, the build-up in its Far Eastern region was to be seem as nothing more than a defensive move. For certain the advent of *glasnost* and the recent signing of various arms limitation and disarmament agreements by the two superpowers, together with the collapse of the Soviet Union and the demise of communism, have created a new geopolitical climate. But even though some of the tension may have been out of the military situation in the Far East, the Japanese still feel apprehensive.

12.7 DEFENCE EXPENDITURE AND SELF-DEFENCE

At present, Japan's self-defence force amounts to just over 155 000 troops, 165 naval vessels and 350 aircraft (Figure 12.9). Since self-defence is the purpose of this force, the troops must be stationed in Japan, however this has been modified by recent relaxations enabling Japan to contribute to international peace keeping forces. Similarly, and strictly speaking, the ships are allowed only to patrol in Japanese territorial waters, and aircraft

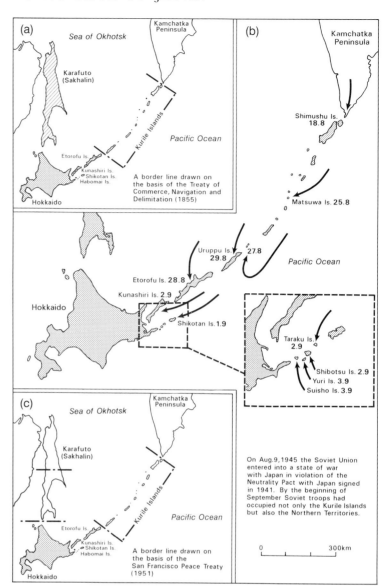

Table 12.6 Expenditure on self-defence (1970–90)

Year	% GNP
1970	0.79
1975	0.84
1980	0.90
1981	0.91
1982	0.93
1983	0.98
1984	0.99
1985	0.99
1986	0.99
1987	1.00
1988	1.01
1989	1.01
1990	1.00

manoeuvres confined to Japanese airspace. The American military presence is now as little as 23 000 troops and 170 aircraft, together with sophisticated hardware for monitoring military movements in the eastern regions of the former USSR and China.

There are two related aspects of self-defence which give rise to much debate both in and outside Japan. They are the level of expenditure and the limits of self-defence. In 1976 the Japanese Government made the decree that the annual outlay on defence should not exceed the equivalent of one percent of GNP. As can be seen from Table 12.6, that self-imposed limit was applied fairly rigorously, but with diminishing success, until the late 1980s. Public opinion surveys in Japan have

Fig. 12.10 The Northern Territories dispute

AID AND DEFENCE

repeatedly shown that the majority of people are strongly against increased defence spending. Two main reasons are given. First, that to spend more on defence may mean exceeding the limits of self-defence. This, of course, raises the interesting question of when does the expansion of a self-defence capability reach the point that the capability becomes potentially offensive? After all, the same military equipment can be readily used defensively and offensively. Certainly, there are still many people who, remembering the Second World War, have a deep determination that Japan shall never again take the role of an aggressor. Secondly, the Japanese readily appreciate that as a consequence of spending such relatively small sums on defence, they have had more money to spend on improving public services and the general quality of life.

Table 12.7 highlights the point about the relative smallness of Japan's defence spending. There are many outside Japan who argue that it should be spending much more. The arguments heard are mainly along the lines that, as one of the world's leading economies, Japan should be (i) spending more on its own defence, (ii) relying less on the USA, particularly so far as the perceived CIS threat is concerned, and (iii) contributing more to the collective security of the West and its allies, certainly in the Asian Pacific region, if not globally. There seem few reasons why Japan could not go some way to meeting the first two proposals. As for the third, many in Japan would argue that the treaties of

1951 and 1952, together with the Japanese Constitution (largely drawn up by the Americans), really allow it only to defend itself, not others. It is a fine point, because one might ask what Japan was doing during, say, the Korean War (1950–53) and the Gulf War (1990–91) other than contributing to the defence of others? Could it really be claimed that Japan was merely defending its own interests?

12.8 THE ECONOMIC BENEFITS OF JAPAN'S SECURITY ARRANGEMENTS

Since 1945, Japan has never been called upon to take an active part in any hostilities. Indeed, it has been expressly forbidden to do so by its Constitution and by international agreement. However, its strategic position and its willing alignment with the USA helped maintain the global balance of power as the USA and the USSR glared at each other across the Pacific for so much of the postwar period. In return for this rather passive contribution to the security of the Western alliance, Japan has been able to reap a number of economic benefits. Japan has obtained defence cheaply from the Americans; defence expenditure has never sapped or deflected the Japanese economy. Thanks to the USA, Japan has enjoyed a much higher degree of security and protection than it could ever have provided or afforded for itself alone. The prevalence of that security and of a largely uninterrupted global peace for nearly 50 years have created the right conditions for the growth of the Japanese economy and the world-wide extension of its economic influence. At the same time, allies grateful for Japan's alignment with the West have felt disposed, if not obliged, to open their doors to Japanese goods and investment. Important economic opportunities have ensued, and Japan has been quick to seize them.

Table 12.7 Defence expenditure: some international comparisons (1988)

	% GNP
Japan	1.0
Saudi Arabia	22.7
USSR	c. 15.0
Israel	14.8
USA	6.4
UK	4.7
France	4.0
West Germany	3.0
Sweden	3.0
Italy	2.4
China	1.9

218

Outlook for the 21st century

13

Domestic issues

In this final section, the aim is to review some of the more pressing issues which confront Japan as it approaches the 21st century. Inevitably, the issues are diverse in character and touch various aspects of the economic, social and political life of Japan, as well as its environment. The issues may be crudely sorted into those which are essentially internal to Japan and those which arise more in an international context. The former will be explored in this chapter, but it should be stressed that some of them do have an international dimension. In short, the simple two-fold classification is not entirely clean-cut.

13.1 A GROWING UNEASE

'The breakneck development of Japan since the early 1960s, the intense,

Photo 13.1 *Emperor Akihito and the new era*

frenetic and, in its own terms, highly successful economic growth, has left the inhabitants of the archipelago a troubled legacy. The theoretical dollar estimate of the wealth of the people is far from matched by the amenities of their lives.' (Ishida, 1988)

'The norms and attitudes which shape Japanese life styles and Japanese society as a whole have undergone crucial changes over the past decade. Indeed a number of tendencies once cited as distinguishing characteristics of the Japanese people actually appear to have reversed themselves.' (Sumiko, 1988)

'The "good life" created by humans has entailed indiscriminate applications of technology. It has become clear however that we are paying for our behaviour with the health of our environment and it is time for a change ... what is needed is a radical rethinking of the relationship among humans and other living things, the earth and technology.' (Nakamura, 1991)

These three quotations, all from Japanese commentators, signal a growing unease that has arisen in Japan as it approaches the 21st century. Interestingly, the concern of the ordinary people of Japan is not only about the economy and likely future rates of growth. Rather there is considerable anxiety about the future of the country and its people in a much broader and less material sense. Undoubtedly, fundamental changes are taking place in the structure of the economy and the nature of society in Japan. A new age is dawning. They coincide with the death of Emperor Hirohito and the end of the Showa era and the advent of Emperor Akihito and the Haisei era of peace and concord (Photo 13.1). The new era calls for a searching reappraisal of where Japan stands and what its people want of life.

Westernisation and maintaining the homogeneity of society

One cause of the current unease arises from a basic conflict. On the one hand, Japan has throughout the postwar period, as part of a much longer historical tradition, sought to maintain its strong custom of focussing in on itself. This it has done in order to preserve the perceived homogeneity of its population and its distinctive national identity. At the same time, however, Westernisation has been seeping into the country. With its emphasis on materialism and the individual, Westernisation may be seen as weakening the consensus and harmony, as well as the sense of order and cohesion, which are claimed to be at the very heart of Japanese society.

The change in values being precipitated by Westernisation is a slow, and to many an imperceptible, process. It does not provoke too much reaction, save amongst the ranks of the elderly and right-wing factions. However, to a wider cross-section of society, a more overt worry is the physical presence of growing numbers of *gaijin* (foreigners) in the country – not tourists, but foreigners resident on a permanent or semi-permanent basis. In particular, they are concerned about the rising ranks of illegal foreign workers drawn to Japan to do low-paid jobs. The number is currently put at around 150 000 and given the growing labour shortage, the number may be expected to increase. Initially, it was Koreans who drew the fire, then people from South East Asian countries, such as the Philippines and Indonesia, and now it is the Iranians. Fears are twofold. First, there is the traditional disapproval of miscegenation, which is seen as threatening what is perceived to be the 'purity' of the Japanese 'race'. Secondly, the irrefutable link between these immigrants and high rates of crime involving property and people is increasingly seen as menacing the very stability and security of Japanese society. It seems certain that the immigrant issue will become even more of a problem as Japan's labour shortage grows. An obvious remedial step is for the Japanese Government to regularise the status of foreigners, particularly immigrant workers. At present, these labourers endure a sort of twilight existence, working, without health insurance and legal rights, for wages significantly lower than those paid to their Japanese equivalents. They are also forced to suffer appalling housing conditions.

The economic base

There are aspects of the economy which give rise to concern. Most have been discussed elsewhere in this book, and it will suffice at this juncture merely to present a summary. Basically, the Japanese, like other people, need to be reassured that the national economy will continue to grow and yield the material comforts to which they have become accustomed. There is a growing pessimism about the economy. Reference is increasingly made to the **bubble economy**, reflecting the insecurity which the Japanese feel, now that by far the greater part of their economic wealth comes from providing services rather than producing goods. The stock market crash of 1987 served to show the potential vulnerability of such an economy. In the opinion of some commentators, the declining economic growth rates of the early 1990s and the recent problems of both industry and services in the face of falling consumer demand at home are evidence that the bubble economy has burst.

Whilst the current gloom does have some foundation, if the Japanese care to look outwards to see how other nations are doing, they might be reassured that they are still faring relatively well (Table 1.1). What also seems clear is that if Japan is to continue to prosper, then modernisation of the economy must be allowed to continue in a co-ordinated manner. In order for this to happen, some painful decisions and adjustments may yet have to be made.

The exposure of Japanese agriculture to the full force of international competition is one obvious nettle to be grasped. Within the secondary sector, there is need to move simultaneously on three fronts by (i) ensuring that Japan maintains its cutting edge of high-tech industries, (ii) selectively retaining and up-dating established 'bread and butter' industries, and (iii) withdrawing from those industries where **comparative advantage** overwhelmingly favours other locations. Acceptance that the service sector has now taken over as the powerhouse of the economy is slow in coming. Here it is the financial services that are the front-runners, with Tokyo now established as one of the financial capitals of the world. A reputation for stability and integrity are absolutely critical to the well-being of this function.

sense, that economic success and its overwhelming impacts on Japan's institutions, infrastructure, environment and the whole way of life took the country by surprise. Many found it difficult to cope with the new order. Although the pace and scale of economic growth may have slackened since the Oil Shocks of the 1970s, the demands particularly on people are no less today as the country strives to make fundamental adjustments to a changing global scenario. Clearly, the prospect for the foreseeable future remains one of unrelenting change.

In some respects, the problems and

Fig. 13.1 *Central elements and interrelationships in the concern for the quality of life and the environment*

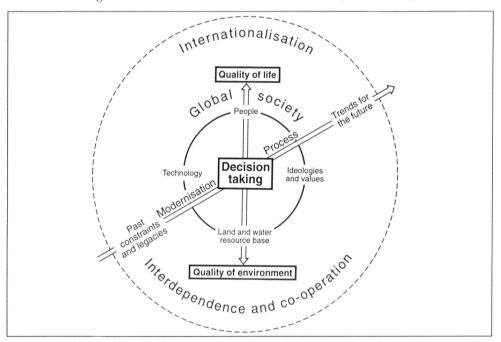

Unhappily, the reputation has been dented by recurrent scandals involving dubious stock speculations and financial dealings, together with an unholy alliance of businessmen and politicians. Two further challenges to flow from the continuing modernisation and expansion of the economy are how best to overcome the growing shortage of labour, and how to achieve further growth without inflicting still more damage on the environment.

Incessant change

The scale and pace of economic success during the high-growth phase up to the 1970s caused immense difficulties, particularly at an individual level. In a

issues which confront Japan are no different from those experienced by all advanced countries as they pass through Rostow's stage of high mass consumption (Figure 3.5). The basic difference is one of time-scale. The passage has been much shorter in Japan's case. The pressure to adjust to profound and incessant change has therefore been markedly more acute. The pressure has been further intensified by Japan's apparent keenness to maintain its postwar pace-setting image and reputation.

The issues generated by the whole modernisation process are numerous, complex and interrelated. However, it is possible to identify three fundamental strands – (i) concern for the

Photo 13.2 *Air pollution over Kitakyushu*

environment and the use of resources, (ii) concern for the quality of life, including but going beyond that of material well-being, and (iii) concern to find a sense of identity and meaning in life amidst all the incessant change.

Before moving on to take a closer look at each of these three recurrent concerns, it would perhaps be useful to place them, and the modernisation process from which they arise, in a contextual framework (Figure 13.1). Fundamental to the modernisation process and its geography are the kinds of decision-taking that ultimately determine both the quality of the environment and the quality of life – the two central concerns of both Japan and the wider world.

13.2 MANAGEMENT AND USE OF THE ENVIRONMENT

One of the ironies of modern society is that whilst today's affluence and mass consumerism came about principally as a result of unsustainable exploitation of the environment, that same affluence and mass consumerism are now part of a new era of environmental enlightenment. Concern for the environment is now a central feature of Japanese Government policy. Surveys show a heightening public awareness in Japan of environmental issues.

Environmental concern is perhaps intensified in Japan by two special

factors. First, there is the meagreness of its resource base, particularly when set alongside the scale of its population. Then there is the legacy of past neglect which is largely the outcome of Japan's obsession with economic growth at all costs during the first three decades of the postwar period. This resulted in abuse of the environment and neglect of the quality of life beyond the immediate aspects of materialism and consumerism (Photo 13.2). As a result of the sheer scale of the abuse and neglect, and despite over a decade of reform, Japan has still much catching up to do in these vital areas.

Within Japan, the most pressing environmental issues today are those to do with the basic resources of land, water and energy. The discussion now turns to a selective look at each of these. It should to be remembered that because the need for resources remains high, and because domestic resources are so limited, Japan must draw increasingly on the potential of overseas environments. In this sense alone, Japan's continued prosperity raises environmental issues in many other parts of the world. This international dimension is discussed in Chapter 14.3.

Land – making the best use and creating more

Japan has always been chronically short of land space and in the past has adopted two ways of meeting this shortage. One was by clearing and terracing the margins of upland areas and the other by reclamation, mainly from the sea. Both methods have a long history and are still very significant today. In the past, much of the reclamation from the sea was to create more agricultural land for paddy rice. Today, the motivation is to provide space for a whole range of urban uses, from office complexes to oil refineries, from housing to leisure amenities. Wetland and waterfront reclamation goes on apace; improved technology has increased the scale of operations (Photo 13.3). Amongst the largest schemes outside the main metropolitan areas are Kojima Bay on the Inland Sea and the lagoons of Naka-umi and Shinji-ko along the Japan Sea coast. Never daunted when it comes to civil engineering challenges, the Japanese are now creating offshore artificial islands. Reconciling all this activity and its obvious impact on habitats and ecosystems with Japan's new found urge to protect and conserve the natural environment is proving very difficult.

Despite the outward signs of greater sensitivity towards the environment, the present economy is, in its own way, proving just as land-hungry as it ever was. By 1990, over 60 percent of the coastline of the four main islands had been developed in some way. It is not only adjacent to major urban areas that

land reclamation continues at a pace. As leisure and recreational activities are developed to meet the needs of Japan's consumer-oriented society, remoter coastlines are also being affected. The most obvious case is the Ryukyu islands (Okinawa) with their sub-tropical climate, palms, sandy beaches and coral reefs. The islands have become one of the most popular destinations in Japan's booming domestic tourist industry. To boost the industry still further, the prefectural Government has recently built a large new airport on land created by filling a lagoon with rock from a nearby hill. Unhappily, the lagoon was part of one of the last living stretches of coral reef in Japan. Much of the reef has already been killed by silting as a result of land clearance for the construction of coastal hotels and for farming to supply some of the needs of the tourists. In addition to the damage to the natural environment, the building of the airport and other developments along the coast threaten the fishing industry upon which coastal villages have traditionally depended.

Pressures on land inland take two forms. One is the clearance of forested upland to meet expanding recreational and leisure needs (Figure 13.2). Such is the Japanese fervour for golf that the demand for more courses appears insatiable (Photo 13.4). This is not only

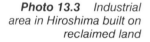

Photo 13.3 Industrial area in Hiroshima built on reclaimed land

leading to the destruction of forest habitat, but contributing to the hazard of landslides and flooding, since such clearance and development greatly increase surface runoff of water. All this is going on despite the Government's and public's commitment to conservation of forest environments (see Chapter 8.6). Legislation seems unable to prevent further encroachment on the upland forests. The situation is not helped by the fact that responsibility for overseeing the implementation of protection and conservation policies is divided amongst a number of ministeries. There needs to be a much more effective coordination of the actions of these various bodies.

The other form of inland pressure is that of encroachment of urban usages onto agricultural land (Figure 13.2). At one time, this was mainly in the form of urban sprawl around the major cities. But with the adoption of a policy of decentralisation away from these areas and revitalisation of rural areas, this encroachment is now threatening not only to take more agricultural land, but also to destroy the character of rural communities.

Currently, there is a great deal of redevelopment going on in Japan. In many ways, this re-use of land to meet the changing needs of Japan's economy and society is being planned with a much greater concern for its environmental impact than were the rushed

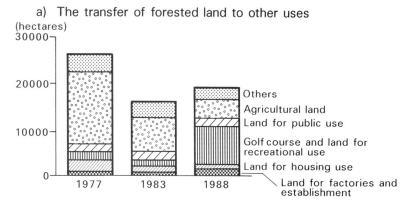

a) The transfer of forested land to other uses

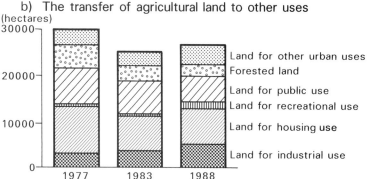

b) The transfer of agricultural land to other uses

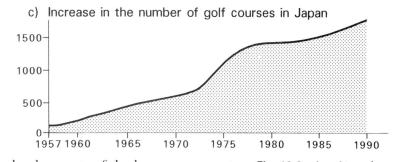

c) Increase in the number of golf courses in Japan

developments of the boom years up to

Fig. 13.2 *Land transfers and the growth of golf courses (1977 – 1988)*

Photo 13.4 *New golf courses carved into the forested uplands*

the early 1970s. Not only are these newer developments visually more attractive, but they take account of the needs of those living in and using the buildings.

Redevelopment is also concerned to actually increase the land area, particularly in view of the astronomical price of land in urban areas (Figure 7.16). This involves a wholesale resort to vertical development, both upwards and underground, made possible by modern civil engineering techniques. The greatest limitation to building upwards in Japan has been the threat of earthquakes. The threat remains, but nonetheless Japanese architects and civil engineers are confident that high-rise buildings of 40 storeys and more can be built to withstand a major earthquake and the impact of the most severe typhoons. Such confidence has led to the recent building of Landmark Tower in Yokohama, the tallest building yet constructed in Japan.

Allied to development upwards, the Japanese are also closely studying the feasibility of large-scale sub-surface developments Subterranean space is already extensively used in Japan's major cities for shopping centres, some office space and subways. But such is only just below the surface. The Government, in particular, is looking at what is termed 'deep subterranean space', at least 50m below the surface, since most of the shallower space beneath the core areas of major cities is already developed. The main use of the deep space will be for urban infrastructure, the expansion of which is essential to relieve the current chronic problems and keep pace with further commercial expansion above ground. Specifically, this means transport arteries, electric power lines, telecommunications and pipes for water, sewage and gas. Warehousing and storage, water tanks and power generation are other possi-

ble 'deep-space' uses.

The main problem associated with both skyscraper and subterranean developments is the cost of construction and maintenance. It is claimed, however, that such is the pressure on land in major cities that further major developments in both directions are to be expected in the near future. Such developments do, of course, have the additional merit of freeing more surface land for the green space and other environmental improvements badly needed to raise the quality of life for city dwellers.

Water supply and associated problems

At present, rainfall over Japan and storage facilities are just sufficient to meet the water requirements of the domestic user and various other demand sectors (Table 13.1). To rule out the possibility of serious water shortages, especially in the metropolitan areas where the risk is greatest, measures have already been implemented for controlling and conserving water supply. To stabilise river flow rates, dams and reservoirs have been built and pipelines laid to move water from areas of plenty to areas of need. Considerable success has also been achieved in conserving and re-using water within the different consumption sectors. Within the agricultural sector, for example, much of the irrigation system is now underground to reduce evaporation and seepage, and the use of water is carefully monitored in relation to need. Today, 75 percent of the water used in industry is recycled compared to 36 percent in 1965. Industrial consumption has actually declined because of the move away from the heavy industries with their thirst for large supplies of water. In contrast, domestic consumption has continued to rise and by 1990 was overtaking industrial usage (Table 13.1). But even here, the rise in demand has been partly met by increased recycling of water.

There are two areas of water management which currently give rise to considerable concern. They are water pollution and the flood hazard.

The concentration of much of Japan's

Table 13.1 *Water consumption (1965–1985)*

Use	1965	1970	1975	1980	1985
			(billion m3 per annum)		
Domestic	6.3	9.4	12.3	13.7	15.1
Industrial	12.6	18.0	18.3	16.5	15.6
Agricultural	–	–	57.0	58.0	58.5
Total			87.6	88.2	89.2

urban development in coastal areas has led to two linked problems, namely land subsidence and the contamination of groundwater supplies by salt-water. The former is caused partly by the sheer weight of the built environment, whilst the latter is exacerbated by over-abstraction of groundwater. Preventing salt-water incursions is proving much more difficult to combat than pollution of water from surface sources such as industrial and domestic effluent. Indeed, pollution from these latter sources has been greatly reduced during the last two decades. Looking to the future, it seems clear that the threatened rise of sea-levels as a result of global warming will increase the frequency and scale of salt-water contamination.

Another serious water problem is the pollution of Japan's lakes, many of which perform a reservoir function in the context of water supply. Lake Biwa, Japan's largest lake, is a case in point. Today, a population of 13 million relies on it for drinking water, and yet, despite the introduction of various anti-pollution measures and controls, it remains highly contaminated. The problem here has been compounded by the fact that that it was not until 1967 that anything was done to rectify the situation. Clearly, it will take decades to correct centuries of neglect.

Flooding is a multi-faceted hazard; it threatens not only buildings and lives, but also contaminates water supplies. A case-study of the Kashio catchment (Kanagawa) clearly demonstrates how the spread of the built-up area, particularly the clearance and use of hillsides, by substantially increasing surface run-off greatly increases the likelihood of flooding (Figure 13.3). For urban Japan as a whole, it is evident that flood prevention measures have failed to keep pace with the rate of urbanisation. Although more recently there has been a move towards more effective flood control and better flood plain management, Japan is now having to pay the cost of failing to take prompt and proper action at the right time (Photo 13.5).

Energy – changing priorities

'Energy is the Achilles heel of Japan and her overwhelming dependence on fuel imports a fact of life' (Crosbie, 1991).

Between 1945 and the first Oil Shock of 1973, Japan depended primarily on imported oil for its energy supply. The vulnerability of that supply was further increased by three factors: (i) the limited domestic sources of energy, (ii) the dependence on heavy energy-consuming industry and (iii) the rise in

Photo 13.5 *Recently-completed flood management scheme*

Over-urbanisation and floods in the Kashio river basin – Kanagawa Prefecture – part of the greater Tokyo metropolitan area

Physical characteristics of the basin

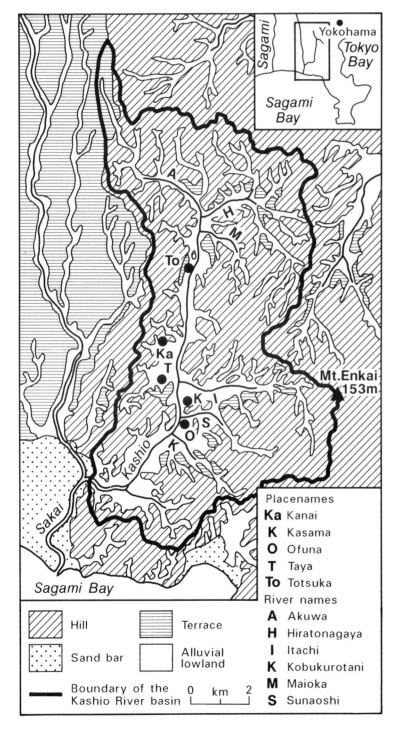

Placenames
Ka Kanai
K Kasama
O Ofuna
T Taya
To Totsuka

River names
A Akuwa
H Hiratonagaya
I Itachi
K Kobukurotani
M Maioka
S Sunaoshi

▨ Hill	▤ Terrace		
⣿ Sand bar	▢ Alluvial lowland		
▬ Boundary of the Kashio River basin	0 km 2		

Figure 13.3

Land development and urbanisation intensifies surface runoff and liability to flooding

1. The straightening of the meandering course of the lower river in 1907 to 1910, associated with readjustment work to make the land more agriculturally productive for rice growing further up the basin, meant flood water was carried more directly downstream causing more flooding after heavy rainfall.

2. With the extension of the rail network into the area from 1889 many factories had also moved into the Kashio lowland from the established industrial zones of Kawasaki and Yokohama. Industrialisation intensified especially during the earlier part of the war, 1941–1945, though many factories

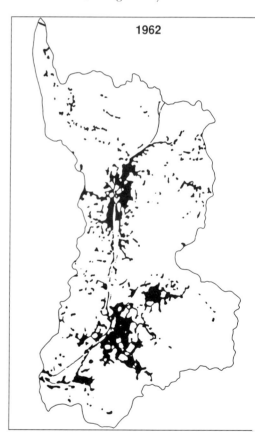

Increase in built-up area

The flood hazard

1. The Kashio River is a tributary of the Sakai River running southwards in the west of Yokohama city. The lowland basin of the Kashio River was formed from deep infilling by sediment of a deeply dissected valley drowned after the Ice Age. The low, flat relief encourages flooding after heavy rainfall.

were destroyed towards the end of the war. But in the postwar boom years many more industries were established in the basin, whilst spread of population from the Tokyo Metropolitan area led to extensive residential spread on the river lowland and terraces above it.

3. From the mid 1960s, land development increased and spread to the hill areas of the river basin with both housing and high-rise blocks being built. By 1980 the population in the Kashio River basin had grown to 446 000 compared to 111 600 in 1960. The basin is now over 50 per cent urbanised. The result has been a drastic modification of the runoff system accentuating the incidence of flooding. Deforestation in the hills, extension of non-infiltrative surfaces and improved drainage have led to an increase in flooding and flood damage.

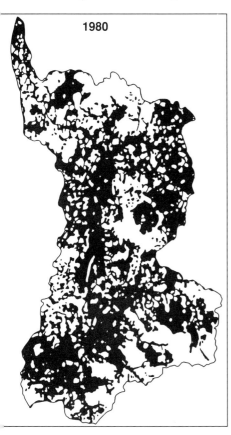

1980

2. Such heavy rainfall is particularly associated with typhoons which affect this part of Japan but it can also occur in the summer semi-monsoonal rain periods.

3. Due to the steep relief in the higher parts of the drainage basin, runoff is rapid giving a sudden rise in river levels and a liability to flooding.

Insufficient drainage and flood management control

1. 1951–1963   Despite typhoon related damage and flooding especially in 1958 only partial attempts were made to prevent flooding by widening the river bed and strengthening the banks in places.

2. 1963–1978   Urbanisation was advancing much faster than flood control measures. The main efforts were directed at increasing runoff flows and the flow of the river. But the rapid urbanisation and thus great extension of impervious surfaces added an even faster dimension to the runoff with which the river could not cope.

3. An integrated scheme was needed to cover the whole drainage basin and this was initiated in 1981. The emphasis was first on controlling further urbanisation in the hill areas so that rainwater could percolate downwards rather than as surface runoff. Developers were also required to put in rainwater control ponds. But these measures only affect those parts of the basin not developed already i.e. about a quarter of it. Runoff remains excessive in the developed areas. To take away excess water a new additional channel needs to be built alongside the existing river as has been done in other areas e.g. for the Kandya River in Tokyo.

Summary – The Kashio basin problem is typical of many drainage basins in Japan where rapid urbanisation has occurred.

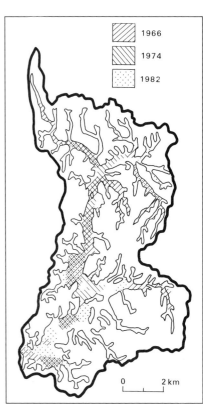

Inundated area of the Kashio River basin due to recent floods

Typhoon effect, September 1982 (Hodagoya Rain Station and Shinko Bridge Hydrograph)

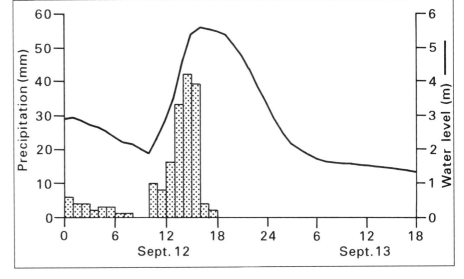

Table 13.2 *Suppliers of oil to Japan (1978–1990)*

Source	1978 %	1985 %	1990 %
Major private companies	65.8	26.1	27.8
Independent companies	3.6	3.7	2.0
Direct deals government to government arrangements	20.7	59.7	61.2
Japanese development companies	9.9	10.5	9.0

Fig. 13.4 *HEP developments in a valley of the Japanese Alps*

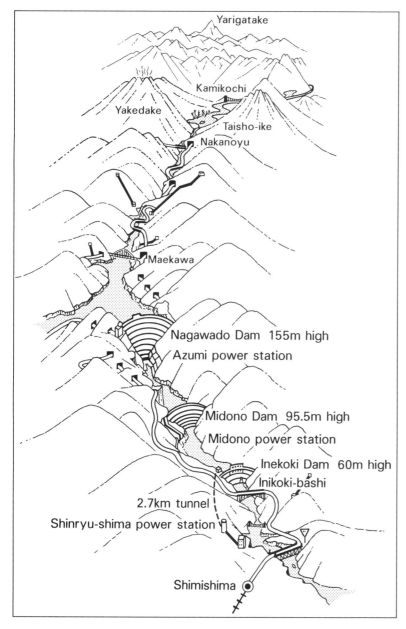

per capita energy consumption which was the inevitable outcome of rising household affluence. Since the mid-1970s, however, the Government has

undertaken and implemented a complete reappraisal of the country's energy policy. As was indicated in Chapter 5.6, in addition to industrial restructuring, the Government has sought to reduce dependence on oil by pursuing three linked strategies: (i) greater energy conservation and greater use of energy-saving technology, (ii) better use of other energy sources, and (iii) research into the use of new and hitherto largely untapped sources of energy, such as wind, solar and geothermal power (Table 5.3).

Japan has already achieved much in terms both of energy conservation and using energy more efficiently. Even so, it may be expected to continue to depend to a significant degree on oil imports, although its contribution to the energy budget is set to decline to about 45 percent by the year 2000. As was pointed out in Chapters 10 and 11, Japan has endeavoured to secure future supplies of oil by diversifying its sources, in particular reducing its dependence on the Middle East, and by moving away from reliance on major oil companies to direct deals with the governments of oil-supplying countries (Table 13.2). There has also been a major shift to the use of liquid natural gas (LNG) rather than crude oil, this more efficient energy coming mainly from the ASEAN countries of Brunei and Indonesia. Coal also looks set to continue to figure in the country's energy budget. Worldwide, there appears to be renewed interest in coal as a fuel, mainly because of its abundance, competitive price and occurrence in politically stable countries. Japan's stocks have dwindled to the point that they only satisfy 10 percent of the current requirement.

Superficially, Japan might seem to enjoy good physical conditions for HEP-generation, so it is not surprising to find it contributing a little more than 20 percent to the country's electricity supply. The main producing area has been the Japanese Alps of central Honshu, close to the Pacific Belt (Figure 13.4). It is unlikely that HEP will assume a greater importance in the future, principally because the rivers do not have sufficiently extensive catchments to support really large HEP schemes. Japanese stations are characteristically small and not very economic. However, it should be noted that these stations have yielded a number of particular benefits. Since many of them are located in mountain areas, they have helped to bring electricity to remote rural farming and forestry areas and are now important in supplying the needs of large recreational and tourist developments in these same areas. Secondly, the construction of dams ponding back reservoirs along forested mountain streams has greatly facilitated river management, resulting in more effective flood control and a better supply of irrigation water. The reservoirs offer much potential for water-based recreation, whilst the construction of roads into these remote areas by HEP authorities have also greatly improved accessibility, encouraging further development.

It is in the nuclear field that Japan looks to increase its supply of energy and to reduce its dependence on imported oil. The decision now gives rise to one of the country's most sensitive issues. Nuclear energy is a technology-intensive form of power; it is also much more highly concentrated, denser and more powerful than other forms of energy now used. As a result, it requires much less fuel and land, and produces smaller quantities of waste in generating the same amount of electricity as other conventional sources. In

certain respects, nuclear power is more environmentally friendly than fossil fuels. The appeal of nuclear energy to the Japanese is easy to understand. With 40 nuclear stations in operation, and with others either under construction or at the planning stage, Japan now has one of the biggest nuclear programmes in the world (Figure 13.5). Roughly a quarter of the country's electricity comes from these stations, and that contribution is scheduled to increase by the turn of the century.

However, expansion of the Japanese nuclear energy industry has slowed in the face of growing public concern for the safety of nuclear reactors triggered off by the Chernobyl disaster of 1986. Public concern centres on the accidental release of harmful radioactive matter and the safe disposal of nuclear waste. A recent minor failure at one of its nuclear power stations has done little to allay public fears, and the voice of protest has become more vociferous and effective to the point that plants planned for Shikoku and Hokkaido have now been abandoned.

Inevitably, this resistance and pressure of public opinion are prompting a reappraisal of the energy budget that emerged in the wake of the two Oil Shocks. For example, the projection for oil has recently been revised upwards from 45 to 50 percent of the primary

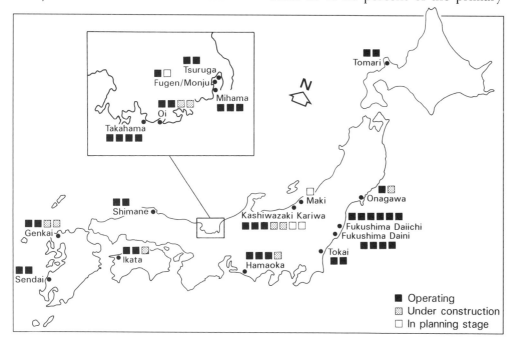

Fig. 13.5 *The distribution of nuclear power stations (1990)*

energy requirement by the turn of the century. Another outcome has been intensification of research into the harnessing of alternative sources of energy, such as wind and wave power, geothermal and solar energy. The costs of developing these sources are high in relation to the potential contribution they can make to the supply of energy. None can be exploited to produce energy in sufficient quantity to be economically viable. Meanwhile, Japan is heavily involved in fusion research, in cooperation with the USA, but this is not likely to yield meaningful results until well into the 21st century.

Assuming energy demands remain strong, it would seem that Japan has little alternative but to stick with the nuclear option. It is a matter of balancing increasing public opposition against the desirability of implementing an energy budget that reduces the country's vulnerability to the sort of blackmail that prevailed at the time of the two Oil Shocks.

13.3 QUALITY OF LIFE

Recent government reports indicate a growing concern about the apparent gap between the high level of material income and the actual quality of life enjoyed by the Japanese people. One obvious difficulty here is to identify what constitutes a good quality of life. Unquestionably, material wealth is an important component, since high levels of spending usually yield the physical comforts of life. Today, the vast major-

ity of Japanese are well fed and enjoy the benefits in their homes of central heating and air conditioning. The typical Japanese home also has its full complement of durable goods, including household appliances and the latest in leisure viewing and listening (Table 13.3). The level of car-ownership is one of the highest in the world. What is more, the urban Japanese especially are geared to luxury items, be it in the form of exotic food and drink, expensive apparel or the latest in high-tech consumerism. The life styles of the younger generations in particular are geared to fashion and change, much of it influenced by the introduction of Western styles (Photo 13.6). It is also noted that consumer products have remarkably short life cycles, surviving only until models superior in design and appearance come on the scene.

What is now being painfully discovered in Japan is that simply adding to people's income by a further expansion of the economy and widening still further the range of consumer choice is not the answer to people still feeling that they do not have the sort of quality of life they perceive to be enjoyed by many in the West, particularly in the USA. Undoubtedly, part of the answer to this problem lies in the fact that there are other aspects of living which also contribute to one's quality of life and which have been insufficiently fostered during Japan's postwar boom years.

Beyond the possession of material wealth, there must be a feeling of physical and mental well-being, a sense of satisfaction with life and a sense of freedom to enjoy what life has to offer. The majority of Japanese people, mostly those living in urban areas, do not have this sense of well-being because of the physical and mental stress placed on them in their everyday living. The traditional obsession with work above the enjoyment of home life and leisure time dies hard and remains a major contributory factor. For many years, the Japanese have been persuaded into believing that devoting all their time to the company was the key not only to improved status and income, but to personal fulfilment as well. Pressure and stress are also generated by the sheer pace of living in a modernised and

Table 13.3 *Ownership of consumer durables (1990)*

	Ownership (% of homes)	Number per 100 homes
Color TV sets	99.4	196.4
Refrigerators	98.2	116.2
Washing machines	99.5	108.0
Vacuum cleaners	98.8	130.8
Cameras	87.2	136.5
Passenger cars	77.3	108.0
Stereos	59.3	67.0
Air conditioners	63.7	114.0
Microwave ovens	69.7	71.0
Videocassette recorders	66.8	81.6
Pianos	22.7	22.9
Push-button phones	39.6	55.1
Personal Computers	10.6	11.2
CD players	34.3	37.6

Photo 13.6 *Fashion-conscious, free spending young people*

rapidly-changing urban society. In Japan's case, this is heightened because the physical and social infrastructure has not been improved and expanded sufficiently to keep pace with economic progress and change. One obvious symptom of this stress and pace, and the general competitiveness of Japanese society, is the relatively high suicide rate (Table 13.4).

13.4 THE QUALITY OF THE BUILT ENVIRONMENT

There is now the realisation in Japan that quality of life is inseparably linked to quality of the environment. So far as the natural environment is concerned, it is appreciated that people can gain pleasure from it and a sense of renewal which adds to the enrichment of life. The rising popularity of outdoor recreation and leisure in modern urban society may be seen as an expression of this therapeutic value. Furthermore, Japanese culture has always had within it some close affinity with nature. However, perhaps rather belatedly, it is now being increasingly understood that the quality of the built environment, in which people now spend so much of their lives, can and does exercise a powerful influence on the quality of life. There are many telling aspects to that environment – from the quality of housing to the availability of commercial and social services, from public parks and open space to ease of movement. But perhaps the most obvious is the degree to which the built environment suffers from pollution.

Pollution

It is quite clear that since the environmental tragedies of the high-growth phase, such as the notorious mercury pollution incidences at Niigata and Minamata, and the outbreaks of *itai-itai* (cadmium poisoning), the Japanese Government has invested much money in pollution control, spending the equivalent of two percent of GNP. Its pollution control legislation is now amongst the strictest in the world. As a consequence, there has been a marked

Table 13.4 *Suicide rates: some international comparisons (1990)*

	rate per 100 000 population
Japan	19.5
Switzerland	24.1
France	22.6
West Germany	19.0
Canada	14.5
USA	12.8
Australia	12.4
Singapore	11.6
UK	7.9

improvement in the quality of both the atmospheric and aquatic aspects of the built environment. However, further improvement is now being hindered by inadequacies in the legal framework to enforce corporations and individuals to comply with the law, and by insufficient support for environmental organisations.

Recent reports on air quality indicate that levels of harmful gases, such as sulphur dioxide and carbon monoxide, are now static rather than falling, whilst nitrogen dioxide has actually worsened (Figure 13.6). The major culprit is the rising volume of urban road traffic. In enclosed water areas and the narrow fronted bays of Japan's coast, water pollution remains at a worrying level. It is further exacerbated by millions of tons of rubble and waste being dumped in bay areas to form the foundations of large-scale reclamation projects.

Fig. 13.6 Energy consumption and emissions of carbon, sulphur and nitrogen dioxides

Two forms of pollution highlighted in a recent report of the Environmental Agency are noise and the rapidly rising volumes of plastic, paper and other

waste resulting from mass consumption and the advent of the information-based age. Fax sheets, computer print-out, circulars, newspapers and magazines give rise to mountains of waste paper.

Complaints about the rise in the level of noise pollution have greatly increased. Some of the increased noise generation occurs in the home from domestic equipment, such as washing machines, and from hi-fis and TVs almost constantly in use. Factories have always been renowned for their high levels of noise, now computer printers, fax machines and photocopiers are exacerbating noise pollution in the office. Construction and traffic are major noise generators. The ears of shoppers are constantly assaulted by advertising on public address systems. Japan is in the throes of urban redevelopment and attempts to restructure transport arteries to cope with the growing volume of traffic, has created a crisis in noise pollution. Without doubt, increased noise is a major factor in the creation of stress.

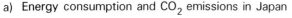

a) Energy consumption and CO_2 emissions in Japan

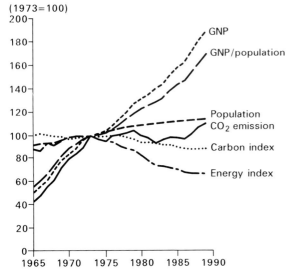

b) Sources of CO_2 emissions in Japan

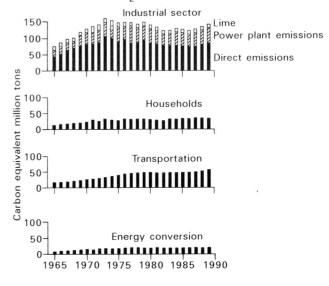

c) Annual average Nitrogen and Sulphur Dioxide concentrations

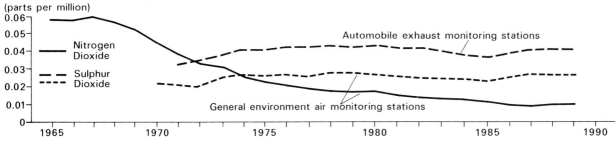

No less serious, but in a rather different way, is the growing crisis associated with waste disposal, an increasing problem for all advanced societies. Between 1988 and 1990, total garbage disposal in Japan increased from 48 to 60 million tons. The problem is most serious for the metropolitan areas which have largely run out of waste disposal sites locally and are now dependent on more distant prefectures accepting their waste. It is not uncommon to find waste disposal trucks making round trips of over 200km to tipping sites. In some of these dumping areas, there is a growing resistance to tipping on the grounds of pollution and health risks. This, in turn, is increasing the temptation to dump in coastal waters. The latter course of action would, of course, promise even greater environmental disasters. At the moment, Japan lags behind the West in terms of the recycling of materials and developing safer ways of processing and disposing of waste.

Housing

One large minus that needs to be set against the high incomes and general affluence of the Japanese is that the general cost of living is amongst the highest in the world. Food is the major living expense (Table 13.5). As discussed in Chapter 8.3, prices remain high because of the Government's price support for domestically produced food and its control of food imports. Expenditure on housing is the second largest single item in the household budget. Over the last 25 years, housing living space has remained cramped, whilst house prices have soared, doubling between 1985 and 1990, largely as a result of the rise in land prices caused by the overall shortage of building land. In Tokyo, the price of an ordinary family dwelling is from 12 to 16 times the family's disposable income, double that for example in the UK. Moreover, in order to find affordable housing, families are forced to live at increasing distances from the central city areas where most workplaces and commercial services are located.

The Government is making urgent moves to mitigate the housing problem with such schemes as subsidised inter-

Table 13.5 *Household accounts (1990)*

	Amount per month (Yen)	US$
Income	**521 757**	**3 604**
Regular	332 026	2 293
Temporary and bonuses	48 644	681
Disposable Income	**440 839**	**3 043**
Living expenditure	331 595	2 290
Food	79 993	552
Housing, fuel and light	56 200	388
Clothing and footwear	23 902	165
Medical care	8 670	60
Education	16 821	116
Reading and recreation	31 761	219
Propensity to consume	**75.3%**	

NB Propensity to consume $= \dfrac{\text{living expenditure}}{\text{disposable income}} \times 100$

est rates on mortgages for intending home buyers. Mortgage facilities are now available over a 50-year period or more. Although house ownership is statistically comparatively high in Japan, amounting to 62 percent, in practice actual ownership is decreasing with long-term mortgages being passed down through the family from one generation to the next. Between 1988 and 1991, the numbers entering the owner-occupied sector fell quite markedly. Young couples wishing to set up on their own simply cannot afford the huge mortgage repayments required by the high cost of housing. Many have given up hope of ever owning a house, and instead now spend their disposable income on exotic holidays and expensive consumer goods. Certainly, the cost of housing is partly responsible for the increase in the number of economically-active women and ultimately, therefore, for the fall in the birth rate.

A major part of the problem remains the cost of land for housing, and indeed for other kinds of construction. How to curb this cost element is a subject of much debate. The suspicion is growing that the price of land is being manipulated by vested interests to maintain it at an artificially high level. If there is such a conspiracy afoot, then how is the bubble to be burst? The Government has recently introduced measures that reform the land tax system and thereby reduce the incentive to speculate in land. It is a step in the right direction, but other actions will need to be taken, such as relaxing the planning controls on the transfer of land from agricultural to residential use.

Another facet of the housing problem is the rising proportion of single-person households (Figure 13.7). This trend inevitably increases the demand for dwellings and also requires adjustments being made in the type of dwellings produced by the house-building industry.

Social services and a silvering population

One of the most worrying aspects of Japanese society today is the growing gap between the wealthier sectors, who have benefitted from the recent boom in shares and land prices, and those on modest or low incomes, for whom there has been little real rise in wages whilst living costs have increased. Japan has rightly always prided itself on being an egalitarian society, with a greater equality of income and status across society than any advanced nation. Clearly, this polarisation is beginning to change that. As it does so, it raises the whole issue of providing public goods and services for those increasing numbers of households without the means to pay for such things as medical treatment and private education. The latter is particularly important in today's Japan, for it provides the passport to higher education and a good job.

There is not space here to explore the

social welfare system in any detail, but in view of the increasing pressures that will be placed on it, if only by the rising ranks of underprivileged households, some consideration must be given. The present social security system covers the three areas of health, pensions and unemployment. In the majority of cases, employers and employees each contribute the equivalence of just 10 percent of wages or salary to pay for these benefits. As far as national health insurance is concerned, people are required to pay 20 percent of the cost of treatment. It is for this reason that many take out additional private health insurance. Similarly, many have their own private pension schemes to supplement the state pension paid to both sexes on reaching retirement age. Also included in the social security system is public assistance which is paid to those households whose income falls below the statutory minimum. The elderly, the sick, the handicapped and single parents are the particular beneficiaries here. Another form of public assistance is the child support programme which is intended to boost the low birth rate. It provides a monthly allowance for each additional child after the third. More recently still, maternity leave of up to one year has become a statutory right for working women.

It is frequently stated that Japan's overall welfare system is a cross between what is traditional in Asia, where the **extended family** network has been the main provider, and the state welfare system adopted during the postwar period by a number of Western European countries such as France and the UK. Even as late as the 1960s, it was still considered that social support for individual members in Japanese society should come basically from within the family as in traditional societies. Perhaps one of the best illustrations of this was the custom for the eldest son and his wife to take elderly parents into their home and care for them in old age. In return, elderly parents gave support in the care and up-bringing of young offspring. Another part of the Japanese tradition has been the provision of pensions and health schemes by the large companies for the benefit of employees; these are additional to the

Fig. 13.7 *Household trends (1960–2025)*

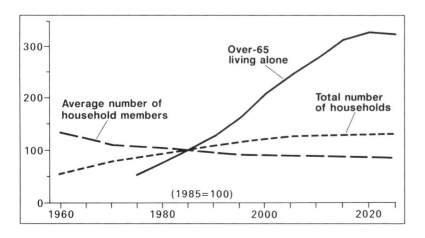

state entitlements. However, the majority of employees in Japan work for small companies or are self-employed in family businesses. For them no such provision is normally made. As a consequence, there has during the postwar period been an increasing propensity for saving to meet the income and welfare needs of old age.

The problem of providing adequate services is, of course, being made worse by the **silvering** of the population. The ageing is the outcome of greatly increased life expectancy and the marked fall in the birth rate since the 1960s (see Chapter 5.1). In 1990, 12 percent of the population was over 65 years old; by 1995 that figure is forecast to rise to nearly 15 percent, and by the year 2040 to 25 percent, the highest amongst advanced countries (Figure 13.8). At the same time, the proportion of the population at work and earning will be shrinking. This poses an enormous problem for the Japanese Government in terms of making adequate provision of relevant services and raising the revenue to pay for that provision. Raising taxes is the obvious way to deal with the latter, but with the economy in a low-growth mode and with the proportion of taxpayers in the population dwindling, there is the real danger of fiscally over-burdening people. So far, the Government has made no commitment to substantially increase its expenditure on public assistance in order to improve the lot of the poor and needy (Table 13.6).

For the wealthy and healthy, retirement today has brought a golden age with comfortable living standards and many leisure opportunities. But there is a growing sector of elderly people, often living alone and obliged to survive on tight budgets determined by diminishing assets and a meagre pension. For these people, much more nursing home provision, sheltered accommodation and support services in the community are needed (Photo 13.7). It is significant that an increasing number of people of pensionable age are undertaking part-time work. In 1990, 35 percent of all those aged 65 or more were still undertaking paid work, the figure being at least 50 percent higher than in other advanced coun-

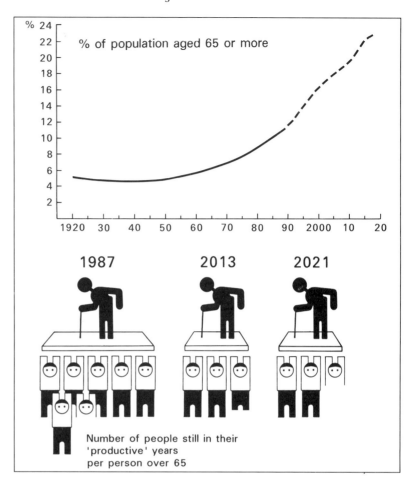

Number of people still in their 'productive' years per person over 65

tries. In the majority of cases, it is financial need which has driven pensioners to seek work. But two other factors serve to boost the Japanese figure. Some pensioners take on work because they belong to a generation basically unused to filling in leisure time. Others have been persuaded by

Fig. 13.8 *The silvering of the population*

Table 13.6 *Government welfare-related expenditures (1980 and 1989)*

| | Expenditures | | |
| | Y billion | | Share (%) |
	1980	1989	1989
Public assistance	1 179	1 513	2.8
Social welfare	2 111	2 270	4.2
Social insurance	20 728	42 625	79.6
Health insurance	9 934	16 795	31.4
Annuity insurance	8 671	22 079	41.2
Unemployment insurance	1 272	2 378	4.4
Public health and medical care	2 270	2 710	5.1
Elderly health and medical care	–	5 520	10.3
Pensions	1 721	1 913	3.6
Aid for war victims	270	402	0.8
Housing assistance	318	275	0.5
Employment measures	144	102	0.2
Total	**28 742**	**53 532**	**100.0**

Photo 13.7 *More retirement care is needed for the population*

recruitment campaigns specifically targeted at the elderly by companies and small businesses desperately seeking ways of overcoming the increasing labour shortage.

13.5 MOVEMENT AND COMMUNICATION

The final issue to be discussed under the broad heading of quality of life is rather different. It involves not just the built environment, but also the natural environment and the whole of the national territory. The point has been made in earlier chapters that the terrain of Japan is not conducive to movement. Densely settled, fragmented lowlands are separated by quite inaccessible upland tracts. Although great advances have been made in terms of breaking down the barrier effects of the uplands by means of national transport and communication networks, those networks have not kept pace with demand (Photo 13.8). In fact, the overall provision falls below that in the USA and leading Western European countries. Japan faces a transport crisis born, as with other contemporary problems, from the

Photo 13.8 *Modern routeways through the mountains, Kyushu Expressway*

sheer pace of economic growth and the failure of government to make commensurate investment at the right time (Figure 13.9).

On the other hand, some of the technical and engineering achievements of Japan in the field of transportation have been spectacular and among the best in the world. Amongst those achievements, one might cite the three *shinkansen* lines, the Seikan Tunnel and the Honshu-Shikoku bridges (Figure 13.9). Impressive though they are, there is the widespread opinion that they have come rather late in terms of helping achieve two basic national objectives, namely the physical integration of the Japanese islands into a single cohesive unit and a much more even distribution of economic growth.

Failure to make proper investment in the transport networks has made two specific impacts on the quality of life. Within the highly urbanised Pacific Belt, the transport networks are now placed under serious strain and suffer acute congestion. For the individual, this means travelling on manifestly overloaded public transport and suffering considerable discomfort in so doing. Car journeys, particularly within urban areas, are characteristically slow and grinding, because the number of vehicles on the road greatly exceeds the system's capacity. Parking is a nightmare. For business, delays cost money and debilitate efficiency. Much of the present transport network was developed in the 1960s and 1970s and is now ageing and requiring costly refurbishment or replacement.

Outside the Pacific Belt, the transport networks have not been sufficiently extended to integrate Japan's remoter regions with the core. Hokkaido, the Japan Sea coast of Honshu and Shikoku have until the 1980s suffered in this respect, their general inaccessibility making it difficult for them to attract economic growth and to retain their populations. For the individual, the feeling of being isolated from the centre of things, the cost, discomfort and time involved in making trips to Tokyo or any other leading city are aspects of the transport situation which, along with other factors, have persuaded many to leave these peripheral regions for good.

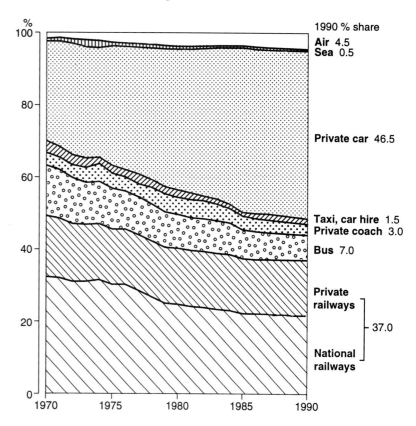

Fig. 13.10 *Passenger traffic (1970–1990)*

There are particular challenges which currently arise in the context of transport and communication, such as the need to reverse the trend in the balance between road and rail for the movement of people (Figure 13.10). For all the congestion and delays, the motor car continues to be increasingly used for commuting, business, recreation and leisure. It is in the major cities, and despite the construction of underground and surface railway lines to link in new suburbs and dormitory settlements, that the modal shift is most needed. Even greater imbalance between the modes is evident in the movement of freight, where motor vehicles carry more than five times more freight than trains (Figure 13.11). The one aspect of goods movement that does make sense, however, is that by coastwise shipping, clearly encouraged by the island character of the country.

From this it can be seen that one of the major challenges for the 21st century is to prise people out of their motor cars and to transfer freight from road to rail. The case is strengthened by the fact that, in general terms, rail is the more environmentally-friendly mode of transport. Alongside this, and no less

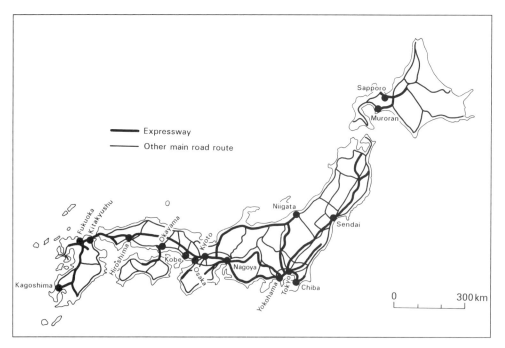

General

Despite developments since the 1960s, the transport networks are inadequate in relation to demand and compare unfavourably with those of other advanced countries as the USA, UK and France.

Why is this so?

1. Rapid economic expansion since the 1960s led to a greatly increased demand which has accelerated faster than transport improvements.

2. Delayed decision-taking on the part of government and transport utilities.

   – Up to 1970 this was due to an overemphasis on economic growth at the expense of infrastructural improvements.

   – After this date the Oil Shocks of the 1970s and the Yen Crisis in the 1980s, though slowing economic growth, also reduced funds available.

3. Long planning and implementation process even after decision to improve and extend the transport network.

4. Physical difficulties – archipelago nature of Japan and much mountainous terrain make construction difficult and costly.

The road network

Despite evidence of a marked switch from rail to road transport since the 1970s, Japan has only recently embarked on a massive road development programme.

There is only one motor expressway route running across the country and this fails to link in the islands of Hokkaido and Shikoku. These are poorly served as are the Japan Sea coast towns, except those of the central part which are linked to the Pacific Belt by two expressways cutting through Japan's mountainous interior. Elsewhere the expressway network is partial only – linkage being via main roads of reduced capacity. The actual pattern is partly a reflection of the difficult physical terrain, partly of demand and partly of inadequate forward investment in roads. Nearly half of the country's settlements are over 1 hour's drive from a motorway.

About one-third of Japan's minor roads are unmetalled, many main roads have narrow stretches, tight bends and steep gradients, comparatively few settlements have been by-passed.

Despite these limitations, the location of economic activity has been increasingly guided by road access rather than rail, especially at motorway nodes and along main routes out of cities.

Among the more spectacular road developments has been bridge building to link Shikoku to Honshu and intra-urban expressway links within the largest cities.

Bridging the Inland Sea to create a west Setouchi economic zone centring on Hiroshima, Okayama and Kagawa

Part of the current major road building includes three bridging links between Shikoku and Honshu. The first link between was completed in 1988, consisting of a 4 lane motorway on the top level and a rail link on the lower level.

But potential traffic has been hindered in using the bridge because the road system either side has been insufficiently improved and toll charges are exorbitant. But the bridge has brought significant economic growth in Shikoku, including by 1990 60 new companies in the Kawaga Prefecture, 20 new hotels to cater for business and tourist visitors who have doubled in number. The bridge link has given a psychological boost to Shikoku's population and improved mobility, since the only previous link to the main island of Honshu was by sea ferry which was slow and subject to disruption by fog and rough weather.

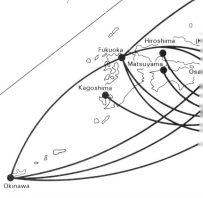

Domestic airways are covered mainly by Japan Air Lines (JAL) but All Nippon Airways (ANA) and Japan Air System (JAS) are also important

Until the 1970s passenger and freight movement by air was insignificant compared to road and rail but is now assuming growing importance, especially for remoter regions such as Hokkaido. Shorter transit times and a decline in air fares are partly responsible, but it is also due to greater affluence and business growth creating a demand. Air fares between centres are little more than double *shinkansen* rail fares and the journey time halved. The growth in high value, small bulk goods industries, e.g. high-tech products, early vegetables and flowers, has led to more air freightage.

Further expansion is hindered by delays in transit from airport to the nearby city destination and limited runway extensions at some major airports, e.g. Narita serving Tokyo where political

Adequacy of the national transport networks

Main inadequacies

1. Densest network coincides with the Pacific Belt but rapid industrial expansion here has led to congestion of much of the network.

2. Within the leading cities, main road and rail/underground arteries are heavily congested and much of it is ageing, making upkeep costly.

3. Remoter areas poorly served due to cost of extending links, though there is a social and economic demand. Also, despite the need, freight and passenger usage insufficient to make land communications profitable, though air routes are more viable.

4. Different transport network modes are not well integrated.

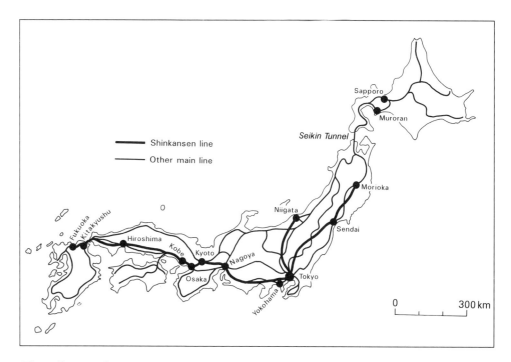

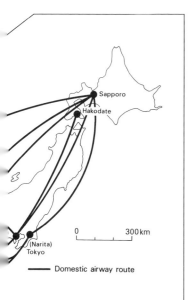

ontroversy has delayed much-eeded developments. Osaka nd Hiroshima have new nternational airport evelopments. But airport xtension and increased air raffic are highly sensitive nvironmental issues.

The rail network

Until the late 1960s, there was an extremely high dependence on the rail network and this exercised a strong influence on the growth pattern of cities in Japan. Even in the 1980s, despite competition from the road network, the railways carried 40% of the country's passenger traffic. But the volume of freight traffic has severely declined since the 1960s due to the greater flexibility offered by road transport and the shift in the economy away from heavy to light industry, for which road transport is more favoured being faster and cheaper.

In the face of a mounting deficit, Japan National Railways were privatised and divided in 1987 into six regional passenger companies and a freight company. There are, in addition, smaller longstanding private companies with profitable commuter lines and serving remoter areas.

The outstanding feature of the network is the *shinkansen* system inaugurated in the 1960s to link together the main metropolitan centres of the Pacific Belt and provide an efficient passenger express service. Further extensions have been made, one through the mountain axis to Niigata and the other as far as Morioka. But important locations still remain without an express link. *Shinkansen* lines have influenced economic growth locations but the rolling stock is ageing and at rush hour have insufficient capacity in the heavily urbanised regions. Plans in hand to replace *shinkansen* with a new super 'Linear Express' network with the Maglev train travelling at 500 kph which will halve journey times. But construction will further focus emphasis on the already overcrowded Pacific Belt.

Within the major metropolitan centres underground and suburban trains also run at overcapacity and lines need to be better linked.

Coastal water transport

As an island archipelago and because of mountainous terrain limiting inland routes, Japan has always relied heavily on movement of freight by coastal waters. To link other islands to Honshu passenger ferries are also important. Coastal freight movement between Japan's main industrial concentrations in the Pacific Belt on Tokyo, Ise and Osaka bays is between two and three times greater in tonnage than that entering international trade. Most major port areas have been extended, old inner areas being redeveloped for other waterfront usage and new outer areas, including docks on reclaimed land for heavy raw material and goods trade, plus expanding container and roll-on/roll-off facilities. Japan's coastal trade continues to expand so that it is likely to remain the leading nation in this form of transport.

Figure 13.9

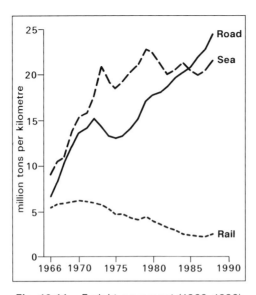

Fig. 13.11 *Freight movement (1966–1990)*

demanding as a challenge is the question of funding. Who is to pay for the much-needed upgrading and extension of the road and rail networks to ensure that they have the capacity to cope with increasing demand? The short answer might be the Government, but given that the economy is now experiencing low growth and competing demands (such as social security and welfare) are being made on a tighter public purse, there is little prospect of requisite amounts of money becoming available from this source. Japan National Railways have now been privatised, presumably in the forlorn hope that the private sector might do better in terms of funding the necessary improvements. What seems increasingly inevitable is that the transport user will be asked to pay more for movement, whether it be higher fares and tariffs on public transport or higher fuel taxes and road tolls. Such moves, in turn, will have profound consequences both for the economy and the cost of living.

Finally, it is appropriate to consider the possible impact of the new communications and information exchange networks which are gradually emerging. Japan is very much at the forefront of the new technologies being developed to serve the needs of the modern information-based society. Amongst the possible beneficial impacts of efficient information exchange and optic-based communication networks is a significant reduction in the amount of personal travel undertaken in relation to work and business. Already, Japanese consumers are using local computer networks for the ordering of goods and services. Perhaps the greatest prospective gains are that better information and communication links over greater distances will encourage significant decentralisation of economic activity away from the currently congested metropolitan areas of the core, as well as tighten national unity. Besides achieving a more equitable distribution of development, capitalising on and fully utilising these new technologies might also help solve some of the transport problems outlined above, if only by reducing trip generation. The danger, however, inherent in the new means of communication is the 'depersonalisation' of community life through the replacement of face-to-face contact by the technological exchange of information.

13.6 THE SEARCH FOR IDENTITY

The discussion so far in this chapter has dealt with the two interrelated issues of the environment and the quality of life. The issues now to be considered have a slightly different focus and embrace two different dimensions of society itself – national character and the political framework. These dimensions need to be considered along the path of time which forms the central axis of the conceptual framework established at the outset of the chapter (Figure 13.1).

Changing national character and the individual

Japan has been described as a corporate-oriented society attaching great importance to mutual relationships and loyalty to the group at every level. Tradition has always placed the group above the individual, along with an emphasis on hard work and consensus. These national traits have certainly contributed to Japan's postwar success. However, since the mid-1970s, the nature of society, its values and attitudes, have undergone a gradual transformation.

This transformation has now reached the point where the great majority of

Japanese find themselves torn between the traditional and the modern. At an individual level, they are obliged to resolve the inherent conflict by finding some sort of compromise between duty, hard work and a respect for the past with the desire for more freedom of choice, a more leisured life style and some degree of individuality. Of course, the extent of this transformation and its mixing of the old and the new varies between the generations. It is least in the oldest and most in the youngest, and has as a consequence opened up sizable generation gaps. Among the elements that remain fairly constant in this changing national character are the importance of the family (now **nuclear** rather than **extended**) and the desire to live in harmony with others (the group) and once again with nature.

The political framework

The Japanese Constitution introduced after the Second World War emphasises the values of democracy, freedom, equality and individual rights. On the whole, it has served Japan well; it has brought political stability and restored a sense of national unity. However, the political system now in place shows major weaknesses. These arise, not because of the Constitution, but because of the way the political system has been allowed to evolve. The situation has now reached the point where those deficiencies threaten to impede the broad modernisation process. Reform of the political system is, of necessity, now moving up the agenda.

One much-needed reform relates to the system of representation. Constituency boundaries remain more or less the same as they were in 1945. The boundaries have failed to take account of the fundamental shifts in the distribution of population. The net result is that the dwindling rural population and farming sector are grossly over-represented in the Japanese Diet. The Liberal Democratic Party, which has held power for most of the postwar period, depends on the support of the rural population for its parliamentary majority. Consequently, it is loath to undertake the redrawing of constit-

uencies and to introduce necessary reforms in the rural sector of the economy.

The political system is also undemocratic in that with the present arrangement, constituencies are of a size that each has three or four elected representatives. In order to secure a majority in the 512 member lower house, a party must on average capture at least two seats in each of the 130 districts. At present, only the Liberal Democratic Party can satisfy this particular requirement. The Socialists find it impossible to do so because they inevitably fall short in rural areas.

A third deficiency of the present system is that within the ruling Liberal Democratic Party there is a number of readily identifiable factions which constantly vie for political influence at the Cabinet level. Government is thus in danger of being dictated by particular factions rather than by party policy as a whole. This represents a lessening of democracy and means that government is open to undue influence from powerful pressure groups, such as the large corporations. These pressure groups are able to back particular factions by providing election funds and in return gain safeguards for their vested interests. Irregular dealings and frequent scandals involving government ministers are symptoms of this unhealthy situation.

These blemishes in the political system mean that the expression of individual identity and preference is being subverted. In the international arena, they bring two unwanted consequences. First, they trigger a loss of confidence in Japan's financial services and institutions. Secondly, they cause a growing embarrassment for Japan, particularly given its keenness to promote the image of a mature and efficient democracy. Given the expectation that in the 21st century Japan will assume an even higher profile in the conduct of global affairs, so the need to repair this weakness in its identity becomes a high priority.

13.7 CONCLUSION

The corporate body of Japan, as represented by the Government and the private sector of industry and business, continue to exercise a strong influence on the future economic and social structures of the country and the spatial expression of these in the landscape. But, within a democratic system, it is the changing personal aspirations of the Japanese people, together with the values and attitudes that shape them, which will be of crucial importance. At the end of the day, Government decisions are subject to the influence of the ballot box and those of industry and commerce to the influence of the market place.

The other fundamental factor affecting the future character of Japan's human geography is the relationship between the core and the peripheral regions. Hitherto, the fortunes of these outer regions have been overshadowed by centralised decision-taking concerned primarily with promoting the prosperity of Tokyo and the other metropolitan areas. Certainly, the peripheral regions will continue to depend to some extent on the spread effects generated by the economic success of the core. However, just as the Japanese people are beginning to exercise individuality, creativity and self-expression outside the constraints of the group ethic, so the regions are taking their own initiatives independent of central authority in a bid to revitalise and shape their economies for the future. Hence the longstanding over-dominance of the Pacific Belt may be increasingly neutralised to give what is urgently needed, namely a more balanced growth across the country.

Japan and the global community

C H A P T E R **14**

In this last chapter, the forward perspective is maintained, but the geographical focus is widened to a global scale. An attempt is made to identify and discuss some of the major issues confronting Japan overseas as the 21st century approaches, at the dawn of what is increasingly referred to as the **Pacific era**. That term is significant in itself, for it implicitly recognises the irrefutable fact that the Pacific region is fast becoming the world's number one sunrise region. Around the shores of the Pacific are to be found countries which collectively already account for about one-half of global GDP (Figure 14.1). Just as the Atlantic region of North America and Western Europe has been the global pivot throughout the 20th century, so the Pacific region is now warming up to assume that role in the 21st century. Symptomatic of the switch is the spatial re-orientation of the North American

economy. For much of the second half of the 20th century, its centre of gravity has been shifting decisively from the Eastern Seaboard to the West Coast. Whether that shift is to be seen as a cause or an effect of the rising prominence of the Pacific region is open to debate. What appears more certain is that, thanks to its location, North America will have been able to play a leading role in both the Atlantic and Pacific eras, providing the continuity, the link between the two.

With the advent of the Pacific era, Japan's location becomes much more centre stage in terms of global affairs. This has a number of possible ramifications, particularly if the economies of Japan and other parts of the Asian sector of the Pacific region continue to expand. By virtue of that regional power, and Japan's contribution to it, Japan might be expected to assume an

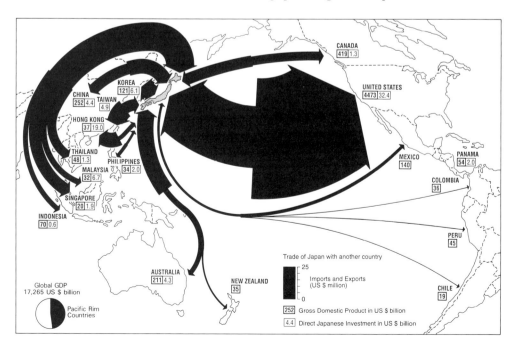

Fig 14.1 *Japan and the Pacific rim countries: trade, investment and GDP (1990)*

CANADA 419 1.3

KOREA 121 6.1

CHINA 252 4.4 TAIWAN 4.9

HONG KONG 37 19.0

UNITED STATES 4473 32.4

THAILAND 48 1.3 PHILIPPINES 34 2.0

MALAYSIA 32 6.7

SINGAPORE 20 1.9

INDONESIA 70 0.6

MEXICO 140 PANAMA 54 2.0

COLOMBIA 36

PERU 45

AUSTRALIA 211 4.3

NEW ZEALAND 35

CHILE 19

Trade of Japan with another country

25

Imports and Exports (US $ million)

0

252 Gross Domestic Product in US $ billion

4.4 Direct Japanese Investment in US $ billion

Global GDP 17,265 US $ billion

Pacific Rim Countries

Fig.14.2 *Cartoon of Japan's balancing act*

dark corner in which she has been sitting and growing slowly but steadily fat and big in the past 40 years. Japan, whether she likes it or not, will have to behave like a great power. That is one thing which is very hard for the Japanese ... to stomach.'

This quotation from a speech, given in 1989, by the Japanese Ambassador to the UK touches on a profound divergence between what many countries expect Japan's role in the global community to be and what Japan wishes for herself. The prevailing view outside Japan is quite simply that Japan, as one of world's most successful and affluent economies, should be willing to assume a much higher profile in global affairs. Japan is thought to have been ducking its responsibilities. In contrast, Japan's view is that it would prefer to be left to do those things which it is good at and with which it feels most comfortable. Japan is without doubt extremely reluctant to step outside the strictly economic realm. Two related factors, in particular, underlie this reluctance.

The Japanese are still embarrassed by the militarist regime which prevailed in the country during the first half of the 20th century; they are not proud of their deeds during the Second World War. The War was a particularly painful experience – it led to a loss of face, the wholesale destruction of the country, and the need to rethink its 'raison d'etre'. The Japanese remain highly sensitive about what others think of them. Certainly, Japan would not wish do anything that might be construed by the global community as signalling that the nation was reverting to its prewar mode.

Secondly, Japan makes the point that real leadership is not derived exclusively from economic influence. It requires the persuasive muscle that comes with a considerable military capability. Here they are quick to point out that the Constitution and the 1951 Peace Treaty confine Japan's military capability and role to one of self-defence.

When it comes to exercising influence in global affairs, Japan's preference is to operate through third parties. It is a willing financial supporter of the UN's

even higher profile in terms of global affairs. Whether it likes it or not, it will be obliged to become even more outward looking; its external geography will become even more complex. Japan may have to take on new responsibilities, for example as a regional and global peace-keeper and as a guardian of the weaker nations of the world. That would undoubtedly call for Japan to perform a delicate balancing act with its own binding commitment to non-aggression and self-defence (Figure 14.2). It will have to address and resolve a whole range of issues that arise from its links with the rest of the global community. A number of these issues have already been touched on in the preceding section. The intention now is to examine them and others in a little more detail. They are diverse in character; they are multi-dimensional. For discussion purposes, however, they may be crudely sorted under four broad headings, as being essentially geopolitical, economic, environmental and humanitarian issues.

14.1 GEOPOLITICAL ISSUES

Global leadership

'Japan...is being propelled blinking into the light out of the warm, nice, peace-keeping operations; it contributes funds to the range of UN agencies, to the International Monetary Fund and to various regional development organisations. When it comes to more economic matters, then Japan is happy to be an active participant in G7 talks and GATT negotiations. But even in the economic realm, the Japanese are highly conscious of their external image and how others perceive them. This is well illustrated by an extract from an official analysis of future economic trends:

'The international community's reaction to the rapid growth and increasing world influence of the Japanese economy has been growing anxiety, and even fear of Japan's economic might.'

So a sort of 'impasse' exists on this issue of a larger role in the global community. The expectation remains, but there is no doubt that currently Japan lacks the will and the military back-up to become a great power in the fullest sense of the term. The view of many Japanese is that their country is used to following rather than leading. They are quite content to play number two to the USA. Of course, Japan cannot be forced to lead. However, even if that preference were to be respected, there are some ways in which Japan might become more active, perhaps more influential. An obvious example is a higher profile in global diplomacy, particularly in the less militarily-minded 1990s. Certainly, there is room for a more effective diplomacy just within the economic arena. Japan badly needs diplomats and politicians to help allay the 'anxiety' and 'fear' created by its economic success. But is it possible that Japan might exercise more leadership even within this more restricted context of global economic affairs?

Regional leadership

It is in its own backyard of the Western or Asian Pacific region that the prospects seem brightest not only for a more assertive economic leadership, but also a more broadly-based leadership. Proposals to create an Asian or Western Pacific politico-economic bloc have been frequently made during the

last two decades. Nothing has materialised to date. The possible reasons range from differences in culture, political systems and economic structures to historical animosities and long-lasting suspicions between potential members. Perhaps as a result of developments on the other side of the Eurasian landmass, in the form of a further strengthening and possible enlargement of the EC, Asian nations are now slowly becoming persuaded that the time has come for them to make moves to establish a sort of United States of Asia. They see the need for a third economic bloc to counterbalance those of Europe and North America. There can be no doubting the potential clout that would come from an alliance of Japan, the NICs and the resource-rich countries of South East Asia (Figure 14.1). In addition, and perhaps surprisingly, China has expressed interest in the idea of regional economic cooperation, whilst the involvement of Australia and New Zealand is not ruled out. There thus begins to open up the even more daunting prospect of a United States of the Western Pacific, straddling two hemispheres.

What seems to be taken as read by all interested parties in the Western Pacific is that Japan would take a leading role. For certain that leadership would have a significant political, perhaps even a defensive dimension. Maybe Japan would feel less conspicuous and more at ease exercising the broadly-based leadership of a regional trading bloc in its negotiations with the rest of the world. One intriguing question surrounding these discussions of some sort of regional union is the possible reaction of the USA. Would the USA be happy to see itself, in effect, excluded from the world's largest consumer market and best resourced region? If not, then what might it do – join it or thwart it?

Defence, expense and the CIS

Defence is a complex issue that is certain to remain prominent. Much has yet to be sorted out, principally under the interrelated headings of role, level of expenditure and relations with the Soviet Union's successor, the CIS. First of all, it is necessary for the global community to recognise that Japan is constrained to perform only a self-defensive role. That was the decision made for Japan nearly 50 years ago. Japan was, and still is, happy to accept the limitation.

It would seem that there are two ways in which Japan might do more in terms of defence and so meet the increasing expectations being placed on it by the USA and many other nations. First, Japan might contribute more to the peace-keeping operations of the UN and be given a permanent seat on the security council. That is particularly justified when it can be demonstrated that by so doing Japan would be protecting its own interests, as was clearly the case in the Gulf War (1991). Secondly, Japan might do more to defend itself and thereby rely less on the USA. That is a point frequently made by the Americans; it is certainly something that Japan could afford to do. The self-imposed limit of one percent GNP on defence-spending does seem to have been something of a red herring. Surely, the guiding principle Japan needs to follow is that its level of defence-spending should be commensurate with the perceived military threat and the military response required to repel it.

Reference to perceived military threat leads the discussion briefly to consider the question of Japan's relations with the CIS. For certain, during much of the postwar period Japan genuinely felt threatened both by the USSR and by the general spread of communism in Asia. The massive military build-up in the Soviet Far Eastern region was both menacing and ominous. However, a totally different geopolitical scenario has suddenly emerged. In the closing years of its existence, the basic attitudes of the Soviet Union changed and so did its priorities. Significant disarmament agreements were reached with the USA. But now that the CIS has replaced the Soviet Union, has the so-called 'threat' also dissipated? Can Japan now afford to be less paranoic and feel less insecure, as the constituent republics of the old Union try to sort out their own internal problems, and as the spread of communism seems to have halted once and for all? Today in the Asian Pacific region, there is more political stability, and therefore greater security, than at any other time in the 20th century.

Two things follow from this greatly improved strategic situation. Japan might volunteer to assume greater responsibility for its defensive arrangements and so come out from underneath the American umbrella. The cost of doing this is not likely to place too much of a strain on the Japanese economy, because today's reduced threat calls for a reduced defensive capability. What is also called for in these days of glasnost is that Japan and the CIS should conclude a peace treaty. That is not going to be easy.

Japan is in a predicament. It has made the return of the southern Kurile islands a condition of any such peace treaty. The former Soviet Union, for understandable strategic reasons, repeatedly stated that the islands were not negotiable. But Japan is readily aware of the great economic opportunities that now lie in store as the former Soviet republics restructure their economies to accommodate market forces. There is promise of resources, a huge market starved of consumer goods and immense scope for direct investment projects. It may be that in the current geopolitical situation these islands are not deemed to be quite so critical, in defensive terms, as they were by both the Soviet Union and Japan for most of the postwar period. There can be no doubt that the member countries of the new Commonwealth desperately need Japan's economic co-operation. It remains to be seen whether or not the Russian Federation, in whose jurisdiction the islands fall, will be disposed to negotiate some sort of deal with the Japanese. To the outside, it would seem a dreadful waste if no compromise were to be reached over this handful of barren islands and if the Northern Territories dispute were allowed to keep these potential beneficiaries apart?

14.2 ECONOMIC ISSUES

All three issues considered under the preceding geopolitical heading are

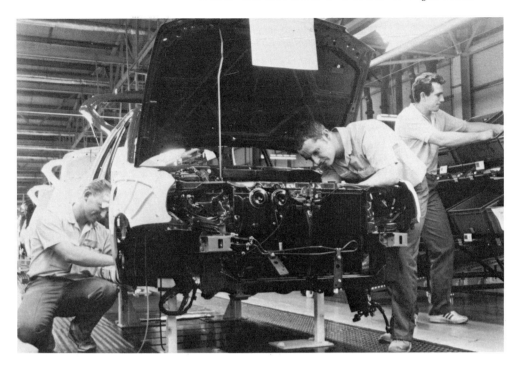

Photo 14.1 *A Nissan Micra produced in Sunderland – a Japanese product ?*

multi-faced and clearly have very substantial economic connotations. Similarly, the economic issues to be examined next have complex political undertones.

Coping with the NICs

The prognosis for the Japanese economy made in the previous chapter was essentially one of continuing expansion, and most likely at a rate faster than that of most other advanced countries. But there is certainly no room for complacency as the equally dynamic NICs increasingly snap at Japan's heels. Competition from the 'tigers' of Asia will continue to require that Japan makes two fundamental moves. First, it will have to persist with the process of industrial restructuring at home. Specifically, this will mean continuing to put more emphasis on the high-tech industries and retreating from those industries where NIC competition is keenest. But the retreat from industries, such as iron and steel, chemicals, motor vehicles and consumer electrical goods, need not be absolute. Rather the tactic, the second move, is the geographical one of switching production offshore. By doing so, Japanese producers may exploit potential economies that exist elsewhere, such as more abundant and cheaper labour and closer proximity to

the eventual market place. It also allows them to shake off the debilitating effects of the yen, which, because it has appreciated so much in value, has blunted the competitive pricing of goods made in Japan. By capitalising on these offshore production opportunities, so Japanese companies will be able to maintain a competititive position in the global market place. There can be no doubt that the proportion of Japanese industrial production achieved overseas will continue to rise. Whilst that, in turn, will mean a maintained, if not increased, world market share, it is most likely to lead to a reduction in industrial jobs back in Japan. For many countries that would be regarded as an unacceptable price to be paid. Not so for Japan, because it currently faces an acute structural labour shortage. Given the silvering of the Japanese population, the offshore option offers a neat way of counteracting the certain prospect of an increasing shortage of domestic manpower.

These structural adjustments to meet the increasing competition from the NICs are simply the recognition of comparative advantage as painfully revealed by market forces. Countries come to specialise in those fields where they are most competitive. It would seem that the same principle might be allowed to operate, but in a much less cut-and-thrust and more harmonious manner, in the context of the sort of economic union discussed in 14.1. Recognition of, and agreement about, comparative advantage reached by round-table discussion could provide a very strong basis for such a union, in that comparative advantage leads to specialisation and to interdependence. Given the diversity of countries to be found in the Western Pacific Region, the potential for interdependence and economic union is immense. But if that union is to materialise and succeed, more conciliatory attitudes will need to prevail, not just in Japan, but also in the growing ranks of the NICs.

Trade friction

Trade friction is an issue which is certain to endure, perhaps for as long as Japan continues to enjoy a large trade surplus. It is perhaps asking too much of any nation to suggest that it should agree to be less successful. Japan has proved itself to be an immensely successful exporter – not by chance, but as a result of meticulous market research and efficient production. Trade has been carefully managed; little has been left to chance. The Japanese Government has been highly supportive of the private sector. The more Japan's trading partners threaten protectionism, the more Japanese producers and investors will be persuaded to go for export substitution. From the Japanese viewpoint, the obvious and sensible counter is to set up branch plants and manufacture near the market. However, it is a suspect strategy as countries – first the USA and now the countries of the EC – place quotas on Japanese goods, and begin to count as 'Japanese', not only goods made in Japan, but the offshore products of affiliated firms. The fairness of that tactic hinges on one simple criterion, namely the percentage of local content in the final product. For example, in the case of the Nissan plant in Sunderland, local content (the EC-produced parts) is now nearly 80 percent (Photo 14.1). To count the cars produced by that particular factory as 'Japanese' and therefore part of the Japanese quota would seem to be grossly unfair. Where the proportion of Japanese content tips the other way, then perhaps the case is stronger.

It is on the import side of trade that Japan has the more scope to make friction-reducing moves. For all its avowed market-opening measures, the criticism that Japan continues to protect its own agriculture are repeatedly voiced by the developed countries of North America and Australasia, as well as by many developing countries. But Japan is not alone here; the EC is no less guilty on this particular count.

The agricultural commodity to draw the greatest attention and feeling is rice. For Japan, rice remains an extremely sensitive, almost emotional, issue. There is much deep-rooted symbolism associated with rice. Although the proportion of the working population involved in rice farming has dropped to insignificant levels, and although rice consumption has been falling for many years, the Japanese people retain a nostalgia for the staple crop that has, at various stages in the past, saved them from starvation. Rice has a powerful economic and political supporter in the huge *Nokyo* or agricultural co-operative movement. The *Nokyo* does not hesitate to use its money and influence over farmers to put pressure on politicians. For example, as recently as 1988 the Diet was persuaded to pass a resolution banning indefinitely the import of rice. But Japan's trading partners are increasingly of the opinion that by completely opening its market to rice imports, Japan could, at a single stroke, do much to improve its international relationships. This would certainly have a profound impact on Japan's rice producers, but they have already greatly dwindled in number. It would also certainly dissipate rural support for the ruling political party.

Again, it has to be pointed out that the formation of some sort of Asian or Western Pacific economic bloc would go a long way to reducing trade friction in this part of the world. Equally, it might be expected to have the opposite effect in terms of trading with the other two major trading blocs of the EC and North America.

Opportunities in the former Second World

In 14.1 attention was drawn to the

desirability of Japan and the CIS resolving the Northern Territories dispute. From Japan's viewpoint, to do so would be to gain access to immense economic opportunities as the CIS struggles out of communism. The openings cover the three principal dimensions discussed in Section C – trade, direct investment and aid. It is the first of these that offers the most immediate interest. The former republics badly need a whole range of capital goods in order to modernise their industrial plant. Slightly longer-term, a huge consumer market may be expected to emerge as and when these countries achieve economic take-off. They are also to be seen as future suppliers of energy (coal and oil) and minerals. Given the high degree of potential interdependence, there is immense scope for much trade between Japan and the former Second World.

In the shorter-term, no doubt Japan might offer aid, particularly in the form of loans and technical assistance, to help put the CIS economy on its feet. In exchange, Japan might negotiate some sort of guaranteed access to the consumer market. As for direct investment, the best prospects would seem to lie in joint-venture projects. At present, however, the risk factor is perceived to be too high. Given the newness of the situation and consequent uncertainties, there is an understandable reluctance on the part of Japanese companies to invest too heavily at present.

Similar opportunities, but of a smaller scale, are now gradually emerging as the countries of Eastern Europe throw off communism and reorient their economies back towards capitalism. There is less on offer here in terms of resources for Japan, with the notable exception of a cheap supply of well-educated labour. That, together with a lower level of perceived risk, could well prove attractive to Japanese industrial companies. In which case, the strategy would be to meet the demands of a growing consumer market with a supply of largely locally-produced goods. Critical decisions for the Japanese company revolve around whether to set up affiliated plants in each country or whether, as in Western Europe, to supply the regional markets from a single production base. If the latter strategy is chosen, then which country should be selected for the task? The obvious choice would appear to be Germany, on the grounds that what was West Germany is securely rooted in the First World and that many Japanese companies are already established there.

14.3 ENVIRONMENTAL ISSUES

The observation is being frequently made in today's mass-media that Japanese industry and consumers have been overcome by 'green fever'. This is supported by a whole range of initiatives being taken by private companies (for example, setting up R and D facilities devoted to environmental concerns) and by government departments (notably the Environmment Agency). However, there are sceptics who suggest this new found green consciousness is superficial and 'nothing more than an enthusiastic embrace of a Western obsession by a nation that considers itself and wants to be considered a member of the world's elite'. The basis for such scepticism is to be found outside Japan rather than within, bearing in mind the basic point that an increasing proportion of the country's resource needs are met from overseas sources. It is clear that satisfying the Japanese demand is generating environmental pressures in those source areas. Three examples may be cited which suggest that, when it comes to environmentalism, the Japanese image may be somewhat tarnished.

Marine resources

The serious depletion of the resources within its own territorial waters are an indicator of profligate over-exploitation. Japan is not the only country to have a history of damaging its own marine resources. However, on some current matters of marine conservation, Japan does seem to be out of line with most of the global community. For example, Japanese fishermen slaughter dolphins, claiming to do so only when they become either 'beached' or inadvertently trapped in drift-nets. But perhaps the most widely-publicised

Photo 14.2 *Destruction of the tropical rainforest*

example of Japan's questionable attitude to marine conservation is to do with the world's dwindling whale stocks. Japan has proved itself to be a highly reluctant signatory to the International Whaling Commission's (IWC) moratorium on commercial whaling instigated in 1985–6. In fact, Japan has continued to hunt the minke whale, and on occasions other species, on the grounds that it is necessary to do so for scientific purposes. But why does Japan have to do this 'research'? What is wrong with the research that the IWC undertakes on behalf of all those nations interested in commercial whaling? Rather worrying is the fact that the 'fruits' of this research are literally ending up, in considerable quantity, on the meat counters of expensive Japanese stores. Thus it can so easily look as if affluent Japanese consumers, with their traditional love of whale meat (and of dolphin meat, for that matter) are prepared to satisfy that taste no matter what the cost.

The Japanese attitude on this whole issue of exploiting the sea was perhaps summed up by the Ambassador in London when he claimed that 'we think we have the right to utilise our resources, provided these resources are not wasted'. But the resources of international waters are not Japan's; they belong to the global community. Is the acid test of resource exploitation not sustainability rather than minimised wastage?

Forest resources

Double standards are also in evidence in Japan's exploitation of forest resources. Whilst a number of Japan's largest trading companies have set up in-house teams to study environmental issues such as global warming, those same companies continue to ignore international calls to restrict their logging of tropical hardwoods and consequent destruction of the tropical forests of South East Asia (Photo 14.2). What compounds the situation is that Japan has considerable hardwood reserves of its own. Sustainable utilisation of these resources could easily meet a substantial part of Japan's current timber demand. Why is Japan not harvesting its own forests? Shortages of labour and difficulties of access provide part of the explanation. But two rather self-centred considerations also carry weight, namely the preference to exploit and exhaust the resources of others first, and the wish not to disfigure Japan's attractive upland scenery. Furthermore, why is Japan not sufficiently using its technological ingenuity to develop and promote alternative materials that have a smaller environmental cost?

Exporting pollution

The suspicion that Japan is willing to let others bear the environmental costs of satisfying its own needs arises in some of the industrial development that Japanese ODI and ODA have backed in developing countries. Whilst the setting up of industrial operations, such as smelting, refining and chemical processing, can be explained in terms of proximity to raw material sources, the accusation is also made that they have been established so as to allow the 'export of pollution'. Is it sheer coincidence that these industries happen to be those that were Japan's prime polluters in the 1960s and the targets of quite stringent anti-pollution measures in the 1970s?

What emerges from these three examples is what might be termed the unacceptable face of Japan. The picture gained is of a country keen to be seen supporting all manner of laudable causes just so long as no actions are required that might disturb the comfort and luxury of the modern lifestyle to which the Japanese have become accustomed. It seems strange that the Japanese are inherently image-conscious, and yet they appear unconcerned that their image is becoming tarnished by instances of the type cited. Selfish, materialistic, exploitive and hypocritical are some of the unflattering adjectives that seem to fit this dark side of modern Japan. Surely, the time has come, and Japan's stature is such, that it should be setting a much better example to others by demonstrating genuinely responsible attitudes towards the environment. On this issue, perhaps more than most, actions speak far louder than words.

14.4 HUMANITARIAN ISSUES

More aid, different aid

One of the things that follows from a nation's economic success is the expectation that help, and perhaps even charity, be extended to the least fortunate members of global society. Japan has not disappointed here. Its sense of obligation and humanitarianism is clearly shown in its ODA programmes, in its substantial contributions to multi-lateral institutions and in things like export credits. However, there are many who think that Japan could afford to spend more on aid than the current equivalent of about 0.3 percent of GNP (Table 12.1). But leaving aside the question of level of expenditure, as was intimated in Chapter 12, there are some suspicions that Japan's aid motives may not be selfless. There is more than a hint of economic expediency and exploitation, in the sense that Japan seems most willing to back those developments in the Developing World that are likely to bear some sort of benefit for Japan, be its resources, markets or dividends.

The sense of exploitation is also intensified by the predominance of loans in the overall aid package. Japan is not alone in this respect. However, the sad outcome is an increasing number of developing countries overburdened and demoralised by ever-mounting debt. So hopefully the time has come for Japan to review its whole aid strategy. In addition to shifting the emphasis away from loans and thus amplifying the giving aspect of aid, two other changes might be considered desirable. First, those aid schemes designed to encourage economic development should incorporate environmental criteria and conditions. In other words, every effort should be made to ensure that the environmental impact of such schemes is minimised. Any development should be sustainable in environmental terms. Secondly, more emphasis should be given to aid that will improve the quality of life for the poorest sections of society in the Developing World. The three priorities here are obvious – education (to include instruction in matters such as diet, personal health and family planning, as well as vocational training), housing (especially self-help schemes) and food production (the promotion of low-tech, low-cost, sustainable farming) (Photo 14.3).

A more benevolent partnership with the Developing World

There is a growing feeling among Japan's partners in the Developing World that more benevolence should also prevail in the strictly economic

Photo 14.3 *Japanese aid for technical training*

fields of trade and investment. There is the feeling that they are dealing with a giant, and that the mechanisms of trade and economic co-operation always tend to work to the benefit of the stronger partner. The stronger partner becomes even stronger, whilst the weaker partner feels more and more exploited. The conviction that they are losing out is compounded by the impression that Japan shows little sympathy or compassion for their plight. A Malaysian Government official has complained that Japan continues to treat developing countries 'as hewers of wood and drawers of water'. A Beijing banker has put it another way; 'the aim seems to be to keep us backward and keep us buying'. A Japanese critic of his own Government's attitudes has been heard to remark, 'To Japan, ASEAN is like underwear – we all know it is down there, we just don't want to think too much about it'. These quotations help to give the flavour of the frustration and perceived victimisation felt by Japan's Third World partners.

So what might Japan do to soften its image as a ruthless economic creature? Within the realms of trade, it was suggested in Chapter 10 that Japan could make its market much more accessible to the agricultural products and labour-intensive manufactures of the Developing World. Indeed, through the medium of JETRO offices, producers might be given even more advice and help about the intricacies of marketing within Japan. As for direct investment, possibly there is scope for more backing of agricultural developments that will improve both the subsistence and commercial aspects of farming. Perhaps this might be paralleled by less support for the really exploitive ventures to do with energy, minerals and timber. Conceivably Japan might do more to encourage its own tourists to patronise the less-developed countries more than they do at the moment. Suggestions such as these might go some way to improving the situation. But the basic question is this – is it reasonable to expect the Japanese business community to become less profit-oriented and more benevolent? Whilst it is easy to preach, it is much less easy to make the sacrifice and deliver.

14.5 HAS THE RISING SUN REACHED ITS NOON ?

The answer to this question would appear to be 'yes' in that the rate of growth in the Japanese economy has certainly levelled off. Since 1975, it has settled down at around the five percent per annum mark. The Japanese are fairly pragmatic about this. A Government official recently admitted that 'no country can enjoy rising prosperity for ever'. In a similar vein, a leading Japanese economist has argued that "the idea of Japan as Number One [in the global community] is ludicrous. We don't have the human assets, resources or political strength to be more than, at best, a good Number Two behind the US." So certainly a sense of realism prevails as to the future scenario.

The notion that the Japanese economy may have passed its peak, in terms of dynamism and expansion, is reinforced by the arrival on the scene of the increasingly competitive Asian 'tigers'. By that is not to say that Japan is now set on a downward path or should in any way be written off. Far from it, Japan has arrived; it is now a key member of the global establishment. Its economy is world-wide in dimension. Japan wields enormous influence on the world economic stage. From the considerable power-base provided by its economy, Japan's destiny lies in a more broadly-based leadership of the Asian Pacific region and a willingness to adopt a higher profile in the general conduct of world affairs. In this sense, Japan has considerable potential. However, in order to fulfil that destiny, a whole range of issues, such as those discussed in this chapter, will need to be resolved. But with characteristic Japanese determination and efficiency, resolved the issues will be, and in so doing there is every expectation that the image of the country will change too.

In all its history, the national emblem of the rising sun has never seemed more appropriate than now as Japan moves towards the 21st century. The dawning of the Pacific era offers Japan the chance to further enhance its international reputation and to gain face of a special kind. In seizing that opportunity, new forces may be expected to impact on the internal and external geographies of the country, bringing new complexions to the changing face of Japan.

Selected Bibliography

GENERAL

Allen, G.C. (1981), *The Japanese Economy* (London: Weidenfeld and Nicolson).

Association of Japanese Geographers (1980), *Geography of Japan* (Tokyo: Teikoku-Shoin).

Atlas Japan in English and Japanese (1991) (Tokyo: Teikoku-Shoin).

Beasley, W. (ed.) (1976), *Modern Japan: Aspects of History, Literature and Society* (Tokyo: Tuttle).

Eccleston, B. (1991) *State and Society in Post War Japan* (London: Polity Press).

Japan: a Bilingual Atlas (1991) (Tokyo: Kodansha).

Pezeu-Massabuau, J. (1978), *The Japanese Islands: A Physical and Social Geography* (Tokyo: Tuttle).

Rebischung, J. (1975), *Japan: the Facts of Modern Business and Social Life* (Tokyo: Tuttle).

Trewartha, G.T. (1964), *Japan: A Geography* (London: Methuen).

Van Wolferen, H. (1990), *The Enigma of Japanese Power: People and Politics in a Stateless Nation* (London: Papermac).

Woronoff, J. (1986), *Asia's Miracle Economies* (Tokyo: Lotus Press).

ANNUAL AND OCCASIONAL PUBLICATIONS

About Japan Series ((Tokyo: Foreign Press Centre).

Changing Japan (Tokyo: Asahi Evening News).

Japan: an International Comparison (Tokyo: Keizai Koho Centre).

Japan: a Pocket Guide (Tokyo: Foreign Press Centre).

Japan Statistical Yearbook (Tokyo: Statistics Bureau, Management and Co-ordination Agency).

Nippon: a Chartered Survey of Japan (Tokyo: Kokusei-Sha Corporation).

Nippon: Business Facts and Figures (Tokyo: JETRO).

Perspectives on Japan (Tokyo: Statistics Bureau, Prime Minister's Office).

Statistical Survey of Japan's Economy (Tokyo: Economic and Foreign Affairs Research Association).

Statistical Handbook of Japan (Tokyo: Statistics Bureau, Prime Minister's Office).

The Japan of Today (Tokyo: Ministry of Foreign Affairs).

Understanding Japan (Tokyo: International Society for Educational Information).

White Papers of Japan (Tokyo: Japan Institute of International Affairs).

PERIODICALS

Anglo-Japanese Journal (bi-monthly) (London: Anglo-Japanese Economic Institute).

Far Eastern Economic Review (weekly) (Hong Kong: Review Publishing).

Geographical Reports of Tokyo Metropolitan University (annual) (Tokyo: Tokyo Metropolitan University).

Intersect (monthly) (Tokyo: PHP Institute)

Japan Digest (quarterly) (Folkestone: Japan Library Ltd).

Japan Echo (quarterly) (Tokyo: Japan Echo Inc.)

Japan Education Journal (quarterly) (London: Japan Information Centre)

Japan Pictorial (quarterly) (Tokyo: Japan Graphic Ltd).

Japan Review of International Affairs (half-yearly) (Tokyo: Japan Institute of International Affairs).

Journal of Japanese Trade and Industry (bi-monthly) (Tokyo: Japan Economic Foundation).

Look Japan (monthly) (Singapore:Look Japan Publishing Ltd).

Newsletter (monthly) (Sydney: Australia-Japan Economic Institute).

Science Reports of Tohoku University, 7th Series – Geography (quarterly) (Sendai: Tohoku University).

Science Reports of the Institute of Geosciences, University of Tsukuba (annual) (Ibaraki: University of Tsukuba).

CHAPTER 1

Buckley, R. (1985), *Japan Today* (Cambridge: Cambridge University Press).

Doi, T. (1981), *The Anatomy of Dependence* (Tokyo: Kodansha International).

Hendry, J. (1987), *Understanding Japanese Society* (London: Croom Helm).

Lowe, J. (1985), *Into Japan* (London: John Murray).

Nakane, C. (1984), *Japanese Society* (Tokyo: Tuttle).

Noh, T. and Kimura, J.C. (eds.) (1983), *Japan: a Regional Geography of an Island Nation* (Tokyo: Teikoku-Shoin).

Reischauer, E.O. (1981), *The Japanese* (Massachusetts and London: Belknap Press).

Tasker, P. (1987), *Inside Japan: Wealth, Work and Power in the New Japanese Empire* (London: Penguin Books).

Wilson, D. (1986), *The Sun at Noon: An Anatomy of Modern Japan* (London: Coronet Books).

CHAPTER 2

Association of Japanese Geogrpahers (1980), *Geography of Japan* (Tokyo: Teikoku-Shoin), part I.

Minato, M. (ed.) (1977), *Japan and its Nature* (Tokyo: Heibonsha).

Trewartha, G.T. (1964), *Japan: A Geography* (London: Methuen), part I.

Witherick, M.E., 'Japan and Korea' in Gregory, K.J. (ed.) (1990), *The Earth's Natural Forces* (New York: Oxford University Press).

CHAPTER 3

Collcutt, M. et al., (1988), *Cultural Atlas of Japan* (Oxford: Phaidon).

Orchard, J.E. (1930), *Japan's Economic Position* (New York: McGraw Hill).

Scott Morton, W. (1973), *Japan: its History and Culture* (Newton Abbot: David and Charles).

Trewartha, G.T. (1934), *A Reconnaisance Geography of Japan* (Madison: University of Wisconsin).

CHAPTER 4

Allen, G.C. (1981), *A Short Economic History of Modern Japan* (London: Macmillan).

Fewster, F. and Gorton, T. (1988), *Japan from Shogun to Superstate* (Folkestone: Paul Norbury).

Nakamura, T. (1971), *Economic Growth in Prewar Japan* (Newhaven: Yale University Press).

CHAPTER 5

Dore, R. (1973), *British Factory – Japanese Factory* (London: Allen and Unwin).

Horsley, W. and Buckley, R. (1990), *Nippon: New Superpower – Japan since 1945* (London: BBC Books).

Nakamura, T. and Grace, B.R.G.(1985), *Economic Development of Modern Japan* (Tokyo: International Society for Educational Information).

Smith, M. et al. (1985), *Asia's New Industrial World* (London: Methuen).

Uchino, T. (1983), *Japan's Postwar Economy* (translated M.A. Harbison) (Tokyo: Kodansha).

CHAPTER 6

Murata, K. (ed.) (1980), *The Industrial Geography of Japan* (London: Bell and Hyman).

McMillan, C.J. (1985), *The Japanese Industrial System* (Berlin: de Gruyter). (New York: Empire Books).

CHAPTER 7

Glickman, N.J. (1979), *The Growth and Management of the Japanese Urban System* (New York: Academic Press).

Hall, P. (1984), *The World Cities* (London: Weidenfeld and Nicolson).

Kornhauser, D.H. (1982), *Japan: Geographical Background to Urban-Industrial Development* (London: Longman).

Popham, P. (1985), *Tokyo: the City at the End of the World* (Tokyo: Kodansha).

Witherick, M.E., 'Tokyo' in Pacione, M. (1981), *Urban Problems and Planning in the Developed world* (London: Croom Helm).

CHAPTER 8

Fukutake, T. (1967), *Japanese Rural Society* (Tokyo: Oxford University Press).

Longworth, J. (1983), *Beef in Japan* (Brisbane: University of Queensland Press).

Moore, R.A. (1990), *Japanese Agriculture – Patterns of Rural Development* (London: Westview Press).

Shimpo, M. (1976), *Three Decades in Shiwa – Economic Development and Social Change in a Japanese Farming Community* (Vancouver: University of British Columbia Press).

Witherick, M. E., 'Japan and Korea' in Tarrant, J. (ed.) (1991), *Farming and Food* (New York: Oxford University Press).

CHAPTER 9

Samuels, R.J. (1983), *The Politics of Regional Policy in Japan* (Princeton: Princeton University Press).

CHAPTER 10

Daniels, G. and Drifte, R. (eds.) (1986), *Europe and Japan; Changing Relationships since 1945* (Ashford: Paul Norbury).

Keith, R.C. (ed.) (1986), *Energy, Security and Economic Development in East Asia* (London: Croom Helm).

Maswood, S.J. (1989), *Japan and Protectionism* (London: Routledge).

Morita, A. (1987), *Made in Japan* (London: Collins).

Nobutoshi, A. (1983), *Japan's Economic Security: Resources as a Factor in Foreign Policy* (Aldershot: Gower).

Ohkawa, K. and Ranis, G. (eds). (1985), *Japan and the Developing Countries* (Oxford: Blackwell).

Shinohara, M. (1982), *Industrial Growth, Trade and Dynamic Patterns in the Japanese Economy* (Tokyo: University of Tokyo Press).

White Paper on International Trade (Tokyo: JETRO).

Yoshihara, K. (1979), *Japanese Economic Development: A Short Introduction* (Oxford: Oxford University Press).

CHAPTER 11

Dunning, J.H. (1986), *Japanese Participation in British Industry* (London: Croom Helm).

Franko, L.G. (1983), *The Threat of Japanese Multinationals* (London: Wiley).

Murray, G. (1991), *Synergy: Japanese Companies in Britain* (Tokyo: PHP Institute).

Ohkawa, K. and Ranis, G. (eds.) (1985), *Japan and the Developing Countries* (Oxford: Blackwell).

Sekiguchi, S. (1979), *Japanese Direct Foreign Investment* (London: Macmillan).

Sekiguchi, S. (1983), *ASEAN-Japan Relations: Investment* (Singapore: Institute of Southeast Asian Studies).

Yoshida, M. (1987), *Japanese Direct Manufacturing Investment in the US* (New York: Praeger).

CHAPTER 12

Akrasanee, N. (1983), *ASEAN-Japan Relations: Trade and Development* (Singapore: Institute of Southeast Asian Studies).

Defence of Japan (Tokyo: Defence Agency).

Japan's Official Development Assistance (Tokyo: Ministry of Foreign Affairs).

Okasaki, H. (1986), *A Grand Strategy for Japanese Defence* (Lanham: Abt Books).

Rix, A. (1980), *Japan's Economic Aid* (London: Croom Helm).

Shibusawa, M. (1984), *Japan and the Asian Pacific Region* (London: Croom Helm).

Shirk, S.L. (ed.) (1985), *The Challenge of China and Japan* (New York: Praeger).

Sinha, R. (1981), *Japan's Options for the 1980s* (London: Croom Helm).

Tabuko, T. *et al.* (1986), *Japan's Defence Debate* (Tokyo: Foreign Press Centre).

CHAPTER 13

Hidaka, R. (1984), *The Price of Affluence: Dilemmas of Contemporary Japan* (Tokyo: Kodansha).

Japan Environment Agency (1991), *Conference on the Environment, 1991* (Tokyo: Japan Environment Agency).

Vogel, E.F. (1979), *Japan as Number One: Lessons for America* (Cambridge, Mass.: Harvard University Press).

Vogel, E.F. (1985), *Japan as Number One – Revisited* (Singapore: Institute of Southeast Asian Studies).

Witherick, M.E. 'Japan and Korea' in Williams, M. (ed) (1993), *Planet Management* (New York: Oxford University Press).

Woronoff, J. (1986), *The Japan Syndrome: Symptoms, Ailments and Remedies* (New Brunswick: Transaction Books).

CHAPTER 14

Armour, A.J.L. (ed.) (1985), *Asia and Japan: the Search for Modernization and Identity* (London: Athlone Press).

Chapman, J.W.M. et al. (1983), *Japan's Quest for Comprehensive Security* (London: Frances Pinter).

Lincoln, E.J. (1987), *Japan's Economic Role in Northeast Asia* (New York: Asia Society).

Linder, S.B. (1986), *The Pacific Century: Economic and Political Consequences of Asian-Pacific Dynamism* (Stanford: University of Stanford).

Morrison, C.E. (1985), *Japan, the United States and a Changing Southeast Asia* (New York: Asia Society).

Okita, S. (1980), *The Developing Economies and Japan* (Tokyo: Tokyo University Press).

Okita, S. (1990), *Approaching the 21st Century: Japan's Role* (Tokyo: The Japan Times).

Scalapino, R.A. (1987), *Major Power Relations in Northeast Asia* (New York: Asia Society).

Index